The Letters and Diaries of Oskar Schlemmer

Oskar Schlemmer, 1932. *Courtesy of Tut Schlemmer.*

The Letters and Diaries

of

Oskar Schlemmer

Selected and edited by
TUT SCHLEMMER

Translated from the German by
KRISHNA WINSTON

WESLEYAN UNIVERSITY PRESS

Middletown, Connecticut

ISBN : 0-8195-4047-1

Library of Congress Catalog Card Number : 77-184362

Manufactured in the United States of America

First edition

IN MEMORIAM

CONTENTS

ILLUSTRATIONS

FOREWORD

The letters and diaries of Oskar Schlemmer, in this first published edition, cover the period of thirty-three years between 1910 and 1943; they record the sum of an entire life. They begin in the midst of the artistic revolution that preceded the first world war, and they end during the second great war of this century.

The material in this book was selected from the wealth of diaries, letters, manuscripts, working notebooks, and notes left by Oskar Schlemmer. A large number of the letters stem from the correspondence with Schlemmer's revered friend, the painter Otto Meyer-Amden. All of these letters have been preserved, and it was always Oskar Schlemmer's wish that they should be published in their entirety.

I hope that no one will take it amiss that the letters and diaries include comments which might prove offensive to certain contemporaries of Schlemmer's. These materials are being published in order to convey a true picture of the times and the events Oskar Schlemmer saw, experienced, and helped mold. Only irrelevant or highly personal details have been deleted. The selection is based on my own perspective and on my sense of what best documents the years I lived at Oskar Schlemmer's side.

My heartfelt thanks go to all those who helped and encouraged me throughout this long and arduous task, but especially to the one friend without whose collaboration I would never have achieved my goal.

Many who knew Oskar Schlemmer as a friend or a teacher loved his winning, cheerful ways, his penchant for jokes and bon mots, his modesty, and his charm; here they may find a different side of his character, for in his private writings he reveals his innermost being.

Schlemmer's intense preoccupation with the art and artists of his day must be taken very seriously. Early in life he found an ideal which remained his guiding light in bright days and dark, in days of hope and days of confusion. Always he strove to be faithful to this ideal, and he was never satisfied with what he had actually accomplished. He was surely aware from the very outset that his path would be rocky, lonely, and narrow, leading far from the broad avenue of comfort and artistic success which stretched seductively before him. In his paintings he constructed a world characterized by the simplicity and clarity which grew out of his infallible sense of proportion, balance, form, and order. The guiding concept of his life was the idea of "man within space."

Another of his passionate concerns was the dance (his best-known work in this field is his "Triadic Ballet"), along with stage design, to which he made revolutionary and influential contributions. For a time he devoted most of his energies to the dance and the theater. It was not merely that Oskar Schlemmer enjoyed this activity—and ideas came flocking to him; he also hoped the theater would provide a source of income. Unfortunately this hope proved unfounded.

Fate allotted him all too short a life in which to develop himself as a painter. He was born on September 4, 1888, in Stuttgart, spent his years of apprenticeship there, and began his studies at the Stuttgart Academy. In his lifetime he witnessed two wars and the changes they wrought. He spent nine years as a master at the Bauhaus, years rich in both pleasure and tumult. For three years he taught at the Breslau Academy where he had hoped to find a more peaceful working atmosphere. There followed a brief period in Berlin at the Vereinigte Staatsschulen [Consolidated State Schools of the Arts], at a time when impending catastrophic events already cast their shadow. In 1933 Schlemmer lost his position as a government-employed teacher and had to retire with his family to the country.

The crucial events of this year and the years during which he was in disfavor deeply wounded Oskar Schlemmer. Economic necessity made it impossible for him to concentrate on his art. To earn a living he was obliged to exchange his country refuge for Stuttgart and Wuppertal. During these years he seldom found leisure for his own work.

His sensitive constitution could not long withstand the strains and irritations of various odd jobs, and he felt acutely the discrepancy between his artistic interests and the economic pressures which forced him to sacrifice all that had made life worthwhile to him. He rapidly succumbed to an illness which he at first welcomed as a reprieve from his uncongenial work. Oskar Schlemmer died on April 13, 1943.

Now his entire work as an artist is finally available in ordered form—the paintings, drawings, sculpture, murals; the choreographic creations, the seminal designs for the Bauhaus Theater. We also have his essays and programmatic statements on art and the theater, the Bauhaus lectures on "Man," and the Berlin "Perspectives" lectures. Only now can the entire breadth of Schlemmer's rich and versatile creativity be perceived.

His life work grew out of a powerful artistic drive, out of an unquenchable faith in life and the future, and out of a yearning, restless devotion to the goal of pure artistic expression.

TUT SCHLEMMER

Stuttgart, September 4, 1958

The Letters and Diaries of Oskar Schlemmer

THE STUTTGART YEARS
(Through December 1920)

Chronology

1888: Oskar Schlemmer born on September 4 in Stuttgart, the youngest of the six children of Carl Leonhard Schlemmer and his wife Mina, née Neuhaus.

Around 1900: After his parents' early death, Oskar Schlemmer goes to live with an older sister in Göppingen (State of Württemberg). Attends the local Realschule [secondary school for modern subjects]. The art teacher recognizes the boy's talent and encourages him in his desire to become an artist.

1903-1905: Two-year apprenticeship in a shop for inlay work. He is already fending entirely for himself.

1905: Through his master, Oskar Schlemmer obtains permission to attend the Stuttgart Kunstgewerbeschule [School of Design].

1906-1909: Oskar Schlemmer receives a scholarship to study at the Stuttgart Akademie der bildenden Künste [Academy of the Plastic Arts]. There he meets Willi Baumeister and studies under Pötzelsberger, von Keller, and Landenberger. In Landenberger's class Oskar makes the acquaintance of Otto Meyer-Amden (1885-1933), who has already studied and worked in Zurich, Munich, Paris, and Strassburg. In Stuttgart Meyer-Amden gathers around him a circle of friends, of whom the most devoted are Oskar Schlemmer and Baumeister.

1910-1912: Following the summer semester of 1910, Schlemmer takes a leave of absence from the Academy and goes to Berlin to work independently. Around 1911 he paints important landscapes such as *Jagdschloß im Grunewald* ["Hunting Lodge in the Grunewald"], as well as self-portraits, still lifes, and interiors, all of which show him striving for utmost simplicity of form and a strict cubistic arrangement of the pictorial elements. Upon returning to Stuttgart in 1912, Oskar Schlemmer becomes a master student of Adolf Hoelzel's. First dance experiments and notes on the dance.

1913: Oskar Schlemmer and his brother Wilhelm establish the Neckarstraße Gallery (1913-1914) where the first exhibitions of modern painting in Stuttgart take place. Paintings: *Rote Dächer* ["Red Roofs"], *Landschaft mit Weißem Haus* ["Landscape with a White House"], *Mädchenkopf* ["Head of a Girl"], *Geometrisierte Figur*

["Geometric Shape"], *Abstraktion 1913* ["Abstraction 1913"], *Figur in Diagonale* ["Figure on the Diagonal"], and others.

1914: Hoelzel assigns his students Schlemmer, Baumeister, and Hermann Stenner the task of doing three murals for the lobby of the main building at the Cologne Werkbund [German Artisans' League] Exhibition. From Cologne the three friends continue on to Amsterdam, London, and Paris. Participation in several exhibitions.

In September 1914 Schlemmer and his fellow students Stenner and Wirth volunteer for military service and are sent to the western front. After being wounded (in October), Oskar Schlemmer is hospitalized near Aachen and then in Stuttgart.

1915: After his recovery, Oskar Schlemmer is sent in June to the eastern front and shortly thereafter receives another wound. First the military hospital in Galkhausen in the Rhineland, then convalescence at his home base. From September 1915 to January 1916 Oskar Schlemmer is on leave to further his education. An important stage in Oskar Schlemmer's artistic development: he says good-bye to tradition. The major works of this period show a decisive breakthrough to abstraction: *Figur von der Seite* ["Figure Viewed from the Side"], *Komposition auf Rosa* ["Composition on Pink"], *Figur von Vorn* ["Frontal View of a Figure"], *Homo,* and *Bild K* ["Picture K"].

1916: Barracks duty. In March, assignment to a surveying unit in Mulhouse, which is later deployed to Colmar; Oskar Schlemmer remains with this unit until the end of the war. In the autumn he participates in the exhibition "Hoelzel and his Circle," shown in Freiburg im Breisgau and Frankfurt am Main; the first showing of Schlemmer's recent works. Toward the end of the year he is furloughed to Stuttgart, where he is to rehearse the dances for a charity fête being given by his regiment. Parts of the "Triadic Ballet" are performed.

1917: Military service in Colmar.

1918: June: Oscar Schlemmer and Baumeister exhibit together at the Schaller Gallery in Stuttgart. He is in Berlin when the war ends and the revolution breaks out. After the demobilization he returns as a master pupil to the Stuttgart Academy, which places a studio at his disposal.

1919: Schlemmer is elected to the student council of the Stuttgart Academy. His attempts at reform are blocked by the professors. His proposal to install Paul Klee as successor to the retiring Adolf Hoelzel is likewise rejected.

In May he receives the manifesto of the State Bauhaus which Walter Gropius has created in Weimar by merging the former Großherzogliche Hochschule für bildende Kunst [Grand Ducal School of the Plastic Arts] with the Kunstgewerbeschule which had been dissolved during the war. Schlemmer works concentratedly on his ballet projects. Paintings significant for his development: *Plan mit Figuren* ["Sketch with Figures"], *Mann mit Fisch* ["Man with a Fish"]; and the first sculptures: *Relief H, Bauplastik* ["Plastic Construct"]. On October 25 at the Württemberg Art Guild he introduces the first show of the "Uecht Group" ["Uecht" = "Dawn" in Old German], formed by the modernistically inclined artists of Stuttgart.

1920: In order to able to devote himself without disruptions to work on the "Triadic Ballet," Schlemmer leaves the Academy in April; he moves to Cannstatt, near Stuttgart. He meets Paul Hindemith, who expresses his readiness to compose music for the ballet.

During the summer a joint exhibition with Baumeister in the Arnold Gallery in Dresden and in Herwarth Walden's "Sturm" Gallery in Berlin. On the way to Dresden he stops in Weimar on Gropius' invitation to visit the Bauhaus and learn more about the position he is to be offered there.

October: Marries Helena Tutein ("Tut").

Simultaneously with Paul Klee, Oskar Schlemmer is summoned in December to join the faculty of the Bauhaus as a "Master of Form." There he joins Gropius, Lyonel Feininger, Johannes Itten, Gerhard Marcks, and Georg Muche.

Diary

Berlin

September 4, 1910

A dream: it is evening, and I am going along the brightly lit Joachimstalerstraße, in the middle of the street, calling out absent-mindedly, "I am looking for a friend with whom I can talk and whom I can love."

The passersby on both sidewalks grin scornfully. The echo of my words bounces off the houses, resounding from street to street.

A Russian proverb: is—somewhere—far, far off a human being?

To Otto Meyer

November 16, 1912

I am now the proud owner of a set of rings *[ein Reck]* attached to the ceiling beams of my studio, and the chambermaid of the late Queen Olga has requested that I be quieter while she is trying to sleep in the room below. From *sich recken* [to stretch] : *der Recke* [hero of olden times] , *der Rekord, der Rekrut, der Rekonvaleszent. . . . .**

To Otto Meyer

Stuttgart

December 12, 1912

I am happy that you have fond memories of my pictures—I have been going through another period of anarchistic revulsion against them.

We had a picture by Baumeister here in my studio, and it looked like an exotic tropical flower in a monk's cell. Someone said this showed the confrontation of two different worlds: asceticism versus sensuality.

---

*Schlemmer frequently indulges in this sort of untranslatable play on words.
— Translator

To Otto Meyer

Stuttgart
December 20, 1912

"Just a monent ago" I received a telegram, according to which I have sold a picture (400 marks). That means I can visit you in Amden, which I had made contingent upon this sale. Is there an extra bed in your house? I shall arrive dressed in full Russian costume, but probably in January at the earliest. I am still considering giving up the studio this spring and retiring to some healthy region where only my closest friends would be within reach—this might represent a final attempt to find my identity. The barometer which in Berlin, and here too, used to stand at "high inspiration" threatens more and more to fall to "inner void." I am still not strong enough to withstand solitude without being overcome by the urge to "cross the boundaries of this external world this very day and never more to dream a shallow dream nor succumb to the intoxication of the world."

Will there be no solution?

Diary

December 1912

Development from the old dance to the new:

Gray: conventional set, with a moon perhaps, to provide a sense of evening! Choreography and music: perfection, thanks to having convention to fall back on, familiar, easy to absorb. The style of Russian ballet, the basis of its success. The dancers first present the type of dance which would assure them of success, which would guarantee the audience's approval.

A demon scurries across the stage (embodying the Dionysian element), provocative yellow-orange color, a mask, and takes up a position in front of the curtain, gesticulating, conjuring; the dancers (their dance interrupted) shrink back, startled. The curtain opens, or a veil-like dark brown drop curtain descends from above and envelops the dancers, gradually becoming lighter, more reddish. The demon has vanished again. The atmosphere has something unclear, groping, about it, as of something just taking shape; the music is dark and confused, melodies and the tempo springing up, then falling back again; the same true of the dancers.

Music in the lower registers, a brown sound. The demon reappears, and at his appearance the brown veils lift. The mood intensifies from red to bright orange. Music and dance full of passionate excitement—erotic delirium. The demon dances along with it victoriously.

The mood climbs progressively from orange to lemon yellow, symbolizing morbid over-stimulation, ecstasy. The movements of the dancers and the music: shrill, high notes.

Then: like a sudden fall into darkest night—black backdrop, the dancers wrapped in gray. The music deep, minor. Mourning.

At center backstage appears a violet dot, which widens into a circle. The circle passes over into a blue square. The music becomes clearer, until blue, deep, pure blue, dominates the stage. The music: majestic, solemn. The dance: measured, noble.

The cherub (an angel in silver, very airy, misty, delicate, indistinct) appears; the mood moves from dark to light blue, growing lighter and lighter until it passes over into pure white (or silver). The dancers brought together, led by the cherub. A white star appears in the background. The music softly fades away.

The demon: dead.

To Otto Meyer

Stuttgart
January 5, 1913

First I must tell you the latest developments in my dance project. Some time ago, a friend and I heard a concert of Arnold Schönberg's melodramas; a lady wearing a modern Pierrot costume spoke to the accompaniment of dissonant, naturalistically illustrative, but very expressive music. We were much taken with the concert and wrote to Schönberg, asking him if he might be interested in composing music for modern dance or if he could recommend a young composer to us. Schönberg wrote back: "My music is completely lacking in dance rhythm, but if you think it suitable, then so do I."

Diary

I am in the best of moods, harmonious, tranquil, as at certain times in the past; I ascribe this to the abstinent life. Often I have to restrain myself from hugging people, and I have visionary ecstasies of the sort normally associated with a high fever. "Is not asceticism a higher form of epicureanism, and fasting a refined form of *gourmandise?*" (Flaubert).*

To Otto Meyer

April 1913

"That Johann Sebastian Bach strikes you as a Philistine"—I have fastened upon this word, confident that he is not one, although I am well aware that Stendhal calls him a German schoolmaster. But yesterday we heard the "St. John's Passion," and it was marvelous. Let's have many more Philistines like that. Meier-Graefe gave a talk on the Impressionists, whom he praised to the skies, while reproaching the moderns for lack of tradition. There was furious debate on the subject in Stuttgart. My principal objection, which I formed years ago when I read his art history, is that he passes over the Germans and concentrates solely on the Italo-Romanesque tradition. Leonardo, Nuremberg, Holbein, van Eyck, the Dutch Masters, Riemenschneider, Caspar David Friedrich, the early Berlin School—do they not represent an equally strong tradition, a world in itself, one in connection with which Hippolyte Taine remarked that certain painters would have been better suited to the study of divinity than to painting (he was referring to the Cologne School, Memling and Cranach). These two worlds were the cause of my inner torments in Berlin. On the one hand the artists of form, on the other the mystics (Flaubert said that if he had not been so much in love with form he might perhaps have been a great mystic).

---

*The German word for *gourmandise* is *Schlemmerei.* — Translator

Diary

April 1913

Baumeister: a wild hodgepodge of influences, skilfully assimilated in his painting. Glowing, delectable color. Flowerlike. But not simple. Without the simplicity of the true masterpiece. He absorbs all the influences of modern art, many of them undigested. The entire process, complete with undigested or purely instinctual elements, enters right into the paintings. Even the upset stomach helps shape his pictures. But he has more of what it takes to produce a work of art than I. "The drop of folly" which I lack. I know too much.

I feel that objective representation of nature would be the way to capture a more profound form of mysticism. The mysticism that is crucial to the painter's vision.

The symbolic force and import of the dot, the line, the triangle, the square, the circle . . . .

And then what I love above all: the astringent, severe style; not flowery, fragrant, silky, Wagnerian, but like Bach, Handel.

Through the study of nature I hope to refine my expressive tools to the point that I can render some great spiritual conception. So first I must turn to the modest still life, and there search for the mystique of vision, unexhausted and inexhaustible.

Diary

May 1913

New territory has really been broken by Cubism, a development based soundly on tradition, if one considers the progression of, let us say, Courbet—Corot—Cézanne—Picasso. Cubism, then, as objective painting, a product of the cultivated eye, certainly guided by the mind, but essentially a question of the eye. The discoveries and achievements of Cubism provided the impetus for Futurism and Expressionism; and none of the artistic styles which run parallel to Cubism is immune to its persuasive power.

Diary

A work of art is a declaration of freedom. There has never been anything so difficult for mankind to bear as freedom.

To Otto Meyer

Stuttgart
June 1913

Baumeister writes that he met Herwarth Walden of the "Sturm," and will be exhibiting in the German Autumn Salon; he urges me to have my pictures photographed and apply to be exhibited along-with. Don't know if I shall do that, i.e. go to market before my fruit is ripe.

To Richard Herre

Stuttgart
June 1913

Here you have my criticism of your criticism: Impressionism at its inception (Manet, Monet) most certainly was a thought, an intention, an idea, and a "preconceived opinion."

For someone whose personality is fundamentally artistic, painting is precisely *not* natural. The artist is a product of the impossibility (inability) to feel at home in life. The artist is sick and ugly (the pearl in the sick oyster), his kingdom is not of this world—he has the ideal. Artists have toiled and worked their fingers to the bone out of the urgent need to express themselves, "to extract style and originality from themselves," but not with the intention of "making something of themselves." Where this inner necessity is lacking, there is no faith, love, hope, or religion; instead one has cynicism, frivolity, charlatanry. Earnestness (which often manifests itself as boredom), "mournful waiting"—those are the virtues of the artist.

In many colors, many forms, with many facets, in different ways, with different media: to give utterance to the One has always been the objective of the artist. (Even Impressionism did not aim for the Many, only for the One in all its multiplicity.) Life will always be the object of the artist's longing (he a stranger to life), and the higher his conception of art, the higher his esteem for this thing called life, which eludes his grasp (which he does not succeed in capturing).

To Richard Herre

Stuttgart
July 1913

Usually I am all too gentle and polite. In the sense that everyone aspires toward the contrary of his nature, or should so aspire, in order to become a richer person (as Goethe says).

I believe in the fruitfulness of resignation, of pain; the sickness I mentioned is of course spiritual in nature. Spiritual wounds. But this Goethean "die and be reborn,"* this spiritual death and spiritual resurrection is something I believe one can observe in the life of every truly artistic person; one might almost wish that this pattern of rising and falling would repeat itself over and over again. Goethe calls it "recurrent puberty." It protects the artist against stagnation.

Resignation: rich soil for the most delicate blossoms. So I shall not make any effort to recover from this sickness.

Diary

July 1913

The Cubists' shared desire for system and basic artistic laws make Cubism appear a style which suppresses individuality. This appearance, however, stems from the external similarity of all the Cubists' works; this similarity results from their shared principles, and merely conceals the fine individual nuances within the general conceptual framework.

Some artists, like Beethoven or van Gogh, have wanted to burst out and establish new laws, but great artists such as Mozart, Bach, Leonardo, Dürer have accepted the existing rules, held themselves in check. The artist should give no scope or encouragement to the sentimental, to "mood"; only to creation, the ultimate, the impossible.

---

*"Stirb und werde," a key phrase in Goethe's poem "Selige Sehnsucht," the eighteenth poem in the first book of the West-östlicher Diwan. — Translator

The earthly lot of genius is toil, trouble, and pain, and only the beholder has the privilege of indulging himself in emotion, in tears.

Not insanity, hypertension; ecstasy, perhaps, when its time is come, in rare, divine moments; but sober, collected productivity based on husbanded strength.

Conceptual vision—an idea—directs the artist's work, guides his hand. The more clearly defined the idea, the more noble simplicity he achieves.

Simplicity—not meagerness; that is the goal.

I believe in the world of the visible. I believe in the painter's mode of vision, i.e. abstraction won of familiarity with nature.

"He who can pluck out Nature possesses her" (Dürer). Study nature, drink it all in, and then render the inner vision.

Diary

July 1913

Respect the unconscious! The hand unconsciously succeeds where calculating reason would remain baffled.

Impressionism's great virtue: the hand was the acknowledged master; its downfall: insufficient understanding of and feeling for the beauty of accidental effects.

To Otto Meyer

Stuttgart
July 10, 1913

They say that an artistic principle in unadulterated form is a horror, and it takes dilution, concealment, to achieve real art. Does any scientific basis exist for this contention? If so, the painter would be a sort of blooming idiot, for whom thought and intellectual understanding meant ruin.

Cézanne and Vincent certainly seem dramatic by contrast with Spitzweg. And they lack the wit Spitzweg displayed in his letters. But I do not say that for the sake of the joke *[Witz]*. You might say, with Ophelia, "You are merry *[Spitz]*, my lord."* I also wanted to ask you who the Hamlet of painting is, although I already know it beyond the shadow of a doubt: Picasso. But you are probably not sufficiently acquainted with him to appreciate the profound truth of my comparison. The writer Jean Paul describes how, after a long inner struggle, a village schoolmaster bites into a gingerbread heart which he had intended to bring to his sweetheart. To restore the heart to its original shape, he keeps taking little bites, each time with an inner struggle, forming the gingerbread successively into a circle, a square, a little heart, and so on.

Diary

July 1913

Corot, Courbet: portrayal of nature as an innovation, a challenge to be met; therefore gray (restraint in the use of color). Cézanne has this problem solved; he can thus devote himself to color. In Picasso a new innovation: abstraction, form; he, too, renounces color, in the interest of achieving greater and greater subtlety.

I should like to trace a monumental form with a line no thicker than a hair. Delicacy of style (like Flaubert).

Delaunay: the straight line as an ideal.

The more color, the less form; my work: more formed now but less colorful.

To Otto Meyer

Stuttgart
End of July 1913

Do you by any chance imagine I am all alone? Oh, no! I have a companion, wingéd, friend to the night, enemy to the sun. One evening she came in through the open window to visit me: a bat. I gave her a box in which to spend the night, and the next morning she ate zwieback from my hand, then flew back and forth in the studio, now and then scrabbling around on the table. I seldom read the newspaper, but on that day of all days I

---

*Hamlet, III, ii. − Translator

happened upon the following item: should one malign the heavenly rays merely because bats flee the sun? Rather a thousand bats should be blinded than that the sun should be darkened on their account! Saadi!*

Diary

August 17, 1913

Just read *Crime and Punishment,* full of admiration for the Russians. Raskolnikov murders out of thirst for knowledge: to see whether he is a man or a varmint; whether he has the makings of a Napoleon. Then Nicolai, the painter, who wants to take up the Cross out of sheer hunger for suffering. Deeds with the greatest potential for spiritual transfiguration. The Russians yearn for transfiguration and have the strength to see it through. Is Germanic coolness an advantage and the Russians' tyrannical subconscious an impediment? Ballast?

Diary

August 1913

What makes Oscar Wilde's artistically perfect pre-prison works less profound than the ones that follow *(de profundis)?* The new theme: pain and suffering? The new theme as a goad and a chalice of discord?

Something really ought to be done.

In any case I must declare war on play, on arabesques, on smiles, on gracefulness, on lapping waves, and perhaps also on unassuming happiness.

To Otto Meyer

Stuttgart
July 15, 1914

Concerning the choice of recognized masters, my thinking runs as follows: if my earlier works revealed unconscious similarities with Corot and Courbet, it was only natural that I

---

*Sheik Muslitiu-'d-Din, called Saadi or Sadi, ca. 1190–1291, one of the most celebrated Persian poets. — Translator

15

should be attracted to Cézanne and follow his lead. Now Picasso is furnishing the logical continuation of this line. In a recently published book, an art critic points out what links these masters; he describes their chief common characteristic as: absolute form. That must be equivalent to the French *peinture*. The critic rejects metaphysical, symbolic painting as long as the symbols do not develop out of the images themselves. Itten is enthusiastic about this book and is devoting a lot of study to theory, to Marées's and Fiedler's theories of art; according to him, Fiedler's major preoccupation is precisely this idea of absolute form. He says Marées makes use of familiar, convenient symbols, or, put more simply: with him, form comes foremost. I shall also mention briefly that I have lately discovered the pleasures of the prism. It inspires me with many ideas for colorful pictures. Are these thoughts the herald of a change in style? I would interpret the move from gray to color as symbolic.

To Otto Meyer

Stuttgart
July 30, 1914

Depending on what comes of the declaration of war, of Russia's decision and the German mobilization . . . .

The mood here is very agitated: demonstrations in the streets, newspaper extras, hoarding of flour, and, as I say, tomorrow the decision.

To Otto Meyer

Stuttgart
November 9, 1914

Have to bring you up to date. For a while I was near Verdun in the Argonnes. Then ended up north of Lille, and just as we were digging in, I got my sprained ankle. A few days later there were bloody battles. A feigned attack by night, during which I came to know all kinds of artillery without being in immediate danger myself; then one night an unsuccessful attempt to blow up a bridge; patrol duty in a very advanced position, in the course of which a rock the size of my head came hurtling past me—those were the perils to which I was exposed! Nights spent in the trenches, exhausting marches, wretched quarters for the night—all part of it. But why did fate have to call me away again, put me back into the civilized atmosphere of a hospital, of home, thrust books into my hands, when I was already completely resigned, had turned my back on life? You wouldn't believe the coincidences that have occurred—enough to drive one mad! For instance: my ankle got sprained overnight, how or why I haven't the vaguest notion.

Another instance: in among cowboy-and-Indian books, patriotic writings, trash—*Niels Lyhne* by Jacobsen. Do you know it? Time and again I run up against myself in the book. He dies as a volunteer.

In Aachen I order a book through one of the nurses: Stifter's *Abdias*. There are no copies available, and I leave Aachen without having read it. The first book that falls into my hands in this hospital, also amidst trash, lying on top of the pile: *Abdias!*

From Lille I came clear across Belgium by train to Aachen, where I spent a week in the army hospital. Then back here for a week. Everything beautifully organized. Good food. Now "discharged from hospital" with a week's leave. Then probably off again with the next troop transport. I would volunteer all over again, even if it were possible to stay in Stuttgart. Around here it is a disgrace for a young person to be seen in civilian clothes. And even if that were not the case—there is only one right thing to do. Stuttgart is changed, or has the uniform changed me? Yes, yes. What better solution could there be for my poor heart than the field—especially the field of honor!

To Otto Meyer

Stuttgart
January ᵽ

Discharged from the hospital now, "fit to serve,"
I feel crushed. I'm no longer the same fellow who v
so eagerly in August. Physically, and especially ₥
beginning was quite simply admirable. But—ev₣

18

that. The situation has changed a great deal. Deeply dug-in positions on both sides, so that taking an enemy trench, which would earlier have been too comical to report, now actually represents an accomplishment. And then: every day a battle report has to be published. Even in the military hospital, where of course the newspapers are read avidly, people were saying that the Germans have now learned to lie.

The theme song: the charts above the beds in the army hospital list the patients' ranks—people's militiaman, reserve officer, wartime volunteer. One of the latter was so ashamed to be a "wartime volunteer" that he obliterated the words on his chart.

To Otto Meyer

Stuttgart
March 11, 1915

I am writing under especially difficult circumstances. I found my studio occupied—despite Hoelzel's promise to the contrary. After all, I did live there. So now I am more or less homeless.

Back in uniform, and again in this sort of trance. The most incredible struggle raging in my mind. Crises that surpass any I have encountered before.

Diary

March 1915

What determines Picasso's use of solid materials in his pictures? His sense for the solid, his passion for experimentation, for the piquant.

What brings him to Cubism, in fact? With him it is not a manifesto for, say, the Buddhistic approach to life. With him, mysticism springs from total form, as with Cézanne from objectivity.

My goal is a sort of mystical objectivity. Would that imply subjectivity, then? Employing materials like silver, tinfoil, dust, sand, silk, etc. for what they can express. Cubism as a result not of logic but of feeling, an attitude toward life.

Basic forms: square, circle (as a line and filled in), right-angled triangle, rhombus, oval, ellipse, star, cross, half-moon. (The Christians and Mohammedans have a sign, a symbol.) (Those who lack one: the Buddhists, the Jews. Why?)

Cézanne, the Philistine, monomaniac, hard worker, woman-hater.—I am thinking of the contrast to the aesthete artists, the "talents," social butterflies.

Diary

Mid-March 1915

At first a soldier through and through. Sense of participation. Exaltation when marching off to war. Pride in one's role vis-à-vis those remaining behind: protector, envoy, hero.

Out in the field, matter against mind, because of the hardships. Apathetic surrender to fate. Fatalism. A human being once more as soon as an idyll is found. Then illness. Then away from the front lines. Military hospital in Aachen. Human inferiority all around, this awareness increasing to the point of misanthropy. Anarchism. Time for reflection. Stay alive at any price. Preserve one's life, even by ignoble means. Paint—and stop reading altogether. Then the insight that there is no escaping, and back to the field with desperate eagerness. A matter of destiny. Premonition of some ridiculous wound. Christ collapsed under the weight of the Cross—also a poor soldier. But now, having come full circle, back to the original state of mind.

That the strength should be there, but not the vision. A profusion of resources, a surfeit of ability, talent, but no vision; what is vision?

Buddha, fasting, asceticism. The thoughts are called upon to justify the attitude, the idea. "I am fasting now"; when I act this way or that, I am acting Buddhistically, ascetically, wisely.

Buddha: perfection, the classical. The ideal, straight line. Only the finest human beings succeed in maintaining such a stance. Weaker beings who may know and live this ideal become weak in the face of it (in their painting concentrating, and how typically, on the *effect*). Conceivable: a painter, an artist who disdains effect. Only artists who are sure of themselves and the genuineness of what they have to offer have the patience to

19

wait until people come to them. They need not curry favor by means of dramatic effects and ingratiation.

Dostoevsky: delve deep into the rich, mad life of mankind.* Here you have Jesus Christ, specifically Grünewald's— earthly, human, demonic, covered with blood and running sores, the crown of thorns in his tangled hair, and this artistic creation is as different from its original, Christ, as Japanese art and Buddha are different. The differences? Is the former more profound?

Impressionism: the absolute in superficial visual impression; carried to its ultimate conclusion, as it were, exhausted. Now pure color will have its turn. This extreme will likewise be carried to its ultimate conclusion—exhausted.

The fleeting impression, and color—these are elements of painting which are more accessible to the less gifted painter than, say, form or drawing.

Looked at pictures of Amsterdam and other Dutch cities again. Fascinating. It must be wonderful to live in a city which awakens such a lively, pleasurable interest in one. When I was there, the city made an even stronger impression on me than Paris. I must have a certain leaning toward bourgeois tranquillity. What attracts me in the early works of Liebermann. I also see analogies in literature—Lawrence Sterne, but even more Jean Paul.

Diary

March 20, 1915

One needs a tremendous amount of patience. The ability to wait, hold oneself back, conserve one's strength, in favor of something superior. Precisely among modern artists one sees so many examples of men who early produced work of high quality and thus established their reputations, but later fell back on a calculated formula and lost the sense of humility which had made their first works worthwhile. Artistic decline as a result of sudden fame or producing in quantity is such a common phenomenon that one should take heed and fight to

---

*A quotation from the "Prologue in the Theater" in Goethe's *Faust*. — Translator

20

maintain one's original outlook, and thereby the youthfulness and high quality of one's painting.

I, unlike other, more fortunate beings, do not regard being a soldier as an end in itself. I love life—the life of the mind. Am I so unbelieving that I question the immortality of the soul, and therefore also that of my beloved, but oh, so unearthly, ideas? But since eternity awaits us in the beyond, and beside it the short span of life fades to insignificance, why not live this life to the full, brief though it may be? I am going off to war because the mystery of fate tempts my curiosity. What does the mighty chaos of war hold in store for me? A bullet through the chest, "with hurrahs on my lips," by night, by day, in sunshine? Will my strength even last until I face the enemy? Or is a field hospital somewhere in Galicia waiting to receive me? Will I be crippled? Will I lose my right hand, my right arm, my sight? A painter—losing his sight! That would be a practical, "appropriate" form of suffering! We shall see what this cornucopia of fate contains for me. Yes, now that painting is denied me, I love it above all else. Only now do I perceive how much one might strive for.

Diary

March 29, 1915

Often memories come back to me. Looking backward! How much I have experienced already. And then I feel like the Prodigal Son—only the other way around; I have no regrets. Everything was good. It was a life, unique, and could not have been lived any other way. No matter where I lift the curtain of the past to peep behind—it was all good and beautiful.

How many things I should like to describe. The trips: Holland—Amsterdam—Paris—London, but the earlier ones, too.

The friendships: first and foremost with Otto Meyer, of course—the greatest experience of my life.

The women.

But also the dreams for the future. Curious, that I should so often think about setting up house. How all my wishes would come together, acquire reality; and I can conceive of the woman who would fit in, too.

21

But that is only one side. I can also picture a life continued in solitude—taking the Cross, far from friends, relatives, in a strange land. In a hermit's retreat. Avoiding human contacts. Waiting for my true calling.

Dairy

April 1915

To avoid too much socialization I choose isolation.

The artist creates out of disbelief. This can be seen in the man who whenever he is not creating doubts his power to produce (Hugo Wolf). It is this very doubt which elicits productivity. Aesthetics for the aesthetes!

Beneficial for the productive artist is anything which adds to the great reservoir within him, no matter what its aesthetic value or lack thereof.

Diary

April 10, 1915

A query on the modern, in painting etc.: what is new about it? What is modern?

So many things achieve artificial modernity by drawing on earlier styles: woodcut style, African style, Gothic.

Woodcut style: the very awkwardness in the treatment of the material accounted for this style's inwardness and expressiveness; its rediscovery thus part of the reaction against Impressionism.

Negro style: also Gauguin's flight to the primitive peoples, seeking an artificial renewal from this quarter. Picasso as a perfect example of shopping around among all kinds of archaism.

Gothic: typical for all expressive style, ecstatic, coinciding completely with contemporary artistic aspirations. The link with Catholicism, Francis of Assisi, etc. Kandinsky: mentions the appeal of every unconscious arrangement of lines, reminiscent of microscopic enlargements, similar to Pankok's sensational discoveries. The "allegorical meaning writ large" of which Novalis is thinking.

Kokoschka: richness achieved through the rumpled, fortuitous quality of his technique.

Creating forms means: Life. Children are creators because they are close to the mystery of their feelings, more so than the imitators of Greek forms. Artists are gripped by the spontaneity with which children express themselves, making sovereign use of their paper and drawing implements and paying perspective and such things no heed. This is important because art today is looking for a pure, concise, hieroglyphic style.

We envy the primitive peoples their strong, native sense of form, the product of a vision which may be primitive but is also genuine and profound.

What does the artist do? He makes the unclear appear clear, the unconscious conscious, the impossible possible; plucks the One out of the Chaos, simplicity out of multiplicity.

Amidst the rush of visions I had, there was one which went this way: the phenomenon itself might be described as bold yet modest. It contained everything of value which had been achieved in painting. The elements of modern painting: conquest of the surface, the secrets of plasticity. As Poussin said: *"Je n'ai rien négligé."*

My moral resolve to abjure charming effects, those unplanned beauties born of hasty work, makes art herself haste away from me.

Diary

April 13, 1915

Lichtenberg: the same felicitous style springing from a sense of one's own substance, from corpulence, from comfortableness, such as one finds in so many Germans—whom I dislike for that very reason. And yet this healthy manner, all strength and energy, represents a real possibility. I have always shunned the comforts of a positive attitude. Was so sarcastic toward anything of the sort. Family, friendships, the beauties of life—I suspected such things carried the risk of shallowness, insipidness. So for myself, castigation, taking up my Cross—not out of Christian spirit, but out of egotism, because only in this sort of life do I see salvation.

My plan of action will have to be as follows: until further notice bury myself, flee the world: people, women—a hermit, a monk, thoroughly independent. But really stick to this, strictly, with determination. What matters is the level on which we live, not superficial breadth. Phoebus challenges the gods. We pray for a long life—but what counts is that it also be a meaningful life, have its great moments. Time should be measured in terms of spirit, not mechanically.

This degree of uncertainty is unusual for me. Every book whets my curiosity. Am thus surrounded by a wild conglomeration of half-begun books, books I have already read, books I want to read. Took Lermontov along with me to Berlin. The heroic, worldly, sensuous Russian type. A dash of Heine, as Dostoevsky said. Robust, with a powerful sensuality. Brought Nietzsche back with me from Berlin. The philosopher of my youth. As a result, memories of youth. Pointed, fine points, finding points. I would like to refute his Antichrist. Artists love Christ. The original Christ, not Christianity.

And then the world of Hogarth and Lichtenberg. The English milieu. And wedged in between, Stirner: his uniqueness. His style proclaims his doctrine. Calmer than Nietzsche's. Factual. Scientific. Then Bjørnson's *The Newly Married*. Nordic, sunny, cheerful mood. Healthy colors. Everything healthy, the people, their feelings. Nature! Nothing that casts a shadow. Color.

The Russians: Dostoevsky deep, gloomy; earth tones, of course. The color of a plowed field under natural light. No artificial color. At the most, blood color. Nordic: robust, glowing color, healthier then, for example, Larsson's, which tends toward English anemia.

France: from the sated splendor of the red-and-gold theaters to the consumptive, decadent pinks and greens of the late period.

Spain: the world of El Greco, ecstatic, religious; Velásquez' pride.

German: I aspire to the Düreresque mode, which in Grünewald reaches its climax, in the form of color and drawing. Truly a merging of all styles: *the* style! Adapting and assimilating everything. This is something I must pursue. My chain of thought was curious: the Rhine, German forests, Weber's *Freischütz, Oberon,* the German fairy tales, Wagner, the *Meistersinger,* Nuremberg, Dürer—Grünewald. And then I had it. There it was. And a great deal more also joins this cavalcade.

Diary

April 22–23, 1915

Birkenstraße, late evening, sitting at the table, piano being played downstairs, a Beethoven adagio.

It lodges deep inside me, as Beethoven almost always does. This adagio stayed with me for the next few days, always running through my head.

The Solitüde. Restaurant. Piano. I enter the house, and the adagio begins. Always sends a little shudder through me. Simply note this sort of thing down, without pathos or amazement. "It exists."

A painter in search of something new. He is full of inner visions, i.e. bubbling over with forms, fantasies, possibilities, new ideas—but he lacks a central concept, a theme, an outlook which would contain all this ferment.

So he produces very strange drawings, meaningless but for the hope that the meaningless may become so familiar that meaning creeps in. Shape experience. The threat of expressionism.

A series of failures, paintings in which I try to achieve something alien to me, is always followed by an enthusiastic mood in which I finally strike the right note. That is how I did the *Selbstporträt* ["Self-Portrait"]. Then the spherical boy in the dance hall. Each time there was calm, reflection, sense of control, coolness. This the mood in which my good paintings have been done.

Create this mood intentionally, artificially? How? By reminding myself of all my past sins? Go over them each time? It is like life. Must one always sin anew in order to attain chastity? The risk inherent in strictly preserved chastity is precisely that one may lose contact with the intensity of life, with its realism.

I am no romantic. List of the painters who are my type:

van Eyck	the delicacy, the hands
El Greco	but without the Spanish element
Chodowiecki	his elongated figures
Memling	the small-headed Madonnas
Holbein	the static element; calm, composure; his drawing
Breughel	absence of affectation

In this connection, Leibl, too. But he lacks grand style, the stature of a type. Confidence in these tastes would be desirable, could form the basis of judgment. For instance, that I am less fond of Rubens, Rembrandt, et al.

Diary

April 15, 1915

Lao-tse says: "He who spies his light and yet chooses to remain in the dark is a model for all men."

To pick out the significant, important forms and lay heavy stress on them, then group the less important ones around them, portrayed less emphatically.

Why does one need nature?

Because nature offers forms which the imagination cannot create, or because the imagination is enriched, stimulated by the forms perceived in nature. To think about: a painter who has to be taken out of circulation; if he is put in the barest of prison cells, for instance. If he is a dreamer, his imagination will conjure up the wildest dreams for him, and he will give them shape. Or the few simple necessities with which he is provided will lend him their forms, and he will create a world out of them. A still life consisting of the most simple objects and forms can contain the basis of an entire mural.

Why do I sometimes stand as if bewitched before an impression nature provides? Like a medium, jerking like a divining rod, electrified, thrilled to my very depths? It means that my instinct has fixed on a certain nuance in nature, in nature as I see it, as I experience it, the form in which it makes the greatest impression on me.

Amazing how in drawing I always end up being playful,

teasing, probably due to the greater flexibility of pencil, or in water colors, the flowing medium. On a wall, character comes immediately. The more unyielding material. "Take a material as unyielding as marble, that you may conquer it with patience" (Delacroix).

Diary

April 27, 1915

I have come full circle. Have returned to Henri Rousseau. That implies a return to the possible, to the lyrical, to the hermit. Consolidating everything accomplished thus far. Simple motifs. But with inner depths, inner depths. No mannerism, no brush technique, not modern. More like Thomas Haider; away from the art-and-industry complex. "Colorful cubism"!!! Art of the people! A folk painter. Draw strength from the local scene.

My earlier garden-house landscapes. Cézanne restrained me: made me draw my inner feelings together, not give in to them.

The pine tree, the acacia, the house. Also the human figure. The type. Rousseau—the colors of Venetian blinds. The wild fantasy of the still lifes, true, but the spirit of Rousseau should make me more inward. I want to paint an unusually beautiful portrait, figure, landscape.

Join forces with the idealists of form. Lehmbruck and Archipenko in sculpture, the Cubists in painting. They form a bridge to architecture, for their paintings are constructed.

Create the sky out of earth-born colors. "Motifs that are not too weighty," the modest still life. Take what lies close at land in order to reach what lies most distant.

Diary

July 12, 1915

We are bivouacked in a Russian village. Already passed through, and in part camped in, Mushaken, Janovo, Kolaki. At noon today Hindenburg is supposed to come and review us. Two long processions of yellowish-brown Russian prisoners passing through the village on their way from the forest. We are divided into "old" companies—those who have already been in the field—and "new" ones which have not yet seen combat. So I'm with the oldies. Who are supposed to lead an attack tomorrow, or so we hear.

Fixed balloons, planes, little clouds of shrapnel, the roar of cannon, especially last night. A rain storm yesterday, from which we fled into the tents we had just finished putting up; a beautiful sight inside the tents: the gray ones translucent and greenish-gray, the brown ones rust-colored—the colors I use in my pictures. I feast my eyes on the splendor of the colors, the different greens of the ground, the gray soldiers; I soak this in, and smoke, and seek the Buddhistic tranquillity which I also managed to achieve on the march. Going from 5 A.M. to 2 P.M. without eating: only cold coffee, a piece of sugar. When we camp, food is prepared: meat, noodles—bustle, hard work; I have laid hands on a bag of rice, my idea being to get by on it for the rest of the march, Japanese-style. A princely meal yesterday. Everyone received a hunk of cold cooked ham, a piece of Swiss cheese, plums, which we later cooked, jam, cigars, cigarettes.

More rain is on its way.

Diary

August 31, 1915

Motto: Persian. Saw the page in the Cologne Library, and then the miniatures, German. Now I have painted a lively painting which has all the charms of the unexpected, all the tantalizing mystery of the unconscious—admirable, original, full of life, in cool, covering tones. It gives an impression of otherworldly serenity. Persian! Buddhistic.

In the Greek vase paintings vivacious drawing is superimposed on the rigid form; does one not find something similar in Beardsley and others, who have managed not to lose any of the original charm?

Diary

I believe in the visible and in the products of the eye, the character, the emotions.

In the paintings of the modern young Germans one finds too much unkneaded dough. Maybe because they take on more than they can handle. Many of their pictures are a wild potpourri full to overflowing. They lack a unifying line. Sharpness, ruggedness, precision. The magnificence of any conception depends on the clarity with which it is perceived.

Time and again they romantically try to take on the whole world. A wealth of promising beginnings, but little application, little patience in thinking things out, in following through on the creative process.

Perhaps a great fiasco will descend upon the formalists. The older forms of art known to us, and especially the art of primitive peoples, are all rooted in a specific world of belief and emotion. It was the mind, the idea, which forged itself a form. Example: the Apollo of Tenea. The way in which he curls his thumb into his fist and extends his arms expresses an attitude toward life. A figure symbolic of a certain body culture. But how about the sculpture of the Middle Ages? Empathy in abstract form.

Just now art's many paths lie before me, unrestricted; I must make up my mind, so as to achieve peace and quiet in my work. I must decide to look neither to right nor left, but to choose a path (at long last) and stick to it. So this is the crossroads.

I must opt for Cézanne or van Gogh, classicism or romanticism, Ingres or Delacroix, Leibl or Böcklin, Bach or Beethoven. I would like to present the most romantic idea in the most austere form. I would like to have such a mastery of technique that the actual painting would present the least challenge. And indeed this is the case: I have the form; what I lack is the vision. At one time the opposite was true. Now I find my hands full and my heart empty. Yet I remain convinced that the idea is the source of form; the spirit guides the hand. My next undertaking will be a series of still lifes in which I will cast a thoroughly romantic perception in perfect artistic form. A non-realistic view of the still life, so to speak; and this form, derived from nature, will someday help me give shape to inner concepts. I shall thus cultivate the still life, which lies close at hand, in order to reach what lies far off. "Do the immediate in order to reach the most distant" (Hebbel).

Diary

Beginning of September, 1915

I am lying under the acacias and thinking of Rousseau, who must always come to mind in this connection. Just as Sisley and Pissarro have put their stamp on certain landscape-moments.

How beautiful Seurat is in his simplicity and firmness. Seurat's painting achieves the ultimate in movement, a dance using the strictest forms (linear, clear).

Düsseldorf and the event: Matthias Grünewald. So many similar aims! The colors of the rainbow plus black. The angels ranged according to the colors of the spectrum. The colossal forms of the pointed arch. The Angel of the Annunciation red-orange, a mass of flames. The garments of the resurrected Christ; a bizarre flower in iris hues. Chrome yellow! my *idée fixe*. I find everything here—most wonderful to behold!

The most Dionysian form and the most Apollonian. Once again the temptation to delve deep into the richness. Stern Memling raises a warning finger. Grünewald has a wild beauty to him. Van Eyck delightfully precious, a diamond.

Diary

September 1915

I vacillate between two styles, two worlds, two attitudes toward life. If I could succeed in analyzing them, I think I would be able to shake off all these doubts.

Characteristics of the first type are: discipline, ruggedness, reserve, restraint, exclusivity, profundity. The effect does not lie on the surface; a first look leaves one cold, but gradually something is revealed to the beholder, by delayed action, as it were. These are probably the essential characteristics of ancient Greek and Roman art.

The characteristics of the other type, then, are diametrically opposed to the art of Antiquity; what contrast could be greater than the Gothic? Or mysticism. In short, anything supernatural, gigantic, Dionysian, intoxicated, enraptured, dynamic. The effect is direct, abrupt, casting an immediate spell, imprisoning one, "bedazzling the senses," overwhelming. These are the great contrasts represented by Antiquity and the Middle Ages. But within them, too, contradictions exist. "Hölderlin, a Hellenic monk."

Given my strong propensity in painting as in life for the rococo, wouldn't the best antidote be to impose the most rigid discipline on myself? But the result would be stylized, sacral art, that other pitfall.

Is it really the drop of folly that makes all the difference? Well then, let us be crazy! Crazy enough to depict things which are only obscurely sensed, apprehended, which defy conceptual thought and reason, which logic has not yet subverted. The truth of fools, the madness which has method after all. If we hesitate, cling to the familiar and what can be readily understood, our grandchildren will have to take the step in any case. But if we forge ahead, we shall anticipate them. The boundaries of awareness will be expanded, and our progress toward solution of the great riddle hastened.

Everything should merge into one great current. Mysticism, the primitive, the most recent, Greece, Gothic—all the elements must be drawn upon.

I must break this spell. Must get back in touch with myself. It is high time. I want to be *me*, even if my artistic ability dies in the attempt. I want to smash the windows of my stifling cell and let in color, world, life, and even more. Enough of being *judicious*—I want to be *audacious*. Let my material be everything human, all of experience. Certainly my inalienable artistic psyche will turn up.

Diary

October 1915

The square of the ribcage.

the circle of the belly,

the cylinder of the neck,

the cylinders of the arms and lower thighs,

the circles of the elbow joints, elbows, knees,
    shoulders, knuckles,

the circles of the head, the eyes,

the triangle of the nose,

the line connecting the heart and the brain,

the line connecting the sight with the object seen,

the ornament that forms between the body and the outer
    world, symbolizing the former's relationship to the
    latter.

Diary

November 3, 1915

All traditions are shattered. The tradition of Classical Antiquity has been toppled.

Artists are surveying the field. Previously neglected or unappreciated styles. Back to the very beginnings: Negro style. The paintings of the Bushmen. Primitive ornamentation. Early Egyptian style.

Also: primal states of mind: children's drawings. Unappreciated: peasant art, the primitive. Almost all of these unrecognized styles have been resurrected in modern painting; each has found an artist to champion it. So where do we find something really new? Absolutely new? In Cubism, one might be tempted to say. True, its forms are derived from *peinture*. Nevertheless, Cubism is a free development, even if one based on traditions. The line is traced with pure, cold calculation; crystals appear; cubic forms.

Universal aspiration toward the mystical. Toward the incomprehensible, unnamable. . . .

There are artists who seek these things in order, others in chaos.

Still fresh and new: the simple, basic forms. The simple

32

form of the square, the triangle, the circle, the oval. The psychology of these forms. . . .

Walt Whitman: "I sing the heavenly square." One must be uncomplicated. . . .

Thus far only the forms have been mentioned. Color should also be considered.

Then comes knowledge of the medium. Some day we may find ourselves fully equipped. The hand, the eye, the sensibility are trained. We have everything we need, but nothing to say. Nothing to express. A creative conception is lacking. Insight. Inner freedom.

Diary

November 7, 1915

Once you reject classical painting and art, the sky is the limit. Everything opens up: the mystical, color, intrepidity—the result must be glorious. Van Gogh offers an example of intentional rejection of classicism. Beauty begins where grace overcomes the monstrous. That is the source of classical beauty. Hölderlin's anguish over his monstrous Germany; the monstrousness of the Goths! Classical painting, *peinture*. Good taste will keep us eternally in shackles. Liberation means embracing the unlimited possibilities.

To Otto Meyer

Stuttgart

January 3, 1916

I guess I must have a powerful imagination. At any rate, I am haunted just now by visions and images of an artistic ideal. Yet I am unhappy about this affliction. The fact is that I am conversant with all the means of artistic expression—but my heart is empty.

I still have hope, however. Unless I am mistaken, my blood is coursing with a rare fire and vigor, and I sense that everything can still turn out well. Perhaps you are amazed that I worry so much about painting. And in fact painting is the major source of my uneasiness, even in the trenches, if you can believe that. At the moment I am enjoying a furlough for continuing at the Academy. When I was in uniform, my mind was buzzing with artistic visions—now that I am supposed to start putting them on canvas, I am left practically high and dry. But if I concentrate and hang onto what I have, I think I can capture something.

Diary

Mid-March 1916

What makes profundity possible in art? Should one throw obstacles in the way of one's own competence? What provides the most effective impediment? Imposing form on an idea? Imposing a new form on a new idea?

This much should be said against complicated materials: it will always be admirable to express oneself by means of a few lines on a scrap of paper. So much for elaborate apparatus.

I am struggling against my Renaissance tendencies. My weapons? Discipline, form, surface.

Forms of the New. No technique, not cute little artistic tricks. Simply registration of the necessities.

The Futurists are crude, hostile toward civilization. But in fact they represent a new world. The future will consist of these elements. Of visionary concept and the few successful works that have been produced thus far. That is truly new. Here we have brand new symbols which have the potential to become the symbols of our times.

A defect in Futurism: it is Impressionism all over again. Presents things which are surpassed by film. Impressionism meets its downfall in photography and the film. These inventions point up the true calling of art. Abstraction. What no form of photography can convey.

What poets achieved before painters: "I am all blue" (Else Lasker-Schüler), or "silver feelings," the "eyes gape inward," "my brain stretches together," "I feel an iron band around my brain," "the cherry-red silk draperies which the hand caresses,"

34

lemon yellow—rose—violet. Everything put at the service of expression. All means are permissible. At the risk of appearing abstruse, pathological. The virtuoso of form comes to despise form. From the pinnacle back to the sources!

Here we find truth. *La vrai comédie* . . . .

Diary

March 20, 1916

Now that I have sung the praises of arbitrariness, of disdain for any and all form, I shall sing the praises of order. Can I escape myself? Intellectually, perhaps, by mental tightrope walking, but not when I am standing in front of a canvas. I have an irresistible urge toward form. In the final analysis I cannot deny my origins. What I have already created exists as testimony to the nature of its creator. I want to establish standards I can follow in my work, so as not to go astray each time I venture on something new. I hereby decree: the underlying conception should be bold, it cannot be bold enough, broad enough, all-embracing enough. But then it must be given shape and form. Since the form-giving part causes me the least difficulty, I must concentrate my efforts on the conception. This is the main thing; it determines what must follow and guides the hand.

Through nature, through this handclasp with the universe, some of the vitality of nature flows into the work of art. Nature can be perceived either through romantic, imaginative, fantastical eyes, or through cool and sober ones.

Diary

March 21, 1916

Spent the evening in the Residenz Café. Back in the barracks had a cup of coffee, which resulted in a night of the wildest dreams and fantasies. I wanted to get up and write, write down all the things I had visualized. These imaginings were crazy, but they keep multiplying, and eventually such inner visions create a burning desire to capture something in form. Then all classicism vanishes, and boundless possibilities open up.

35

Diary

March 23, 1916

Manifesto: its name is Henri Rousseau!

In the military hospital in Galkhausen, I finally touched terra firma, after roaming, ill and exhausted, through boundless, drifting, formless realms of the mind; similarly yesterday, depressed and tired, I at last found my way back to the world of the visible, to acceptance of myself, to my past, to my desires. The process: fresh from a walk and a bath, I sit and sketch the tantalizing planes of a photograph. First uninterestedly, then with ever-increasing interest. The first drawing turns out cool and precise, the second richer in form, more creative. Now I am using the colors of the mind.

Greetings, Rousseau!

Diary

March 1916

If one simply follows one's instincts, one can brush true depths, perhaps very, very rarely reach them, but unconsciously, like a medium.

Diary

End of March, 1916

Just as the French were ahead of us in aviation, so, too, they were ahead of us in a discovery: aerial photographs provide a hitherto unknown view of the earth's surfaces and forms from above, combined with the enormous tonal effects of photography, and the French immediately perceived that this technique can derive new, untried stimuli from the visible world. I can think of nothing more fantastic and stimulating to the imagination. It has mainly to do with the treatment of the surface, be-all and end-all of painting, an art which, it so happens, chooses the surface as its field of expression.

Good paintings drop like ripe fruits, the product of crises that have been weathered.

Harsh punishment awaits the artist who tries to work before the right moment has come. Harsh punishment is the reward for cheap repetition. The "unique" work of art always conveys a sense of exceptionality, originality; one feels the palpitations of an artist as he gropes and hesitates, still unsure of the effect. This is a far cry from the "flighty" product which results when no obstacles exist and the artist keeps to a well-worn groove .... It is all a question of choice; art means choosing among the riches of nature.

Extremes: the ultimate in line, the ultimate in surface treatment.

The great peril: the desire to be a certain way!

This self-consciousness dulls the creative process. Everything should be the result of ineluctable necessity. In that sense one cannot go back to anything. All is destiny. Creativity likewise. No!: there must be no return to conditions of the past; that would be death! I am a modern man, and there is no help for it. Now new possibilities again; we have come full circle once more.

No "artistry," no *"peinture,"* no technique.

Diary

April 4, 1916

True excellence will not be found on the surface.

The life task of the artist: to assemble and portray his best, most precious visions.

I am on the point of sacrificing everything in order to save my soul. If the rich man is supposed to rid himself of all his possessions, why should I not rid myself of my hobby of painting, now that I have realized how half-baked all my efforts are.

I am superior to the half-hearted—once I have recognized them for what they are.

I shall have to learn not to boast about that. To cling to an old attitude and refuse to give it up, even after seeing a better course, is sin, and it is the first step toward spiritual death. Even greater simplicity, purity, and directness of expression exist. The idea, insight into the essence of art is all-important—the artistic conception is all-important and determines the making of the work of art.

Van Gogh imported a concept from outside—the idea of the primitive, the pathological—and tried to fit it into painting. Cézanne took artistic form as his starting point. For him, as for the French in general, form came first. Others, like Beethoven, van Gogh, wanted to burst out, establish new rules. But some of the great artists, like Mozart, Bach, Leonardo, Dürer, accepted the existing rules, imposed restraints on themselves. Just as the barbaric forms part of the transition to nobility and sophistication.

Some artists register all the phases of their development, every mood; others wait, knowing they can afford to wait, and leave us only those works that are truly free of blemish.

What taxes an artist's strength the most is to let an idea ripen. To keep from rushing ahead impetuously, to be able to wait for perfection. To carry an idea as if one were pregnant and to assure its healthy development by living sensibly.

To Otto Meyer

Stuttgart
May 10, 1916

In my recent paintings I alternate between emphasis on form and emphasis on the underlying conception, and this confusion, this unclarity has occupied my thoughts for a good while, and very intensely. Some observations based on experience: form-oriented pictures have more scope, in the good sense, a monumentality which does not occur in pictures based on an idea. The latter are lyrical, the former related to the spirit of the epic. For the moment I have rejected on principle anything lyrical, lovely or tender, probably because I already have more than enough of this weakness.

Since this letter deals with my dicta and contradictions, here is one more: I vacillate between the greatest sophistication and the greatest simplicity—a contrast like that between the folk song and spiritualism. I am steered toward the former by my heart, my feelings, and my earlier work, which at least gives hints of something similar, in a few of my pictures. Jean Paul and Spitzweg might be mentioned as fairly good examples of this world. My rational mind and my obligation to modernity steer me toward the latter. Yet even if I chose the first course, I would still want to be modern. Here the result would be "obligatory forms," and a marked tendency to shoot off "into the blue." When I quote you thus, this choice is sufficiently discredited. Another factor in favor of the first choice is "the voice of the people." It almost looks as if the few successful paintings among the modernists' works were simple folk songs.

Herwarth Walden has invited me to exhibit in Berlin at the "Sturm" Gallery; but the fact is, I would rather wait until I have mastered a clearer artistic language. He knows my work.

To Otto Meyer

Stuttgart
May 30, 1916

It so happens that I am farther from Christianity now than I was ever close to it. Especially the cherubic element; I have put Angelus Silesius aside for when I am better prepared to appreciate him. My entire capacity for belief is swallowed up by my ideal of a very definite formal style. Perhaps I am preparing the bottles into which the wine will be poured. But I should also consider the vineyard. If it is still a good year . . . .

In a revolutionary play by Büchner,* a grisette says, "It all adds up to the same thing, whether one rejoices in bodies or images of Christ, wine glasses, flowers, or children's toys; it is the same feeling: he who enjoys the most prays the most."

My strongest link with Christianity is (at present) Christian music—Handel, Bach—and, I must add, the style of Christian painting. I revere the style without paying attention to its sources. I make a distinction between the cherubic and the dramatic. The latter I find in the Russian characteristics of Dostoevsky and Strindberg, and also in what Wilde achieved later in life. That is, the motif of suffering. The former suggests divine love, ecstasy, Francis of Assisi.

---

*Georg Büchner (1813–1837), *Danton's Death,* Act I. — Translator

To Willi Baumeister

Stuttgart

August 28, 1916

Your letter received, with lamentation and rage about mail and non-receipt thereof, but in the meantime mine own good Will will have been reached by a letter. Next you will be the recipient of the finished catalogue for the exhibit, parcel post. A meeting with the printer today to select the paper, ditto type and the color of the cover. An orange was not in stock, nor was the coloring matter for a lemon yellow; what remained was merely preserved, but life-preserving, a not-so-bad geranium red (or Germanium?). The catalogue promises, insofar as it is able, to be good, varied, and, we hope, finished by September 2. The pressure we are exerting fits in with high and low pressure systems (of printing), the total cost: 750 marks. From the Hoelzel Foundation: 400 marks. The rest is supposed to be covered by catalogue sales, our coverall. Itten was at first all puffed up, predicting triumph for his magnificent photos, but now that he has been stuffed into the catalogue uni-form and trimmed of his megalomania, he seems somewhat chastened, since your work appears better to him than his own. My contributions are practically out of the running, being drawings. You will see. Your impressions may be shared by quite a few.

Tonight two more declarations of war. Two new enemies— and two less reasons to need friends. All last week large-scale call-ups. Me, too: fit for combat duty and waiting to be transferred at any moment. By now even the palace guard has been declared fit for combat duty; yet appearances have to be maintained—impossible to remove the fellows; though perhaps austerity measures: bearing arms and no presenting by the veterans. Let's see what happens.

To Otto Meyer

Stuttgart

September 7, 1916

The exhibition "Hoelzel and his Circle" in Freiburg has already been promised to Frankfurt and probably also to Cologne and other cities. I feel rather uncomfortable about all this, would rather have the pictures back in my studio.

In the midst of the excitement I was declared fit for combat duty and am supposed to return to the field. There is a German journal appearing in Zurich, *Die weissen Blätter,* * which has bitter things to say about the war. All the parties to the war are heaping guilt upon guilt, and no end in sight.

Diary

September 1916

Klee is the finest among the better-known moderns; yet his most uninspired imitators find more understanding among the art critics than he, the genuine artist. Klee is simply wonderful. He can reveal his entire wisdom in the barest of lines. That is the way a Buddha draws. Calm, composed, unmoved by any passion, the least monumental line of all, searching and child-like, out to capture true greatness. He is everything: intense, tender, and many other superlatives, and this above all: he is original. Here we find, as Blake says, greatness of conception resulting from precision of conception. The accomplishments of all significant men are rooted in a simple but comprehensive insight into the nature of things. To have found this means to have found oneself, and thereby the world.

Today is another great day. My furlough ended, back in uniform. The heavens filled with visions of future projects. Vow: read nothing but the best, things that will nourish the highest aspirations; be very selective. Think and draw. Pursue the One Significant Thing, even if that leads me by tortuous highways and byways. I indulge myself in voluptuous drawing. "Lack of moderation leads to the palace of wisdom."

To Otto Meyer

In the field

October 6, 1916

I have landed in topography, which means map-making for military purposes, using a magnifying glass, utmost exactitude. So I am spared life in the trenches.

The White Pages, edited from 1915 on by the Alsatian poet René Schickele (1883–1940). – Translator

Summer is gradually drawing to an end. You feared for the Germans this summer. They have survived it well, I think. It could have been much worse. Hoelzel is director of the Academy for the next two years. During this time he will want to push through some of his projects, for instance the developmental gallery. He wants modern exhibitions to be treated as conferences at which current issues in painting can be discussed and decided, with the paintings serving as illustrative material. This may be appropriate to the pedagogic character of Hoelzel's and Itten's pictures. Itten in particular wants the painting to "prove" everything. For instance, he is annoyed at my pictures because, as he says, I pay proof little mind, simply go ahead and paint; because he does not find their meaning self-evident. He calls them subjective, and *that* a picture is not supposed to be—or it does not belong in an exhibition. The same old song. Enough!

Diary

Fall 1916

To be strong a thing must grow piece by piece, of most urgent necessity, and simply *have* to be done.

To Otto Meyer

In the field

December 1916

Today I am on leave, or rather, tonight. The mind has not yet fallen under dictatorship, but the passage for its freedom* is considerably narrowed when one's life and limbs are at the disposal of the state. Small consolation that "whatever befalls us is for our own good." Now Germany is making a peace offer. Its reception by the enemy will at least show us where we stand. I myself am pinning considerable hopes on this either-or situation and have them tied up with the thread of my patience, which is near the breaking point.

---

*An echo of the words attributed to the famous fourteenth-century Swiss hero Winkelried, who, at the battle of Sempach, is said to have thrown himself on the pikes of the Austrians, crying, "A passage for freedom!" – Translator

To Otto Meyer

In the field

April 15, 1917

Conversations with my friend Dr. Pfleiderer. Discover we both admire Vermeer. Among other things, he said that Vermeer concentrates so much on *how* to portray a thing that the objects themselves become meaningless; I countered that the choice of subject matter was an integral part of the spirit of his painting.

One of the first things we agreed on was our admiration for the Russians. When the French are unusually good, they come close to the essence of the German; when the Germans outdo themselves, they almost achieve the essence of the Russian.

Now that I am back in the field, or rather ahead of the front lines, our letters are more newsworthy than usual: censored and passed through many hands, the style accordingly of necessity cryptic. Perhaps we can still communicate sub some art-ificial rosa's.*

Started out in a town which brought me closer to you geographically than at any time since Amden (graphically I was always close). Standing on a hill there, I thought I could almost make you out, your mountains. Am now in a more northerly town, one which would be experiencing a flowering of the arts, if it were only peacetime. The war has driven it away, and at the moment it is undergoing restoration in a city which is the city par excellence of restaurants and breweries and *Theken* (i.e. Pinako's).† I am in a surveying unit. You would like the *sur*realism of it. Could there be anything more marvelous for my purposes than maps? aerial photographs? After all, aren't they aspects of nature, seen from a long-neglected perspective? Photography has much to contribute, and I prize it highly in the form you pointed out to me. Am surrounded by vast sheets of paper and colored inks and geometry, and still I complain. I am becoming aware how important independence is to me. I am alienated from myself, uprooted.

---

*A well-nigh untranslatable pun: *"Vielleicht können wir uns doch durch einige Kunst-Blüten und -Blumen verständigen"*. — Translator

†*Theke* means "eatery" in German; the Alte and the Neue Pinakothek are the Munich art museums. — Translator

What happens to a painter in a prison cell? If he does not scribble on the walls, he will be burned out by his inner visions.

Diary

Summer 1917

We do not know what was the most inspired thought in the history of mankind, or whom it occurred to. Christ, they say, "for example." One would have to choose from among men and ideas that really existed. Perhaps the most significant idea dawned in a brain which proved fatal to its human host.

The same is true of the most significant feat of strength. Legend gives us Hercules. Man and woman; human lust. When the flames intertwined most intensely.

The most profound pain; its sting to be sure is softened by death, which in fact appears on the scene whenever man oversteps his measure. Release or punishment?

This double life. Why not take the decisive step to the true one, the inner one?

Because external life provides the natural source of strength which is necessary as a safe channel (after the searching mind has done its pioneer work). The philosophers claim that reality means the death of potentiality, but that is not quite true: reality is fulfilled, active potentiality.

Socrates proved the immortality of the soul by pointing out that disease of the soul (sin) does not consume the soul as disease of the body consumes the body.

Despair!—(spoken to aesthetic man), for he who despairs finds the eternal man, and as eternal men we are all equal. Doubt is despair of the mind. Despair is the doubt of the personality.

Nature painting is and remains a branch of the plastic arts. I would not like to see it dismissed entirely, for nature is a source of strength. At the moment I must stick to my guns, not let nature impressions influence my painting, because I have something better in mind and feel an inner obligation to live for the new. Mine is the restlessness of the prospector who hopes his find will change his life—greed of the spirit. Nature and the real world are and must be the basis of everything spiritual. But what is nature? The painter bases his impressions not merely on the "motif," the felicitous detail, but the entire wealth of daily experience.

A few great painters in various periods have indeed succeeded in capturing this all-embracing feeling, even in nature pictures.

But there is another possibility: to break the link with nature and to abstract, following the flight of one's feeling; to seek the more precise, the simpler form. One thing the modern schools of painting have in common is their concern with the *means* of portrayal, which are being made purer and more effective. Thus the major innovations until now have been largely formal in character; if the two central aspects of the work of art are idea and form, form has now more or less monopolized the role of the idea. It is rare that discovery of a new idea should go along with conquest of a new form; I can think of only a few artists who manage this. Usually one finds old subject matter in a new form, or, as I said, form for form's sake.

The more all the constituent elements are present in a painting, the more comprehensible it is. If the absence of a clear subject matter or an idea makes the form difficult to understand, how much more will that be the case when both parts— form and idea—are new. And should that not be so? It must be so, it comes about naturally, since any new form transforms the idea, but the new idea calls especially for a new form. Only a new conception can fill the new art with the great mission which is expected of it, i.e. weltanschauung, religion.

In this connection, the artist must be especially well rooted in the feelings of mankind, or: the conception must be ethical, the form can be aesthetic.

Diary

Recognition of his inadequacy and limitations led the painter to restrict himself to the "picture," a slice of nature reproduced on a smaller scale, and to the realization that his business is imitation, translating the given into the available medium. Art begins where these resources are brought into harmony with the object which is to be portrayed. In a sense they are also part of nature, for they possess strength. Study of the character of the painter's media and of the effects they could achieve led eventually to artistic forms which were felt to be deviations from nature and which sometimes did violence to nature in the name of total application of the media, in the course of which the subject matter was partly or wholly negated. Thus paintings were produced in which the medium became a purpose unto itself; subject matter, on which paintings had previously been based, was replaced by a mental element, the idea (the idea consisted of the form). What abstract media painting uses in comparison to the other direct arts, and what rules and requirements these media imply! Paper, canvas, their structure and format, the oily substance of the color, the range of nuances, oils and varnish and the methods of applying color, brushes and the spatula. Special emphasis on any one of these media was sufficient to identify entire schools and artistic periods: Pointillism, with its scattered, pure color; the brush strokes of Trübner; Liebermann's spatula technique; the soft as well as the solid coloration of Cézanne; the azure, the thick application of paint. Here the media were employed for the depiction of nature. In modern painting the nature of the media receives much greater emphasis; the texture is often enhanced by the introduction of completely abstract materials; all the possibilities are tried out.

The right-angled surface, for instance, is such a compelling fact in itself that the painter, obeying a feeling fully as admirable as the respect he once paid his subject matter, has begun to adjust all his forms to this surface, so that they mirror the basic form (the right-angled surface) and stand in a distinct relationship to it. This victory of form over subject matter is an essential characteristic of modern painting. Form can be an end in itself and is by nature aesthetic. It provides a sort of framework and the tools with which to capture an idea as it wells up from the ethical realm. In modern art the idea is expected to create a new visual world, the religion of our times. Should this religion be conveyed through inherited forms? Or should one transpose traditional subject matter and ideas into new form?

Only renewal of both form and content can successfully forge a new spirit. In these times everything cries out for renewal. Entire philosophies and religions are being called into question or collapsing. In the midst of this chaos, the artist must seek stability within himself. Out of the absolute subjectivity of many individuals who share the same attitudes the spirit of the new age will arise.

Diary

September/October 1917

In science, the mind's anarchies are accepted (even if not yet understood) as soon as their utility and purpose have been demonstrated. No matter if this implies the overthrow of entire systems. Art, however, has no specific purpose, or rather, its aims lie in an area as irrational as that of the soul.

Diary

November 1917

A copse near Colmar. When I am feeling tired, empty, and sluggish I go there. A narrow path and the gently soothing greenery usually conjure up beneficient spirits. Hölderlin appears, bearing numerous blessings. I have the reputation of being a Peter Schlemihl, a man without a shadow, whereas actually they are seeing the shadow without the man.

On the Rhine steamer Björne comes upon a dandy who is entertaining the company with off-color jokes; ostentatious vest and so on. The man falls asleep in a corner, a book tumbles out of his pocket; it is Jean Paul's *Titan,* scribbled all over with notes and marginal comments: there you have the German.

My life here is not that much different. The *Titan* is an external similarity. With my fellow soldiers I am careful to keep my intellectual life in full incognito.

Creating out of disbelief!

The pitiable state of the artist when his creativity is blocked, internally or externally. The doubts in himself that set in. So perhaps creative work is simply affirming of one's identity.

Perfecting oneself is also part of it. Does that make the artist an inferior type by comparison with the philosopher?

To Wolfgang Pfleiderer
In the field
November 10, 1917

Bruckner's "Mass in F-Minor" was glorious. It seems to me that this music beautifully sums up everything that was to come later, and that makes the simplicity with which it conveys such multiplicity all the more amazing. It shows us a man whose great, childlike heart resists the blandishments of art. The contrast to Bach and Handel was very striking—in Bruckner everything appears somewhat differently facetted, which makes it stranger, newer, sweeter. While listening to the music I again found myself thinking in terms of forms.

Chagall: I attribute the basic element of primitiveness, of undigestedness to the Russian in him. But then I also feel that works as forceful as his must have solved their formal problems. In fact, the formal solution is precisely what makes them so effective. It seems to me that the moderns tend to overemphasize form, thereby destroying the balance, because the idea can no longer keep pace with the form; or else strong, confident form tempts the artist into presumptuous ideas, which then spoil the enjoyment of those who approach the picture from an intellectual angle. I admit that I admire many of the moderns, although with considerable reservations, especially the Russians (for instance Kandinsky); for they help me perceive my own ideal more clearly as antithetical to theirs. Among the moderns Chagall stands out brilliantly; it is easy to judge the whole movement by one strong representative. But one should always remember that he is one of the group, and a Russian with the Russian's idiosyncrasies: decorative, colorful, in tune with folk art. But others will appear, including Germans, I hope, to give this period its characteristic face.

To Otto Meyer

In the field

November 20, 1917

An idea which much preoccupied me at times: might one not achieve a felicitous combination by putting the most abstract depictive methods at the service of the visible world—in a Shakespearean blend of fantasy and reality, fantasy referring in this case to the method of depiction. Having myself lurched from one extreme to the other, in my present extreme I was often afraid of losing the ground under my feet. The result: my spirits, masks, dolls. If the visionary ever got both feet firmly grounded in reality, he would not tumble into the abyss to which Schiller assigns him. On the contrary, I have observed that involvement with abstraction increases one's sensitivity to reality.

To Otto Meyer

In the field

February 11, 1918

In connection with a charity performance by my regiment (in December 1916), Burger was invited to perform parts of my ballet. I received a furlough to supervise the rehearsals, and the results were not bad at all, I think. Some of the critics misunderstood completely, others were highly appreciative, as were the aesthetically minded circles of Stuttgart.

Things did not stop there; the director of the Hoftheater [Royal Theater] wanted to meet me, and I was supposed to design more ballets for the theater. Then I was shipped off to combat—and the war continues. I myself took the first step, and now I am expected to follow up with more. In addition, this involves me directly, for I am planning on dancing my own inventions; after all, if the copy was effective, the original should be all the more so. I certainly see great possibilities in the realm of the ballet and the pantomime, both of which are much freer of historical ballast than the theater and the opera; this is why I believe that this relatively minor but more independent branch of the theatrical arts will provide the impetus for a renewal. I mentioned in a previous letter that I had flung myself into this heart and soul. My inherited passion for the theater refuses to be suppressed.

I have reason to believe that this ballet job brought out an aspect of me which usually remains invisible; I felt transformed and struck people as being very different. The new artistic medium was a much more direct one: the human body. In Kierkegaard I recently came across an idea which goes like this: the most abstract idea conceivable is sensuous, erotic genius, and its one and only form of expression is music. The dance must also belong to this realm, for it, like music, portrays the directly erotic as "a succession of moments," in contrast to painting and sculpture, which are completely present in any given moment.

To Otto Meyer

In the field
April 15, 1918

As to the taste of the people: ordinary people should be precisely the ones able to leap boldly over the prejudices in which the educated are mired—and which they so cherish. The people, with its untapped resources (see Dostoevsky's great expectations for the Russian people), should be precious to the artist for its originality and its capacity for appreciation. I have a truly mystical concept of the emotional and perceptual make-up of the people, and in this sense I have real faith in the people as a natural source of strength. The Russian people seems to be the ideal example, but this native energy can be found in any people unspoiled by education and left to its own devices. In the part of the country to which destiny has assigned me, there are said to be people like the early Christians who at night struggle on the mountain with the angel, and girls gifted as mediums.

Draft of a letter to an unknown recipient

In the field
May 1918

The tremendous difference between the artist today and the artist in the past is that the artist used to be part of an entire people with its own set of values and its own religion. What a wealth of individual art works was inspired by the common ideal of Christianity! African sculpture and Greek statuary grew out of the culture of entire peoples, for whom the artist functioned as a medium, fashioning the gods and idols. But nowadays! Dilution, discarding, and destruction of old ideals. That explains the bewildering array of artistic trends and the desperate search for standards. Is it surprising that the artist of today withdraws into himself? Thus necessity attains what artists in better times earnestly aspired toward: introspection. It seems to me that this acquisition of self-knowledge provides the best justification for any artist's making himself a center and focal point; if every artist strove with utmost integrity for self-knowledge, the true source of our energy, all the many centers together would yield the whole. Does anything give more eloquent testimony to the immortality of the soul than when two distant souls happen to arrive at the same idea?

To Fräulein Martha Luz *

In the field
June 9, 1918

You shall have your letter at last. The "author's preface" I had in mind has not yet been printed, due to production difficulties. Then, too, I was held back by the renewed realization that the painter should not attempt to justify himself; you remember the old saying, "he who defends himself is his own accuser." And then, so much is being babbled about modern painting, and usually to its detriment, that I was reluctant to add to the growing body of discussion.

But I am glad that you are so involved, and I shall try to help you. One thing which we all need is a conference at which uniform terminology and definitions could be worked out. Contradictory use of terms is responsible for a good deal of the mess in which we find ourselves. If the *elements* that go into the work of art are *idea, material, form, medium, object,* and *nature,* my definitions would be as follows: *idea* means the intellectual or spiritual element; *material* means the visible form of the intellectual element; *form* means creatively molded material; *medium* means the raw materials and tools used for depic-

---

*Later Frau Helmut von Erffa. — Tut Schlemmer

51

tion; *object* means the form in which visible nature appears; *nature* I interpret pantheistically as energy. As one can experience nature, one can also, since everything is active energy, experience *object, media, form, material,* and *idea.* The most decisive factor is the type of experience. In addition one must consider the qualitative difference between objective and subjective experience.

If correctly grasped, these definitions would provide the key to understanding the various artistic styles, for each style is determined solely by the way in which the elements are fitted together and by the relationships among the individual elements. In modern painting, for instance, Cubism is a style based on the experience and development of form, and is thus a form of classicism, while Futurism and Expressionism tend to mirror the mind and nature and are thus deficient in shape and form, expressing themselves chaotically instead. It was only natural that crosses between these artistic strains should evolve—the Futurists learned from the Cubists' superior sense of form, and the Cubists learned from the Futurists' broader horizons. Significantly, the father of Cubism is French Classicism, the master par excellence of form. Futurism originated with a group of Italian painters; in many respects it might be considered an intensification of Impressionism, but the best Futurist works show a decided advance in the direction of conceptual content. German Expressionism is firmly rooted in nature, with form and idea playing a more or less auxiliary role.

Naturalism attained its high point in the Impressionists' objective representations of nature, its low point in the abysmal kitsch of exact copying of nature, a perversion which reached its natural conclusion in the cyclorama and the waxworks; the natural reaction against this abuse can be perceived in modern painting. Instead of concentrating on a given object, the artists began to study the means by which they might portray it, considering all the effects that could be achieved. Use of these new effects produced the art forms which were criticized as deviations from nature. These forms ultimately resulted in "violations" of nature, which was partially or totally negated in favor of purely formal considerations. In some works the form became an end in itself and the idea was identical with the form.

Thus quite a few present-day artists are bending their efforts toward capturing new form. Form provides the guise and the framework within which the idea manifests itself. I would like to devote myself completely and absolutely to pure form until I have it at the beck and call of the idea. Others are working on renewing the conceptual framework of painting. Form is by nature aesthetic, related to the realm of beauty and play; whereas the idea is rooted in the ethical realm. From this realm modern art is expected to derive the new symbols and the new perspective for our times. Can this new conceptual framework draw on the old concepts of form? Might it be sufficient to deck out the old materials and ideas with new form, with "contemporary" ornamentation? No. Renewal of form and renewal of concept are inseparable. Of course, the more traditional components a work contains, the more readily comprehensible it will be. The isolation of the modern artist cannot be denied. Our times lack a great unifying idea or religion. The artists are striving to create one, and the way to it appears to lead via absolute individual subjectivity. Like the mystics, today's artists hope to pass through total self-absorption to oneness with God and the universe. Everything is part of nature, part of the fabric of the universe. The man of our times cannot shut out the richness of everyday experience, the fullness of the Creation and of history. Thus everything functions together to express the essence of the universe. "What was once perceived by the imagination is today perceived as reality." The kingdom of painting is not only of this world, and more than ever, art's aim is to make the invisible visible. Imagination, but not unbridled fantasy. Fantasy rambles off into the thicket of possibilities and goes astray, while the imagination follows inner necessity and ultimately finds fulfillment.

And understanding? That is the last thing the modern painter can expect from the acknowledged artists of his time, for self-preservation dictates that they cannot and will not understand him. Educated, aesthetically inclined comtemporaries will understand him, once they rid themselves of their most recently acquired tastes and are more or less free again. Worst of all are the half-educated, with their good common sense. Immediate comprehension will be found only among the painter's own kind and—do not laugh!—among the receptive souls of simple, uneducated people. The less educated, the more predestined. When the sparks leaps the gap between the complicated, intellectualizing artist and the simple, strong soul of the people, the circuit of cause and effect will be closed. So, although much in modern art is not understood, at least not consciously, the effects will be felt in secret. Painting, unlike other art forms, does not depend on direct impact. It can wait. Many pictures now in museums had to wait for centuries. Modern art will plant a seed which will slowly take root and receive nourishment, often from an unexpected quarter. A seed needs time to come to fruition.

To Konrad K. Düssel

In the field
June 13, 1918

My friend Baumeister writes me he has been frustrated in an attempt to see you. What he had to say is something which I now feel I must communicate to you in connection with our exhibition at Schaller's. It concerns our relationship to Professor Hoelzel. Hoelzel is a man the likes of whom cannot be found at any of Germany's academies of art, and I dread what will happen to Stuttgart's art world once it is without a man of his caliber in a leading position. A sure instinct, not to say political acuity, leads him to ally himself with youth and with artistic freedom. This stance has brought Hoelzel his students. The stronger ones were attracted by the freedom implied by his general philosophy, the weaker ones by—the lack of freedom in his theories. To be sure, he has the sensitivity not to force these theories on anyone whom they do not suit. This was true especially of Baumeister and me. In point of fact, we stand diametrically opposed to his theories. For instance, the linear quality of my work leads him to false conclusions: he suspects my pictures of calculated "construction" where none is present. Our pictures originate in completely different ways. Hoelzel begins by covering his canvas with a network of lines, by means of which he plots the structure of his picture. But then he destroys this fascinating texture, "to veil the process," and usually ends up with the chaos and accidental effects he so highly prizes. He starts with the calculable and proceeds to lose himself in the mystique of the incalculable. Let nothing be said against this; I merely want to point out the contradictory nature of this method. Baumeister and I take the opposite tack; in the beginning feeling and emotion reign supreme, and form develops out of the conditions set by the materials; the result is order, freer and more original than any pre-established order. (At this point Hoelzel would attempt to determine the rules that apply, to capture them and rope them into the service of art.) One would think that this essential difference in approach would be apparent from the pictures; but we have been designated "pupils of Hoelzel," and this label has encouraged people to interpret difficult pictures in terms of easily grasped theories, with much misunderstanding as the result.

Diary

June 21, 1918

Our (dead) age sees African sculpture as caricature, although no one could doubt the creative passion which went into its making. The sublime and the ridiculous. The fate of passion in our times will be the same. The religion of our time is the operetta, the musical revue.

To Otto Meyer

In the field
June 25, 1918

I remember how deliberately I at one time turned against anything that excited me, against temperament, against the artistic, thinking I was saving my energy for something better. I was also aware that this decision was leading me away from the traditional concepts of painting, at least away from the concept of the pictorial, and toward a subsidiary relationship, to architecture, perhaps. It may simply have been that purely aesthetic considerations could not satisfy me in the long run, and I was in search of the ethical. Kierkegaard said in this connection that he who lives aesthetically sees the future in terms of possibilities, whereas he who lives ethically perceives duties and obligations on all sides.

Now I am experiencing a total reaction, and the swing of my pendulum seems unusually violent. Perhaps I have gone astray after all, in the realm of the fantastic, for the possibilities before me reveal such wild forms, such reckless abandon that I cannot find a firm footing. Perhaps the circumstances under which I am living are partly to blame for the fact that my visions remain formless, existing only in my imagination, and assailing me from all sides.

To Willi Baumeister

In the field
June 30, 1918

Our exhibition is over now. Your Royal Highness departs in no more cheerful a mood. But the critics have had a delightful time with ten years of work by two men. I do not care to comment . . . . There remains the material benefit: you sold a picture, on which I heartily congratulate you, and I sold a drawing to the Kupferstichkabinett [Copper Engraving Collection]. The stipulation: instead of 180 marks, only 150, and agreement not to have the sale reported in the newspaper. Strange, no? As I see it, this behavior by the purchaser results from fear of publicity, of compromising himself by supporting this kind of art. One is left with the cautious hope that a soul here and there may have been touched; that the seeds one has planted may someday, somewhere, blossom; and that time will be kind. It was a mistake to have a show in Stuttgart. They will not be seeing me again for a good while, those dear fellow townsmen of mine. There will have to be a period of intense work, and then, perhaps, the Forum in Berlin. We will make a dent on Stuttgart only if we win our laurels elsewhere. Can you imagine: a Kokoschka début in Stuttgart?

To Willi Baumeister

In the field
July 4, 1918

When I wrote my last letter to you I was depressed from the nasty reviews. The very next day the *Tagblatt* arrived. The *Süddeutsche Zeitung* is supposed to be favorable. There must be quite a commotion in Stuttgart. My brother writes that Inspector Schmidt, the spokesman for the professors at the Academy, was ranting and raving that the police should step in. We now have a reputation in Stuttgart, and people will have to take us into account.

Diary

July 12, 1918

Where did Goethe's Olympian calm lead? To epigonic followers, eclecticism, lack of freedom—then the storms and stresses burst upon the scene like a refreshing downpour: Kleist, Lenz, Büchner, and others. But with them it was a matter of temperament, of inner ferment, not of calculation; that is how we must be now. They perceived the unfortunate state of affairs, and their reaction spawned something new and different. In the natural course of events, every artist should have his years of storm and stress, which naturally give way to a classical period, in accordance with the normal course of human development. Someone who *starts out* a classicist strikes me as suspect.

What Pericles wanted was not external beauty but greatness. This greatness renounced individual, living features, and thus resulted in a form which seems empty and hollow if one compares it with Egyptian statuary and statues of the Buddha.

Nietzsche: everything excellent has intermediary character. "The strong, free man is unartistic."

Talent: the gift of having extreme feelings and expressing these in an even more extreme fashion (Socrates: verbal epilepsy).

Art: as expression of the greatest human need as well as of human joy; born of deprivation and of plenty. Art as affect or art as a product of character; forced or elemental. "Still waters run deep": Schiller on Goethe.

To Otto Meyer

In the field
July 21, 1918

All my feelings seem to run in contrasts these days. In connection with Jean Paul I once again became aware of the contrast between nobility of mind and high intellect. The latter appears to be allied with irony. True, Jean Paul does not seem to me a pure satirist; that one should probably seek among his beloved English writers (Sterne, Swift, and others). Then there is Voltaire, who seems related in some way to Jean Paul. When I try to imagine Jean Paul's face, I cannot manage without borrowing a few features from Voltaire; some of the many. In Jean Paul pathos and humor seem to be harmoniously distributed.

Hölderlin, whose letters and late poems (some of them) I have only just read, has had a powerful effect on me. I was amazed to see how the young Hölderlin so reverently modelled himself on the classical authors, and how at his peak he lost his sense of proportion and plunged into Dionysian excess (usually the reverse: Goethe, for instance), and it is precisely this late Hölderlin who apparently arouses such enthusiasm in today's young poets. Is the above-mentioned contrast identical with Schiller's distinction between naive and sentimental?

Hölderlin is said, like Pericles and Christ (this latter according to a Russian), "never to have laughed."

To Otto Meyer

Stuttgart
August 19, 1918

During this furlough I have felt acutely homeless, despite all my old love for the city and rushing from friend to friend and from relative to relative. But I have no place which I can call my own as I could the studio. I am not looking for diversion and entertainment. Nevertheless, I have been able to fulfill a few of my favorite dreams: to wander undisturbed in civilian clothes through the parks early in the morning, to fool around on the piano.

I consider the absolute and counterpoint in painting products of the intellect. Kandinsky has struggled to achieve musical painting, without even coming close to finding anything similar to the laws of music; in fact, the mere search for such a thing seems to me to reveal the futility of it all. The Cubists might be closer, but where an absolute order appears to have been found, a closer look reveals sterile rigidity. Theory lies like a great barrier across Hoelzel's path. I do not believe that study of color theories will be particularly fruitful for art. What I am after are the undercurrents, a "theory of the subconscious." And the divining rod should be feeling. But there is one thing in contrast to earlier. I am nursing an ideal which in happier moments stands clearly before my eyes. This is almost the only positive factor I can see, but it provides the impetus for all my efforts. Everything pertains to it, the surface of the work field, the surface of the work, and the thing depicted. If I could hold the visions at bay better than I can at present, I might be able to analyze more successfully. For the picture used to crystallize out of feeling, and provided a marker in the midst of chaos; but now that I cannot paint, everything is flooded with feeling and remains vague.

To Otto Meyer

In the field

September 6, 1918

My last letter was a bugle call for the day before a birthday, insofar as time has anything to do with it: thirty years are up. So an appropriate moment for retrospect and reckoning.

Should I give you an idea of how my days are passed? I often think this could easily end in mental derangement. If this brought the consummation that one *is* because one must be, then t'were devoutly to be wished. The casual way in which I put up with these conditions indicates weak nerves; if I had real depth, the catastrophe would have come long ago. Just now the external circumstances are especially unfavorable. My job has changed; I have to familiarize myself with a whole new area, which makes greater demands on the mind than the other, demands which unfortunately extend into my free time. I have barely enough time to unwind before the evening meal and inevitable night close in. My new work has to do with photography, and I hope that something positive comes of all these negatives. Aerial photographs. I get to see nature from a completely new point of view, and from such an elevation that the earth's surface often appears not to have any. I have learned to admire objective photography, and if I seem to be adding a subjective element, I am merely channelling its useful aspects, greatly to the benefit of itself, of me, and of beauty. Everything would be different if I could paint, or at least think, in material. I might even say that a man becomes a painter when he is incapable of thinking non-pictorially. I always had the deluded notion that painting ought to be considered more than pleasing free play. I still find it difficult to accept the idea that painting should be the mere handmaiden of an intellectual concept, even given such changed circumstances as we have these days: lack of an intellectual concept and the attempt to create one through signs and symbols. Can it be that painting is incapable of using its unique methods to create a special form of expression, to which the intellectual concept would be a handmaiden?

It would require a fundamental readjustment for me to abandon this idea. To be sure, history is against me. The great intellectual concepts were hostile to art. The sort of painting I have in mind would thus be hostile to the intellect. Yet here the old form-content business comes full circle.

To Otto Meyer

In the field

September 23, 1918

I can easily see a connection between Hölderlin and Beethoven in terms of the Apollonian-Dionysian contrast. Hölderlin is so absolutely exalted. It made a deep impression on me to see how his Greek concept of form exploded upon contact with a broader perspective. Christian and Dionysian are here not contraries but one and the same. The biographical fate of Hölderlin and Beethoven is similar: in each case failure of the most important organ: the brain and the ear, accompanied by overwhelming inner intensity. Beethoven in relation to Mozart—Hayden: more dramatic—as a result of subjectivity? Hölderlin versus Schiller—Goethe: subjectivistic; more dramatic? The moderns Dionysian; the Apollonian: a flash in the pan. Yes: that would be precisely what I wish the moderns. The catchword "Expressionism" emphasizes this exclusively Dionysian aspect even more.

A *largo espressivo* by Bach is a beacon of what is worth striving for: consistency matched by rich inner resources.

Diary
October 10, 1918

The exalted contest in the arts. The more powerful man is recognized, loved, enthusiastically venerated. Only the interference of something impure, of commerciality can change the picture. Our present war: is it dictated by commercial considerations, or is it an exalted contest? Battle among nations as a touchstone of their inner worth? Is it necessary? And with such methods? Wherein resides the blessing of war? In blood and death and rising from the ashes?

Why did the voice of civilization remain silent at the outbreak of the war? Why did England, America, and the neutral countries fail to utter a resounding veto against war? It would have been heard! If civilization and mankind are at stake, one must use human tools, not tools that make a mockery of man, such as war, violence, cannon. For these latter lure us away from what is truly noble and inspire such mighty hatred that nothing good can come until exhaustion has set in. Reconciliation of the enemies. Blessings. To proceed from these generalities to the specifics, i.e. reality, is as hard for me as to proceed from abstractions about painting to the actuality.

But I can anticipate the happiness of being allowed to go back to work. I shall really apply myself and take care of the most important matters first. Even after four years of systematic depersonalization a good deal is stored up inside me—I hope it will all prove fruitful yet.

To Otto Meyer

Berlin

October 15, 1918

May this be my last wartime letter! The present high tide of events interferes with letter writing. My thoughts circle in fascination around the possibility of peace.

To Otto Meyer

Stuttgart

November 22, 1918

I am in the process of moving into a studio, which should bring me peace and quiet and the right atmosphere. I witnessed the revolution while I was in Berlin, having been sent there for an officers' training course. As an officer I would have been able to write every week, because I would have been relieved of the daily drudgery. Now I am relieved in the fullest sense, and unexpectedly so—discharged and a student once more. But the waves of revolution are swelling mightily, especially here in Stuttgart. I arrived in the midst of such a whirlpool of events that it took me days to become even slightly reoriented.

And to tell the truth, I am not yet reoriented—there are too many unpleasant things going on. The Social Democrats have a tradition of competent organization, and now their left wing is organized again—and the bourgeoisie is desperately trying to resist their massive onslaught. Bourgeoisie has become a dirty word—now we have the *"Rat geistiger Arbeiter"* ["Council of Brain Workers"], which is pressing for seats and votes in the Workers' and Soldiers' Council. Everything previously unorganized is now being organized. The institutes of higher learning, and that includes the academies, and therefore their students. I am a student delegate to the Council of Brain Workers! My election came after the institutes of higher learning had quietly picked their directors to go to the Council; this move created a lack of confidence and led to the demand that the delegates should be students.

I had to accept for the time being, hoping that a more suitable representative would be found later. For the issue at stake is reform of the Academy—I cannot accept a moderate plan, and the directors would never allow me to carry out my own extreme one.

To Otto Meyer

Mid-December 1918

I cannot make up my mind; and if one were to try to characterize the German's nature and worth and arrived at *indifference* as the essential feature, that would probably be correct. The important question is: does this imply "decay before maturity," as a Frenchman has said, or might this unique condition betoken a great future? The war represented an attempt to break this spell of indifference, and the revolution is another such attempt, its very failing proving the force of that indifference. I volunteered during the war and am equally ready to join the ranks of the revolution. As to the Academy issue, I was equally ready to recognize the status quo or to work out a reform program; accommodation on the one hand, opposition on the other, and the only thing that really seems to matter is independence, personal freedom.

The maelstrom of events and people here is almost impossible to follow and to understand. The Council of Brain Workers, entirely the product of compromise, carries the seeds of its own destruction, and is thus trying desperately to prove its right to exist.

Christ and the early Christians have acquired new meaning, without anyone's declaring himself openly in their favor; that is, no one has unambiguously invoked their authority—to help organize the masses.

Diary

December 18, 1918

Like all the other institutions in the new Germany which continue to exist according to their old principles, the academy, the art school, has become questionable. In the past it ministered to the prestige of the royal family and more or less clearly served the interests of state, to which it owed its existence; now that these things have changed, the academy should likewise alter its character. Long before the war, the increasing trend toward individualization in art created a demand for the end of the academies. And the demand was made on artistic grounds, by men firmly committed to progress in the arts, not by utilitarians, although they, too, spoke out against the academies.

Diary

January 4, 1919

Accident does strange things. A line, but even more a tone, painted in response to necessity, yields a truly amazing profusion of accidental effects. Matisse uses this method, and it actually achieves an immediacy of line similar to that in the works of the primitives.

This is what Corot means by not *planning* to make something beautiful. With the Cubists, form becomes purposeful, intentional. In the successful early landscapes I was unpurposeful in this sense.

To put things down in writing the way they occur. Glorification of the results. People may call them accidental effects; they are the ultimate in profundity; they are mysticism, soul.

Everything else, everything that has been corrected, is bad, intentional.

To Otto Meyer

Stuttgart

January 25, 1919

A student petition to the Minister of Cultural Affairs in an attempt to keep Hoelzel on; parallel to it another petition to the professors, along with the students' declaration in favor of Hoelzel and suggestions for reform: for example, that the students have a seat and a vote in the Faculty Council. In Munich the students took a more militant stand, demanding that professors be elected by the students and hired only for a limited number of years, subject to reelection.

The situation is as follows: the professors have formed a bloc against Hoelzel, whose departure would be welcomed by many; the professors' pets (pupils) have launched a counter-petition against one-sided (Hoelzel-style) modernization of the curriculum. The Minister for Cultural Affairs remains under the sway of the cultural official of the old régime, who speaks for the professorial majority, and therefore for the student majority. Now, in support of the petition by Hoelzel's pupils, a second one by former pupils of his, along with seminar leaders and art critics. The ministry is trying to postpone the matter until later. So a more permanent government will have to decide whether the Academy is to be or not to be. (In Berlin they want it dissolved.)

Baumeister is once more my studio neighbor. I already feel: you take the high road and I'll take the low road; that is, he will stay and I shall have to flee.

The Spartacus movement can be suppressed only by governmental force. Even painters who are only slightly modernistic are dubbed "Spartacuses." Intellectual matters are being identified and confused with political matters in a most stupid fashion.

News from Russia has finally arrived. Moscow is said to be flooded with Expressionism. They say Kandinsky and the moderns are splashing whole quarters with color, using blank walls and the sides of houses as the surfaces on which to paint modern pictures. An artificial spring conjured up, with giant sunflowers, flowerbeds in a potpourri of color, silver trees. The fallen art of Czarist Russia replaced by Tolstoy, Dostoevsky, Jaurès, Robespierre. Russia: the youth of Europe. The German revolution a pale imitation of the Russian, which in its westward march is being blocked by newly awakened Western imperialism; we shall be lucky to get a measly democracy. At the moment I see precious little intensity in Germany. A clash between Western and Eastern principles, but no German ones. Yet perhaps the present confused scene cannot be evaluated, and its blessings will become apparent only with peace. Jean Paul—oh, what realms I have lost contact with!

To Otto Meyer

Stuttgart
February 10, 1919

Before me I see only new areas, uncharted territory, and the order of the day: to put my ideas into execution.

Baumeister is impressively productive, at least one picture a day. Should I be happy or resentful: he lives off my work, paraphrasing it so cleverly that it is scarcely recognizable, at least to the innocent observer. He succeeds so masterfully because he is the fortunate possessor of a nucleus, a core which can absorb and assimilate anything. Tell me—is this why you broke with him? I can see it coming: the mortar which binds us together—our common alienation from the local art scene—could be dissolved by the acid of such insights.

Diary

February 19, 1919

Ecstasies, presentiments of spring.

Had hardly thought it possible, but I am on the verge of a new decision, a new breakthrough; had thought everything was over, that I had gone hopelessly astray. But no: the beautiful old feeling of impending rebirth has returned. How did that come about? A few days of calm contemplation, reading, quiet, self-absorption, helped me overcome severe nervous tension and find myself. The sky has opened up again. First I was too conventional, preoccupied with models and tradition; now I am too arbitrary, too much a loner. Now comes—must come—the purification process, pure form, the combination of both possibilities. Mastery, classic form, the steady compass. I must succeed, will succeed, if I fix my attention only on the essential and refuse to let myself be drawn into turmoil and confusion, which only alienate me from myself. Life itself is at stake!

To Otto Meyer

Stuttgart
February 23, 1919

On the 28th, if all goes well and Munich stays peaceful, I shall be going there with a group to see Grünewald's Isenheim

Altar and various other things; I shall also try to look up that man Klee, who lives in Munich. Klee has a sort of devoutness and deep insight which inspire him to childlike forms of play.

Diary

February 23, 1919

"The Germans are neither rebels nor slaves; they have not had anyone in between and are still waiting to discover their own strength," says Jean Paul; I now imagine he must have said it with the same despairing faith with which Dostoevsky said certain things about the Russians. Today it looks as though the in-between location (geographically) were a grim misfortune; reason and necessity point to the West, instinct and hope to the East. It is no comfort that the new structure will be built on compromise. But then it can hardly be considered a new edifice; rather, a half-destroyed old one will be patched together as best it can. There are even certain educated, intelligent people asking merely that the state provide peace and order, in short, the things that made the old Germany so admirable. Such a demand strikes me as egotistic, given the tremendous factor of revolution, which must work itself out, slowly, and perhaps even contrary to people's wishes. The world must vomit up all its accumulated evils; no one has a right to ask for peace and order until that has been accomplished.

To Otto Meyer

Stuttgart
April 12, 1919

My long silence is due to the strike, to political and personal upheavals.

I am well aware how much I owe to city life, especially to Stuttgart, my natural home, which I am coming to love more and more wholeheartedly after a period of unfaithfulness (in earlier years); I realize what a blessing it is to emerge after days of relative isolation in my studio and plunge myself into the richness and diversity of sights and sounds. For instance, display windows become windows into a theatrical world, the revelation of a special style. More than anything else, however, I need solitude, and this is precisely what eludes me. The succession of exhibitions and campaigns on my behalf (more than I really want) has given me the reputation here of being a modern painter; add to this the current vogue for modernism, and you see why many a day goes on visitors, who unfortunately come only out of curiosity: especially architects, perhaps the most genuinely interested. Others are merely seeking stimulation: arts-and-crafts types come hoping to filch some ideas; the most despicable of all are the painters, who are actually just collecting "material," which they then with a notable lack of compunction transform into cheapened or distorted imitations, for which they garner critical acclaim, thanks to assiduous politicking. But this latter could easily be prevented.

A more serious problem remains: the political uproar in my circles. I cannot manage to shut it out. Attempts to bury my head in the sand, to act apolitical, indifferent, while in the streets shots are being fired and the students are being called upon to arm themselves and defend the government . . . .

Diary

April 30, 1919

An artist's work: small aggregation of implemented ideas, suggesting the range and the potential of his imagination; how little opportunity one has, given the infrequency of good moments and the shortness of life, to plumb one's own depths and mold their treasures into tangible form. Add a streak of pessimism as to the possibility of actually accomplishing anything; or a philosophical bent that obstructs action, or the insight that it is senseless to add new fantasies to the existing chaos—fantasies which merely complicate a world in which even the simplest things have not yet been grasped—why, then the very foundations of the creative impulse are undermined.

I must admit that I feel more drawn to philosophy, to the analytical approach, and paint almost unwillingly. Perhaps I sense that many things are still in the embryonic stage, not yet matured, and nature is hinting that I should wait patiently. Imperturbability—not indifference.

One could picture an artist who is ahead of his times; the

revolution comes—an experience he has already inwardly surmounted (there are also artists whose state of mind coincides with the revolution); his art already depicts the post-revolutionary world—cleansed, a new Greece, purity: what benefit can this artist derive from the revolution?

Should he retrace his steps? Act ecstatic and Dionysian? True, an artist never puts unrest, revolt, death and resurrection behind him—but what matters for the individual is the dominant mode: Apollonian or Dionysian. Since the artistic revolution began so far ahead of the political one, reconstruction should command all the more attention.

The hour of the manifesto is past; the slogans have been coined, the dividing lines drawn; now it is time to take stock, and the German method of bringing order out of chaos can come into play.

To Otto Meyer

Stuttgart
May 6, 1919

What do you think of the Dadaists? Arp and the others in Zurich? A lot of it seems to be hollow decoration.

Diary

May 7, 1919

The drawbacks of our times: mediocrity, conformism; expressionism, paucity of original talent. Kandinsky, Marc, Chagall, Klee, Archipenko, Picasso are the few really original artists.

What is the situation in modern art? Either: sensationalist jesting à la Dada—Jankó, Wauer—disintegration into merely decorative, handicrafts stuff, and not even very good at that, using art nouveau forms. Or: ecstatic, expressive over-stimulation; Meidner, the weltschmerz types—agitators all; collapse. Or: African style, peasant painting. What is missing: intimacy, noncontemporaneous but subtle, tender, modern but in an unobtrusive way, free of crass effects. True values, personalities, original talents.

69

To Otto Meyer

Stuttgart
May 7, 1919

Today I received the enclosed documents and the program of the reorganized former "Academy" of Weimar, which may well become the model for academies throughout Germany. Gropius wrote me a very friendly letter, expressing his willingness to give further information.

The situation here is as follows: the entire student body issued a declaration of solidarity with Hoelzel; it has gone unanswered all this time; or rather, the answer which the directors of the Academy gave after repeated inquiries was that Hoelzel had been offered the opportunity to deliver a few lectures each year. Insulting and unacceptable, since our goal had been to have him play a very different role, setting up the entire preparatory or elementary curriculum. So Hoelzel is no longer at the Academy, and the students have thereby lost their only representative of the recent trends in art. This alone would be sufficient reason for the students to demonstrate. The very least the young, modern students have a right to demand is a modern instructor, for in fact they have none now. Paul Klee has been mentioned.

To Otto Meyer

Stuttgart
June 3, 1919

Today I received a copy of *Der Austausch* ["Exchange"], put out by the students at the Bauhaus in Weimar; it is full of gratifyingly sharp self-criticism; there is no doubt that something is in the making in Weimar. This represents a challenge to those cautious souls who first like to see which way the wind is blowing. I do react somewhat skeptically to the thought that here in Germany yet another attempt is taking place to create something from scratch; that style and beauty and art are to be designed, made according to plan. Another fear: that the good old German pretentiousness may now manifest itself in art, having failed in the political realm. But nevertheless I see this venture as beautiful, wonderful.

I do not believe there will be a boycott against German art, much as I might wish for one, as a sort of Great Wall of China to make us more self-reliant. In point of fact, the German intellectual world, especially the art world, displays a vitality and ferment which one could hardly find in such intensity anywhere else. Gropius is not alone. In Dresden Poelzig has designed some architectural projects which can only make one regret that current economic conditions render their realization impossible.

Perhaps the coming ten years of enforced introspection will be beneficial; many things will have a chance to mature and be tested until they are truly perfect.

To Paul Klee

Stuttgart
June 28, 1919

It will be necessary to mount an exhibition of your works here. Could you arrange this yourself, or should we get in touch with the "Sturm"?

It looks as if we shall have to face considerable resistance in the Academy. We want you to take over Hoelzel's composition class, but we have been informed that only an assistantship is vacant. There will be a struggle, for if worse comes to worst we shall demand the retirement of one of the older professors.

To Otto Meyer

Stuttgart
July 2, 1919

Paul Klee has said he would accept an appointment to the Academy. But there will be a struggle. Still, it is the advanced students who demand he be hired.

To Paul Klee

Stuttgart
July 9, 1919

Your letter meant a great deal· to me, because in it you set forth your ideas on teaching.

One of the chief accusations against which we have to defend you here is that an artist as "unworldly, visionary" as you would "in all likelihood" hardly be the teacher to advocate modern style with the vigor necessary in a city like Stuttgart! Well—perhaps the gentle manner is the more effective, and others can be trusted to proselytize for the new art; Stuttgart has no lack of such types. "Playful," "feminine" are other terms expressive of skepticism; we reply that "power" is sufficiently represented at the Academy in Waldschmidt's monumental musclemen and in Altherr's baroque style, and that you promise us a sophisticated contrast which will mean a real enrichment of the curriculum and teaching . . . .

If we lose in your case, as we did in Hoelzel's, when the entire student body was in favor of his reappointment (that case seems to be closed), we shall protest publicly and if necessary call a strike.

Diary

October 1919

Result of an exhibition:

Immense gulf between art and public.

What seems dangerous today will be perfectly normal tomorrow.

Everything which today is a reality was once perceived only by the imagination.

Cubism: the forms best suited to the four-sided surface; a circle will demand circles, a square squares. The fractured quality of our age, the dismemberment of time, fragmentation, are reflected in the paintings of the Cubists.

Cubism the most decisive, important achievement of modern art. Formal element of construction, of structuring, an element of expression. Enrichment of the expressive possibilities. A current which sweeps everything before it.

What is the style of our times? We have none, or our style is precisely to have no style. A clever *aperçu* which tries to make light of a sorry state of affairs.

It is a grave mistake to seek style deliberately or to try to create it. Style already exists, or it is at this moment being born; the rudiments are present, and finely attuned artists feel them out, and extract the valuable from the chaos.

We are accused of negating, when actually we only emphasize, extract, underline. Radically, in order to achieve clarity. Pure technique is the province of the epigone. Genius can afford to be a dilettante.

Every human being, and even more every artist, has his own unique sense of form; this enables him to enter into a relationship with the outside world and to withstand the chaos (of reality).

The evolution in art from Impressionism to today's new style, from objectivation to abstraction, demonstrates the "plucking out of Nature" which Dürer mentions. One can perceive a particularly clear, logical progression in the following series: a landscape by Ruysdael, for example; then the leap to Corot and Courbet; from them to Cézanne; from him to complete abstraction. One can trace the increasing tendency to single out colors and forms, the steady movement away from objective nature, and the benefits that accrue from using the full force of the artistic media themselves. Previously the artist was guided by his feeling for the subject matter; now he must be guided by something no less valuable: when working on a picture, he must follow the spirit and the concept of the surface, so that all the forms on that surface relate to its possiblities and limitations.

Diary

November 1919

My pictures: "pictures" in the familiar sense they are not, canvases which draw on all the illusionary trappings of space and light in order to capture a slice of nature, or world, and are destined to live out their peculiar existence in salons and museums between four pieces of golden frame. Rather, they are tablets which burst out of their frames and ally themselves with the wall, thus becoming part of a large surface, a larger space than themselves, thus actually becoming part of an ideal architecture. Compressed in them, reduced to a miniature scale, is what should furnish the laws and form of their surroundings.

In this sense: Tablets of the Law.

The portrayal of man will always remain the great symbol for the artist.

To Tut

Stuttgart

November 12, 1919

My true self—which, in fact, is my innermost being—is usually surrounded by a shell formed by the outside world. If I accidentally reveal some of it, it is always in the form of a joke, or between the lines—and they need not be written lines. Perhaps the most accurate reflection of my true being can be found in my art. Indeed, that is the purpose of my art, to reveal that true self, in the purest way possible; and if people fail to perceive or understand, well, that is just the form in which my real self is expressed. A man is an artist or becomes one if he lacks the gift or the ability to express himself in life in the simplest form. Such a person seeks a mouthpiece, a means of indirect self-expression. One way to reach my innermost being would be to understand my art. But you want to take the direct path to me. Up to now I have had that path to myself. I would have to learn to share it with another person; and I wonder whether destiny will allow me to travel it other than alone. Perhaps these doubts are merely the product of boyish defiance, which must be overcome, melted away. My previous course proved worthwhile; it made me what I am today. Wouldn't the simplest conclusion be that I should stick to this course, since in retrospect a pattern reveals itself? Was it youth, body temperature, freedom, solitude, humility—or all these things together; I don't know. The future is dark, and decisions bearing on it difficult.

Perhaps I am simply mistaken and cannot believe that my youth is over and the time has come to be a man. My great dream was always to preserve my youthfulness forever—old conservative that I am! What about progress? What am I afraid of?

As Nietzsche said, I have my work—I do not strive for happiness! I have always been wary of happiness. Art, the sublime, is born of suffering. The closer I feel to my work, and that happens far too infrequently, the more distant I am from human beings; Jesus Christ, the Buddha, and others like them chose their mission in place of happiness—and I have a mission to fulfill. Sometimes I feel a wild urge to destroy all my pictures, despite their present success at the exhibition, for it could all be so much better, so much more profound; at such moments I realize that what I have to give is mine alone. Just a little more exclusivity, a little more concentration—no, "a little more" is ridiculous: I need all the energy which gets dissipated in daily life—and then I could "create the One Thing which surpasses those who created it." That is my credo in art.

To Otto Meyer

Stuttgart
November 27, 1919

The death of my unmarried sister Henriette, and an exhibition with a group of local painters and the Berlin "Sturm," presented in unaccustomed grand style in the Kunstgebäude [Art Center]. Unexpectedly strong public interest and attention; a campaign in the press against the Academy and the critics in connection with the battle over Klee (who has now been definitively rejected by the Academy and by the Verein der Kunstfreunde [Art Patrons' Guild]); the gas being turned off; a shortage of electricity which shortens the days and forces me to use the most valuable part of the day, the evening, for visits; and ballet rehearsals; things hardly calculated to give me the peace and relaxation I need.

Diary

November 29, 1919

Ensor—Redon—Rousseau—Carrà.
The noble synthesis of everything great in art.
Goals: truth, no self-assertiveness, no senseless mysticism; the forms of reality at the service of art.

75

Instead of artificial stimulation, grandeur of conception.

Slow, deliberate, thoughtful, consistent work. No subservience to architecture.

To Paul Klee

Stuttgart

November 29, 1919

You have probably received my pamphlets; they were a necessary part of our campaign. Unfortunately they will only provide a feeble epilogue to your case here. The Academy says no. I am enclosing a copy of this art-historical document.

The Academy's decision clearly bears the stamp of the opposition. In this instance, the director seems to be the wolf in sheep's clothing. He is reported to have opposed you with utmost determination, all while he was assuring us of his good will, his deep agreement with us, etc. When it was announced at the student meeting that you had been turned down, I got up and said: half a year ago we demanded that Hoelzel be reappointed and were turned down. Our next campaign, for your appointment, was likewise rejected; would the students put up with this? A lively debate ensued, ending with the decision that no, they would not put up with it. They had been promised the appointment of a modern teacher, and they were going to insist on it.

Immediately following my appeal, which was seen as a motion against the Academy, the authorities are said to have decided on my expulsion. True, I have little to lose, since my studies will be completed by the end of this winter. Should we start a revolution? A small minority could be rallied. It would mean an exasperating struggle and a great loss of time. And I have a burning desire to get to work. What would you advise?

What are your plans now? You can imagine our sorrow. All that remains is hope that the next few years will bring our revenge. The spirit of your art will hover over us.

To Otto Meyer

Stuttgart

December 28, 1919

First the ballet project with the Burgers! What we are doing now, rehearsing the dances, makes it thoroughly apparent that I am the key to them. What suits my body is determined by my kinesthetic sense and cannot be adequately reproduced by other bodies.

Let the world belong to the dancer, as Nietzsche would say. But isn't dance pure effect? From my father I received love of effect, a typical Rhineland heritage—my better part comes from my mother. I am very conscious of these two souls in my breast; they contain the germ of constant new conflict.*

I wanted to give you a brief report on the Klee affair. He was rejected by the Academy (Faculty Council), on the grounds that: 1) no position was available, 2) "a thorough examination of Herr Klee's past and recent work revealed his work to be playful in character and lacking the firm commitment to structure and composition which is rightly demanded by the moderns." The student body protested the decision on the grounds that it contradicts the earlier promise to appoint a new man. The young moderns, eight or ten of them, and I first and foremost, were to be expelled by resolution of the Council for our press campaign on Klee's behalf. The Ministry refused, since it held a different opinion of the newspaper campaign, whereupon the Council withdrew its proposal. Waldschmidt, who has taken over Hoelzel's chair, is trying to act as lightning rod by dangling an assistantship in front of me, provided we cause no trouble! This place is buzzing with cabals, and Klee is only one case in point. At any rate, I am leaving the Academy in March and shall put it all behind me.

To Tut

Stuttgart

Beginning of April 1920

Swam in the Neckar again yesterday. Very jolly, many children. Am now reading Spengler's *Decline*. All power to

---

*This passage contains allusions to Goethe's little verse in the *Zahme Xenien* on his parental heritage and to his *Faust*. — Translator

anyone who can claim it does not apply to him. When I have done some work and can get a sense of perspective, all will be well. Then I will know! Until this happens you will find me a hesitater and a dreamer, a man who thinks of himself first. Please don't take this amiss—it has to be this way, and this is not laziness on my part.

To Tut

Stuttgart
April 8, 1920

General gloom here. Demonstrations against the inflation, with people getting killed. Not in Stuttgart, that is. But it is simply unbelievable how prices are going up.

Big storm over the ballet. Imagine, Meyer, strangely enough, is for it. Was glad from the very beginning that I am doing it. A mystery to me. I plan to leave in a week.

To Tut

Stuttgart
April 24, 1920

You see, this is my situation. I have to finish up the ballet project, and that will take the whole summer, but by autumn it must be all set. That means I will simply have to be in Stuttgart until this thing is taken care of. I realize more and more what all this entails. But you see, I feel we really must wait. I don't even want to tie myself down to Lake Constance, which might be the best of all possible worlds. All this, the where and the how, I shall think out at the end, when I calm down and can go over my life thus far. Right now Amsterdam does not suit me, and I have even considered Italy of late. But I am thinking all the time, and the moment will come when all the possibilities are resolved into one. Then I shall know what to do and I shall act.

To Tut

Today the Landesgalerie [Regional Museum] had its formal opening. I am best represented among the moderns, with four paintings. Let's see what the press says. Redslob took all sorts of risks, but he intends to take an even stronger stand. I listened to his speech and then slipped away.

You want something to read: Knut Hamsun always comes to mind first. You should read his *Pan*; you would like it. He would strengthen your existential sense of merging with the universe; you find the same thing in Walt Whitman, whom I like but secretly find less profound than I would wish; perhaps profundity is what I am looking for in the philosophers, who may disappoint me in the end, leaving me to fall back into the clutches of art. For I have become skeptical towards art. Perhaps that explains my present mood. My public success as an artist gives me a terrible sense of responsibility. And when I notice that I unintentionally exercise an influence over others, I feel responsible for every step I take. I have reached my age of skepticism. Whatever happens in the future should, and must, be well founded, a true expression of my character in the best sense; the moment has come for a summing up, a synthesis. My earlier work has to be reconciled with my recent pictures, my conservative pictures with the revolutionary esoteric ones, and a certain middle ground must be found that will give me the courage and certainty to continue. Even though I seem to be placing great hopes on this middle ground, and I am, there is no danger of sudden revulsion. All these thoughts apply only to painting. But I may even give up painting. Perhaps life lies ahead, and painting will play only a subsidiary role—I must mull this over during the summer. Everything further will depend on this, but the decision is crucial, lest in the future the same situation arise again, leading to a renewed necessity for thinking things out and coming to a decision.

I should also like to tell you about a key idea I found in Keyserling's book. He writes: "A man who seeks progress looks for new possibilities; one who seeks God looks to fulfill those he sees before him." He keeps posing the alternatives of progress, in the sense of broadening one's horizons, one's possibilities; and self-fulfillment, in the sense of achieving greater profundity, intensity. The latter independent of time and circumstances, universal; the former timely, modern. Thus, he says, the genius of perception is typically characterless, while the genius of action has a clearly defined personality.

Think about it. I shall too. It goes to the heart of my crisis, in connection with what I said before.

I often wish I could see you again. You know that longing in any form is a great stimulus to the artist. For many an artist it has proved the moving force in his creative life. And isn't that the role longing always plays?

You know, it is a precious thing to have one's life, one's resources in one's own hands, to be able to pick the most promising course, to venture at one's own risk, to risk one's life for an idea. Of course, Schrempf says: "I do not live, I am lived." Individualism, egotism, self-centeredness, self-knowledge, all represent attempts to take control of one's life, protests against being lived. Schrempf then comes to the conclusion that: "I am lived, but it is certainly *I* who am lived, and I cause myself to be lived." Perhaps you will ponder that one; I shall, too.

To Otto Meyer

Cannstatt
May 25, 1920

I have already written you about the changes in my outward circumstances. Am no longer at the Academy, have exchanged my opulent studio for a simple room in Cannstatt, not far from the Kursaal [spa auditorium], not far from the Neckar, the bathing establishment—various things to conjure up memories of days past.

Looser ties, thanks to the geographical distance from Stuttgart and my friends and fellow artists; I see Baumeister less often than all the others. The mews in Cannstatt: upstairs a large hall with a dance stage, where for the past six months the special designing and sewing of the costumes has been going on; downstairs I have my room. You perceive the two-way division, or rather three-way, for the room next door is inhabited by my brother, who, however, is not home during the day.

I have begun to entertain great doubts about art, to a degree unprecedented with me. In retrospect, my development as a painter falls into three stages: I pleased the conservatives with my naturalistic paintings à la Corot, then I continued along the French path to cubism, and in my recent works I struck a revolutionary note.

I see two possible avenues open to me: I might try to follow up my hitherto erratic development with work that was more even, less subject to outside influences, a combination of the best of the old and the new. The prospects seem appealing. I might evolve a style very different from current trends, not an attempt to be interesting, but rather the result of striving for a depth and intensity which, as I have become painfully aware, modern painting grievously lacks. I often find my thoughts wandering unexpectedly in this direction, unexpectedly because at the moment I am more preoccupied with the other alternative. Perhaps my abstract paintings might be interpreted as a transition to life? I incline of late to see my artistic development in this light. I have now come around to rejecting art and am instead ready to affirm life as never before. I think I can actually give up practicing my art; or I might satisfy my slight remaining drive casually, on Sundays, for instance. Perhaps! On the other hand, these days I seem to be living simply, without ambition. It would not really matter what I did, since the spirit would be the main thing: I am devoting myself to questions ethical and moral.

I feel that I have neglected some side of my life, that somewhere there is a gaping hole. Perhaps I shall put art aside for a time and devote myself to human matters.

To Otto Meyer

Cannstatt
June 12, 1920

Remember: abstraction as a transition to life. A state in which it does not matter *what* one does, but *how*. You should see my skepticism about the aesthetic in this light; for the aesthetic now appears to me a small branch of the ethical, which I would consider from the root point of view to be a tree.

I should let Schiller undertake my aesthetic education perhaps; maybe I indulged in unconscious play too long, maybe I have finally become skeptical of the hegemony of form, realizing that form cannot survive without a conceptual basis. And yet I am becoming interested in the dance.

Once upon a time, dance was totally alien to me, and I am amazed to see how this inherited aspect of myself, which I had denied and cordially hated, as if out of guilty conscience, has come into its own. Give a temptation an inch—and it takes a mile! Should I be cheered or frightened by the thought that this is just one temptation among many? Does one live, or is one lived?

Victory for the aesthetic? I have moved from the geometry of the one-dimensional surface to the half-plastic (relief), and thence to the fully plastic art of the human body (the paradox may be that the more plastic the figure, the flatter it is, that surface-painting is the most plastic form of all). There is also a geometry that applies to the surface of the dance floor, though only as part of and a projection of spatial solid geometry. I am working out a similar geometry of the fingers and the keys on the piano, in an effort to achieve identity (or unity of movement and bodily form) and music.

In my last letter I intended to draw up a list of themes, taking up the unfinished ones first. As for the new ones, I think a dictionary would provide everything. Looming over me is Jean Paul, whose introduction to aesthetics I am currently skimming. I was reading "On the Comical" when your letter arrived. Jean Paul remarks that the grave Spaniards have more comedies than any other people, often two Harlequins in one play; also that the serious-minded clergy produced the greatest humorists (Rabelais, Swift, Sterne, and others), and that solemn nations (for instance Britain) are the ones with a deep, intense sense of the comic.

I was interested to learn that Swift and Sterne "were in real life quiet and serious," and that Carlin, the most famous Harlequin of early Italian theater, died in Paris an incurable

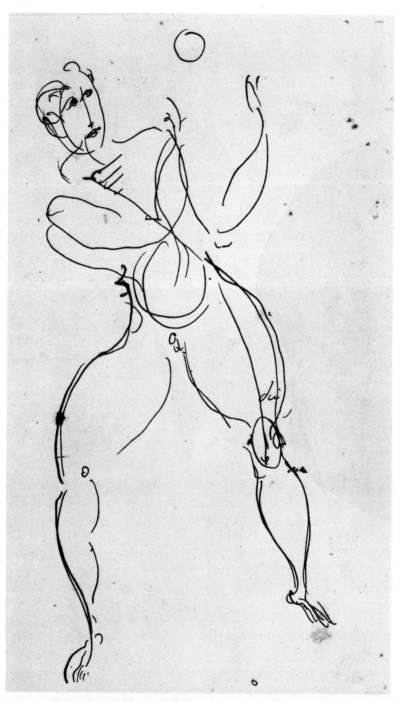

The Ball Player, by Oskar Schlemmer; pen-and-ink drawing, ca. 1913.
Courtesy of Tut Schlemmer.

The Dancer, by Oskar Schlemmer; pen-and-ink drawing, 1922. *Courtesy of Tut Schlemmer.*

hypochondriac. I know of many similar examples. Certainly it was not gnawing worry about ethical questions!

To Tut

Cannstatt

June 14, 1920

The Utopia publishing house in Weimar wants reproduction rights to my works. Altogether, there are supposed to be people in Weimar who want me there. Don't know what I would do if it came to that.

To Tut

Cannstatt

Beginning of July 1920

Work busily upstairs every day, have to make some progress, am managing, have to prepare things, because in mid-July I am going to Dresden and Weimar. Tomorrow the composer Paul Hindemith is coming from Frankfurt; he does dance music as well as orchestral. I am very pleased to have him, since I was chiefly worried about getting the right music. He has composed a little opera to a text by Kokoschka, to be performed next winter in the Landestheater [Provincial Theater] in a production designed by me.

Saturday evening was invited to the Hildebrandts'—quite a party. A psychiatrist from Heidelberg, Dr. Prinzhorn, formerly an art historian, gave a talk on the drawings of the insane—very interesting illustrative material, with surprising similarities to the moderns; to Klee, for instance, who has seen these things and is enthusiastic. Gives one to think.

For a whole day I imagined I was going to go mad, and was even pleased at the thought, because then I would have everything I have been wanting; I would exist totally in a world of ideas, of introspection—what the mystics seek.

The Doctor also displayed a drawing with the caption: "Dangerous to look at!" This keeps going through my mind. The drawing showed delicate symbolic signs for love, life, childhood, humor, systematically arranged. Of course the whole business is used as an indictment of modern artists: see, they paint just like the insane! But that is not so, despite the similarity; the madman lives in the realm of ideas which the sane artist tries to reach; for the madman it is purer, because completely separate from external reality. One must admit this is a dangerous game the moderns are playing, and Goethe certainly knew very well what he was doing when he kept such a firm grip on reality and lauded healthy common sense; he must have been aware of the dangers of letting the imagination roam into the trackless wastes. I am much preoccupied with these questions.

To Tut

In transit

July 10, 1920

Yesterday in Darmstadt. Exhibition. Valuable impressions. The Germans bad. The French: good classicism—Baumeister bought one; he is capable of touchingly childlike ecstasies. Sunday in Frankfurt, where I visited Hindemith, a quicksilver young fellow, works like a demon. Lives in back of the main opera house in a nice, quiet street, his mother and sister downstairs, he upstairs in his musical garret. Many cigars for me and schnapps for both of us. Discussed everything; he is the right man, although not the perfect one; too bad I don't have his ability—I know what would be just right. For that we might wait forever. In the evening he has to go to his "factory" (the Opera—*Fidelio*). I don't want to go back until ten o'clock, am sitting now in the Groß-Frankfurter-Variété [Great Frankfurt Variety Show].

Now, Monday morning, in the rattling train on the way to Weimar. Due to arrive there at two-thirty.

Shall be glad to get home, plan to work hard, to finish up the ballet as soon as possible. Have to restrain myself from wanting to paint—because I had all sorts of things in mind, wanted to exhibit something in the next autumn show, but I will not take part, will not paint. A lot still has to take shape inside me, and once more something new is in the making.

To Tut

In transit
July 13, 1920

Am now en route between Leipzig and Dresden.

Saw all kinds of things in Weimar. Gropius, the director of the Bauhaus, wants me to come, offers me a studio. Thus I was greeted everywhere with, "So you are coming to Weimar." It is a lovely, quiet spot, historic ground, on which the young, high-spirited Bauhaus crew is playing its pranks. Most of them in Russian-style smocks. Ate in the cafeteria, good and cheap; even the director eats there. They are being viciously opposed by the reactionaries. Have great plans, but are hampered by lack of resources, dissipate their energies in various games. It has its drawbacks, despite all the attractions. No place to swim, except the Ilm, which is shallow and muddy. Many leave; in general it seems that after the first joyous meeting reflection sets in and the group breaks asunder again.

Now I am on my way to Dresden with Baumeister. But would like to head for home Sunday or Monday. In Weimar I slept in Itten's studio, a little old house built for the Knights Templar, in the middle of the park near Goethe's garden pavilion.

Have now arrived in Dresden, am staying at the Hotel Hospiz; am going next to the Arnold gallery, where our show takes place. Pictures and sculpture all arrived safely, will mount tomorrow. Sunday the opening lecture by Dr. Paul Ferdinand Schmidt.

Dresden lovely. Green roofs, the Elbe, much nobler and finer than Frankfurt.

To Otto Meyer

Cannstatt
August 7, 1920

It is high time I wrote to you. The dance of temptations has become very turbulent, but I am glad to describe it and will gladly open this can of *turbellarias* (that means "whirlpool worms") to give you a peek.

Temptation number one: to exhibit. A pressing invitation from an enthusiastic city museum director who saw my work here and to my surprise perceived lines leading back to Runge and (my secretly admired) Caspar David Friedrich; he also saw the contrast between my work and the ecstasy-Expressionists. You will be happy to hear that one of the things he said was that I create the mathematical and constructivist elements around which Baumeister twines his flowers. In general he preferred me. I am not exhibiting in order to sell paintings; but rather to elicit a few opinions I feel I should hear if I am to be properly skeptical toward what goes along with recognition and say "humph!" with sufficient firmness. And then a very definitive caesura is injecting itself into my life, so decisive and terminal that this seems the right moment for parting with my paintings.

Temptation number two: the road would lead to Weimar. Gropius invited me to join the Bauhaus and placed a studio at my disposal. I told him that at present I am wrapped up in ballet skirts and will be tied to them until spring. Gropius had to sustain heavy resistance from the Landtag [Regional Parliament] and the old Academy, but now the Bauhaus is supposed to be out of danger, although perhaps not quite as independent as Gropius had planned; the Academy will remain in existence. Gropius hopes to gather a good group of young people and form a phalanx. Incredibly, the workshop equipment, which was in beautiful shape before the war, was sold during the war, so now there is hardly even a planing bench left; and this is supposed to be an institute "based on craftsmanship." Building, even in the most utopian sense, can hardly be considered.

Temptation number three: close to Dresden a friend has set up a factory for textile printing, supported by the Werkbund and several benefactors. Another invitation to weather the coming vicissitudes in art and economics by working in a field "based on craftsmanship."

Temptation number four: the girl with the golden eyes and the big handwriting. Sooner or later she will be my wife.

Temptation number five: Count Keyserling, who is setting up a "school of wisdom" in Darmstadt, with the support of the former Grand Duke and other aristocrats. His writings appeal to me greatly, and I have been sorely tempted to enroll as a pupil.

To Tut

A letter at last! What proofs must I give you that we are one, that together we shall face life, which is so complicated that one person can hardly manage alone, at least not without love. You see, you will be my storage battery, collecting all the currents of life, my hearth when I am cold, and all the beautiful things the poets say and which I hope to tell you and make you feel in the course of a lifetime. Yes! See, I shall show you my last traces of doubt; the old uncertainty about whether I wasn't born to be a monk, the sense that I ought not squander myself if there existed a chance of attaining The Goal. The idea that the energy of modern man must be husbanded more than ever before, concentrated on what is most important; if monks did this in the past, how much more must they do it today, when they are so much more tormented, open to temptation, unbelieving. And then you know, and know about, the man I admire most—Otto Meyer—who is strong, keeps such solitude and creates something with eternal value. You do understand that all this can make a man very troubled?

To Otto Meyer

Cannstatt
September 9, 1920

I shall soon be married! Up to today I have been enveloped in a hubbub of rejoicing, applause, doubt, and dismay, balanced only by what provoked it all: the deed! This makes it easy for me to have an opinion, and here it is: my years of apprenticeship and wandering are over. Luther and Bach were also married and had many children—the highly civilized Chinese consider being married the most natural thing—man and wife are biblical concepts—I had begun to grow chilly, and I long for the warmth of life. So along with the dance, I am devoting myself to the question: how shall I build my house?

To Tut

Cannstatt

Mid-September 1920

Do you know our house is called Tutwyla? See, we must have a beautiful garden; we'll plant all the seeds and cuttings we can lay hands on; everything should grow in wild profusion; how lovely the flowers were in Nussdorf for the procession.

Tull will teach Osk what constancy means, because he is a dreadfully unstable type. And constancy is precisely what he needs for his art, because it alone yields true intensity. Intensity—that is what really matters, and consistency, which means slow, steady growth from deep sources. Will I succeed? I certainly hope so.

I want to ally myself with warm life and youth while there is still time—and I am also thinking of art. I picture my future as a beautiful unity; I shall bring my mathematical, constructivist art into contact with life, lest some day I find myself alone on an icy pinnacle. You see, I want to give my life a style of its own; in this you must let me take the lead, for I must make sure that everything converges—hopes, ideas, dreams. It will be lovely; you will be pleased. You should feel your way, enter into my being.

Did some drawing this morning, like the old days! Have trouble taking up the thread. Am amazed how long ago it all seems. It will look foolish to have dropped something halfway through—perhaps I shall yet have occasion to drop many things in favor of something clearly superior. The question is: will it work? Am facing the future with joy and apprehension—we do not know what life holds in store.

To Otto Meyer

Cannstatt

October 4, 1920

It almost looks as if my good intentions will pave my way to hell unless I change soon. If I had taken all my experiences deeply to heart I would be very different; instead, I suffer from the great forgetfulness, and I am inclined to believe Keyserling when he sees the bane of the Occidentals (as opposed to the

Indians) in their lack of memory. I am tumbling and leaping, unfortunately not to the primeval rhythm, although I still hope; indeed, to capture that is my great goal. I have made a bigger gamble than ever before; am giving up a tried and true way of life in anticipation that the new, unfamiliar one will be an improvement. I am not calculating at all, yet am also calculating very intensely. Love causes this vagueness; I am being rocked (by the waves of a sea with which I am little acquainted, landlubber that I am). My sweetheart is the bewitching siren— she laughs at my dusty old art, destined only for the storage bin.

The wedding before mid-October; almost certainly in Mannheim.

To Otto Meyer

Cannstatt

November 4, 1920

Weimar-Bauhaus. Gropius strongly urges me to come. He writes that the reactionaries' stubborn resistance is slowly crumbling; he will be given complete freedom; the old Art School professors are beginning to find the air too brisk and are withdrawing, leaving him with chairs he should fill if he wants to keep them. A position with a salary of 16,000 marks would be available for me sooner or later. What to do? First of all: my initial step was to write that I am involved from now until spring with a ballet which I cannot leave hanging in mid-air; I proposed that my presence in Weimar remain a formality until I am free (to me that means: until I have made up my mind). The appointment would not come through immediately in any case. An offer is also being made to Klee, who will probably accept at once. This whole business crosses up my plans, which included, as I wrote you, privacy, life in the country (this was the condition on which Tut agreed to marry me; above all she does not want to play "the artist's wife"). But can I be sure I would accomplish what I had hoped to accomplish there (in the country)? I only know that the greater my isolation, the better my work. My wife's gay, tempestuous temperament might tip the scales the other way.

Gropius seems more interested in getting artists than in getting devoted teachers. Itten is the exception and indeed stands out brilliantly among the quieter men who make up the rest of the faculty.

To Tut

Weimar

November 24, 1920

Found a room at the Elephant Hotel. But to come to the point: things look good for the Bauhaus! Today another meeting for Gropius—he must act, lay claim to rooms, present a list of appointees; he thinks I should stay here for a month and then come permanently in the spring, should put together an exhibition for the students and the government, should send to Mannheim for my pictures. Everyone here considers my coming so definite, so obvious, that I myself can no longer think any differently. It could be wonderful here—Klee will almost certainly come. He plans to visit at the end of November or early in December; I would have liked to meet him at long last.

They picked out a studio today for me; I would have a handsome one on the ground floor, in a quiet part of the building. I have the choice between two. And just think, there is an open site here where the students are to build. All in all, the plans are conceived on a grand scale and will take time to mature. The surroundings of Weimar lovely; the day after tomorrow I hope to look around, walk out into the country to see if we might live there eventually.

Diary

December 1920

Should I make a getaway at the last moment? Not accept the appointment? That would be madness, some might say, but not some who are in agreement. Advantages—disadvantages. What will be best for me: living under primitive conditions, under the pressure of circumstances, but free? What do I want? Art? I tend to doubt that, since I think Spengler is indeed right when he says that painters should become engineers, lest they remain charlatans and fools. Can a composition in materials by the Bauhaus people—or by the Dadaists, in whose footsteps they partly follow—compare with a technical, industrial product?

WEIMAR
(Winter 1921 to Summer 1925)

1921: Having accepted the appointment to the Weimar Bauhaus in December 1920, Oskar Schlemmer spends the next few months alternating between Weimar and Stuttgart, where he continues work on his ballet project. In March he is assigned living quarters in one of the courtiers' houses at the Belvedere Palace in Weimar. He designs the scenery and costumes and decisively influences the choreography for two premieres at the Stuttgart Landestheater, Oskar Kokoschka's one-act *Mörder, Hoffnung der Frauen [Murderer, the Hope of Women]*, with music by Paul Hindemith, and Franz Blei's *Das Nusch-Nuschi [The Thingamagig]*.

At the Bauhaus Schlemmer is put in charge of the mural workshop; for a time he also teaches nude drawing. As director of the Bauhaus, Gropius constantly finds himself confronted by difficult situations both outside and inside the institute.

In the summer Gropius appoints Lothar Schreyer to set up a stage workshop at the Bauhaus.

1922: Appointment of Wassily Kandinsky to the Bauhaus. In a reshuffling of the workshops, Oskar Schlemmer takes over the stone and woodworking section as a "master of form."

Certain basic conflicts have emerged within the Bauhaus. Schlemmer attempts to bring about free discussion and clarification by meeting with the students. In the summer he goes to Amden and then to Stuttgart, where he makes final preparations for the performance of the "Triadic Ballet"; it takes place on September 30 in the Small Theater of the Stuttgart Landestheater. Once back in Weimar, Schlemmer devotes himself primarily to painting. Pictures of this period: *Tänzerin* ["Female Dancer"], *Tänzer* ["Dancer"], *Figur von der Seite* ["Figure from the Side"], and his major India ink drawings.

1923: In the spring Itten leaves the Bauhaus and is replaced by László Moholy-Nagy. When Schreyer likewise does not renew his contract, Schlemmer assumes his duties in addition to his own.

The major event of the year is the big exhibition (August-September), at which the Bauhaus offers a comprehensive survey of its theoretical and practical work and accomplishments. In addition to exhibiting pictures, Schlemmer makes the important contribution of decorating the workshop building with murals and reliefs. As part of the "Bauhaus Week," the Jena theater, remodelled by Gropius, is used for performances of the sprightly Bauhaus theatrical experiments. The "Triadic Ballet" is performed to great acclaim in the Weimar Deutsches Nationaltheater [German National Theater]. Somewhat later the ballet is also performed in Leipzig.

The Berlin Volksbühne [Popular Theater] takes up contact with Schlemmer, and he is commissioned to design the production of Carl Hauptmann's drama *Der abtrünnige Zar [The Deserter Czar]*. Other commissions follow.

Schlemmer produces *Tischgesellschaft* ["Dinner Guests"], *Paracelsus, Mythische Figur* ["Mythic Figure"], *Sitzende in Weiß* ["Seated Lady in White"], and a series of lithographs.

1924: Grave new difficulties arise for the Bauhaus when rightists come to power in the government and a vilification campaign against the Bauhaus is launched in Weimar. Since the appropriations barely cover the costs of the workshops, the amount budgeted for the theater, painting, and sculpture workshops is reduced. For Schlemmer, as director of the sculpture studio and a projected experimental theater, this means a radical reduction in the scope of his work. In the summer a trip to Amden.

Schlemmer writes "Mensch und Kunstfigur" ["Man and Art Figure"], published in 1925 in the fourth volume of the Bauhaus series.* In September all the masters are informed they may be dismissed on April 1, 1925.

Gropius receives many expressions of sympathy for the Bauhaus, both from within and outside of Germany; he founds the "Friends of the Bauhaus" under the trusteeship of a group of prominent intellectuals.

The year 1924 sees the creation of what Schlemmer calls the "gallery pictures": *Vorübergehender* ["Passer-by"], *Sinnender* ["The Thinker"], *Frauentreppe* ["Women's Stairway"], and others. Murals in the house of the Weimar architect Adolf Meyer. Exhibitions in Stuttgart and Berlin. Productions for the Berlin Volksbühne and the Weimar National Theater.

1925: By January the cities of Frankfurt am Main, Mannheim, Hagen, Darmstadt, and Dessau have all offered the Bauhaus a new home. The choice falls on Dessau. In April a number of Bauhaus members move to Dessau. At first Schlemmer is not considered for a new post. The Berlin Volksbühne offers him a contract, but he realizes that this position would not be right for him. Otto Bartning, who has in the meantime set up the Staatliche Bauhochschule [State Architecture

---

*In *The Theater of the Bauhaus,* translated by Arthur S. Wensinger (Middletown, Conn.: Wesleyan University Press, 1961). — Translator

School] in Weimar, makes him several offers, which, however, do not meet Schlemmer's requirements. The prospect of a teaching position at the Stuttgart Academy fails to materialize. Schlemmer decides to wait it out. In his Weimar studio he paints his famous pictures, *Römisches* ["Roman Theme"], *Ruheraum* ["Resting Space"], *Konzentrische Gruppe* ["Concentric Group"], *Akt, Frau und Kommender* ["Nude, Woman, and New Arrival"]. With these pictures he leaves pure abstraction behind and after painful inner debate commits himself to his life-long theme: "Man in Space."

In the autumn Gropius summons Schlemmer to Dessau. He entrusts him with the task of developing an experimental theater. Gropius's design of the new Bauhaus Building includes an experimental stage. Schlemmer will live in one of the "Masters' Houses" Gropius proposes to build. In September he goes to Dessau.

To Otto Meyer

Weimar: the contract has been signed, covering the period from January 1, 1921 to April 1923. The move will take a while, since living quarters are difficult to find. I also have permission to stay away until the ballet project is finished.

Did I write that Klee has also been appointed? I finally met him, and found him strangely caught up in materialistic concerns: questions about food prices, rental costs. I mention this because his insistence on such matters bordered on the ludicrous. I could say many things, and sometime I shall, about the Bauhaus, especially once I am part of it. Fortunately it looks as though I will not have to be a real teacher, to give systematic instruction. Only Itten has such responsibilities. Lyonel Feininger, for example, sees students only one day a week. I foresee that the students, who are free to choose their teachers, will work with me on my projects—I am thinking largely in terms of a practical, flexible cooperation, which should automatically reveal the particular interests and needs the students have.

The Bauhaus runs the risk of becoming little more than a modern academy of the arts (the nature of the appointments suggests this), for the essential distinguishing feature, the crafts, the workshops, is treated as peripheral. For instance: the workshops lack the most basic equipment. And the students apparently have little enthusiasm for practical craftsmanship; the chief ambition is to become a modern painter. On the positive side, Gropius plans to give himself and the Bauhaus time; nothing is to be exhibited publicly for the first five years.

But I am looking forward to Weimar and my work there. It is a peaceful little town, and I hope to salvage some of the dreams which were supposed to be fulfilled on the banks of Lake Constance. Our stay there will merely be postponed, I say, and Frau Tull says it even more insistently. Then, too, the Bauhaus takes a three-month vacation!

To Tut

I want to get out of the Pension. They are relatives of Count Keyserling. Lunch today. Next to me a princess. Before and after the meal there are prayers. And then every time I turn around it is "Herr Professor this," "Herr Professor that." Even Klee calls me "Herr Professor Schlemmer"! This morning I planned out my exhibition. Invited to Gropius's this evening, tomorrow night to Itten's. Klee will have no place to live until April. Until then alternating every two weeks between here and Munich. He does not plan to begin in earnest until fall.

To Tut

Weimar

January 20, 1921

The weeks are terribly long in Weimar.—Well, I moved. Feel more comfortable, but I have a cold.

Last night there was a Bauhaus lecture on Russia. The speaker traced a connection between the sweep of the Russian landscape and the sweep of the Russian soul. Much beautiful description. At the piano afterwards he played and whistled the march which the demonstrating Russian mobs sang. Then the funeral march for the fallen of the Revolution. Later the masters and a few musicians at Gropius's house—until 1 A.M

This morning I visited Feininger in his studio. He likes me, it would seem. Klee is also nice and sticks close to me, feels lonely. Tomorrow morning I am supposed to conduct Feininger and his wife through my exhibition.

Went house-hunting yesterday: nothing.

To Otto Meyer

Cannstatt

February 3, 1921

Have you heard the battle cry of the moderns: Picasso paints naturalistically! (It is a mixture, or cross, of Gulbransson and Millet!)

I do not know whether this new slogan, superimposed on one that people hardly understand yet, will prove a blessing or a curse. I see gruesome confusion in the making. Or does the trend make no difference, provided the essential thing, meaning, is preserved? Still, there should be A Sign in which Thou Shalt Conquer! Might it be the same situation as with the religions and the rings in Lessing's *Nathan?* What is truth in art? What, in fact, is the truth? Is there an absolute truth, an absolute art; or are there only truths, relative and approximate?

I found myself somewhat insecure in the face of such questions, which came up in Weimar during conversations with my nephew Hermann Müller, who is a student there. In Weimar an "apostle of truth" has turned up, "speaking truth" by quoting Jesus Christ, Lao-tse, and Nietzsche. This man claims to be the first activist of the word, no mere listener. His great deed: to leave family and possessions (which he lost in the war; he was a champagne manufacturer in France); now he moves from city to city, from prison to insane asylum, released each time on the basis of apparently glowing doctors' reports. I am telling you this because of his impact on Weimar: almost twenty students of the Bauhaus proclaimed that "art is a grind," threw up the whole business, and set out on foot without cares or money for the South: Spain and especially Italy; some of the students follow Häusser's (that is the name of this man of God) disciples around everywhere (the girls seem to be especially in favor of direct following; the young men express their inner confusion by throwing aside conventions and inhibitions and sliding into the Great Indolence).

The fact that the Bauhaus does not shun the spirit of the age, even when there is an obvious risk involved (the Bauhaus evenings demonstrate this); the fact that the Bauhaus program has attracted a fearless band of young people (we have a crazy sampling of modern youth): all this means that the Bauhaus is "building" something quite different from what was planned—human beings. Gropius seems very aware of this; to his mind the academies make a grave mistake by neglecting the formation of the human being. He wants an artist to have character, and this should come first, art later. Yet at times he appears alarmed at the outcome: no work gets done, but there is a great, great deal of talk. He would welcome a temporary wall around the Bauhaus and some monastic solitude. The pillar of calm amidst the student chaos is provided by the teachers. I am witness to two attempts to take the situation in hand. Itten tried it with dictatorship, exhibiting such ruthlessness and schoolmasterly pendantry that the students finally cried coercion. Klee will try it with exactly the opposite means: indifference (or the semblance thereof); if students come to him—and they will come more readily than one might think—they may be surprised at how warmly they are received. By the way, Klee's appointment seems to provoke the greatest head-shaking, for he is considered a *l'art pour l'art* type with no conceivable practical contribution to make; I personally find such a judgment short-sighted. We shall see.

The situation is this: the Bauhaus was intended to be an arts and crafts school, an architecture school, and an academy of the arts rolled into one. That did not work: the Academy wants to preserve its independence. Right now the issue is being fought out: should the Academy be made an integral part or be dissolved?

Once I am properly established in Weimar (at the moment I am still here temporarily), I trust I shall gain a good deal of insight, experience, and information.

To Tut

Weimar

February 25, 1921

Back from a walk to the Belvedere. Coatless, in sandals, glorious weather. Had the castellan show me the apartment in the "Clock House": one rather large room, a kitchen, and three or four smaller rooms. Could be made very pleasant.

Covered the distance from the Bauhaus to the Belvedere in less than half an hour. Ate lunch with Feininger at the "Fountain of Youth" for 5 marks, afterwards coffee. Feininger is a fine man; walked back with him through the park, where he perks up: "Ah! It really is beautiful in Weimar!" He is right, Tull—it will be very, very beautiful. I can already see you rushing hither and thither, and I am looking forward to showing you around.

Letter to an unknown recipient

March 2, 1921

I received the living quarters I had applied for: in one of the courtiers' houses at the Belvedere Palace, half an hour's walk down the Avenue from Weimar. Here, as everywhere in Germany, there is a housing shortage and short-sighted housing supervision. I should be skeptical toward such great good fortune; but then it is not completely unclouded either.

The student resignations continue (Italy conspiring with springtime); fewer applications this year. Attacks in the press. And then today the latest: the government has decided to revive the Hochschule für bildende Kunst, formerly reduced to three professors, now to be made part of the Bauhaus. Gropius is out of town, and Itten informs me that we are in for a no-holds-barred struggle. This latest plan would degrade the Bauhaus to an arts and crafts school. Gropius had presented sufficient arguments against the Academy to the government, outlining what had happened elsewhere in the country when academies and arts and crafts schools were merged for economic reasons. Before the war, the city of Halle was outstanding for its cultural institutions and resources and supported them unstintingly. The City Council has now decided that "a realistic appraisal of the situation" demands eliminating the entire appropriation for the arts, which will mean closing the theater, firing the distinguished museum director, halting the purchase of paintings, and so on—on the grounds that other things take precedence. Of course Gropius dreams of dispensing with government support and controls as soon as possible; but this is utopian, for even with its subsidy the Bauhaus barely scrapes by.

I am amazed at the bad will toward Gropius among the students I know. They claim he is no longer what he was at the beginning, when he lived—and suffered—in true communion with them, a "Father Gropius." They say he has changed greatly, that it even shows in his eyes and the expression around his mouth; and the present program of the Bauhaus contains no trace of the inspiring original program. Similar criticisms are voiced against Itten. They feel his initial élan is hardening into an inflexible set of rules. I simply cannot judge yet whether this process forms the necessary follow-up to the optimistic beginning, whether these particular students preferred a blazing fire to a still glow, and whether indeed the present situation represents such a glow. We also have a group of students who deeply and seriously believe in quiet and concentration; they feel that the students who have left are no loss; the valuable ones are those who are just now arriving and those who return. It speaks well for Gropius that he so ardently wishes the Bauhaus to be left in peace to work; the aforementioned Wall of China.

On the positive side: the cafeteria, for example, where the cooking follows vegetarian, organic principles (Mazdaznan recipes); some of the girl students work there, voluntarily giving up time that might be spent on their art studies. The cafeteria is frequented by students and masters alike, with some of the former receiving free meals. Connected with this, the "building site," a piece of well-situated land where fruit trees and vegetables are to be planted. Later on, the first building it receives will be the garden house. The building site, which is uppermost in our minds, due to the time of year, is intended to dissipate the widespread prejudices against the Bauhaus. Gropius also hopes to set up dormitories for the students; altogether, his plans run along boarding school lines, one of the chief reasons being that he has concluded from recent events that the students must be tied more closely to the institution. Many of them sooner or later break with their parents and are left without financial resources. It is heartening to see how readily the girls recognize these economic necessities and voluntarily undertake various services.

What the students actually produce in the way of art or handcrafted objects can only be called meager. Almost shockingly so. One may say with some justification that the Bauhaus is a beautiful facade, a concept, an idea for Germany, shored up by the names of a few artists and a program. Many things will be decided during the fierce fight against the Academy—perhaps even the collapse of the Bauhaus.

To Otto Meyer

Weimar
March 2, 1921

Picasso. I have borrowed from the Bauhaus library a new book on him, which covers even his more recent period. The author places the greatest value on the problematical (cubistic) works, which he sees as the expression of a highly cultivated "sensibility" (a term he uses time and again). In connection with the recent works, he says that Picasso has grown weary, the stars have left his eyes; and perhaps also: anxiety at the labyrinth into which he has ventured. I was amazed at the versatility of the man. An actor, the comic genius among artists? For everything is there: he could easily assume the role of any artist of the past, or of any modern painter. I am not sure whether Picasso started everything (they say Braque invented Cubism). But Picasso certainly strikes me as the great initiator, the tightrope walker (the comedian who courts danger); others, less hot-blooded than he, seem to have lit their fires from tiny sparks of his fireworks. For Picasso plainly contains the germ of all the French Cubists I know. I find Picasso's latest works revelations, exposés. They reveal the Spaniard who lives in Paris; by that I mean: naturalism provides a touchstone. Show me how you portray nature, and I shall tell you who you are.

I became intensely aware of the non-Germanic quality of Picasso's new work, and of the fact that he is so Spanish or Latin in nature. The author of the book quotes a philosopher who says, "Man spends the first third of his life among the dead, the second third among the living, and the third third with himself"; the author hopes that the need for rest expressed by Picasso's return to older forms signals the advent of the third stage. He concludes by expressing the highest hopes for Picasso. The figurines for Picasso's Russian ballet interested me for two reasons: human figures dressed from the knees up in conventional garb, below the knees spreading into gigantic structures, borrowings from his cubistic paintings. A trace of Dada, actually vulgarizations or persiflage of his pictures—and then, simultaneously with these, to judge by the date (1919/20), a portrait of his wife in evening dress and holding a fan, and not, for heaven's sake, "like Ingres," but rather postcard-style kitsch. *Voyez-vous moi?!*

So far I have had no opportunity to display or practice "pedagogic method." Not until the summer session will I see whether I have pupils, and if so, which ones. In the summer the students are free to choose their teachers. In the winter they have a compulsory class on form taught by Itten. As I said, I would like simply to work and let the students follow that example. A dialogue will spring up by itself. I am also tempted, however, to do my paintings at home and bring them to the studio as a fait accompli. This will have to wait until I am actually painting again; in the year and a half of abstention I have almost forgotten how; for it has been that long!

To Tut

Weimar

March 3, 1921

In strict confidence now: things look bad for the Bauhaus! Six more students want to leave for Italy. Few new ones. But the most important thing: under pressure from the rightist parties and certain other forces, the old Academy is supposed to be revived, under the same roof with the Bauhaus, with one administrator for both, one building superintendent, and so on, but of course different directors; this promises constant friction, not the least among the students. Altogether, a mixed-up mess, just when Gropius wanted to have everything neat and tidy, with "ideologically irreproachable" men in the various positions. Gropius considers the fashion in which the restoration of the old Academy was broached and implemented a slap in the face. He feels that this is it. We must stand firm, which may mean drawing the consequences and—resigning. He would be ready to do that himself, but the masters of course have to back him. We could only gain by it. For then the issue would come up before the Landtag, and there the leftist parties approve of the Bauhaus for its handicrafts orientation. And then outside support. Klee has been summoned by telegram, and decisions will have to be made rapidly.

To Tut

Cannstatt
April 24, 1921

Worked hard today. Made a plaster model for Kokoschka and all the figures for *Nusch-Nuschi.* Yesterday Hindemith came over and played through all the music for me. Worked so hard today that I was done in, then sat in the Kursaal park and read your letters; wonderful, soft air, Stuttgart air! And this softness pervades all of nature here. I looked my fill at a green meadow. The birds here sing very, very beautifully, more melodically, it seems to me, than in the Belvedere. What is wrong with me? Why were the theater sketches I did in my Weimar studio such a mess, while being here seems synonymous with clarity and the ability to work? I shall not look for an explanation. It might be something else entirely; perhaps the atmosphere of the workshop in Cannstatt and the proximity of the costumes have put me back into the right frame of mind.

To Tut

Cannstatt
April 29, 1921

Cannot suppress the sense of belonging here; it is in the air, the light . . . . When you come right down to it, I must be a Swabian after all; you, on the other hand, love the wide open spaces, the unknown.

To Tut

Cannstatt
May 14, 1921

Guess what time it is! Half-past five! In the morning! I worked straight through the night. The birds are twittering, day has come, I have just turned out the light. I feel marvelous—not tired in the least. I am full of "Dionysian over-alertness." Realize once again that serious accomplishments must be fought for. This is what happened: I was dissatisfied with *Nusch-Nuschi,* despite all the praise; I rehearsed and rehearsed, did a thousand sketches, became jittery. I felt I did not have the solution yet.

Yesterday morning we had the stage rehearsal (only the sets), stacking wooden boxes, and so on. Learned a lot, noticed that I was undecided about many things, which merely intensified my insecurity. Did this and that during the afternoon, then came home, only to find a room full of people. Couldn't get to work until eleven. Finally the guests left, and I sat down at my drawing board. Did sketches, over and over again. At three-thirty an idea came to me in a sudden flash. The simplest solution; all is well, the road ahead clear, tremendous relief, almost prayed. You see, despite the "master" title, nothing can be won without a struggle. The fact is, I have forgotten how to work properly. In Weimar I shall have to give up many a night's rest, and spend the days in the woods or out in the sun. It is a precious thing, the night's peacefulness.

To Otto Meyer

Cannstatt
Whitsunday
May 16, 1921

My theatrical projects: two operatic one-acters, one in grand theatrical style, the other "for Burmese marionettes," with an idiotic text—comical, erotic, Indian. One of them (the Kokosch-ka) can be done in dull or earth tones, the other very bright. And I shall also have a say in the direction, which may prove my only satisfaction. I would like my influence to be decisive. But right now I wonder whether this will be possible, given the singers' conceitedness. The dances must also be rehearsed; I hear that the ballet master is delighted with me. "Inimitable!" I should be happy, but I am not. I have discovered how untalent-ed I am at improvisation (of visual effects); I work slowly and painfully, and usually nothing will gel if I have a problem to solve from one day to the next. The ballet will be far superior to the rest of the production, for it has had a long gestation period and is now solid. I notice that when something is expected of me (usually on the basis of a misconception as to my intentions) and I do it just to be obliging, the results are dreary.

In Weimar Itten teacher "Analysis." He shows photographs,

and the students are supposed to draw various essential elements, usually the movement, the main contour, a curve. Then he shows them a Gothic figure. Next he displays the weeping Mary Magdalen from the Grünewald Altar; the students struggle to extract some essential feature from this complicated picture. Itten glances at their efforts and then bursts out: if they had any artistic sensitivity, they would not attempt to draw this, the noblest portrayal of weeping, a symbol of the tears of the world; they would sit silent, themselves dissolved in tears. Thus he speaks, then departs, slamming the door!

To Tut

Cannstatt
May 16, 1921

This morning a special delivery letter: Gropius just arrived. Around ten o'clock I went to see him at the Hotel Marquardt— we talked a great deal. Then I sent word I could not attend the rehearsal, and I showed him the costumes for the ballet; he was much taken with their solidity. He said my endeavors would dovetail very neatly with what Lothar Schreyer has in mind. He takes a positive attitude toward theatrical matters, thinks we should work on costumes and such at the Bauhaus.

Gropius mentioned he had set up a course in nude drawing for the sculptors; would I like to be in charge? I accepted with alacrity, and he promised to make the necessary arrangements. He considers study of the nude figure a necessity. This might turn out very well—I am looking forward to it!

To Otto Meyer

Weimar
June 14, 1921

The theatrical adventure in Stuttgart is over, and I am back in Weimar now.

I had a difficult task in Stuttgart, but it afforded me much valuable experience, at the very least. As you know, I became deeply involved: prepared the dances, directed the singers' movements; fear of failure constantly threatened to overtake me, yet in the end, the initiates recognized my touch, as you had predicted. The performance was a success; from backstage I heard my name being called, louder and louder, and I was dragged onto the stage, to face an audience of 1,400! I understand the production won over people who had previously been unable to make head or tail of my painting. I ascribe this to the production's being a compromise; I have a general tendency to see this success in a gloomy light. But all this took place the first evening. The next day the newspapers appeared, pouring a flood of filth over the whole evening because of obscenities in the text of the second piece. (i.e. the castration of the royal field marshal). Everything was interpreted pornographically, every form seen as phallic; and the uproar effectively drowned out any mention of the music and the production. The second performance was already noticeably inferior to the first, because the theater people were upset and angry; and then the press got the scandal it wanted: the final curtain brought a chorus of catcalls and boos. The press is attacking the theater management and demanding that the plays close.

It would not make sense to discuss every factor in detail. The scandal has no bearing on my own efforts. I should say, though, that I enjoyed working with the theater and found my talents in this direction confirmed.

I noticed one thing, which became especially clear from the perspective of the Bauhaus: much of modern art nowadays tends toward practical application, toward architecture. The economic crisis may make building impossible for years to come. There are no noble tasks to which the utopian fantasies of the moderns might be applied. The illusionary world of the theater offers an outlet for these fantasies. We must be content with surrogates, create out of wood and cardboard what we cannot build in stone and steel. Perhaps Gropius shares this idea: he has appointed Lothar Schreyer to the Bauhaus, a theater man and poet who had opened a "Theater of Struggle" in Hamburg. So now the Bauhaus has a commitment to theater, which makes me happy. Theatrical questions will henceforth play an important role among the subjects we treat.

Are you familiar with Spengler's *Decline of the West?* His notions on painters run as follows: today's art is inevitably eclectic, incapable of completely original creation; therefore an artist nowadays must be either a charlatan or a fool. Our age stands under the aegis of industrialism, and he advises the poets to join the merchant marine and the artists to become engineers. This advice probably aroused merriment in the painting world; but the idea haunts me, for the following reason: development following Picasso was toward increasing formalism. The basic concepts were: the functional, the dynamic, the tectonic. Some of the works produced so resembled the structure of machines that they differed only in not being real machines. Machines are supremely functional; these pictures, by contrast, seemed so romantically unfunctional, as if begging for salvation. I myself have tendencies in this direction, and I am worried about the trend. You once described machines as abstract compositions. However, machines owe their existence not to abstraction but to pure considerations of functionality. Are they teaching art how to rid itself of romanticism and be concrete? Like Stendhal, who read the *Code Civile* and then set out to write his novels in a factual, unromantic style.

Diary

June 23, 1921

I sit in my studio every day, half obliged and half resolved to produce something. I pick up this or that, then let my hands sink into my lap. It has hold of me again, and with a vengeance.

Am I suffering the effects of premature fame, of my position at the Bauhaus, which cripples me instead of spurring me on? The fact is—and how unusual for me that it should be so—that once "an angel has offered what I desired" I am unhappier about it than before. Is this just a mood, a temporary failure of nerve, or am I simply not equal to the situation? I spend a lot of time on the art of the past: the early Greeks and the like, the Old Masters, classicistic works. Compared to all this, especially to the works of Antiquity, much of modern art (and I mean myself) strikes me as sheer folly. The title of a book by Adalbert Stifter, *Das Narrenschloß [The Castle of Fools]*, haunts me whenever I think of the imperative contained in that classical formulation by Goethe: Antiquity, conjury, magic has style; the modern does not. Antiquity and conjury are nature. The modern, on the other hand, is purely cerebral, fantastical. Antiquity is sober, modest, moderate. The modern is undisciplined, intoxicated.

To Otto Meyer

Weimar
June 23, 1921

A *Putsch* brewing at the Bauhaus. The best people here are criticizing Gropius, and I myself am a secret *Putschist* (for the moment). Or I fancy myself one, largely out of a sense of responsibility. The basic conflicts have become even more obvious now that I am near Itten again (and Itten is Gropius) —even in Stuttgart I was already involved in a constant, though friendly, feud with him over principles about which I turned out to be right. I see the faults in an undertaking which has the potential to be truly great but is not great, or not great enough. Not, to be sure, that I have the power to change anything, or at least not now.

To give you an idea: the Bauhaus has no course in architecture, with the result that no student wants to, or rather is able to, become an architect. And yet the Bauhaus stands for the primacy of architecture. The blame falls on Gropius, who is the only architect at the Bauhaus but has no time for teaching. A program could easily be set up (theoretically), but it would be hard to implement. Then, too, the original program has been dead for a long time, replaced by a set of statutes which hardly differ from those of any school of the arts and crafts. I am not resentful and eager for a *Putsch;* rather, I am concerned for the fate of an undertaking for which I feel partly responsible. What I would like to see is this: more architecture at the Bauhaus, more discipline in the other fields; the Bauhaus should seek out, collect, and preserve all the possible laws of artistic production—old and new.

What the Dutch accomplish in the way of architecture is remarkable. Every city in that small country has its modern architects, each working on his own, but all linked by such basic agreement on principles that already a new architectural style has emerged such as one finds nowhere else; in addition, this style has won an undisputed place in the awareness of the people. At present the Dutch are the best builders. This may explain the strong impression Amsterdam had on me; at one time I wanted to live there.

For the vacation, i.e. the summer months, I have been assigned the sculpture workshop and nude drawing. This week I must take over, and I do not know where to begin. To get a sense of each student's interests, I circulated questionnaires, which were either not filled out at all or else only cursorily and pretentiously. Some of the students want correction or advice, others will have none of it. The students tend to ask for many different positions to draw, whereas my plan was to have them concentrate intensively on one position. Enough sloppy work is being done already, cultivation of cheap effects and the like, and I should like to follow the principle of Matisse, who told his students that until they could draw like a Dürer they had no right to invent facial expressions. I shall harp on solid work and hope that they leave expressions alone until they have mastered the nude model.

As director of the sculpture workshop I shall of course have to devote myself to that branch. But I find myself resisting, as I always do when I am forced into something. When I was working under Hoelzel, I secretly turned against him. Now I am mustering all kinds of arguments against the Bauhaus and sculpture. I refuse to be a good boy and let myself be pinned down to a specialty. But it seems my destiny to be praised for achievements I consider less important (in theater, ballet, sculpture). A good reason for being on my guard.

To Otto Meyer

Weimar
July 14, 1921

I wrote you that the Bauhaus kitchen was introducing the Mazdaznan diet or trying it out. Itten and a few faithful Bauhaus disciples have been following its precepts for some time now, and Itten returned very enthusiastic from a Mazdaznan convention in Leipzig. This method will produce "the new man," he contends, and according to him, the thought processes and emotions must be transformed before that goal can be attained. All I could reply was that paying so much attention to the stomach and to what passed one's lips might rob one of one's spontaneity and distract one from essentials—such as the word and the spirit; and I was not sure that purity was guaranteed by a pure stomach.

I mentioned Balzac, who could work well only on a full stomach. (Itten: "But just look at his kind of work, and besides, it is only for other people with stuffed stomachs.") Yet the carnivorous Dutch produce great painters. Itten wants to turn the Bauhaus into a monastery of saints, or at least monks; I suspect from his pilgrimages to Beuron that he has a similar organization in mind, and there I cannot withhold my admiration. This much is now clear: Itten and Muche and a few loyal disciples are shutting themselves off from the others and following their own course, its exclusiveness intended to both attract and repel.

Diary

July 23, 1921

It is clear, and there are good reasons for my present state of mind: once again I face fundamental decisions. The death-and-resurrection business in particular is getting me down! Should my work degenerate into the decorative, become merely "animated," and end up in mannerism and aridity—or: can the principles of high art still be rescued?

Diary

July 28, 1921

I dislike my way of fighting so keenly over principles. Why not simply accept the undeniably good aspects of the dietary program, instead of going to extremes in my protest, to the point that I become an advocate of gluttony? Especially since back in Stuttgart I myself was getting people interested in Mazdaznan, living according to its ideals, albeit only for a time, while others observed them longer and more faithfully. The

111

Indian and oriental concept is having its heyday in Germany. Mazdaznan belongs to the phenomenon. It strikes me that the life styles of the different races and peoples are as varied as their languages. Indian–oriental abstinence—Dutch gluttony. Austrian pastries and Swabian *Spaetzle;* both made with eggs. And everywhere one finds people who live to be one hundred, everywhere human beings. Nowadays an unprecedented exchange of ideals seems to be taking place. The western world is turning to the East, the eastern to the West. The Japanese are reaching out for Christianity, we for the wise teachings of the East. And then the parallels in art. The goal and purpose of all this? Perfection? Or the eternal cycle?

To Otto Meyer

Weimar

October 5, 1921

Your letter arrived almost on the very day, September 17, and contained a correct guess, a daughter. A son was anticipated, the name chosen (Tilman), but nature's decision was quickly and reverently accepted in light of the miraculous event. Nature must know what she is about, or at least better than the parents, and I am sure she does not prevail blindly, as people claim. She almost did prevail: there was half an hour when the child had the umbilical wound twice around its neck and life hung in the balance. In half an hour it would have been twelve midnight, Sunday—and dead; it was a brilliant night with full moon. Karin is the daughter's name, with an Eva in front of it (like all of them), to dispel any doubts as to the gender of the middle name.

Diary

November 1921

Simple form and nobility: I cannot fully advocate them, since in some sense they are not genuine, i.e. they contain an element of reflection, of intention, consciousness of the impact; the underlying idea does not totally permeate them.

So what then? Wait until the form comes to fruition? The

fate of today's artists: to have form, a wealth of form, without content to match; we have the techniques but lack a conception.

Artists? Time and again one of them delves into the midst of life. Lovingly draws upon his techniques. Even descends into the depths, reaches the heart of the world, nature . . . .

Possibilities? One might be a last flowering, dance on the ruins, unthinking, with the pungent scent of decay all around—Klee. Could one be historical? Simultaneously vary the silence, change, a transformation artist. Picasso—Chirico. Should one be strange? Seize the depths of the subconscious without formulating any meaning intellectually.

Diary

November 7, 1921

What creative task to set oneself? Over and over pure form, a ventriloquist's trick, sleight of hand, product of the restless, fearless imagination, senseless, driving toward senselessness?

To Otto Meyer

Weimar

December 7, 1921

Events here induce me to write sooner than I had intended. The Bauhaus is in the midst of a crisis, and no minor one at that. I shall have to fill you in. As I already wrote, Itten introduced the Mazdaznan doctrine. Returned this summer from a convention in Leipzig and was, as he put it, completely convinced that, despite his previous doubts and hesitations, this doctrine and its impressive adherents constituted the one and only truth.

But the consequences: first the kitchen (the student cafeteria) was converted to Mazdaznan principles. The argument being that only with this sort of cooking could we afford to keep the cafeteria open these days. The meat eaters must give in, and some claim they need the meat. But that is not all: Itten allegedly carries Mazdaznan principles into the classroom, differentiating between the adherents and the non-adherents on the basis of ideology rather than on the basis of achievement. So apparently a special clique has formed and is splitting the Bauhaus into two camps, the teachers also being drawn in. Itten has managed to have his course made the only required one; he further controls the important workshops and has a rather considerable, admirable ambition: to put his stamp on the Bauhaus. To be sure, he has been stomping about on it since its inception (three years ago). Gropius, the only other person who qualified as a director (the "Council of Masters" has been in full existence only six months), let Itten have his way, since he himself was too much taken up with organization and administration. Now Gropius has finally taken a stand against Itten's monopoly and asserts that Itten must go back where he belongs, i.e. to his pedagogic tasks. So Itten and Gropius are duelling it out, and we others are supposed to play referee.

Now this is the situation: Gropius is an excellent diplomat, businessman, and practical genius. In the Bauhaus he has a large private office, and he receives commissions for building villas in Berlin. Berlin, business, and lucrative commissions, partially or hardly understood by the students (whom Gropius wants to help get jobs this way)—these are scarcely the best prerequisites for Bauhaus work. Itten is right to attack this practice and demand that the students by allowed to work undisturbed. But Gropius contends that we should not shut out life and reality, a danger (if it is a danger) implied by Itten's method; for instance, workshop students might come to find meditation and ritual more important than their work. Itten's ideal would be a craftsman who considers contemplation and thought about his work more important than the work itself, and who does not envy his neighbors and their fine workshops. Gropius wants a man firmly rooted in life and work, who matures through contact with reality and through practicing his craft. Itten likes talent which develops in solitude, Gropius likes character formed by the currents of life (and the necessary talent).

The first ideal results in little that is tangible (the saying goes that at the Bauhaus one sees nothing, and one is always asked to be patient), much talk about work and the necessary conditions. The other ideal results in superficiality, even officious bustle with as few tangible products as the quiet one offers.

Oskar Schlemmer as "The Dancer" in his *Triadic Ballet*, Stuttgart, 1922.
Courtesy of Tut Schlemmer.

Poster for *Triadic Ballet*, Donaueschingen, 1926; the figure in foreground represents "The Abstract," a role sometimes performed by Oskar Schlemmer. *Courtesy of Tut Schlemmer.*

These two alternatives strike me as typical of current trends in Germany. On the one hand, the influence of oriental culture, the cult of India, also a return to nature in the *Wandervogel* movement and others like it; also communes, vegetarianism, Tolstoyism, reaction against the war; and on the other hand, the American spirit, progress, the marvels of technology and invention, the urban environment. Gropius and Itten are almost typical, and I must admit that once more I am caught in the middle, half pleased, half displeased. I affirm both possibilities, or at least I would like to see cross–fertilization between the two. Or are progress (expansion) and self-fulfillment (introspection) mutually exclusive?

What position does the Masters' Council take? Klee remains the most passive; he says next to nothing. Feininger talks about general feelings. Muche acts as Itten's second and assistant, although remaining much more tolerant than Itten. Marcks, Gropius's intimate, seconds him. Schreyer, the theater reformer, wants to effect a reconcilation. And I—well, I would also like to, but I would further want to see the areas of activity clearly assigned according to talent and capability, and this would mean expressing truths which I do not feel equal to.

Diary

February 20, 1922

How can I possibly spend as much as an hour on anything but my ideal!

Wasting an opportunity to capture the One and Only, the Divine. Or does the daily confusion, the distraction from my true path and vision, actually help me perceive it all the more intensely, since I glimpse it so seldom?

If I were more sensitive, more fragile of nerve, I would perish of impatience before the very portals of the realm into which I must enter!

Diary

February 1922

The New Series! White plaster plates as a basis, these hollowed out, shaped in relief, pierced—and on them—in them, glass, glass pipes, mirror glass, colored glass. Painting behind and in front of glass, several pieces lined up in succession, to be placed against the light; wire made of nickel, brass, copper, steel filaments.

Polished, sculpted woods.

Not machine, not abstract—always man!

To Otto Meyer

Weimar
March 13, 1922

Now I am interested in having the ballet appear at last—it will reveal a different, unfamiliar side of me. I note with curiosity that those whose opinions I most prize keep telling me that I should be in theater. Of course, I myself helped create this opinion at the Bauhaus Carnival, a costume party for which I staged a performance by mechanical figures; to motivate the whole thing, I had to play a crazy professor, and since then my theatrical reputation has been growing. What should I do? Plunge right in or feel ashamed?

By the way, the theater is gradually being admitted to the Bauhaus. Schreyer was the opening wedge—he is both a poet and a painter, but in the realm of the "holy." That leaves me the dance and the comic element, which I gladly, i.e. unjealously, acknowledge to be my department.

The Mazdaznan business has long since subsided—or rather, it is at low ebb—and many new waves have since washed over the Bauhaus. Now building and the concept of the "Livingmachine" come uppermost. The Bauhaus wants to build houses on the "building site," or rather, "pour" them; standardized, yet preserving as much latitude as possible for individual wishes.

Diary

March 1922

A task for the Bauhaus: codifying all the valuable formal and qualitative insights of the past and the present. Headquarters for superior industrial design.

116

Subject: art and the crafts, past and present. I suggest the pyramid. Question: why? All men are equal before God. And one can establish standards of measurement only for things one can actually measure, for better or worse—not where measurement becomes impossible in the face of the infinite.

The do-nothing, the creator. The baker, the artist can both be complete, each in his own way. There are only good bakers and bad bakers, good bread and bad, good pictures and bad.

To Otto Meyer

Weimar

End of March 1922

What keeps me awake at night is the Bauhaus. Just picture it, almost without a fixed pole, assailed from all sides. In point of fact, and outsiders confirm this: the name "Bauhaus" arouses certain expectations, and justified ones. You might expect architecture and building to be the main thing, and instead you find a modern art school. With workshops, to be sure, in which students chip and whittle away, following their aesthetic stirrings, somewhat better than at an arts and crafts school. The instruction could provide a model for keeping the art academies alive. The construction and architecture class or workshop, which should be the core of the Bauhaus, does not exist officially, but only in Gropius's private office. His commissions for factories and houses, carried out with more or less finesse, thus provide the center around which everything else is supposed to revolve. It is an architectural bureau, its aims directly opposed to the schooling function of the workshops. The better products of the workshops are turned to a practical use, with varying success, by the architecture office. This defect in the Bauhaus causes me, and has always caused me, my greatest sorrow. If only the Bauhaus would admit to being a modern art school! As matters stand, there is nothing specifically wrong, just constant unrest, vulnerability to attack, and so on.

One of the most vocal opponents is van Doesburg, the Dutchman who advocates architecture so radically that for him painting does not exist, except insofar as it mirrors architecture. He defends his notions most eloquently, drawing the Bauhaus students under his spell—especially those interested chiefly in architecture, who deplore the Bauhaus's deficiency in this area. The Bauhaus lends itself readily to his rejection of it and its masters. So far I have been the one of whom he was most likely to approve, although I "still" use "soft" forms. He rejects craftsmanship (the focus of the Bauhaus) in favor of the most modern tool: the machine. Exclusive and consistent use of only the horizontal and the vertical in art and architecture will, he thinks, make it possible to create a style which eliminates the individual, in favor of collectivism.

It seems to me that the laws of architecture differ from those of painting. When painting serves a function within architecture, it must, of course, obey its laws. Kandinsky tried to make painting be music; now it is trying to emulate architecture or the machine. Painting should remain what it is, perfect itself within its own limits, just like music, architecture, the machine, technology, and science. I firmly believe that the laws of painting have not changed now and never will. It would be a laudable achievement to restore them to their former glory, thus counteracting the confusion of artistic standards for which one can blame much of what is going on today.

Contemporary art is developing in two directions. On the one hand we have the trend in which art transcends the individual, taking up the rhythm of technology and the machine, and in turn lending support to them; this implies a negation of painting in the old sense. On the other hand, painting is finding itself again; after overstepping its boundaries, it came to recognize them and is now beginning to *se humaniser*. I find it unnecessary to go so far back, and this is probably where the different races part ways. The Latins cannot help reverting to historicism once they have taken form as far as it will go. It is curious that the French (and Italians) can abstract themselves totally from the object—specifically from the still life—and yet never leave it behind, so that when the reversal comes, they go right back to their historical subjects again. The Germans seem to have reached a crossroads. Either they will cooperate and keep faith with the Latin—classical ideals of form and construction, or art will witness a development similar to the one which moved Hippolyte Taine to remark that certain painters were more suited to the study of divinity than to painting. Nowadays another kind of learning is supposed to be decisive, one in which the German "is ambitious and idealistic but spoils his own chances through form." Perhaps the Germans have learned enough to get over this "through form" business. Yet I think it more likely that the earlier parallel will be repeated. A fate . . . .

Should I say something about my beloved daughter? She inspires much admiration, is called "lovely young Greek" and "Mantegna child." I myself feel she has excellent proportions. She is very good when it comes to waking us up at night (she almost never does), and she will probably be self-reliant, for she can lie awake a long time and keep herself fully occupied. This might change, of course.

While writing this letter I was trying to catch a mouse in the studio. It kept rustling more and more inconsiderately in the wastepaper basket. So I placed a bucket of water next to the wastebasket, built a bridge out of cardboard and scattered sugar on the end that was suspended over the bucket. One strip of cardboard fell into the water, and the mouse leaped back into the basket. The next time the gimmick worked, that is, the mouse fell into the water and swam desperately about; I wanted to hasten its end by pushing it under. The pail, elevated on a little box, tipped over, the water spilled all over me, and the mouse escaped. All that remains is the stench, probably from the cold sweat—I trust the mouse won't catch cold!

The busybody editor of a German art journal has taken a survey on Neo-Naturalism, probably to orient himself so as to know where he should meddle. I skimmed the answers he received, found that the painters summed up the phenomenon more ineptly than all the others; but one thing a contemporary philosopher said has stuck in my mind: he felt the recent naturalistic phenomena might result from an attempt "to bind the metaphysical."

Diary

Beginning of May 1922

I cannot discuss my old pictures, for they lie behind me, their mission fulfilled. Others might want me to explain their genesis, to analyze. That would be tantamount to analyzing myself, which I must avoid in the interest of self-preservation. I cannot discuss my unborn pictures, for if I could, I would not need to paint them.

Diary

Beginning of May 1922

On impulse I tried to give the Bauhaus something halfway between instructive lecturing and pleasant entertainment, feeling that the divergent elements had to be drawn together somewhere and somehow. We need a synthesis to balance all the analysis. Such a synthesis naturally raises basic questions. I consider it valuable and absolutely necessary that we clarify our fundamental position. I do wonder, however, whether this can be achieved through debate and discussion. Isn't action much better? Let the deed speak for itself and show us the way.

I feel that our times need ethical commitment, not aesthetic commitment, and we at the Bauhaus should be especially aware of this.

Diary

May 1922

When modern mathematically minded artists examine the paintings of the Old Masters for classic proportions (the Golden Section, the Pythagorean formula) and find them present to a striking degree, this still does not prove that the Old Masters painted according to mathematical principles. There are many such startling examples of sure instinct, guided perhaps by the proportions of the human body, the hand, the characteristics of the joints.

The eternal values may be found in the human, the divine. And thus in their depiction. Progress possible only in this endeavor, but this is the key to everything.

120

Diary

Topic: the "Livingmachine." The misunderstanding that Philipp Otto Runge would have been against the Bauhaus. Kurt Schwerdtfeger wants a course in which a model of this house would be constructed. I say we cannot handle this sort of purely technical problem; that should be left to an engineer. Franz Singer claims that I use Runge as a Bible, but that the important factor is precisely that Runge is *not* a Bible. Nowadays, Singer claims, all sorts of things are called religion. But a true religious spirit is the fundamental prerequisite, and since the Bauhaus lacks this, nothing can be expected. Quarrel over this. Schwerdtfeger, after equating intensity of feeling and sensibility with religion, asserts that anything one does with intensity is good. Steal well, lie well, paint well, build well. I say: art and religion would be outlawed if the state had its way. What would matter would be the man who went right ahead, regardless. I mention Adolf Loos, who said: the best things have already been done, and one can spare oneself the work of doing them again. He stated he would take the best carpet he could find, likewise the best chair, table, and so on. Schwerdtfeger: "In short, an antique lover!" Dörte Helm: "What is the unifying factor?" I: "The idea of saving oneself work." Singer: that is all wrong; every child must learn everything from scratch, language and so on, and likewise no one can spare himself anything, and nothing is genuine unless it has been experienced and acquired through struggle. I draw the conclusions: if consistency demanded that everyone make and create the chair he sits on, then everyone should bake his own bread, weave his own shirt, make his own shoes—the ideal Bauhaus member!

Singer: this is a misunderstanding, like everything else people keep saying here. Someone else: "We should concentrate on concrete matters here." Suggestion: each should think about how he would build his own house.

Fräulein Grunow spoke of measurements. The basic sense of proportion which every sensitive artist carries inside him. Klee instinctively uses very specific, biologically accurate measurements, she saw. The sense of proportion a man bears within him necessarily permeates everything he creates.

Someone else: one should determine these measurements and set them up as principles for those who lack a natural sense of proportion.

Diary

May 1922

In art I am focussed on one point where everything comes together; this point determines all the relationships. If I lose it, reality gains the upper hand, and I am reduced to nothing. I become weak, fainthearted, despairing, almost intolerably restless, irritable—and if I rediscover that point, I feel comfortable, good ideas come to me unbidden, I am devout, in harmony, and all is well.

Diary

May 22, 1922
(Mother's birthday)

I am tired. I am *expected* to make art, whereas previously it was a matter of inner necessity. Maybe my pictures have achieved the utmost perfection of which I was capable; maybe art has already fulfilled its mission in me, a mission of purification and perfection?

I no longer need art, can live without it. All is well, and I understand everything. But when artistic form captures high points of feeling and insight, these can provide *points d'appui* in the confusion of everyday life. One needs tremendous energy to manage without them.

Diary

June 18, 1922

Waking dream ("Dionysian over-alertness").

I saw everything: a perfected glass culture, no longer industry, civilization—the glass pictures: chiselled, polished, colorful—anatomical—metaphysical man—it was glorious!

Feeling: what should I do? Do nothing? Begin to make it a reality?

I have seen the future.

122

I saw broad perspectives, looked into the future, the future of art and of evolution—it lames my hand for creation in the present. Doing this or that—what significance can it have in the face of eternity? Present fame, posthumous fame—how long, oh! They have lost their attraction for me.

To Otto Meyer

Weimar

June 1922

I wrote you about the duel between Itten and Gropius. For a while it looked as if it would have to be either one or the other. Then a peaceful settlement appeared to have been reached; Itten was forced to limit his sphere of influence, a step Gropius justified by pointing to the newly appointed masters and their fields of activity. Gropius expanded his influence all the more. Itten ostentatiously withdrew from teaching and the workshops in order to devote himself to his own work: he went back to painting from nature and doing his panel paintings. And of course, Mazdaznan. His hopes of spreading the doctrine met with especially strong resistance in Gropius, who feared sectarianism at the Bauhaus. And indeed this danger did exist. As Itten confided to me, he wants to become a lecturer at the University and the Kunstgewerbeschule in Zurich—and I am not the only one to suspect that he is putting out feelers in Switzerland with the idea of staying there and abandoning the Bauhaus. Perhaps he will issue an ultimatum; perhaps he will not even go that far. It would certainly mean a loss for the Bauhaus. Pedagogically he is more skilled than the rest, and he has a decided talent for leadership. I sense all too keenly the lack of those qualities in myself. Furthermore: when Gropius need no longer fear the strong opposition of Itten, he himself will constitute by far the greater threat. But Gropius already has a new man up his sleeve: Wassily Kandinsky!

I have too much to do and thus accomplish nothing. Can I want to build? Can I want to become a servant of architecture? I can't do anything—when I am told I have to!

I can only do what I want to do and what I have learned.

To Otto Meyer

Weimar

End of June 1922

Well, well: so Frau Tut wrote. I thought as much. She is absolutely determined to "pack me off somewhere." I would be glad to come—if I only knew when. Here is how things stand: I still have to go to Berlin and Hamburg, but to Dresden too. I had to agree to be in Stuttgart in August and September, because in October the ballet will be performed. The Bauhaus also has claims on me. Right now everything is impossibly hectic. In addition to your house, my wife has also written me off to Lake Starnberg (where Klee lives) and Saxonian Switzerland (as a substitute for the real one). I can only say maybe. But since I once again have things of the deepest consequence I want to discuss with you, I shall add a hope and a probably.

Diary

June 1922

Turning one's back on utopia.

We can and should concentrate only on what is most real, the realization of ideas. Instead of cathedrals, the "Living-machine." Repudiation of the Middle Ages and of the medieval concept of craftsmanship, and ultimately of craftsmanship itself, which merely provides schooling and the means for achieving the end of artistic creation. Ornamentation necessarily degenerates into unconcrete or aesthetic craftsmanship based on medieval principles; it will be replaced by concrete objects which serve specific purposes.

To Otto Meyer

Canstatt

August 22, 1922

So the beautiful days in Amden-Aranjuez* are past. The postcard must have informed you of my safe arrival in Stuttgart. In the meantime I have established myself here and feel very much at home.

---

*An echo of Schiller's *Don Carlos I, i.* — Translator

The Burgers had been back only three days, still heady with vacation ecstasy. He uttered a mighty thought with perfect calm:† "Well, it looks as though we have to finish up the costumes and the dances." By today we have reached the point of no longer just talking; we are doing it. There is a great, great deal of work involved, and I wonder if we will be done by the end of September. It would be a miracle.

The days are taken up with arranging and organizing, with duty visits to friends and relatives, and today I shall have my first swim in the Neckar. The air is soft and mild; this time it feels thoroughly southern to me, sensuous. There are even real hot days.

Stuttgart struck me as rather dilapidated, dusty, neglected. But the hills are as lovely as ever. A lot of building is going on, and it is good. I like it.

I was interrupted because I had to run out to fetch money and go shopping, the haste necessary because the mark is falling and falling. The people best off are those who "equipped themselves" for a lifetime before the war. Next best off are those who did it during the war, and in a relatively good position are those who are doing it now. Burger is the one pressuring me to lay in a good supply of the most essential items (clothing); he gives the ballet as an excuse, which as a passport to the outside world must step out in a good jacket, hat, and cane. He who says "B"(allet) must also say "A."

Otherwise, we are deep in rehearsals. I knew what was in store for me; what could be a pleasure has become a burden. By the way, we are doing a Handel dance, a *Passecaille* or *Passacaglia,* that means an old Spanish dance or turkey strut. I liked the name *Passecaille,* and I was pleasantly surprised to find out what it meant. The name of the ballet? my pseudonym?

To Otto Meyer

Stuttgart

September 23, 1922

Just this note—am too busy to write at length: the ballet will have its premiere on September 20, its name: "Triadic

---

†An echo of Goethe's *Iphigenie,* I, iii. — Translator

Ballet." One dancer is called: Walter Schoppe (need I say more?). I urge you most cordially and insistently to come. But: I shall be overwhelmed with work until the very last minute; you would only be able to stand by and observe—I can neither look nor hear to left or right. And then I must rush off to Weimar the very next day. But it would be nice if you came along. Even so: there will be a big crowd; half the Bauhaus plans to come to the performance—friends, relatives, acquaintances!

Diary
September 1922

Ballet! Of the basic forms of the dance, cultic soul dance and aesthetic mummery, ballet is the latter. The former characterized by nakedness, the latter by costume, shrouding. (And in between one finds the skimpiness and flutteriness of today's ballerinas, whose halfway position makes them shun nakedness as much as costume) .... A temple to nakedness, a temple which we do not, however, have and which calls for bodies of a beauty as rare as the mind which shapes them;* but costumes fit the theater, which, although alienated from its true calling, still provides a place where an event is more or less consciously "made" or "played." The theater, the world of appearances, is digging its own grave when it tries for verisimilitude; the same applies to the mime, who forgets that his chief characteristic is his artificiality. The medium of every art is artificial, and every art gains from recognition and acceptance of its medium. Heinrich Kleist's essay *Uber das Marionettentheater* ["On the Marionette"] offers a convincing reminder of this artificiality, as do E.T.A. Hoffmann's *Phantasiestücke* ["Fantasy Pieces"] (the perfect machinist, the automata). Chaplin performs wonders when he equates complete inhumanity with artistic perfection.

Life has become so mechanized, thanks to machines and a technology which our senses cannot possibly ignore, that we are intensely aware of man as a machine and the body as a mechanism. In art, especially in painting, we are witnessing a search for the roots and sources of all creativity; this grows out of the

---

*An echo of Schiller's *Es ist der Geist, der sich den Körper baut."* — Translator

126

bankruptcy brought on by excessive refinement. Modern artists long to recover the original, primordial impulses; on the one hand they woke up to the unconscious, unanalyzable elements in the art forms of non-intellectuals: the Africans, peasants, children, and madmen; on the other hand, they have discovered the opposite extreme in the new mathematics of relativity. Both these modes of consciousness—the sense of man as a machine, and insight into the deepest wells of creativity—are symptoms of one and the same yearning. A yearning for synthesis dominates today's art and calls upon architecture to unite the disparate fields of endeavor. This yearning also reaches out for the theater, because the theater offers the promise of total art. Yes, today we have good prospects of achieving this goal, albeit with surrogate materials: we shall build with canvas and cardboard if stone and steel become utopian dreams.

Theatrical dance, the original form from which opera and drama developed, is languishing these days in the shape of ballet. Once upon a time the situation was different: world history manifested itself in the dance of that noncommittal Muse who says nothing yet signifies everything. In 1699 Louis XIV made his last appearance as a dancer, in the ballet "Flora." Dates which historians consider the milestones of an ascent actually mark the stages of decline: in 1681 female dancers performed for the first time—previously female roles had been danced by men. In 1772 face masks were abolished: the handsome Gardel appears adorned only with his own blond hair and vanquishes Vestris, who always danced in an immense black wig, with a face mask and a large gilt sun made of copper on his breast . . . .

Now theatrical dance can provide the starting point for the renewal. Not burdened with tradition like the opera and the drama, not committed to word, tone, and gesture, it is a free form, destined to impress innovation gently upon our senses: masked, and—especially important—silent.

The "Triadic Ballet": dance of the trinity, changing faces of the One, Two, and Three, in form, color, and movement; it should also follow the plane geometry of the dance surface and the solid geometry of the moving bodies, producing that sense of spatial dimension which necessarily results from tracing such basic forms as the straight line, the diagonal, the circle, the ellipse, and their combinations. Thus the dance, which is Dionysian and wholly emotional in origin, becomes strict and Apollonian in its final form, a symbol of the balancing of opposites.

The "Triadic Ballet" flirts coquettishly with the humorous, without falling into grotesquerie; it brushes the conventional without sinking to its dismal depths. Finally, it strives for dematerialization, yet without seeking salvation in the occult. This ballet should demonstrate the elements which might form the basis of a German ballet, a ballet so secure in its own style and worth that it could hold its own against analogous developments in the dance that for all their admirable qualities remain foreign to us (Russian, Swedish ballet).

To Hans Hildebrandt

Weimar

October 4, 1922

In general and in particular: I consider the symphonic character of the ballet so central that the individual dances could easily be given musical or symphonic designations; for example, the *Eroica* character of the third part; the scherzo character of the first. The second is hard to pin down. At any rate: first a burlesque, picturesque mood; not an earnest, festive one; and finally heroic monumentality. Another thing I would stress is the "floor geometry," the configurations which determine the paths of the dancers; they are identical with the forms of the figurines. Both are elemental, primal. I should like to do more with the choreography; I mean the graphic representation of the dancers' paths, a problem which has not yet been satisfactorily solved because too much would have to be portrayed within too small a space, resulting in either confusion or lack of completeness. For instance, one dancer might move only from back to front, following a straight line. Then come the diagonal, the circle, the ellipse, and so on. This idea was not based on any particular "intellectual" considerations. It grew rather out of inventive, aesthetic pleasure in mixing opposites of form, color, and movement and shaping the whole into something which conveyed significance and an underlying concept.

Anyway, dance is not intellectual but Dionysian in origin. This unconscious activity must be precise if it is to achieve definitive shape, form, and proportion. Thus one always discovers remarkable correspondences to music which one could never have reasoned out. First came the costume, the figurine. Then came the search for the music which would best suit them. Music and the figurine together led to the dance. This was the process.

I have nothing more to say for now, except that in its present form the "Triadic Ballet" represents a beginning for me, a stage; I have on tap ideas for a purely comic ballet, as well as for a transcendental one. More and better dancers; the technical resources for producing the figurines, more appropriate music: those are the things I hope for.

To Otto Meyer

Weimar
October 25, 1922

Well, one can say it was a success. At least in Stuttgart—the audience was certainly very considerate, putting up with long intermissions and parts of costumes getting lost right on the stage. Curiously enough, not one of the reviews, even the most hostile, mentioned or exploited these mishaps. At the performance some of the costumes were onstage for the first time; to this day I have not seen them, so busy have I been with directing and acting my own part. People told me they found this detail or that beautiful; all I can say is: maybe— unfortunately, I did not see it myself. For instance, the performance was the first chance I had to try out some costumes which so interfered with movement that they had to be completely revised. Who was my supervisor and helper? My imagination or the mirror. Add to that stage fright, worries about the whole performance, everything unrehearsed—the theater had allowed only a very brief rehearsal, at which we had to attend to all sorts of things and never got to rehearsing.

So in spite of it all. I realized that I should direct dances but not be a dancer myself. I can say what has to be said and keep an eye on everything if I am not participating; I can control the smallest detail. I realized that the Burgers do have a perfect grasp of theatrical technique; they are simply accustomed to moving on these boards and under these lights. She mustered all her forces and was apparently very good. He was relatively good, too. Some of these opinions I collected from the Bauhaus people, of whom more than twenty came, Gropius included; they felt the whole thing was a victory for them, they said. The enthusiasm still lingers on.

Schoppe, by the way, is taken from Jean Paul, from *Titan* and *Siebenkäs*. He also appears under the names of Leibgeber and Löwenskiold. He takes off after his alter ego, which becomes confused and no longer knows which one he really is. So that is the explanation; I also wanted to help those in the know to recognize Schoppe as the *Leib-geber* [body-giver], whom I imagined myself to be. Baumeister tossed me a wreath, the ribbon of which read "To Schoppe from Leibgeber."

Diary

October 25, 1922

Expressionism revived form, which had died. Free and unfettered in non-objective painting. Russia—Kandinsky. In the more form-conscious countries it introduced the elemental, lapidary forms. But it had been robbed of its foundation, reality, and needed a new one. This it sought in architecture and in functional objects. Picasso translated into furniture. Artistic craftsmanship, for simple craftsmanship also fills the simple needs. This is the mission of Expressionism, if it is indeed a mission. Should this be rejected, the old style of painting will return—classicism, romanticism.

Marcel Breuer (voluntarily and certainly at a cost) abjures painting, at which he would be talented, and does cabinet-making instead.

I am "full of inner images." Is that no longer right, no longer permissible? Or should the inner "images" be made realities? Renounce being all "image" (yes, image), and make tables, chests, pitchers—for the sake of a principle, a demand, existential necessity? Existential necessity in the sense that I would sacrifice a favorite piece of glass if it could be used to repair a window through which a cold wind is blowing into the room. Sacrifice a piece of metal for the kitchen, a piece of wooden sculpture because I have no firewood?

Unpretentious, free art which captures its world with paper and pencil, a world which can turn the familiar world topsy-turvy! How can one hesitate when there is only one thing that matters!

What can the theater offer by comparison? What can architecture offer by comparison? Building requires subordinating oneself to a practical purpose; fulfillment is possible there, too, but directed toward life.

Was art ever as much free play as today? As devoid of purpose? In the past it was always at the service of an idea, and everything was merely a vehicle for the idea.

To Otto Meyer

Weimar

November 11, 1922

As regards future work on the ballet, the situation is as follows: in early December one of the best small theaters in Berlin (the Kammerspiele [Chamber Theater]) will present a matinee of the best dances in the program, with the press and a carefully chosen audience invited. I must bear the expense, for that is the only way one can break in these days in Berlin. Everything will depend on the outcome of this venture. An agreement on performances in Berlin and in the rest of Germany, and especially in other countries.

This summer will bring the first Bauhaus Exhibition. I shall be deeply involved; I suggested that we do paintings and reliefs for the entrance hall of the Bauhaus, which still has plain white walls and ceilings. One possibility would be to have the students do sketches; I would choose the best designs and help by giving advice and directing their execution. This would be in the spirit of the Bauhaus. Or else I could be my own supervisor, with the students following instructions in the customary fashion. I would prefer the latter course, and as the initiator of the idea I have a bit more say. The project is challenging and might turn out very well. I am much preoccupied with it; at the moment I keep vacillating between abstraction = shorthand and universal intelligibility = beautiful painting. I wonder: what do people expect? Can we take the liberty of painting mysterious puzzles on the walls of an area also used by the old Academy, with which we share the building?

A special exhibition hall is planned, and opinions on it still vary greatly. You can see that I have already moved on to something entirely different from dance and the theater. I am afraid of having too many strings to my bow, i.e. dissipating my energies. I still do not know where my true calling lies.

Diary

November 1922

The decoration of the Bauhaus vestibule for the planned exhibition will provide an excellent example of the Bauhaus theory of architecture. The new structure will have to be simple, allowing little latitude for the painter as a muralist and even less for the sculptor. And that also explains why the wall painting and sculpture workshops at the Bauhaus are problematical; their scope remains limited, for the Temple of the Future, the Cathedral of Democracy, the Edifice of Socialism will be some time in coming. For the present we have our simple building and must take the representative where we find it. The vestibule cries out for creative shaping. It could become the trademark of the Bauhaus; within the space created by van de Velde we shall combine wall painting with sculpture, displaying them in a context which normally seldom presents itself. But we must show them in this context if we ever hope to receive jobs of this sort, and even better ones.

The mural has always been prized as the form of painting which, unlike the self-sufficient easel picture, with its risk of becoming *l'art pour l'art,* exists in a close relationship to space and architecture; the Bauhaus must provide a refuge and a good solution for this form. The mural must be given ethical underpinnings; the idea it depicts must be one of universal validity or should at least contain the values necessary for acquiring such validity. It falls to the mural to express the great themes. This function still remains—in fact, today more than ever. The will to fulfill this function is present today, specifically in German painting.

Disturbed by developments in the Latin countries, which are either nurturing a new naturalism or else negating art altogether, we in Germany hold the fate of art in our hands, so to speak, for we must protect it against both conservatism and anarchy. That is how I interpret Kandinsky's meaningful statement that our exhibion is a "world event." At stake here is finding a middle way, usually so despised, for it alone promises the ardently desired synthesis between architecture, painting, and sculpture.

Diary
Beginning of November 1922
In connection with the current general debate, I must present to the Masters' Council my views on the teaching of form, something I have been asked to do before.

The workshops have been assigned, each naturally having its own sphere of endeavor, and now we should introduce a similar fair distribution of responsibility for instruction in form. Each of the masters would have to give an approximate description of the areas he intended to cover, so that all the gaps could be filled and coordination achieved.

I shall jot down here the subjects which previous experience and insight suggest I would most enjoy teaching, and in which I feel I have something to offer.

I would place the human figure at the center of my investigations. "Man, the measure of all things" provides so many possibilities for variation and for relationships to architecture and craftsmanship that one would merely have to extract the essentials. Therefore: measurement, proportions, and anatomy; typicality and special features. The various guiding ideals of the different artistic styles. The dynamics of the body. Movement. Dance. Kinesthetic sense. Man in his relationship to the world about him.

Diary

Mid-November 1922

Rededication to art, to what is unique with me, the things I have always strived for and been most preoccupied with, which for that very reason are all my own.

I must not waste time on commercial art or the crafts, for that would mean a dilution of the highly concentrated content one finds in true art.

I must not devote myself to doing murals in or on houses.

I should not direct myself toward building houses, except the ideal house which my paintings imply and anticipate.

I should not try for something which industry can do better, or which engineers can handle more expertly.

What remains is the metaphysical: art.

Diary

November 1922

At seventeen Arthur Rimbaud was finished as an artist. He created utterly unique masterpieces—then dropped everything and set out to travel: he set out into life.

Does this symbolize the fulfillment of art, that it made him ready for life, that more difficult art?

That shows admirable courage and freedom: to be able to burn one's bridges, once a type of perfection is achieved which could gain further scope only in a completely different arena (life).

So do without sentimentality what the inner voice demands. Who sets us tasks in art? Who stipulates, or could presume to stipulate, an artist's course of development? Anyone who tries this has not grasped the meaning of art.

I am aware of the danger that lurks in the merely decorative, the degradation of high art to commercial art.

Diary

November 1922

The Bauhaus and me:

What do I want? To create a style in painting which springs

from a necessity beyond fad and aesthetic form, which can hold its own against the perfect utility of functional objects and machines.

This style must thus necessarily be ethical in nature. Depicting life in order to "raise the level of self-awareness."

I want to accomplish this through self-sufficient works of art, which, however, naturally require and shape their own fitting surroundings—primarily architecture.

I do not believe in craftsmanship. We cannot restore the crafts of the Middle Ages, any more than we can restore the art of the Middle Ages, not even in an approximate modern equivalent. It has been made obsolete by modern developments. Handmade *objets d'art* in the age of the machine and technology would be a luxury for the rich, lacking a broad popular basis and roots in the people. Industry now provides what the crafts once provided, or it will when fully developed: standardized, solid functional objects made of genuine materials.

The same applies to architecture. Technological progress has resulted in bold innovations. Magnificent example: Frank Lloyd Wright's country house. These developments flow naturally out of a spirit of objectivity which rejects grandiose artistic ambitions.

I do not believe that craftsmanship as practiced at the Bauhaus can transcend the aesthetic and fulfill more serious social functions. "Getting in touch with industry" will not do the trick; we would have to commit ourselves and merge completely with industry. But we cannot make that our goal; it would mean turning our backs on the Bauhaus.

To Otto Meyer

Weimar
December 19, 1922

On December 2 at 9 A.M. a girl, Ute Jaina, was born.

We tell ourselves that Providence must have its reasons for giving us nothing but girls, and Providence alone has a right to decide these matters. My wife needs little helpers around the house, to make things a bit easier for her and more comfortable for me—who needs soldiers? So far the "new one" takes after the Tutein side, while Karin is a Schlemmer. She is blond, light-eyed, and sunny; the new one is dark and serious, apparently. Frau Tut also accepts this ruling of fate; the thought of a goatee rapidly dispelled any interest in having a boy.

The reason I did not get to write sooner: urgent business of a literary and organizational nature, in preparation for the Bauhaus Exhibition. The students elected the exhibition committee, consisting of Muche, me, a crafts master, a journeyman, and an apprentice: a sort of action committee with almost dictatorial privileges and obligations. This exhibition, which will decide the fate of the Bauhaus, is so much at the mercy of attacks from right and left, shortage of money, and the spirit of the times, that it becomes a question of survival, of victory or total destruction.

No further progress with the walls—or on them. I plan to spend the vacation on the preliminary sketches. The students will do likewise. A figured (romantic) treatment contrasted with a purely linear, constructive one, which has caught on like wildfire among the students. The latter somewhat derivative of van Doesburg, a trend which, by the way, also seems to have many adherents among the Russians.

Yesterday the Bauhaus Christmas celebration. In each of the joke packages (from the girls of the weaving workshop) I received a child, nothing but girls: Parsley, born 1924; Constructiva, 1925; Abstracta, 1926; Pabulum, 1927; Little Mary, 1928; America, 1929; Rosina Sultanina, 1930 (in the form of baked goods) and so on. I realized how much they like me; at one point I was tossed up in the air to the accompaniment of wishes for long life and happiness. And indeed, I have a very positive attitude toward the Bauhaus, and this, it seems to me, makes itself felt.

To Otto Meyer

Weimar

February 12, 1923

The Bauhaus with all its "affairs" is a complicated and distressing thing. I would rather not talk about it. The year 1923 is supposed to bring bad luck—Saturn complications. That I can well believe.

This week I am supposed to speak at Griesebach's in Jena, on new art, before an audience of about twenty-five students. He says he senses "the pedagogue in me," and is sure it will be a success.

Zurich will be getting its first look at a piece of Bauhaus, in the form of Itten. I imagine the "reaction" will be precisely that.

Our neighbor, the Academy, refused us permission to paint the vestibule of the main building, although we had made the conciliatory decision to depict the basic forms and colors and the fundamental principles which both schools share. We shall have to apply to the government for a ruling.

All these goings-on and battles have made me more anxious than ever to return to my own work; many things have built up and are begging to be expressed.

Freedom exists only in the realm of dreams.

To Otto Meyer

March 20, 1923

I am doing lithographs, also modelling in the sculpture workshop and preparing surfaces for painting. Yet I also want to do work for the Bauhaus. The result: either nothing gets done—or I am most useful, even to the Bauhaus, when I think of my own needs. Man does indeed grow by setting himself high goals, but "what he gains in breadth of vision he loses in insight." It is a painfully protracted process or something endless—and when Picasso says, *"je ne connais pas nègre,"* I might say, *"je ne connais pas Bauhaus!"*

The Russian Kandinsky will probably, or certainly, be followed by the Hungarian Moholy-Nagy (Itten's successor). Now I understand why Klee corrected a phrase of mine in a Bauhaus essay to read "art in Germany," instead of "German art."

To Otto Meyer

Weimar

March 30, 1923

The Bauhaus Theater, hitherto directed by Lothar Schreyer, gave a trial performance which failed miserably, condemned by masters and students alike. Schreyer will thus leave the Bauhaus. As a result they now come to me, as the next in line, and someone whom they feel has proved himself more than once: I am supposed to do various theatrical things for the exhibition this summer.

The evening in Jena went well. The whole business ended theatrically. I said I had a mental image of two larger-than-life heroic figurines, masks, personifying such abstracts as Energy and Strength, or Pride and Courage. I said I pictured their gestures and had a vague sense of their words, but that the poet who would write the poem of our times had not yet been found. That aroused great interest, and it seemed as if the result of the evening might be that one would come forward. The students were fascinated to see that an optical conception can develop out of a dramatic one. Here, too, I have searched for a poet and found none. That is how I would imagine a Bauhaus play.

Diary

End of March 1923

At the Bauhaus anything is still possible. A dictatorial director might perhaps have achieved an outer semblance of unity, dressed the different personalities alike and lined them up for review. The Bauhaus resembles a canvas blocked out by Poussin, whose motto was, *"Je ne veux rien négliger."* Supporting structures, false tones rectified only in the final version: these fail to convey the picture's unity to an outside observer.

The Bauhaus acts as a seismograph for international developments in art; it remains to be seen whether it gets dragged into the undertow of fashion or achieves a style of its own. This style will have to be national and different, in spite of internationalism, developed according to the unique laws of a specific landscape, people, idea.

Diary

June 1923

The Bauhaus represented the first serious attempt at merging craftsmanship and academic work, and it did pioneering work in that area; so, too, the Bauhaus was intended to be shaped not by a dictatorial administrative system with insignificant "subdivisions," but rather by a multiplicity of minds and interests. Four years of Bauhaus constitute a chapter in art history. But also in the history of the times, for the Bauhaus mirrors the fragmentation of the German people and of the period. Pioneering work, then, in all different fields, under the most difficult of circumstances, and yet with results—these facts should dispel all doubts as to the value of the undertaking.

This is the time for quiet, preparatory work. In the practical realm, so that we will be ready when the order of the day comes through; and in the artistic realm, where we want to provide for a mighty, spiritual idea that is on its way.

The unique structure of the Bauhaus can be perceived in the person of its director; it is characterized by flexibility, adherence to no dogma, receptivity to anything new, with every intention of assimilating it. Also the intention of stabilizing this whole complex, of finding a common denominator, a set of standards. The result: an unprecedented battle of the minds, whether declared or veiled, a constant unrest which almost daily forces the individual to take a position on very profound and basic issues. Depending on the temperament of the individual, he either suffers from this multiplicity or finds himself confirmed in his opinions by it. (From the rough draft of a declaration).

To Otto Meyer

Weimar

Beginning of June 1923

In strict confidence: the students (the familiar battle array) are "only" waiting for the exhibition before they go to Gropius. They want to get rid of the "decorative" masters, the billboards, the publicity names, sometimes called the "corridor masters" because at most one meets them in the Bauhaus corridors, never in the workshops; they want the money thus freed to be used to improve their own lot (which is certainly often very bad). More on this if and when it comes to a head. As to me: I am not on their list, in fact anything but. And yet I was thinking of voluntarily getting out if the occasion presented itself, since the new line does not appeal to me. Kandinsky has become Gropius' chancellor.

Stage Director at the Bauhaus? Not really. First, Schreyer will still be here until October, although he will do no further productions. My only duty is to supervise the students' theatrical experiments. These center almost exclusively around the mechanical, the grotesque, and the formalistic.

The future development of the Bauhaus stage lies in darkness. The Bauhaus lacks the first prerequisite, a stage, and Gropius ignores all suggestions to this effect. Literary theater is avoided almost on principle; therefore, formal matters. Mobility, portable backdrops. Mechanical effects, lighting. At the very most dance, which naturally suits the craftsmanship-oriented Bauhaus students better than acting. I regret that somewhat. The poem of the times still slumbers. The poets have failed us.

To Otto Meyer

Weimar

June 23, 1923

Unfortunately I can think of nothing but the Exhibition. In a moment of enthusiasm I offered to paint the rooms in the workshop building and to do reliefs for them, and now I am realizing how much I have taken on. But I am enjoying it and must try to stay in this frame of mind.

Diary

June 25, 1923

The alternation between abstract and non-abstract techniques has almost become a sign of the times, here at the Bauhaus as well. I myself have succumbed to it and am trying to establish some principles, so that the two modes can coexist side by side when that seems meaningful and so that one can understand why one mode or the other was chosen for a given project.

The new technical discoveries as new media for artistic expression. Just now these possibilities fascinate me. Is oil color the one and only medium for the painter, marble for the sculptor? Ignoring "modern technological developments"! Don't film, airplanes, electricity make those media a little less absolute? Would a van Eyck of today discover oil color all over again? Would Phidias again choose marble? I recollect something Keyserling says: perfection can be conceived only within a familiar framework (he is thinking of religion). Might this be the key: a Catholic can still be saved, despite Enlightenment and Steiner. An oil painter can still be an artist, in spite of film and phosphorescent paint. But today's artists do seem to have reached a crossroads, similar to that "abstract or non-abstract" controversy. Some seek out new possibilities for the sake of their novelty, as a supposed source of new ideas; others seek to fulfill the familiar possibilities.

I think I can ascribe a good portion of my inner turmoil to the fact that I too readily allow myself to be fascinated by those fascinating new possibilities; that I imagine I can attain the whole, or *a* whole by doing a huge variety of things, all at the same time. With the intention of establishing order, of course, but it is too much for a little chap of my constitution. How can I curb myself? I think it will come about of itself, I tell myself that the Bauhaus Exhibition will help clarify matters. I shall find out what direction to follow. In the art line I am displaying "free" art, in the workshop building "applied" sculpture and painting (development of the walls and the architectural space). There will be the ballet, and the "Figural Cabinet" will take care of the humorous angle. I shall certainly not rely on the opinion of others, but I shall listen to it and add my own.

Diary

July/August 1923
Principles for the painting and sculptural adornment of the workshop building of the State Bauhaus in Weimar: what we

have to work with—van de Velde's treatment of the space, the sober, whitewashed walls, for which one generation of young painters pleaded passionately, hoping that such walls would deliver them from sterile picture painting.

It should be mentioned that in the secular modern world any art based on the great themes occupies a peculiarly solitary position. All the foundations which once supported it have tottered or vanished: the collective unconscious, ethics, religion. The new is still in its birth pangs—disputed—unacknowledged. And yet one great theme remains, ancient, eternally fresh, the subject and form-giver of all times: man, the human figure. It has been said that he is the measure of all things. So be it: architecture is the noblest form of measurement, so unite!

It should be mentioned that man's innate sense of proportion can, when used creatively, constantly express itself in new ways and produce new phenomena. Granted: geometry, the Golden Section, the laws of proportion. They are lifeless and unproductive unless they are experienced, touched, and felt. We must surrender ourselves to the miracle of the proportions, the magnificence of the mathematical relationships and correspondences, and derive our laws from the results. Counterpoint will never be achieved in art, or if it is, it will, in contrast to music, provide only a meager skeleton. The reason is that the creative processes in the two arts are entirely different. Quite by accident the numbers 3, 5, and 7 cropped up in a great variety of forms and combinations in the painting of the workshop building. Instinct decided and reason confirmed it ex post facto. The same applies to the forms and the colors. The trinity of primary colors, red—blue—yellow, increased to five by the addition of the non-colors white and black, and the resulting numerical series of combinations have their counterpart in the basic forms of the surface and the reliefs, but they suggest only the rough dimensions of the incalculable dynamics of the whole.

The fundamental element in figural painting is the type. Distillation of the type represents the final and ultimate task, and it may be impertinent to attempt it if the prerequisites for success rest in the hands of Providence. Variations on the figural theme are executed plastically (in relief), in color and in line. As

abstractions, the figures' proportions are exaggerated accordingly, to be either much larger or much smaller than the living
human being; man should furnish a measuring stick and a focal
point.

The technically necessary use of earth tones that can take a
varnish (non-chemical colors) creates a naturally harmonious
range consisting of the primary colors of English red—
ultramarine—ocher (white as a basis and black) and the secondary colors of *caput mortuum,* called burnt umber, and indigo.
In addition the metallic tones: gold, silver, copper—blue silver,
violet silver.

To Tut

Berlin

September 4, 1923

This morning on my breakfast table your letter for my
birthday. Liked your little painting very much.

Advance of fifty million. Wanted to buy myself a white
shirt, but now it costs twenty-four million!! No, better to
accept the odium of being considered an uncultured fellow.
That dog of a cashier gives me two and a half million in
five-thousand-mark notes; that makes five packets as thick as
two fists. I protested—to no avail. Stuffed it into my pockets.
How to get rid of it? The post office won't accept it, the banks
are closed. The shirt too expensive—a nice little tie? Brood a
while, decide against it. A book? Check with the bookstore, six
to eight million for one book. Decide against it and go—it is
four o'clock by now—to a restaurant. Can hardly sit down for
the bundles in my pocket. Thank God the waiter accepts it.
Then, after leg of mutton and macaroni, go to the Café Bauer,
light as a bird—this evening Kleist's *Käthchen von Heilbronn* at
the Staatsschauspielhaus [State Theater]. Tomorrow evening *As
You Like It* at the Lessing Theater. Thursday the *Merry Wives.*
Saturday Handel's *Julius Caesar.*

After the café I shall buy myself the indispensable grapes,
what I always have for my birthday.

So I am reborn, far from home and the hearts of my loved
ones.

Weimar

September 29, 1923

Tomorrow marks the end of the Bauhaus Exhibition. A great, great deal might be said about it—where should I begin?

With the things on exhibit? With the exhibitors? With the objections one could make—no, I don't know where to begin.

Imagine—Kirchner has invited me to visit him in Davos and stay at his cottage, should I get to Switzerland this year.

Well, the ballet was performed in Weimar. And it was a big success—the next day there were many cheerful faces in town. The performance was better than in Stuttgart. We were urged to tour other cities.

To Otto Meyer

Weimar

Beginning of October 1923

I cannot tell you much about Grosz and Dix—I have seen little of their work, and nothing for ages. Grosz sticks primarily to political themes, which he handles very well. He would be the right man for *Simplicissimus,* if *Simplicissimus* were still revolutionary. His painting did not particularly impress me. Dix has become a great man. I saw pictures in many different styles by him, but no new ones. I have the impression that the revival of Naturalism will be accompanied by a return of parallels with the past: take your choice! The treasures of the past lie spread out before us. Every year new parallels to new old styles—that promises material for an entire generation.

Things are in such a mess at the Bauhaus. These days Gropius is wishing his painters would just go to the devil. Van Doesburg has almost certainly received secret assurances that he is in line for a mastership. Right now the gentleman is here, back from Paris, having given up trying to impress the French with his ideas; he still finds the Bauhaus the most fertile ground. Will you believe me when I say that I am completely isolated here, especially now? No links with either the masters or the opposition, the constructivists' guild. But constantly under fire from both sides. And greatly weakened ties with the students.

At one time I would have welcomed such a position; it is the position Feininger has occupied for years. Now I should be able to work in peace, without being bothered. But that requires strong nerves, which are not so easy to come by here.

Theater. I originated the idea of finally starting a puppet theater. That is being done now, using a tale from the *Thousand and One Nights.* Freely adapted. I wanted to do a Thuringian folktale, the "Smith of Apolda." It could have been performed for the farmers in exchange for farm products. The students opposed it as too boring and moralistic, but primarily because the suggestion came from a master. They want to run things themselves. That way their hearts are in it and any project will succeed. Cardinal principle: the students must think the idea originated with them.

To Otto Meyer

Weimar

October 21, 1923

This letter should have been written yesterday, to be mailed before the latest insane rise in postal rates. But we are rushing so fast toward the billions that a few millions seem a mere trifle.

I got back from Berlin a few days ago; it was a success. The production was a real production, which rather amazed me, for I had considered it somewhat insignificant and was already afraid I was introducing myself to Berlin inauspiciously. The circumstances proved favorable. It was the debut of the new director of the Volksbühne, who had been brought to Berlin from Stuttgart; it was therefore an important evening to all of Berlin's theater critics, who had come to look the new man over, and got me into the bargain. Berlin's critics are very exacting, and they rarely give special mention to the stage designer—this time they did so almost to a man, and some of them even praised the sets to the point that the play, the actors, and the director came away second best.

I must say, the job was both annoying and rewarding. The daily struggle with the assistants: first resistance, then gradual acceptance, finally enjoyment. Rehearsing the props, the lighting, the actors; the dress rehearsal; the evening itself. Calls for the lead actor, the director—and suddenly for me, too, and what an uproar! A theater that holds two thousand. Several friends also praised the way I had conjured something out of nothing— the French "atmosphere" of the production, the German quality despite the Russian play (all things Russian are the rage in Berlin just now)—the alfresco quality of the stage set.

People were saying the evening belonged to the painter.

All this does nothing to mellow my dissatisfaction—my longing for something better. Still, getting involved in a thing does increase one's appetite for it. I am really determined to try this métier. It also seems as if all the threads were coming together now: the triumphant success of the ballet in Weimar, commissions for various productions, pictures based on theatrical undertakings, my taking over Schreyer's position as director of the Bauhaus theater workshop—and in addition: my relative failure in monumental murals and reliefs, and not one single picture sold at the Bauhaus Exhibition. Well then, should success alone determine the decision? Purely external matters? How about the future? That's what I keep wondering.

Muche: when I came to Weimar, Muche was Itten's assistant, and during the feud with Gropius he defended Itten. Itten leaves, and Muche becomes Gropius' most faithful adherent. Speaks out against Itten's major accomplishment: the preparatory course which Muche, as Itten's assistant, had recently directed according to Itten's specifications. I urged that we at the Bauhaus should no longer ignore the machine, technology, and engineering as scornfully and carelessly as we have done. I cited van de Velde (Gropius' predecessor), who perceived their new beauty and sang their praises. At the time Muche replied testily that this new beauty was highly suspect; but whom do you find today the greatest proponent and advocate of this American form of beauty—Muche. So much so that I found myself in the curious position of leaning over backwards to restore equilibrium. I do like Muche, though.

The history of the Bauhaus is a long story, an endless one. I could never reach the end; I have merely traced one strand—let's drop the subject.

Kandinsky's classes: scientifically strict study of color and

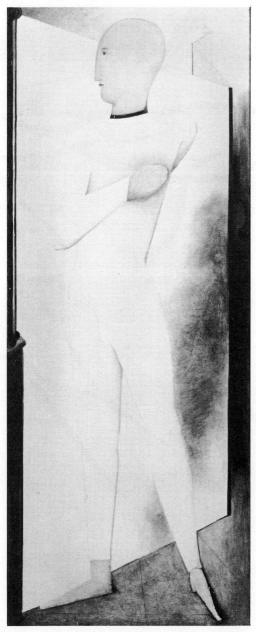

The Dances, by Oskar Schlemmer; oil on canvas, 69″ x 27¾″, 1923.
Courtesy of Oskar Schlemmer Archiv, Staatsgalerie Stuttgart.

Kneeling Figure, by Oskar Schlemmer; pen-and-ink drawing, 1928. *Courtesy of Tut Schlemmer.*

form. For example: the search for the three elementary colors that correspond to the three basic forms (triangle, square, circle). The decision was reached that yellow went with the triangle, blue with the circle, and red with the square—once and for all, so to speak.

Diary

October 1923

Statements by famous contemporaries:
p o e l z i g: "the people needs bread and movies."
g r o p i u s: "we have to clean up around here."
k a n d i n s k y: "the circle is blue."
s c h l e m m e r: "the circle is red."
g r o p i u s: "art and technology—a new duality."
b r e u e r: "the chair gets sat on until it breaks."
m o h o l y: "v–o–n–d–e–r–f–u–l."

Diary

December 29, 1923

Acceptance of the present as far as art is concerned? Architecture accepts the present in that it utilizes the latest technological advances and thereby produces daring new forms. Thus something external, or the addition of something external, can give the impetus for innovation; this includes new materials, new discoveries in statics.

What would be the equivalent in painting and sculpture, which have not yet moved beyond the old media: canvas, oils, stone, marble, metal?

One thing is certain, and that is that the application of scientific principles to art is now widespread. Basic forms, laws, numerical configurations. Anything connected with the psyche has become suspect. When applied to the human figure, this scientific approach would yield what one might expect to see at a hygiene exhibit: a portrayal of the blood circulation in action, the movements of the soul portrayed in such a way as to "raise the level of self-awareness." One can see the contrast to Greek statuary, also a version of perfection.

Such an approach, if it were "strictly scientific," would remain in the realm of science. The question is: would the inclusion of art have an intensifying effect, would it add a monumental, ethical dimension, or would its effect be disruptive, beclouding the purity?

Times like these, times of collapse and of renewal, raise the ultimate questions as well as the basic ones; they lay bare the roots of all being and becoming, as part of the attempt to rediscover meaning.

Human beings and life styles are destroyed and new ones come in their place. Miracles occur, signs appear in the most sensitive reflector of the human spirit, art; art anticipates events in the exterior world, and presents in perfected form much that has not yet emerged from the chaos of external reality.

In the arts, awareness of everything original and elemental is peculiarly distinct and sometimes takes on purely scientific guises: analysis, abstraction.

Diary

January 8, 1924

The essence of sculpture must of course be illustrated by means of three-dimensional sculpture, the purest form; and the contrast to the painting, which deals in flat surfaces, should be made clear.

The plane presents itself in two dimensions (height and breadth). Furthermore, the entire plane can be taken in at any given moment and from one vantage point.

Sculpture is three-dimensional (height, breadth, depth). It cannot be grasped in any given moment; rather it reveals itself in a temporal succession of vantage points and views. Since a piece of sculpture does not yield a total impression from one angle, the spectator is obliged to move, and only by walking around and adding up his impressions does he eventually grasp the sculpture. Thus any piece of plastic art which does not offer the viewer a series of surprises as he walks around it, but merely repeats one segment (and this is true of all stereometric bodies), has no validity as sculpture.

Besides, I can create any kind of stereometric body by

means of projections, which should not be possible with real sculpture. I can also portray stereometric bodies in one plane so convincingly, simply by manipulating light and shadow, that the other sides need not even be projected. This, too, could not be done with a true piece of sculpture. In fact, the sculptural quality of any sculpture can be measured by the number of individual facets that can be viewed.

The "purest form of expression" can probably not be defined; only the prerequisites for it yield to conceptualization. An alphabet is far from being a language, an instrument from being music. Could one ever dip into the rich supply of sculpture from the past, find an ideal, from it derive a canon (which would be worthwhile only if it proved itself alive and fruitful)? How about it?

To Tut

Berlin
February 5, 1924

Almost didn't get in the door. Out of matches; the lock worked the opposite way from what I had remembered. Only after a long struggle. Was already picturing spending the night walking the streets. Slept well after that. This evening: stayed at the Volksbühne until five-thirty, then ate finally, then to the library to study palms and such, cannon and Greek gods.

Am now having coffee. After this, home. Still a lot to do at the theater. Have to take care of every little mess. General sloppiness and high alcohol consumption. At the same time I have to race around Berlin looking for this or that and can't get away. Oh, well!

To Otto Meyer

Weimar
February 13, 1924

Your letter arrived just in time to catch me in Weimar, back from Berlin (preparations for a production), on sick leave for a few days, exhaustion break, half welcome, half un-. The success of last year's production earned me a commission for the same theater this year. *King Hunger,* by the Russian Leonid Andreyev. The job is not satisfying, because of course I cannot go as far as I would like; I have to subordinate myself entirely to the play, with the result that any effects I achieve will be limited. My only pleasure lies in putting my stamp on the whole production, making a thread—red—run through it. Given the circumstances, the production will remain only a sketch, a preliminary design. For this sort of theater does not give one sufficient time for ripening and perfecting, and many other things are lacking as well. The subject matter is too powerful, too demanding, and agreement among those involved, even among the two or three main people, too precarious.

What I do like about the Volksbühne, probably Berlin's most lovely theater, is that, almost alone among Berlin's innumerable theaters, it tries for grand style. Imposing dimensions, two thousand seats, the largest stage: all this has a hold on me! And you are well aware that this "grand style" is a cherished idea of mine, perhaps a risky one. Yet the Volksbühne is also a theater for the Socialist organizations; thus its first requirement, as I understand it, is that a play have a political slant. *Nie Wieder Krieg [No More War],* a Twilight of Mankind with proletarians hiding out in caves, *Don Carlos,* because the Marquis Posa is a pacifist, the play *The Marriage of Figaro,* because Figaro rebels against his master and the aristocratic privileges— and accordingly, *King Hunger,* in which the author actually exposes the "rich" and the "hungry" equally lovingly, will be slanted to say that the hungry are good, the rich totally bad. That is the Volksbühne's Achilles' heel.

Other theatrical news: The ballet is supposed to be revived; nowadays it seems worthwhile to make such efforts in Germany again.

The Bauhaus Theater! Let this be all I say about the Bauhaus.

I have discovered that nothing is so ill received, by Gropius as well as the students, as a suggestion that comes from one of the masters, once he no longer sticks to theoretical neutrality, but actively expresses his own ideas. The students want to do everything themselves, or at least to have the illusion of having done it themselves. Therefore they favor the master who stays neutral and benefits them the most in practical terms. They hate a master whose objectives coincide with theirs. And now see if you can make rhyme or reason of the fact that in the discussion of the cutbacks (which are just around the corner), the students sided with Klee and me.

Elections just took place in Thuringia. The previous Socialist government, which supported the Bauhaus, has been replaced by a middle-class one. All sorts of things will be happening in the days ahead. Gropius has anticipated and worked out a plan which calls for taking the Bauhaus workshops out of government hands and incorporating them. The state government would then pay just a small number of faculty members. I know about these plans only from hearsay—I am farther from the throne than ever. Kandinsky, who, like everyone else, was very close in the beginning, gradually became disgusted and has already been displaced by Moholy, the newest member. But enough of that.

Diary

March 18, 1924

The Bauhaus is going through its March Evolution: theoretical and practical suggestions issued by the younger Bauhaus members for our Bau-Haus, permanently under construction. It took until March before last summer's experiences and insights could be formulated. The proclamation strikes such a firm and convincing note that one feels obligated to clarify one's own position.

It should be an encouraging sign when the commitment to good architecture is stressed. There are increasing numbers of students who earnestly want to devote themselves exclusively to architecture, and now that this young guard of architects exists, it is hardly surprising that they plan to fight for the basic prerequisites of their studies. I would guess they want to set up a workshop which would have standards, rights, and obligations similar to those of the other workshops, and through which they could pursue their practical and theoretical objectives. I never understood why this most important workshop of all did not exist at the Bauhaus; I have long been calling for a strong architecture workshop, and I feel that it must be established, no matter what the objections. I am sure that the danger of producing "drawing-board architects" is a paper tiger. And then times have changed, too. The period of wild stylistic eclecticism, when drawing-board architects flourished, has now been followed by a new interest in the actual materials and their uses, and this has created an entirely new set of circumstances.

Once we have such a workshop at the Bauhaus, other questions, such as that of the dubious building site, will be resolved or will become easier to resolve.

I do not know whether the call for this workshop came in response to the threat posed to the Bauhaus by certain successful undertakings. For the ceramics and weaving workshops are well on their way to becoming the hallmark of the Bauhaus, if they are not that already. The label of a good arts and crafts school should thus come as no surprise.

Another gratifying and healthy feature of the student declaration is its rejection of artificial style, of cheap effects, cuteness, mannerism, fad, quickie methods. The clear distinction between "mode" and "modern," between art and technology, technology and handwork. The consideration that Bauhaus unity should result naturally when each specific area of endeavor is developed in the most skilful fashion. Such an insight seems truly inspired. For it reminds everyone where he belongs and demands that he give his very best. For devotion to one's task, not insistence on conformity, leads to artistic unity and shapes a particular image of the world. This insight would furnish the basic premise the Bauhaus so sorely needs in order to fulfill its mission by itself and in its own way. And isn't that what we want?

The declaration referred frequently to the artist, a term and a type which are actually taboo at the Bauhaus. Well, how about the artist? According to Molnár, he is merely an intelligent house painter executing the commands of "higher necessity." I happen to believe that the architect of the future, as chief exponent of the functionality concept, will think in terms of materials, including color, and exercise a decisive influence. What will go by the board: the craftsman responsible for the arts and crafts, which now place art in such a difficult position. We shall be left with a lowly but solid corps of untrained workmen—and the artists, the creative inventors. In spite of secularization and the "cul-de-sac of abstraction," art still has a role to play. Future inventions, scientific progress will not encroach on art's preserve. Possibly a National Art Warden could forbid the painting of pictures for ten years or so, until the housing problem is solved.

I view future developments as follows (the general outlines are already more or less visible): the ways will part. The architectural, constructivist trend in recent art will be channeled into direct application, the answer to many of the problems we are experiencing now. Application: shaping the objects of everyday use, or better yet, designing houses and their entire contents. At the same time, the rumor of art's demise will be laid to rest; it was originally spread by the advocates of applied art (the *real* constructivists, who do not paint); as I see it, the picture, painting, the metaphysical, will be rescued by precisely those constructivist methods which can either be applied to the real, practical world or used to express the realm of the ideal.

"Absolute" art, the art of "pure" form and color, belongs to architecture and all that implies. Painting needs a medium borrowed from the visible world. The most appropriate subject matter: man. Does that suggest a restoration of the old aesthetics? I believe it does. Certain old principles seem unshakable, eternally fresh. If their restoration in a new guise were not a reality, someone would have to invent it.

Proud, new, noble tasks ahead.

To Otto Meyer

Weimar

May 20, 1924

Peace and quiet seem more unattainable than ever. The next few days—or weeks?—will bring a decision as to whether the Bauhaus remains alive, with or without Gropius, with or without faculty. The rightist government of Thuringia, the bourgeois circles, the master craftsmen, the local artists, who claim to be fighting "with their backs against the wall," are all raising a hullabaloo and slinging slogans about. The papers are rustling mightily with pros and contras. Gropius circulates a summary of the favorable press opinions; a counter-brochure appears, then a pamphlet, a newspaper campaign, pro-Bauhaus posters designed by the students. Although I do not clearly perceive the outcome, I am only mildly curious. According to our contract, we have until the spring of 1925.

One more enemy: the Academy, which feels threatened by our comprehensive program and would be happy to see the Bauhaus reduced to an arts and crafts school once more.

At the moment I am very busy with a publication on theater for the Bauhaus series; I am to contribute several essays. I have seized this opportunity in the awareness that the future does not look especially bright for theatrical matters. The Volksbühne in Berlin has made me an offer, just in case the Bauhaus . . . .

Diary

May/June 1924

The role of the plastic artist in relation to the theater, the writer, and the actor, has up to now been subservient. The body matters more than what clothes or shelters it; if the plastic artist cuts loose and achieves creative freedom, it happens at the cost of the writer and the actor. This circumscribes the area within which such freedom is possible. This freedom should obtain where language falls silent (or fails), where costume is not de rigeur, and where the setting requires no illusion of nature. It can be found wherever the stage is a tabula rasa.

Man appears on this stage as an abstract organism which fulfills the set laws of his organism and of his environment (space). It is pantomimic dance.

Diary

September 1924

The Volksbühne: about ninety percent of my work consists of secondary chores I must perform in order to get to the ten percent I consider really important. Thus I am ninety percent involved physically and psychically and should be wholly involved. The economies insisted on by the Volksbühne make it impossible for me to create anything complete; compromise. But I can get my ten percent better there than anywhere else: familiarity with the stage, experience with the personnel, the connections in Berlin, dancers, other theaters, above all opera. Kestenberg. Piscator.

I lack the peace and quiet needed for my own work.

Postcard to Otto Meyer
Weimar
September 30, 1924

From Basel I had to continue straight through to Berlin, have been in Weimar a week now; next back to Berlin until October 15. In Berlin I am supposed to do another production at the Volksbühne. As was to be expected, the whole Bauhaus has been provisionally fired for April 1925.

To Otto Meyer
Weimar
October 20, 1924

Postscript to an agonizing Berlin premiere: *Der Arme Konrad [Poor Konrad]* was torn apart by the Berlin press; that is, only part of it, but largely the part that counts. When I was mentioned in connection with the set design, it was, as has often been the case, to the detriment of the author, the actors, and the director.

But for now I am sick of compromising myself in the service of writers. For when you come right down to it, this kind of work simply means following the way each individual director's wind is blowing, and they blow and buffet one from many directions.

I had to spend almost three weeks in Berlin. Now back here, curtly reminded by Gropius of my duties in Weimar. This Wednesday should bring the decision. Gropius has formed a circle of "Friends of the Bauhaus," the most notable members of which are Hans Thoma, Gerhart Hauptmann, and Albert

Einstein. Individuals and groups. The Thuringian government is said to have received about seven hundred testimonials—despite all this I am now only half here; unless miracles occur, not of preservation but of reorganization of the Bauhaus.

November 1924

I am still very fond of this idea of Runge's: "Strict regularity is urgently necessary precisely in those works of art which spring directly from our imagination and the secret depths of our soul, without external subject matter or plot."

November 12, 1924

"Abstract" figures, completely divested of corporeality, and mere hieroglyphs: mysterious marks, cliff paintings, stone engravings are, see in this light, one extreme. The other would be embedding the figure in space, coloration, *valeur*. Objective: a felicitous synthesis of nature and abstraction which—still—seems to be the criterion of true art.

This style of depiction: imbedding in space, coloration, *valeur,* will appear conventional, and in a sense it will be just that, for it incorporates the old, proven truths of painting. Nevertheless, or perhaps for that very reason, this method will be capable of revealing the most profound original insights, and Otto Meyer's great wisdom consists in his use of a comprehensible language to express new, unheard-of visions. It looks like compromise. Perhaps the ultimate wisdom is: compromise.

Developments in Germany and in art are being cut off before their prime. They are falling victim to the tempo of the times. I feel absolute freedom and metaphysical fulfillment have not yet been attained; the degree of formal perfection, or of classic form, necessary to the development of grand style has not been reached.

We are now witnessing a relapse, and one which threatens previous gains. The relapse may stem from the realization that abstraction meant the risk of losing the ground under one's feet, of hanging suspended in the void, at home neither here nor there. It may stem from a desire to "bind the metaphysical," to give it substance and clothe it in comprehensible language. If neither of these realizations motivates today's artists, they run the terrible danger of sinking into banality. We might witness the triumphal march of empty impressionism; the specter of the Glass Palace might rear its head; and certain art experts who "knew it all along" will celebrate an illusionary but potentially disastrous victory.

To Otto Meyer

Weimar

November 22, 1924

Serious deliberations on measures to be taken if the Bauhaus were torpedoed. It was not—only the National Socialists were in favor of that; the German National Party approved the establishment of a corporation for Bauhaus products, reduced the budget appropriation from 146,000 marks to 50,000. Yet Gropius has great hopes. Founds the "Friends of the Bauhaus," picks a board of trustees consisting of prominent intellectuals, so that we are now obliged to meet certain expectations. But we should not count our chickens yet; the full Landtag must still grant permission, which might become an epilogue with far-reaching implications. In short, we have not yet had the longed-for clarification, especially as regards the Bauhaus internally: who will go, who will stay.

As to Léger, and the similarity. A confession: not conscious, since my attitude toward him is more negative than otherwise. I would say it is more a question of lapidary style. I was surprised to see this cropping up in France, also. Something else, but also similar, then appeared in Italy—irrational—mysterious.

Theatrical matters now. Assignments: the next one at the Volksbühne: *Hamlet.* Another here at the Nationaltheater: Grabbe's *Don Juan und Faust*—no less mighty a theme, and one which attracts me more than ever; it will give me an opportunity to show what I can do. Perhaps a small ballet there as well, for a little opera in the most advant-garde style. In spite of everything (Bauhaus-security and our theatrical doings here), I am debating whether I should move to Berlin. The struggle between the two souls in my breast—one painting-oriented, or rather philosophical—artistic; the other theatrical; or, to put it bluntly, an ethical soul and an aesthetic one—this struggle has not yet been resolved; it underlies these doubts, or, as the case may be, decisions. One cannot serve two masters—when both are powerful and demand one's utmost (if it can be given at all). Some element will probably have to come from outside to bring about a decision.

To Otto Meyer

Weimar

December 15, 1924

Nothing decided as yet about the Bauhaus. But I have practically made up my mind not to stay here. The conversion into a corporation will industrialize the workshops; those which by nature do not lend themselves to industrialization will be at a disadvantage from the very outset.

I am writing for another reason, i.e. Stuttgart. I have been told unofficially but reliably that a chair in modern painting is to be established at the Academy (for the time being it will remain a lecturership, not part of the regular funding). The choice apparently fell upon me, and I am to be informed in the very near future. I am besieged by doubts on several scores. Some of them whisper: Berlin it must be. And others whisper just as firmly: Stuttgart. I say: in Berlin emphasis on theater to the exclusion of all else, which implies various compromises. I shall hardly have a chance to paint, to pursue my own work, which, after all, means a great deal to me. In Stuttgart: emphasis on painting, relative independence, a peaceful working atmosphere (Tut sees a danger of settling into bourgeois stolidity)—influence within a small sphere. Certainly, other considerations, too: my native turf, source of strength, Lake Constance, proximity to Switzerland.

In Berlin I saw an excellent play done at the Staatstheater [State Theater]: *Das Leben Edwards II. von England [The Life of Edward II of England]* by a young, very up-to-the-minute playwright, Bert Brecht. At the king's right sits his wife, to the left his boy companion (a nasty fellow), on the throne. The latter is hanged, Edward is murdered by degrees, the relationship having become the pretext for a war. In Berlin the critics and the audiences are split into two hostile camps. The "splash" is apparently fantastic. The author is timely in the sense that the play was written for the present situation in Berlin (the play was adapted from Marlowe, Shakespeare's predecessor).

To Willi Baumeister

Berlin
January 16, 1925

Your last letter hurtled me out of the clear blue sky into a huge rain cloud—or something very like one! I was actually no longer counting on Stuttgart, but was also growing skeptical about Berlin. It would really represent quite a compromising descent into the popcorn-chewing audience, with only dim prospects of finding fulfillment, since the people simply fall short of what we would wish them to be. I am still tempted by the wider possibilities open to one in Berlin, which, as Paul Westheim says, is the only city in Germany worth being in—but I have the distinct feeling that, for a while anyway, I would be unable to work there, at least on my painting, which I do still want to do.

In the meantime, the Thuringian Landtag is in an uproar over the Bauhaus—although our days in Weimar are past in any case. But the Bauhaus is a sort of merry widow, and the suitors keep multiplying. The handsomest one will get her. Since "he" is a "she," that is, a city between Stuttgart and—, I have not said a word, and if you think you have an idea, you are wrong, so who knows where we shall end up.

Postcard to Tut

Berlin

January 28, 1925

Chaos at the Volksbühne. Heinrich George wants to get out of the play—he's right! Gerda Müller—broken collar bone. First act of *Schluck and Jau* enough to make one turn tail and flee. Clashed with Piscator, who also has no idea what he wants. No—this is not the place for me! Utterly impossible. If I have to carry through on this, I am done for, that much is clear!

Postcard to Tut

Berlin

January 31, 1925

Sent a telegram to Mayor Hesse of Dessau: "Request extension." I am going to present the Volksbühne with a bill of particulars, including the demands which will have to be met before I commit myself. So Gropius will succeed after all in reuniting us. Amazing! One cannot deny that being together has its value. That becomes apparent when one gets to know the outside world better.

It would be impossible for me to visit Dessau now. Monday lighting rehearsal, tomorrow costumes—every day crucial. The week will pass quickly. I can't help it—I feel fine, very cheerful.

Diary

Middle of February 1925

Painting as a depicting art will exist as long as photography, moving pictures, or any other technical process cannot match its visual effects. Application and display of "pure media" does not exhaust art's possiblities. As long as there are ideas which can be portrayed neither philosophically nor technically, but only through the medium of painting, the "pure idea," like the "pure media," must remain the province of art.

It is not the function of art "to adorn and beautify life." Today less than ever. Today art is a form of display, often only this. If its roots reach no lower than the surface, it is not rooted at all. Then it may be a lovely, glittering surface; but not an organism that grows from within, forming visual evidence and images, whether superficially beautiful or not, into a universe determined by man and therefore small but still all-inclusive.

To Otto Meyer

Weimar
February 17, 1925

My chickens are not yet hatched, that is to say, I do not yet know where I shall land. I mean to give the heart its due, and the head likewise. Stuttgart is still up in the air. The Academy and the Ministry have decided in my favor. But the German Nationalist prime minister, Bazille, came out against that fellow Schlemmer, who is a modern and a leftist. The Academy protested this usurpation of authority.

Why am I flirting with Stuttgart? Berlin—at least the Volksbühne—would mean selling ninety-nine percent of my soul. The remaining one percent consists of my real interest there: theatrical innovation. To be an employee of the Volksbühne means playing shoe-shine boy to the egocentric actors and directors. Where would I find the inner strength to subordinate myself to a play I found uninteresting? Certainly I have seen some top-notch theater in Berlin, unforgettable actors; Shaw's *Joan of Arc,* for instance, but that is not my field.

The German cities' dance around the Golden Bauhaus is drawing to a close. The lukes have parted company with the warms, the hots with the scaldings. This leaves Dessau (this in confidence), a smallish city between Leipzig and Magdeburg—ambitious, coming up in the world, not without economic resources—and willing to take on the Bauhaus. "Actually" I did not want to be involved any more. But several factors made the city and the circumstances worth considering: the promise of a thorough reorganization, the dismantling of the Gropius autocracy, the enticing prospect of keeping the good students and masters together, opportunities for building (immediately), theatrical opportunities for me, and, last but not least, the proximity to Berlin (two hours). In addition there is the Elbe.

For a time Frankfurt am Main seemed to be in the running, also Mannheim.

In Weimar the "true" father of the Bauhaus, a Berlin architect, will be appointed, and apparently he plans to start from the opposite end, commencing with actual building, out of which all the rest is supposed to develop naturally, provided, that is, the Thuringian government gives him the chance (which it did not give Gropius).

What do you think of the wave of reaction in Germany? The rejection of any abstraction in art, even in the theater, is momentous. As protest against an exhibition of mine in Jena not one single word appeared in the press; an exhibition in Erfurt had to be cancelled for fear of the consequences. In the theater old-style acting (humanity) with painted backdrops is having a comeback. There is precious little I would consider positive in Germany today; the French are at least being clever, the Russians honest, the Americans bold—here something is brewing; I do not know whether it will be civil or aggressive war.

To Tut

Berlin
March 30, 1925

Today, Sunday, I slept late, because I was locked in—the door to the stairway, which is never shut. What to do? I threw leaflets out the window: man locked in! Then two young men arrived with the wife of the concierge and released me. Like Harold Lloyd.

How are things? I think about you all the time! Really. How is child Number Three? Couldn't you wait another week? That would be best. Because I won't be home for Sunday. On the way I might go via Dessau. For of course the particulars in Dessau are important. Apartment, length of contract.

Things are getting crazier and crazier here. Don't know whether I'm coming or going. What a drain on the nerves!

To Otto Meyer

Weimar
April 1925

I wish to report briefly:

1) The birth of a son, named Tilman, on April 1. At any rate this Ram child promises to be a born leader, hardheaded, tough—qualities which this family, to which he is the heir, urgently need. But we also have to take into account the influence of the Crab—perhaps everything will go backwards, hard to say. A Bauhaus member is at this very moment working out the horoscope, a widespread custom in Germany just now. Mother and child are doing well, and the little girls are happy to have a brother. As I see it, the "Triadic Quintet" is now fully assembled and we can turn our attention to other matters.

2) Transfer of the Bauhaus to Dessau/Anhalt, an industrial city which seems smaller than Weimar but is actually bigger, two hours from Berlin, ten minutes from the Elbe, with a royal prince, a smattering of tradition, a sense of obligation toward things theatrical, and the willingness to take us on. A new Bauhaus will be built, as well as houses for the masters—which would be just dandy if Gropius had not used the opportunity to seize control; now he is bestowing the blessings of his favor in greatly varied measure. Only four of his paladins have been full beneficiaries of his generosity. In order to scrape by, I shall have to supplement my income elsewhere; Berlin naturally offers a possibility. At the Bauhaus I shall henceforth be responsible only for theater work, which means I am receiving a firm shove in this direction. Gropius' conduct was not irreproachable, and we barely avoided a break; even now I am suspicious, although Gropius has been making an obvious effort to see I am adequately provided for. I shall keep my eyes open; in any case it will take the whole summer before the buildings in Dessau are ready to be moved into.

The sets for *Hamlet* in Berlin were acknowledged by most of the reviewers to be handsome; it was regretted that the actors did not know how to relate to them. I suggested to the Volksbühne that I be allowed to do some abstract experimental projects on the side, but I was turned down on the grounds that the theater's regular audience would not understand such experiments. That had been my hope for Berlin.

All in all, my growing longing for peace and leisure to work might cause me to consider Stuttgart after all. I wonder how this will turn out, and I envy soothsayers, who can foresee everything—yet without taking advantage of it.

At the New Bauhaus the anti-art and anti-painting, pro-industry trend will probably become more marked. This trend has already partly split the student body. It is only natural that the concrete tasks of building and furnishing the dwellings should push picture painting into the background. The advocates of progress claim that the slogan "every man his own movie theater" replaces the idea of the individual painted picture, which uses old-fashioned means, especially if it represents something, i.e. is not even abstract = non-objective.

Recently I saw some new Russian theater, Tairov, which revealed a sense of discipline almost foreign to Germany, coupled with scenic audacity and tremendous versatility on the part of the actors, who are excellent actors but no less excellent singers and dancers. The critics noted this superiority of the Russians, as well as the existence of modern theater in France and the almost complete lack of any such thing in Germany. And my ballet was singled out as the only comparable attempt. So to this extent certain hopes are placed in me.

Diary

Spring 1925

Contemporary art:

A glance at the present situation in art reveals that the three stylistic trends of cubism, futurism, and expressionism have consolidated into two: constructivism and verism. Now these two are in opposition, and, depending on their objectives, will move farther and farther apart or else merge. If the latter occurs, the phenomenon will still need a name that covers the most particular *and* the most general, provided one does not simply call it art.

Constructivism pushes the conventional picture to absurdity in order to fulfill its most valuable function, i.e. the creation of real material, applied art in the best sense, rather than illusionistic pictorial elements. Engineering with an added spiritual dimension will therefore be the next stage.

Yet the constructivist is still painting, and his pictorial elements, no longer tied to the object, consist of basic (geometric) form and basic color (the spectrum). These elements signal the ultimate, abstract fulfillment of one objective of art: to provide a feast for the eyes. An aesthetic effect which just happens to have ethical implications.

Verismo is principally slanted—for no art exists free of a slant—toward the political. This slant can be perceived in the treatment of figure and object and the obvious stress laid on these elements. Here painting becomes *Moritat**, often dangerously close to mere illustration. But it has rescued the honor of painting, reintroducing brilliant, technically skilled *peinture*. Yet with its "Back to Nature" slogan *Verismo* will also unleash all the inclinations toward copying nature which Expressionism frustrated. *Verismo* will steer art back into the old groove.

No! This is the moment to unfurl the standard of art and issue the call for a return to art's ancient, yet inexhaustible, ideals. The work of art represents a marriage of form and content. According to Leonardo, the work of art consists half of fantasy, half of reality, united in him in equal portions. According to Delacroix, art should provide a feast for the eyes, but should also go beyond that. And just as surely as the art work of the past fulfilled these specifications, so these specifications exist today, providing art with its raison d'être. And art will continue to have a raison d'être as long as there are things which it alone can portray and convey, despite technology and new inventions. In fact, it is precisely film and photography which help bring out the unique quality of painting, i.e. its capacity for abstraction. And no people has such a gift for abstraction as the Germans, to whom it is a curse if they run aground on its problematical aspects, a blessing if they succeed in solving that most difficult of tasks: achieving perfection of form and profundity of thought.

All great art contains as many constructive elements, yes,

---

*A narrative ballad, usually describing sensational deeds or events. — Translator

even constructed elements, in the form of real and metaphysical mathematics, as it contains living, actualized realities. The work of Philipp Otto Runge and Caspar David Friedrich struck their contemporaries as constructed and geometric!

Diary

April 28, 1925

Abandon the tack I took in 1923; instead pursue the idea of metaphysical spaces, metaphysical perspectives, the metaphysical figure. Brightness, absence of mannerism. A constant flow of new formulations. Figures in outline, not differentiated individuals. In abstract spaces of the future, of translucency, of reflection, of optics, of multiple figuration of man.

What are my origins? The simple palette of Corot, Courbet, and those who followed them; the simplest mixtures, uncomplicated materials.

I arrived at abstraction—Picasso, Archipenko and others. The essential element: simple forms. Deeply personal. Profundity does not suit me. But the simplicity of optics does, it makes drastic depiction possible.

Diary

May 22, 1925

Sculpture continues to fascinate me, wherever I encounter models or pictures of it.

The early Greeks (forever and aye!). Maillol. The Goddess of the Berlin Museum.

And probably the classical element which can always be discerned in France's best painters (Corot, Seurat).

Mystical power of expression: the carrier of spiritual dynamics. Light and shadow.

Themes: the nude and the clothed figure, next to each other, confronting each other, juxtaposed, half-right, left, on a slant.

The figure in white, in black, the nude in rose, burnt sienna, burnt umber. Violet shadows. A series, a gradation of nudes.

To Tut

Dessau
June 14, 1925

Well, I set out for Dessau at 6 A.M. on Saturday, got there at 10, and saw Gropius at 11. I explained my letter, and Gropius was deeply hurt that I should take such a tone with him when he was doing his very best for me! It almost came to a break. He said that if that was my attitude, the next step would be legal action; he would bring up the affair before the Masters' Council, etc. I could of course go to the Mayor, but, he said, I should bear in mind that that would definitely mean the end, etc. Yet I couldn't care less whether it is the end or not; I want to be paid. He is writing to the Mayor at once to explain my situation. At least I accomplished that much. Gropius says it is now up to me to do something; that he owes to the City Council. I reply: as soon as I am in a financial position to do so, depending on how I am paid. I shall stay here until Monday. Am staying at the "Filthy Sack." Monday back to Gropius to see about the theater, which must finally be worked out in detail.

We sit in Dessau's only café and talk, talk, talk.

To Tut

Weimar
June 17, 1925

Your last letter sounds rather mournful. Surely you received something a long time ago. I am doing the accounts, trying to see where the money goes. For the Dessau trip I had to borrow from Otte. Have to pay Kandinsky back. On the first of the month things will look up, I hope. It really is stupid when life turns into an endless exercise in arithmetic!

Well, to my interview with Gropius. Once more we escaped the worst. He promptly wrote to the Mayor and suggested that as an interim solution he be authorized to draw the necessary sums from the general budget.

Sunday I was invited to dinner at the Muches'. Gropius dropped by and asked me to visit him that evening. Moholy, Breuer, Albers, and a few others were in Berlin for a summer festival. I had been supposed to go along, but the prospect was too much for me. I only saw Moholy briefly. Muche returned Saturday evening from Berlin in a truck with seven looms which he had bought there for an outrageous price, to the horror of poor Gunda. Muche: he is tired of being a businessman. He complains bitterly about his job: he wants to create a "fashion" of his own.

The houses for the Bauhaus masters have been approved, Gropius says. On Monday, June 22, a big parade, City Council, exhibition; permission for the new building is supposed to be granted then. Now Kandinsky and Klee have to commute once a week. Monday they are also expected to be present, as am I, which will mean another trip.

My impression of Dessau has not changed much. Not even under the influence of the Elbe and the Hollow. Everything so dreary and bleak. No life. Especially after Halle. I was puzzled. Marcks still manages to laugh. It is terribly windy and dusty in Dessau. I do not place great hopes in General Manager Hartmann, a theater expert who takes no risks, steers clear of experiments. The theater schedule for the year offers the usual bill of fare. The ballet master is said to be a student of Laban, is bringing a troupe with him.

To Tut

Weimar

June 18, 1925

I am really worried. Today is Thursday; nothing this morning, nothing at noon. Or are you sticking strictly to the agreement to write only on Sundays? Can you even wait that long? Nonetheless, I keep writing to you, and you must be receiving something every day! I have no news to report, except that I am turning into a financial wizard. Every day calculations, payments, borrowings. Aside from that I feel fine.

I am drawing up a detailed work schedule for the Bauhaus Theater, so as to have something to show Gropius. The thing must be well organized. I am setting up a curriculum which assures me the initiative and makes it possible to build up gradually, step by step. I am also painting.

To Tut

Returned from Dessau, found both your letters waiting. So things are all right. I am living in an admirably orderly fashion, wherefore I categorically decree: in the future I must have a room to myself, just for my work. Jean Paul had one, too. Wife and children are only permitted to visit!

So Monday and Tuesday I was in Dessau. Everyone was rather battle-weary, especially Muche. But the big project has been ratified unanimously. Now Gropius will have to see to it that the building costs remain within the approved limit. In the evening a celebration with champagne: Klee, Gropius and his wife, Muche and his wife, Moholy, Scheper, who had invited me to dinner, also Gunda Stölzl and Rudolf Paris. Home at half-past two. Tuesday morning at nine went with Gropius to see the Mayor about my case. The Mayor is now taking a realistic position, sticks to the facts; as far as he is concerned, no substantial changes are permissible, at least not for the time being.

Klee is here now from Monday to Friday. Poor Klee! It is deadly boring. The two days were quite enough for me. Was the only person at the swimming pool. Still weigh 142 lb.

Postcard to Tut

Weimar
June 17, 1925

Mme Kandinsky in a state. All Weimar is "a vale of tears." They were happy here. Very depressed.

Tomorrow, Sunday, dinner with Klee. In the evening everybody going to the circus. Am supposed to go along. They all send warmest greetings, especially to you.

Diary

July 8, 1925

Why did the Old Masters paint in brown, asphalt tones? Why not green? Why did Poussin often paint such unnatural terra-cotta nudes? Why were Renoir's carmine? Because the medium of color was more important to them than the realities of nature. They painted nature, but translated into the natural media of their palettes. Vermeer's blue and Constable's green were great achievements. Really. They made the gamble succeed. But it failed for those who conceived it as a step toward the banal verisimilitude which enabled them to use the media ever more unrestrainedly and unartistically. Not until the Pointillists did something like a principle temporarily reappear (Seurat), that of spectro-analytical color. The present barbarous chaos perpetrated in the name of nature could be overcome by a return to the fundamental, primary media.

To Tut

Weimar

July 9, 1925

Gropius has sent new house plans. Strike at the moment, work at a standstill. They will certainly turn out well, those houses. But seem unable to apply myself to the plans just now.

Am actually working. The one as a result of the other. The secret is concentration. Bombing pause, during which one works. Says Klee. He lets no one interfere with him. I have a big pitcher of lilies and Canterbury bells on the floor. Have this longing to have flowers around me, now that you, my flower, are no longer here. The Tut picture hangs before my very nose over the bed. Often stare long and hard at it. Really!

To Tut

Weimar

Mid-July 1925

Sunday on the veranda. The blue Canterbury bells are a foot and a half tall. I was especially pleased that you wrote so quickly. I kiss you on the shoulder in my thoughts. I shall also try to be satisfied with that, or with even less, since you love Til "so terribly." A fine rival I have begotten. Should I be jealous of the little fellow? I've been stood in the corner to be fetched out when needed . . . . Well, I still have my artistic offspring and the lovely memories. And I'm still young, and handsome as a Greek. See for yourself! I have a beautiful pair of white linen trousers and a narrow belt to match. An idealistic Schillerian shirt, white shoes. Yesterday I wore all this to the Klees'. My Lindau costume.* It has transformed me completely. The open collar is a blessing; I never want to wear a stiff collar again. Frau Klee to her Paulie: "Why don't you wear something like that?" "No money!" I tell them what it cost. I say what one says at such moments! No, he replies, I am mistaken, it is true that they have no money. He is breaking his contract with Goltz, who keeps wanting to lower the prices. He, Klee, wants them maintained. He has 800 marks a month, but that is as inadequate as the 250 marks earlier. Everything is relative, he says. A rich man with 3,000 marks a month has no money either—because he has needs and desires to match.—Attempts to soothe him.—What will become of us if this is what befalls the celebrities?

Diary

July 13, 1925

Paint this renunciation! My last picture.

I am filled with doubts, and thus cannot reach the ear of God. I am too modern to paint pictures. The crisis in art has me in its grip. Perhaps I am not stable enough. I approach my work with great trepidation. Agonize more than I paint!

Theater! Music! My passion! But also: the scope of this particular field. Theoretical possibilities that suit my disposition, because this is natural to me. Free run for the imagination.

Here I can be new, abstract, everything. Here I can be traditional successfully. Here I need not stumble into the dilemma of painting, relapsing into an artistic genre in which I secretly no longer believe. Here my desires coincide with my temperament and with the contemporary mood. Here I am myself, and yet a new person. The only one in the field, without competition.

A late realization, but perhaps not too late. Sense of liberation!

---

*Lindau: a small town on Lake Constance. — Translator

To Tut

Weimar

July 14, 1925

Painting or the stage! I really want very much to do "metaphysical theater." Am working on the schedule for the Dessau theater, my head buzzing with ideas. Everything is being put in order according to plan; we can begin with the simplest, most straightforward methods, which are perfectly respectable. I now believe it is my personal calling to do this kind of theater in Germany. Apparently the many voices encouraging me are right.

Painting! Yes, I did a bit more. But not to my total satisfaction. When I paint, I get hundreds of ideas. When I think of the theater, I likewise get hundreds of ideas.

That time we had the champagne in Dessau we all looked at each other's palms. Klee's left hand revealed a few, simple gifts, the right one promising rich development. The opposite with me. Many gifts, unused, and simple application; large, plain lines. Might be correct! Gave me to think.

To Tut

Weimar

July 16, 1925

So now you plan to send me to the seashore? But I already have a southern journey mapped out: Lake Constance—Berchtesgaden—Salzburg. All for partly practical, partly useful reasons—the ocean would be pure pleasure, which I cannot afford now. I hope, for instance, to get to see Reinhardt in Salzburg.

Last night at the Feiningers'. She and their son Laurens are the only ones still home. He and the other two are in Deep on the Baltic. The Bauhaus has vacation for the whole month of August. Gropius had wanted only two weeks. Great outcry. And even a month is not much. Art academies take three months.

The farewells were touching. The masters' wives kissed each other. Mme Kandinsky had a cold. But Frau Feininger did not let that bother her. These families—the Klees, the

Feiningers—have a certain calm fullness to their lives. We by comparison are nervous wrecks. Perhaps we shall succeed, too, someday.

To Tut

Weimar
July 23, 1925

I am glad you enjoyed the photographs of the paintings. Have begun another picture, by the way. The work is going well now. Shall keep at it, accomplish as much as possible. Because after this will come the great interruption, the motor will run down and have to be cranked up again. But now I realize what concentration can mean, how Klee, Feininger, and others benefit from their undisturbed concentration; one picture seems to flow naturally out of the other, almost by itself—the entire secret of originality and creative energy. And in fact I am constantly getting new ideas these days. I would be a fool to neglect painting simply for the sake of a theory (theater). Painting is the right thing just now. It would have been folly not to use the studio for its intended purpose, namely painting. The pictures are now stacked up in threes. Twelve of them, too, some pretty good-sized.

When I plan to come? Unfortunately all the holiday trains are sold out. Depending on the weather and the course of events I shall either wait or set out. Also depending on the work. There are still a few things I hope to get out of the way.

To Alexander Schawinsky

Egghalden on Lake Constance
August 12, 1925

Your letter gave me, and us, great pleasure. Especially since it rained today, and yesterday as well, and the usual pleasures such as swimming in the brook and the lake had to be abandoned for indoor activities.

We have a perfect Bauhaus here. The living room often presents the ideal *Exposition internationale des arts décoratifs*

173

et infantiles, made out of blocks, with a corso of doll carriages, a fashion show of wet or dry colored diapers and wraps, a balloon which will not hold its air. A make-believe Seine—a *scène* which alternately materializes and disintegrates into a flurry of cleaning rags, snail hunts, fly catchers, home cine and house Chinee, rose beds and red hose, horse flies, mysteries, village bands. One step and we are international: in Austria, Bavaria, Germany. We inhabit a house of boards (in which we have our exits and entrances) and of glass (fragile!); it has, as the dernier cri, a sloping roof (the latest spoof!)—and if one looks very carefully, one can see the mountains. The "Gaurisankar,"* as my wife says, but actually it is just Sankt Säntis. Interruption. Child crying. Fill a new pipe. Heartfelt thanks from one in another life for your condolences on the occasion of my Bauhaus death. I did not know that at headquarters I had been proclaimed dead and done for, and I am most eager to know whether this came from above or from the nether regions, in what form and with what accompanying circumstances. Was I at-tacked on the bullet-in board? When will the obsequies be held? Are you planning something for the mourning after? Will a satire be performed or a hymn? A farce or a burlesque? Since my (ahem) contract as an instructor in this area officially remains in effect through April 1, my son's birthday, and since he has rolled another year around, this would be an opportunity to direct the play myself, to die and let (myself) live.

Too bad about the Theater. I was really looking forward to finally doing something concrete and building from the ground up. But since my death has been officially registered there, I shall simply have to renounce steadfastly.

Work! and not despair—that is the sole solution, solution and con-solation, which I can con-sign to you. But keep me informed of the spheres and atmospheres; the factions aside, I remain anxious, yes, morally obligated, to help and sustain you with words, as long as deeds are denied me. I shall write a festival play second to none, and, like every really good piece of writing, impossible to perform. Here I stand—so help me God! For the time—which is announced here punctually with cuckoo

---

*A mountain in Nepal. The Säntis is in Switzerland; *Sankt* means saint, and is added just for the pun. — Translator

calls and rattling of chains by the Black Forest clock—I have nothing more to report.

To Tut

Weimar

September 12, 1925

Arrived safely. The good old Weimar Bauhaus Company is being decimated. Gropius lays claim to Otte and Arndt.

Gropius has intimated to Bartning that it is not fair to snatch people away from Dessau, after *he* hired them. The former Bauhaus now has an uncomfortable atmosphere. More and more art students from the old Academy are moving into the studios. Haven't seen anyone. That makes leaving easier.

Diary

September 13, 1925

The desire to emulate more harmonious times misled Ruskin into preaching a return to beauty, but the gushing romanticism and nature worship he espoused were actually a mockery of natural evolution and reality. Like him, Morris resisted the industrialization of the crafts, calling instead for work based on love and emotion. Van de Velde, less romantic than "extraordinarily rational," combatted the general decline of standards and taste by taking as his model the precision and functionality characterisitic of the work of the engineer and the machine builder; he expelled imagination from realms where it did not belong, trying thus to bring about neutral conditions under which everyone would follow the dictates of reason.

To Otto Meyer

Weimar

Mid-September 1925

In the haste of departure, just this quick note: the Rubicon cube has been cast!

Stuttgart postponed indefinitely. Who knows the reasons, can count the traps? Simultaneously Gropius offered new enticements (still paltry enough)—a free apartment in the new house that is to be built. But the big new Bauhaus building will contain a theater which will be my very own exclusive domain; the proximity to Berlin will also promote my theatrical activity; and recently the prospect has arisen of collaborating with an international mime company, which would mean reviving the "Triadic Ballet." So everything is pushing me, half-willing, half-unwilling, in this direction, and now I am giving myself an occasional shove, too.

DESSAU
(Autumn 1925 to Summer 1929)

1925: The Bauhaus settles in Dessau, in temporary quarters at first. The masters are assigned studios in the Museum. Schlemmer immediately formulates a plan for systematically building up the experimental theater, to be devoted primarily to study of types.

The faculty of the Bauhaus has grown; G. Marcks has left for a position in Halle, and Feininger is not teaching, but the "young masters"—Josef Albers, Herbert Bayer, Marcel Breuer, Hinnerk Scheper, Joost Schmidt, and Gunda Stölzl—join the remaining masters. The first books of the Bauhaus series appear, among them the volume *Die Bühne im Bauhaus [Theater of the Bauhaus]*.

Schlemmer designs productions in Berlin. Exhibitions in Dresden and Berlin.

1926: The first party at the new Bauhaus is called "The White Festival" and proves a great success, thanks to the Schlemmer-inspired theatrical presentations. In July the "Triadic Ballet" is performed at the music festival in Donaueschingen, and later as part of the *Große Brückenrevue* ["Grand Bridge Revue"] in Frankfurt am Main and at the Metropol Theater in Berlin.

In August the family moves into the Masters' House at No. 5 Burgkühnauerallee.

On December 4 the solemn dedication of the new Bauhaus building takes place. The Theater opens with a presentation of basic theatrical elements: dance of forms, dance of gestures, dance of backdrops.

1927: In March Schlemmer delivers an illustrated lecture on the elements of theater before the "Friends of the Bauhaus." In April he turns over most of his house to the architect Hannes Meyer, appointed to direct the newly established architecture department; his wife Tut takes the children to the Ticino for a year. In May the Bauhaus Theater performs at the German Theater Exhibition in Magdeburg; for this occasion the third issue of the Bauhaus journal is devoted to theater and Schlemmer acts as editor, offering the first comprehensive report, with pictures, on the goals and methods of the Bauhaus Theater.

The brilliant success of the Bauhaus summer party can be attributed in large measure to the theatrical performances. At the end of the summer semester, Muche leaves the Bauhaus. In Ascona, where

Schlemmer goes to rejoin his family, he finds Hermann Scherchen, with whom he discusses possible collaboration.

On his return, he considers working with Erwin Piscator, for whom Gropius has sketched out a project for a total theater.

In the winter semester Schlemmer instructs the second-year students in drawing the human figure. In December he persuades the Bauhaus to put on a "Fete of Slogans" and shortly before Christmas a "Silent Christmas" party. At the end of the year he visits his family, now moved from Ascona to Mittelberg.

During this year he has no time for painting. Exhibitions of his works in Wiesbaden and other cities.

1928: At the beginning of January, debate over a new course and budget matters. In spite of great concern at the Bauhaus over the financial squeeze, the usual *Fasching* party is held under the device, "Party for the Beard, Nose, and Heart." Gropius decides to resign, and leaves the Bauhaus. Moholy, Breuer, and Bauer join him. Hannes Meyer becomes Gropius' successor. For the farewell party Schlemmer writes a chronicle, *Neun Jahre Bauhaus* ["Nine Years of the Bauhaus"], which is performed with student participation. At Easter Tut and the children return and move back into the house, while the Meyer family moves into Gropius' house. In June the Bauhaus Theater has a successful guest stand at the Dance Congress in Essen.

Hannes Meyer introduces decisive changes in curriculum, in connection with which Schlemmer conducts the required course for third-semester students, taking "Man" as his topic; he continues his work for the stage as well. In the meantime he also has a few periods of concentrated work on painting, resulting in paintings like *Interieur-szene* ["Interior"], *Gegeneinander* ["Opposition"], *Gruppe mit Sitz-ender* ["Group with Seated Woman"], *Fünf Männer im Raum* ["Five Men in Space"], *Fünf Akte* ["Five Nudes"], and the series of great watercolors.

In the autumn Schlemmer is commissioned to do a series of murals for the Folkwang Museum in Essen.

He stages ballets in Hagen and at the Dresden Opera. His pictures are exhibited in Berlin and other cities. In Düsseldorf he receives the Gold Medal at the German Art Exhibition.

1929: In February the traditional Bauhaus *Fasching* party takes place, the most splendid yet: "Metallic Party." In March the Bauhaus Theater accepts an invitation to present a matinee at the Berlin Volksbühne. It receives great acclaim and subsequently undertakes a tour to Breslau, Frankfurt am Main, Stuttgart, and Basel. Despite these outward successes, there is opposition within the Bauhaus to the direction the Theater has taken. Hannes Meyer and some of the students demand that it be politicized. Since Schlemmer rejects this demand as incompatible with his views, he decides to leave the Bauhaus. In July he

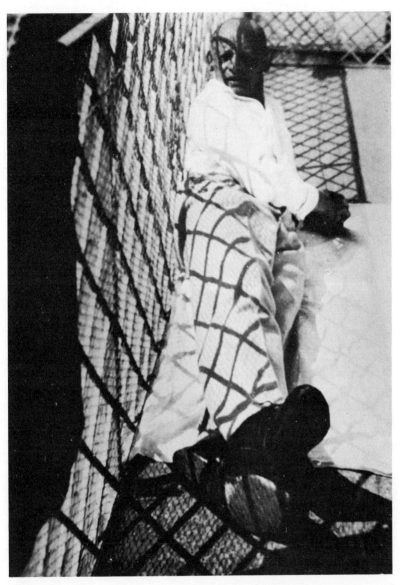

Oskar Schlemmer at Ascona, 1927. Photo by L. Moholy-Nagy. *Courtesy of Tut Schlemmer.*

Oskar Schlemmer and associates at the Bauhaus Theater, 1927. *Courtesy of Tut Schlemmer.*

accepts a professorship at the Staatliche Akademie für Kunst und Kunstgewerbe [State Academy for Art and the Crafts] in Breslau.

While still in Dessau he manages to complete the preliminary sketches for the murals in Essen, as well as such paintings as *Bekleidete und Unbekleidete in Architektur* ["Dressed and Undressed Figures in Architecture"], *Fünfzehnergruppe* ["Fifteen Group"], *Blaue Frauen* ["Blue Women"].

The Künstlerbund [Artists' Guild] in Cologne confers a prize on Schlemmer. Exhibitions in Cologne, Basel, and elsewhere. Before beginning his new job in Breslau, he takes a vacation with his family at the Samland seashore.

To Tut

Dessau

October 8, 1925

At the museum I now have a table and chair, and my office is open for business. Heaps of work. Shall soon get up and hit into it. A slight run-in with Moholy over the theater book. Called Gropius in to arbitrate.

Muche keeps wailing: no money! I am already concerned about how this operation will be run. Without people, without means. Gropius does intend to put a theater fund at my disposal. But think of all the people it will have to support! When you come right down to it, you can't conjure something out of nothing.

The townsfolk seem to have a hostile attitude toward the Bauhaus. The city ballet members are ashamed to be seen in our company. The teasing they must undergo is the least of it. Also: people are being urged to come to a protest rally against the Bauhaus. Well, well.

Meeting yesterday at Kandinsky's. They were complaining as if this were the last gasp. The rent payments were called exorbitant and unfair; the price of meat had gone up, so salaries should be raised; they could not afford to have any furniture made. What was I supposed to say? I sat there looking blank most of the time. When one perceives the injustice in a thousand trivial points, it takes genius to remain calm, cool, and collected. The general attitude: Kandinsky said he had had a member of some ministry to tea, and this man had mentioned that something had to be done in the way of lectures or exhibitions to placate the townsfolk. The Mayor gives the opposite advice: just keep quiet, the best course is to remain invisible! The ministry official mentioned that some were calling for impeaching the Mayor and paying the Bauhaus people their salaries—simply to send them packing;—that was the real mood. This was greeted with uproarious laughter. Ha! If that happens, we can build our villas wherever we please! All evening I felt uneasy. It does not look to me as if we shall enjoy being here. The whole thing is too incredible. I was shocked when I saw the houses, the first of which has gone up already. I suddenly had a mental vision of the homeless poor standing and staring while the Lord Artists sunned themselves on the flat roofs of their villas.

To Tut

Dessau

October 31, 1925

So yesterday things were supposed to get underway: a lecture by Gropius, before an audience of three hundred invited members of society. Then in the very dignified *Messelhaus* a reception for the Mayor and his *cercle,* with beer, open sandwiches, tea, and coffee, served by twelve blond Bauhaus girls; also an exhibition of our products. Toward eleven o'clock a serenade by the three Triadics, I in a dark suit with only a silver mask as my costume, beating a gong to lead the way; then a young student in Turkish costume, a second as a golden sphere, and then Schawinsky with the balls. The effect was brilliant, great applause. Roesslin apparently reacted with great enthusiasm, and rushed about trying to find suitable music for an accompaniment. In the Winter Garden until half-past two. The "Circle of Friends," which was energetically publicized, gained sixty new members; that means that we are firmly established in Dessau. The Bauhaus people assert the costumes clinched it. Nonetheless, I have the feeling that yet again I played the decisive role in making things turn out well for my dear colleagues.

Dessau society definitely does not have the stature of Weimar's. The ballet master said: the "Triadic Ballet" should be revived no matter what—the usual song and dance. The *Magdeburger Zeitung* carried a report on the jury members and my pictures. The Dessau newspapers reprinted it, and the article was discussed all evening, the Mayor reading it aloud at his table. But what good does that do? Who really understands my position at the Bauhaus?

To Tut

Dessau

November 5, 1925

Your letter this morning depressed me greatly—why so full of despair? You shouldn't let it get you down. What has happened to all your courage, your indomitable defiance, your spirit of contradiction? The children of Scorpio have fallen upon hard times now, that's true; the stars do not lie, as you can see. But when these bad times are past, other people will have to take their turn. Not the Virgos, I hope!

Where do you feel most vulnerable? Of course I do my best to make you happy with me and my work. It gives me an excellent incentive when I know that this way I can help you, and only this way; but it cannot be forced. This simply happens to be a period of suffering, and we must be steadfast.

Klee said something interesting while we were working on the new house: we (the next generation, who come after him and Kandinsky) will be on better terms with fame; in a few years things will go better with us than with them, who were scarred by the war and the post-war period. That makes it easier to see why these men want to get the most out of their reputation and their success; I suddenly understood certain human failings they display. I know you perceived this long ago.

Schmidtchen keeps very busy in theater matters. Yesterday a grand debate with Gropius over the outfitting of the theater. Schmidtchen wants a purely mechanical theater. Out of the question, as I had foreseen; and besides, that is not what I have in mind. It would cost thousands, and Gropius must watch every penny. The general situation is catastrophic. It is a miracle that an undertaking like ours should even be possible in Dessau in times like these.

Schmidtchen wants to do something with the Theater, Schawinsky also has ideas, but I am going to insist on my plan for a type stage. Other projects will have to take a back seat for a while. But if I find myself blocked by the egotistic interests of others, my days here will be over. I am very firm on that.

As soon as I have the equipment ready—a curtain, leotards, fabric—the time will have come for me to hold an open meeting and invite participation. Then I shall stir up the workshops and theatricalize the Bauhaus.

To Tut

Dessau
November 15, 1925

Gray, dreary Sunday. In Dessau a dance and the carpenters' fête for the Bauhaus. Crazy goings-on, which ended only after the theater; many others there: Klee, Kandinsky, Moholy.

To Tut

Dessau
November 28, 1925

How are you? Muche agreed that the Scorpios are having a rough time. It is bitterly cold in my studio, also in the others. This can't go on; I would rather return to Weimar, where at least it's warm.

All sorts of excitement: Kiessler may commission me to go to Paris, Berlin, and Dresden to gather material for an exhibition in the United States. It is snowing.

I am sending you the theater book. On my suggestion the Bauhaus members are going to Halle dressed alike: blue mechanics' overalls, the masters included, and all the girls and women in pants. Will you come along? I shall have no money unless Otte invites me for the fourth and fifth of December. We must work like crazy if we hope to have a performance ready by next fall. And we must have something, because that is when the decision will be made.

To Otto Meyer

Dessau
Mid-December 1925

Between pauses for breath—yes, between—Berlin, Dessau, and Weimar, I am mailing you the Bauhaus books. You will be delighted with Moholy's photography and probably also with

Klee's book. Perhaps you will like the theater book, and the Mondrian I have not yet read myself. But will you agree with the author of the book of photographs when he wipes the slate clean of anything that might be called painting? That is the crucial question at the Bauhaus, and in part of the art world as well; in some places the issue has already been dropped. Moholy is so aggressive on this score that he sees, like a soldier, only the enemy (painting) and his victory (photography). Since at the moment he is also Gropius' prime minister, he possesses great, almost enormous, influence in the art world. He himself continues to paint, a sort of copying, with an eye on the demands of artistic circles. He had his photographs enlarged, and I must admit they are very beautiful. But I can also picture one of my costumes enlarged, or one of my paintings, and I would find them beautiful, too. Does painting still have a raison d'être in the face of such photographic achievements?

Yes, it does, I say, if only for the sake of contradiction. True, when I see such marvels as Man Ray's "Hand with an Egg" I am tempted to try such figural things myself. Ray, by the way, gave Moholy his inspiration. The traditional painter and the photographic painter: arrest them both and put them in a jail cell; whose vital existence will be more threatened? That of the man with the camera or of the man without? Have you any suggestions for saving painting? I must undertake figural experiments. I am burning with eagerness to get started!

The general economic depression is spreading. People are saying that anyone who hangs on until spring will be ruined, too! The art market has collapsed entirely. The theaters are going bankrupt. Where are we headed? I think of the Russian Revolution; during the wildest confusion the theater remained intact, and afterwards it actually developed into a very important factor, unique in Europe. In Russia the theater has once more become a "moral institution" in Schiller's sense, a tribunal of world history. In France one has the theater of esprit, of grace and playfulness; what about Germany? Will the concept of "metaphysical theater" I have in mind make sense to anyone? For that is where I see things happening, and where I should like to put my energies to work.

I know that the ballet would be a triumphal success. Some

184

of the costumes must be redesigned; that requires money, which is so scarce at the moment. I am constantly on the lookout for possibilities. The success of the ballet was overwhelming and so it continues to this day, because there is nothing else like it, either in conception or in precision of execution. And it had appeal for everyone, because it adhered to a single line, from the conventional to the abstract; it had a great deal to offer, something for everyone. It is as far from the body dance of modern dancers as from the ever more naked ornamental kitsch found in revues.

My plan is to begin here with a theatrical ABC; I want to create a theater of types, I have more ideas than I know what to do with. But it is so hard to undertake this sort of project when one has tasted the independence of the artist, and suddenly finds oneself forced to rely on collaborators. Still, Gropius is building me a stage which will be a pleasure to use, despite its small dimensions.

The artistic climate here cannot support anything that is not the latest, the most modern, up-to-the-minute. Dadaism, circus, *variété*, jazz, hectic pace, movies, America, airplanes, the automobile. Those are the terms in which people here think. In painting the non-representational, the "abstract" = non-objective, all the stronger because of the outwardly powerful positions of Kandinsky and Moholy. I am considered a man from bygone days, or perhaps a deserter, because I paint "classicistically." The artistic trend in that direction is labelled "reactionary." That's the Bauhaus opinion. Elsewhere things are viewed differently. My recent exhibition in Berlin brought in many enthusiastic letters, which does not usually happen.

The theatrical concerns naturally tie in closely with this prevailing mood at the Bauhaus. See the aforementioned slogans and attitudes—humorous pieces, Dadaism, mechanical experiments, cinematographic effects are the current rage. Any sort of emotion, sentiment, and in fact anything serious is passed off with a smile. However, I plan to try something in that line, treated in a very special way. For the time being I shall begin with the simplest musical sounds and dance movements. The dramatic element will come later, bit by bit; I shall be cautious, letting it develop of itself if possible. Since beginnings are supposed to be fun, I should like to begin in that vein. Therefore: stories taken from newspapers or any other useful sources. But what sort of fun? Dada is fun—I can imagine a gracious, emotion-splitting form of Dada's being attractive, cheerful. But I can already hear the Bauhaus people's reaction! They would reject it for the same reasons that make many people prefer the movies or the *variété* to the theater. A spirit of anti-pathos? Are decisive transformations underway, or are these attitudes merely ephemeral? Is urban man all that matters nowadays? What really counts, man or progress? Does progress change the human qualities, and can these shrivel in its absence? "A man who seeks progress looks for new possibilities; one who seeks God looks to fulfill those he sees before him" (Keyserling). It is worth noting that the sculptor Barlach, the best modern dramatist we know, is a God-seeker, and his search has helped him find a new form. Yet he is considered representative of only one aspect of modern art. The other aspect is represented by the writers who treat contemporary events in a political and social vein.

Experimental theater again: I want to continue with the geometry of the dance, using carpets with various geometrical patterns (chessboard, etc.) on which to dance. Each field will be numbered, and during the dance the numbers will be called out. A similar procedure with the instruments (the simplest percussions), and likewise with the colors, the space, and so on. I realize such hints do not mean much. They must be carried out. The immediate goal: discover the principles that govern the different areas: space, movement, form, color. More of this later.

Yesterday Kandinsky gave the Bauhaus lecture. In places he spoke rather pointedly, thus arousing my inner resistance. The natural development of art toward non-objective abstraction. Everything else mere regression, reaction, romanticism— Biedermeier, Goethe's *Faust,* the Kurfürstendamm in Berlin (!). But romanticism is still alive, in the cinema. Three heroic types: the criminal and the detective; the athlete and the artiste; and the eccentric, the latter being the synthetic artist. In traditional art one had: content, romanticism, the ideal. In the new art one has: form, concreteness, calculation.

Kandinsky spoke fluently, likably. Pan-Europe would be equivalent to a "pan-art." International. He also spoke with resignation of his own isolation, of the fate of the modern artist.

Endless food for thought. But I am dying to speak a word on this subject myself.

To Tut

Berlin

December 15, 1925

Tremendous difficulties in Dessau as a result of the miserable economic situation. The masters will in any case have to take a ten percent cut in salary.

I still have not heard whether you are recovered. I think about you a great deal. I guess I just want to have you beautiful!

To Tut

Berlin

December 24, 1925

I am writing because I happen to be in the mood and it is so beautifully peaceful here (in the Romanisches Café, early in the morning), and I have no idea how it will strike you when I return from Berlin all battered and burned out. I have more or less overcome the initial unhappiness and am on top of the situation again. To get on top and stay there is the be-all and end-all in this curious struggle for "life," which in spite of everything, or perhaps just for spite (and especially in adversity), I refuse to stop trying to seize by the tail. Hand in hand with you we wish ourselves a relatively merry Christmas.

To Andreas Weininger

Weimar

December 1925

The motto for our lottery, says Otto, is, "Something must be done."

Long live the world stage, long live life and so on, long live writing and in-fighting, long live the Ilm and the film, and long live the Elbe, well, I'll be!

So Andy, take heart! Wine and song, etc. In five hours the world will be one year older—I shall be in Dessalia on the 6th or the 8th (at the latest); enjoy yourself, and a thousand greetings! Cheers!

To Otto Meyer

Weimar

January 3, 1926

Lest I forget an important matter, I shall begin with it. Some time ago Kandinsky conducted a survey. On a piece of paper were a circle, a square, and a triangle, and one was supposed to assign the colors red, blue, and yellow to them. At the time I did not participate. The consensus, by I do not know how many votes was: the circle blue, the square red, the triangle yellow. All the experts agree on the yellow triangle, but not on the others. Instinctively I always make the circle red and the square blue. I am not quite sure of Kandinsky's explanation, but it goes something like this: the circle is cosmic, absorbent, feminine, soft; the square is active, masculine. My contrary contentions: a red circular surface (or ball) occurs in a positive sense (actively) in nature: the red sun, the red apple (orange), the surface of red wine in a glass. The square does not occur in nature; it is abstract ("Nature works to destroy the straight line" — Delacroix) or metaphysical, for which blue is the proper color.

Kandinsky builds an entire system on this dogma: every curved line he considers part of a circle, therefore blue; every straight line red, every point yellow, and so on with variations ad infinitum—when he lectures, only a few shy voices dare to ask why. And when "neutrals" free of preconceptions also decide that red = circle and blue = square, I can only ask: why do I paint my circles red? Should I sacrifice my instinct to a rational explanation?

Mondrian: he is really the god of the Bauhaus, and Doesburg is his prophet. Perhaps Doesburg's fanatical role as an agitator and prophet has distorted what started out a good thing. Mondrian *is* a god, and what he does is perfectly consistent with a certain type of Dutch architecture—and in fact I see Mondrian's "pictures" as typically Dutch, despite the absolute for which they strive. It is probably immaterial that economic necessity compels Mondrian to paint flower still lifes, which he embarrassedly pushes out of the way when one visits his studio. And what else could he do, given his practically unique contribution to painting? It is like the Russian Malevitch, whose great feat consisted of presenting a red square as a picture, and who said with irony that now one could go back to cherubs' heads again. At the Bauhaus, which always wants to keep up with the times, a saying is making the rounds that Square + Flower = Art.

In point of fact, anything contemporary is automatically great and noble; that is, those two categories no longer exist; they are passé, like the ideal. The contemporary alone is great. And timeliness is the current fad. Kandinsky's lecture still has me upset; I plan to reply (indirectly) in a talk I shall be working on soon, "Theater at the Bauhaus." A hint: I shall be obliged to say critical things about the Bauhaus, and to discuss basic principles, in order to break the ground for my projected theatrical endeavors. For my theater must do more than mirror the prevailing chaos and fence with its own shadow. It must—God grant it success!—offer "enchanting pedagogy," and become a Schillerian tribunal. Oh, I so hope we succeed with the basic conception, the setting, the language, the speakers, and the audience! A theater thus conceived could become a powerful force for order at the Bauhaus. I must give it my all in the days to come—put aside my painting until further notice, until autumn and winter, I fear.

Diary

January 17, 1926

In a chaotic period like this the aesthetes can think of nothing better to do than to laugh at the times, to indulge in nonsense until something different and better develops.

The ethical minds are busy developing it, or at least looking for possibilities.

Nihilism—play—dance of death. Construction—seriousness—
new life.

January 28, 1926

It is already being shouted from the rooftops that soul,
pathos, ethics are nowadays considered suspect. But the babies
are being thrown out with the bath; for there is soul and *soul,*
pathos and *pathos,* ethics and *ethics;* and the likelihood is that
what survives will not be the extreme reaction to those things,
but the rediscovery of the old values in response to that extreme reaction.

To Tut

Dessau

February 5, 1926

We are making gradual headway here. My part of planning
the Theater is finished. Which is good, for now the others have
to adapt and adjust to it. But the work progresses slowly
because every point must be fought out. I handed Gropius an
inventory of things we need, only a fraction of which we can
receive right away, of course.

I am in charge of the *Fasching* party, which will take place
in February or March, and I am calling it "The White Festival."
Four-fifths white and one-fifth color. This will be: "dappled,
splotched, and striped." Why don't you want to come?

It turns out that the houses will in fact not be ready before
June. In Weimar marches and demonstrations are taking place,
under the motto "Not a Penny for the Duke," etc.

Postcard to Tut

Dessau

March 16, 1926

Almost every day we work until two or three in the
morning. Even so, little gets accomplished. But perhaps the
party will turn out better than anyone expects. Don't you give

up hope, and I shan't either. I want you to come. At all costs. And furthermore, you must be beautiful. A colorful vest with silk ribbons, all colors. Silver? Seems somewhat cold. Quite a rivalry has sprung up among the women: I was designing the Kandinska's costume (in the form of a little Kandinsky); the Gropia floated off with the sketches and was no more to be seen. I am curious.

The weaving group, or Gunda, really, is preparing fine cakes, beautiful flowers, eggs. Everybody is busy. So of course there have to be some minor scandals. The Klees and Feiningers are coming, too, aren't they?

To Tut

Dessau
March 22, 1926

Did you arrive home safely? Have you gotten over Dessau; where does the emotional thermometer stand at the moment? From Weimar things must certainly take on another aspect. Just as I look different from a distance. I did dance triadically, after all; that always used to arouse you.

Will you demand the totally triadic next? Will you refuse to speak to me until then? Today an inquiry arrived from the ducal music director in Donaueschingen. Hindemith has suggested that the ballet be performed there for the music festival in July. Now I must act quickly.

Today much dismantling and carting away, doing of accounts—perhaps a deficit after all, unless something is left over from the carpenters' fête. Today we filmed, I in Hart's costume, along with Lis Beyer, and Schmidtchen as a clown. I am curious to see how it comes out; certainly a good study.

The latest: on April 1 Neufert is off to join Bartning. That will certainly have repercussions for the new building, for Neufert was completely in charge. Poor Gropius?

To Tut

Dessau

Palm Sunday, March 28, 1926

Thank you for your Sunday letter. So I shall remain here over Easter and work very hard. Shall straighten out everything with the dancers. May end up dividing the music for the "Triadic" in three—Stuckenschmidt—Toch—Hindemith; that would correspond to the three parts. Donaueschingen is a fine thing! I shall try to expand the three parts (series) of the ballet so that each one can stand on its own.

To Tut

Dessau

April 1, 1926

This morning at eight I went over to the new building. The construction is still behind schedule, the mortar and plaster still wet, won't be ready before June, but I shall certainly be able to move in before then. In the morning sun it is lovely, of course. So many things are coming together. April, May, and June will be spent on the ballet. After moving out of the Mariannenstraße apartment with a handcart today, I shall set myself up in the museum tower. Shall wake up much earlier and get right up, in general start a new life. April 1 and the change will see to that. Instead of coffee for breakfast I shall have yoghurt. Am wearing an old but brightly colored slicker and a felt hat which transform me, and quite becomingly, too. Have sloughed off my winter skin; but of course they are old things.

Your, my, our flowers are still fresh; I took them with me to the studio.

To Tut

Dessau

April 16, 1926

This summer there is to be no Klee-class. But the weaving workshop put in a request for "formal instruction." So Gropius asks Muche. The weavers reject Muche as an instructor and—two birds with one stone—declare that Muche is "not needed in the workshop." Apparently the written declaration was sharply worded; Gunda is not involved; it all comes from the weavers, who are now prepared for the worst; the student body is backing them and considers this a test of whether it still has any say or not.

To Otto Meyer

Dessau

April 22, 1926

These are the concrete matters I have to report: it looks possible, or from fairly probable to certain, that part of the "Triadic Ballet," the best part, will be performed in July at the musical festival in Donaueschingen. Since a noted composer, Paul Hindemith, has taken over the musical side and is writing mechanical music for it—that is to say, music for a player piano—through his name and one-tenth through mine and a few tenths through that of a famous woman dancer we hope to engage, the desired triumphal progress of the ballet is practically assured.

I am now immersed in theater, contrary to my intentions, and painting seems a dim, faraway memory. Will this harm me? If the ballet does not succeed—and I have ambitious plans in case it does—then I shall simply creep home to my painting, which "still and all" has its beauties and its advantages.

Diary

April 1926

Do not complain about mechanization; instead enjoy precision!

Artists are willing to convert the drawbacks and perils of their mechanistic age into the silver lining of exact metaphysics. If today's artists love the machine, technology, and organization, if they aspire to precision and reject anything vague and dreamy, this implies an instinctive repudiation of chaos and a longing to find the form appropriate to our times, to pour new wine into the old bottles: to formulate them in a unique and unprecedented manner. That is saying and demanding a great deal.

There is no universal recipe. In the beginning there is only the path the individual takes at his own risk. Perhaps he will remain a loner, perhaps his path will become a major thoroughfare. Anything original usually proves identical with the elemental, and this in turn with the simple. One can begin over and over again with the ABC, one can always return to the basic elements of art, since simplicity contains the energy essential to all innovation. Simplicity, understood as the fundamental and the typical elements from which anything complex or particular develops, simplicity understood as a slate wiped clean of the eclecticist embellishments of all periods and styles; simplicity should show the way—into the future!

To Tut

Dessau
April 27, 1926

I have stopped smoking! I have introduced Tut-days on which I really do not smoke. And I am gradually cutting it out entirely. As a result I am already getting better and better.

Yesterday evening Hindemith arrived, and now he is already on his way to Frankfurt; he was coming from Prague. Just as before, he is deeply committed to the project and will certainly produce something good. He has very firm opinions and rejects many aspects of modern music. Very strong-minded. So it is in the best possible hands.

Hm, moonshine. No one shines here, it just stinks of circus. (Refinery.) No, you would have to look long and hard for any romanticism in this place. This morning Gunda said, "Isn't life awful?" In the evening Moholy: "Isn't life beeootifool? Vat do yoo tink, Schlemmarr?"

To Tut

Dessau
May 1, 1926

Meeting yesterday. Five minutes before it opened, the students delivered a declaration saying that they stand united behind the weavers. Muche wanted to find out the masters' position, before he "drew the consequences." Kandinsky, Moholy, and Breuer criticized the weavers' tactics. The others said nothing, or at least nothing in Muche's favor. Today the weavers' group and the student representatives will be summoned to hear how impossibly they have conducted this affair. They are so furious that things look very bad for Muche. Gropius is handling both sides very calmly. All this was preceded by a discussion of finances: the deficit, economy measures, making full use of all our resources, no extravagances. The overture to the Muche Case.

To Tut

Dessau
May 2, 1926

I must admit the nightingales sing beautifully in Dessau. Heard them for the first time. Yesterday was May 1 and we were allowed to take the day off. No teaching. At six in the morning I drove to Wörlitz with Gunda, a good hour's drive, a lovely and pleasant atmosphere in Wörlitz. Thought of you a great deal and wished you were there.

Oskar Schlemmer in Dresden? An exhibition or in person? No! Moholy is giving a lecture at the Salon Fides, where my pictures were also supposed to go. Grand "Internationale" in Dresden. Bauhaus not in a body; Moholy and Kandinsky were in Dresden. Moholy is now back here.

To Tut

Dessau
May 19, 1926

Yesterday Gropius' birthday; an unusually nice mood downstairs in the Theater workshop. He was very happy with his reception. Will tell you more later.

Postcard to Tut

Dessau
May 20, 1926

Glory be! Advance of 1000 marks for Donaueschingen, so work on the costumes can begin immediately. The directors very obliging in other ways, too. Still have heaps to do if I hope to get out of here by Whitsuntide.

Now: to find a female dancer!

Dairy

July 5, 1926

Notes on the performance of the "Triadic Ballet" at the music festival in Donaueschingen:

Why ballet? Which, they say, is dead or dying. Because the heyday of ballet may be long since past, and the old courtly ballet is certainly dead, but today's entirely changed circumstances give good cause to believe that this particular art form can be revived. Now we have eurythmics, the chorus of movement developed out of them, and a new cult of strength and beauty; one is thus justified in reviving their opposites: the brightly colored masquerades once so popular with the people; theatrical costume dance; and also ballet, to be born in a new form. For human beings will always love bright games, disguises, masquerades, dissimulation, artificiality, as they will always love any festive, eye-catching, colorful reflection of life. This speechless theatrical dance, this non-committal Muse who says nothing yet means everything, contains possibilities for expression and articulation which an opera or a play could not offer in such purity; theatrical dance, originally the form from which opera and the drama sprang, is free of constraints and thus predestined to furnish time and again the starting point for a theatrical renaissance.

Why "triadic"? Because three is a supremely important, prominent number, within which egotistic one and dualistic contrast are transcended, giving way to the collective. Following it in importance comes the five, then the seven, and so on. Derived from trias = triad, the ballet should be called a dance of the threesome, ringing the changes on one, two, and three. One female and two male dancers: twelve dances and eighteen costumes. Other such threesomes are: form, color, space; the three dimensions of space: height, depth, breadth; the basic forms: ball, cube, pyramid; the primary colors: red, blue, yellow. The threesome of dance, costume, and music. And so on.

196

Why Hindemith? Because here a musician who creates "directly from the imagination and mystic depths of our soul" has found a theme with which he can range from the cheerful grotesque to full pathos, and he has attained such mastery over his musical handiwork that he adds a spiritual dimension to everything he touches.

And why a player piano? Because the mechanical instrument corresponds to the stereotypal dance style, dictated in part by the costumes, if not set as general objective; this in contrast to the spiritual and dramatic exuberance which music is usually used to convey these days. On the other hand, this music provides a parallel to the costumes, which follow the mathematical and mechanical outlines of the body. In addition, the doll-like quality of the dances corresponds to the music-box quality of the music and this should furnish the unity implied by the concept of "style."

One might ask if the dancers should not be real puppets, moved by strings, or better still, self-propelled by means of a precision mechanism, almost free of human intervention, at most directed by remote control? *Yes!* It is only a question of time and money. The effect such an experiment would produce can be found described in Heinrich Kleist's essay on the marionette.

To Otto Meyer

Dessau

August 27, 1926

I have very exciting weeks behind me, and I am still under their spell. Donaueschingen was followed by Frankfurt am Main, with performances of a revue and the ballet; then Berlin, where the ballet was integrated with a larger revue. Everything at a good clip; in the middle we had the move from Weimar to Dessau—the house unfurnished, children crying, Bauhaus troubles, and so on. Vacation out of the question. Maybe in the winter. My need and desire for it great.

197

To Willi Baumeister

Dessau

December 21, 1926

I was sorry not to see you among the great throng of guests at the Bauhaus dedication. I hope you can make up for the missed visit some other time, and I should like to invite you right now to consider the Schlemmer house your headquarters. Stuttgart was well represented; we were very gratified, and our new friend and house-sharer Hannes Meyer-Basel is a great addition. He also made a definite impression on the chief Bauhaus people, thanks to his sound opinions and his winning ways. The aestheticism of the other houses was getting on his nerves, and he was delighted to find that we had children; perhaps they also reminded him of his own, and he had a grand old time playing with them. We had good talks with Elsaesser and May from Frankfurt; they were among the survivors, those who stayed another day; the majority of the big names were present only for the large gathering. I saw little of them, because I was so taken up with the Theater. Its debut did not take place under favorable auspices. And no wonder: the previous day the theater was still full of workmen and scaffoldings, since Gropius had waited too long before putting the necessary resources at the disposal of this fifth wheel on the Bauhaus cart. Now that it is more or less ready, we can finally get to work, and I have hopes, despite the undeniably difficult situation, due largely to the shifting and unpredictable make-up of the ensemble. We have painters, young people just out of school, an occasional dancer, an actor, temporarily; and with these people one is supposed to stage revolutionary theater. Perhaps time will change all that; more and more people are joining the department, and we may gradually succeed in putting together a group capable of action and good enough for performances even outside Dessau (for what good is Dessau to us!).

In the face of these struggles with the material world, with people's lack of initiative and other inadequacies, and with financial restrictions, my other, perhaps better, half always comes forward and reminds me that I used to be a painter. Oh, happy colleagues in the house next door (Klee, Kandinsky,

198

Feininger): they can lead a relatively contemplative painter's existence and spend a few hours a week setting forth to their pupils the theoretical bases of their work! If the Theater is to be effective, I must give it everything I have; in addition, this field is so many-faceted and my human material so inadequate that I must also act as educator, a task which almost exceeds the capability of one person (especially when he has another soul within his breast). I do often consider changing this otherwise comfortable Bauhaus-Dessau constellation, and I confess that an offer to go to New York did not leave me cold. So now you have a brief sketch of my loves and sorrows here.

Postcard to Otto Meyer

Dessau
March 31, 1927

Wife and children are going to Lugano, and Hannes Meyer will share part of the house. I am a straw, art, and life widower.

To Tut

Dessau
April 1, 1927

Dearest Tullbritsch, last night at ten the Hannes Meyers arrived. Two nice, chubby children, bigger than ours, the wife small, lively, all of them brunette. Slept yesterday for the first time and well at the Prellers'. Don't have everything over there yet; office and household things still have to come.

To Tut

Dessau
April 7, 1927

How was it? I am so impatient for your first account! Yesterday I was with you in spirit and hoped you were getting your first look at Lake Lugano and breaking out with oh's and ah's. Is that how it was? Write! write! write! What do the children say, what are they up to? Endless questions.

Today I am moving back from the studio, after much

back-and-forth with Meyer. I have decided I prefer to keep the studio in the house, living upstairs in the Lena room, which is fairly empty because they can't get their big armoires up the stairs; and I have the roof garden, which I plan to fix up.

April 9, 1927

"The Cathedral of Socialism." The original phrasing was: "The State Bauhaus, founded after a catastrophic war, amidst the chaos of revolution and at the peak of an emotion-laden explosive style in art, will begin by first providing a center for all those who, committed to the future and defiant of established orders, wish to build the Cathedral of Socialism."

This sentence was taken from a programmatic statement written for a Bauhaus exhibition in 1923, and supposed to provide a chronological survey of the developmental stages the Bauhaus had passed through. The "first" makes this clear enough. It is thus meaningless and malicious to lift the sentence from context and present it as the manifesto of the Bauhaus. The sentences that follow make it perfectly clear that this developmental stage was soon passed and was replaced by other objectives, just as the political makeup of the Bauhaus, if indeed it ever had one, soon changed: among the students one could find rightists as well as leftists; or the political wave yielded to a religious one.

One need not deny that theorizing was going on at the Bauhaus and still is, and the Bauhaus therefore mirrors a piece of our times and their history. And then, too: didn't the majority of the German people want to build the Cathedral of Socialism in 1918? Weren't the revolution and the constitutional democracy launched in the name of a people's state? And what is a people's state other than socialism? Furthermore: does socialism necessarily imply the Social Democrats or the Communist Party? Isn't socialism a concept, an ethic, not limited to any specific party?

To Tut

Things are fine here. We are gradually getting used to one another. I have now set up my studio with Lux Feininger. I sleep upstairs. The Meyers are becoming acclimatized. Sundays I am now regularly invited to dinner at the Klees'. Fridays at the Feiningers'. Coffee at noon at the Schepers', who are overjoyed with the house. And it is certainly going to be very handsome. Here everything is turning green with a vengeance. The children are missed, by me as well. A year is a long time, but all things eventually come to an end.

I am a stickler for neatness now. Very dignified, clean: first-class order. I am sure I shall get a lot of work done, since I am completely in charge of how I spend my time; total independence, or, shall we simply say, changed circumstances of life. The justification for this period must be: work, find a new vantage point, right?

Piscator was here; unfortunately too one-sidedly political, but compelling in his way. He does not understand what we are doing, considers it frivolity. Yet he thinks—he hinted at this— that we might establish an actors' school in Berlin together, but of course with a strong leftist orientation.

To Otto Meyer

Yes, it is of course high time that we saw each other and talked. I am placing my hopes on the summer, when I shall be going to Italy by way of the Ticino in any case; for my wife and children are in the Ticino, in Agnuzzo, near Lugano, for a good while, a whole year in fact! The house has been rented for that long, and Tut wants to enjoy relative freedom with the children this year, because next year they have to start school, and she figures this is the last chance. But there was also an element of flight in her decision, flight from conditions in Dessau, some of which are not too pleasant, due to shortage of money; there was also Tut's love for change, for roaming around, the nomadic life. By the way, I am not completely banished from the house; I still have the studio, a bedroom, and the roof garden. So far I have felt all right without the family. I shall have more time to myself and shall thus be able to work more.

And Hannes Meyer is also here. He came for the dedication, when I made his acquaintance. He severely criticized various aspects of the Bauhaus. He frankly used such phrases as "glorified arts and crafts," "Dornach," "decorative aesthetics," and often he was right. He stayed a day or two, longer than the other guests, and met several members of the Bauhaus. He obviously made a good impression, and one had the sense he could contribute something the Bauhaus needs. Gropius was looking for a man for the architecture department he was finally setting up. He tried to get the architect Mart Stam, who was here with Hannes Meyer. Stam refused, thinking he lacked the necessary pedagogic skills and commitment. Hannes Meyer received an invitation to visit Dessau again and feel out the architecture students. He presented a small exhibition of his works, among them a very interesting project for the League of Nations in Geneva.

One motto of his work as an architect is: "organization of needs." But this is to be understood in the broadest sense, and certainly does not exclude spiritual needs. He said that what impressed him most here were the pictures (mine and Moholy's), not the rooms in which they were hung. He especially liked some of my abstract things, at least much more wholeheartedly than the more recent ones. He was not interested in Klee; he says Klee must be in a perpetual trance; Feininger does not appeal to him, either. Kandinsky because of the theoretical underpinnings. In terms of character he feels closest to Moholy, although he is very critical toward much about him—his manner (officious), his false teachings (which the students also see as such and reject); he was not interested in Muche's steel-construction new building, since steel is the least important element in it. Gropius can count himself fortunate to have this honest fellow as the latest feather in his cap.

We have done all sorts of things with the Theater, including a public lecture on "Elements of the Theater," with demonstrations on the stage, and it would be a worthwhile line to pursue.

But since the Theater is considered peripheral, something to be enjoyed but kept on a short tether, it will not really have a chance to develop, unless I assume the mien of a robber baron; for this reason I remain skeptical, despite my devotion and enthusiasm.

To Tut

Dessau
April 25, 1927

The Theater is staging a mini-revolution, aha, aha! The central issue: a Schlemmer theater or a Bauhaus theater! I say it is all up to them. Schmidtchen is the spokesman for mechanical theater, I for figural theater! I have declared I refuse to let myself be pinned down or be dictated to. I was doing mechanistic theater when Schmidtchen was still in swaddling clothes.

All is well in the house. We are getting along amicably. We often play ball on all the terraces, which is great fun and brings an unusual spark of life into the neighborhood. Meyer often gets very high-spirited. But his wife seems troubled. He certainly is hardheaded, a man of principle, and for all his love, totally inconsiderate. So you see, all that glisters is not gold.

To Tut

Dessau
May 1927

Theater! The State of Anhalt has approved an extra 200 marks for our Magdeburg production. Within the Bauhaus we can claim a moral victory; Gropius, Pia, and others are pleased.

I shall edit the third number of the Bauhaus journal, devoted to the theater. It is supposed to be brought out in time for the Dance Congress on June 21.

Female dancers are hard to find. Doubly hard if one cannot give monetary assurances. We are working on a "play": *The House of Py.*" Wrote it myself. The structure will do nicely. Very difficult to find the "word." Everyone was looking for a story. In the end it was left up to me again, and I have the first act ready. After an unsatisfactory evening of discussion, during which no one had any good suggestions, I presented the first act the next evening, and it was accepted. It is strange to do a play this way, but it seems to be working out. On July 15 there may be a summer party, and the premiere can take place then. People keep joining us; we are a good-sized group, and the mood is as promising as when we were working on the elements of theater.

A smear in the *Centralanzeiger* on Muche, Meyer, Kandinsky, Moholy.

To Tut

Dessau
Mid-May 1927

I took along this piece of stationery when I went to Magdeburg Thursday, planning to write to you in a quiet moment. But none came, and today it is Monday, and our moment of glory is already past. Well, our booth was the most modern at the exhibition, which is not saying much, at such a second-rate affair. A great deal of mediocrity and poor staging. No unifying line. Still, instructive and a chance to see all sorts of things I had not seen previously.

Here we are not yet ready, and the lack of a technical supervisor can be felt acutely. I cannot handle everything. Well, we were also invited to a banquet paid for by the city, from three-thirty to seven; I sat with Molzahn.

Gropius is doing a theater project for Piscator, who might collaborate with me; but if he tries to bring in politics while excluding modern form, I shall have to decline.

I have—had—a bad cold all over again, from which a night of working straight through in the completely unheated exposition hall did not exactly help me recover. Still have a fever. Shall make myself another grog.

To Tut

Dessau
May 1927

May Revolution at the Bauhaus, under the leadership of Volger. Against the egotistic masters and the lazy students.

Demands have been formulated which must be accepted, or the student representatives will resign. Meyer, Gunda, Scheper, and I enjoy a position of trust. Kandinsky angry, Gropius in a fix. Likewise a Breuer crisis. I wonder what will come of it.

In the theater we are hard at work on the models. Good photos by Lux Feininger. Schawinsky is also back, but will probably leave again, since he will not get a studio. Meyer has become a sort of Bauhaus Marquis Posa, supposed to help with everything, our new broom.

Well, that's the general gossip, which may interest you.

To Tut

Dessau
June 1, 1927

A play is actually in the making. Ironic that I, the one who am most skeptical towards the whole business, should turn out to be doing everything, writing the play, demonstrating it for everybody, directing it—at the moment I am irreplaceable! Parts of it will certainly be good; when I have it all together I shall send it to you: *The House of Py, or the Home in the Stars! Dedicated to My Wife.* The roles in the play: astrologer, female dancer, young man, revolutionary, passer-by, general, his wife, their child, the mysterious one, three thieves. The first act can stand as is, the second is one-third done. Often we rehearse until late at night, starting at eight. Individual rehearsals in the morning, often in the afternoon as well, from three to seven.

To Tut

Dessau
June 5, 1927

Theater: I may cancel our *House of Py,* against the advice of the others, and devote myself entirely to gesture dance, triadic and figural matters. The only way to provide an opportunity for Siedhoff and others to earn some money, to develop my ideas, and to get out of the present mess. Now I am bending all my efforts toward having something ready for the Dance Congress.

Am very busy now with the journal. Then a lecture for Magdeburg. Then many rehearsals. It looks as if more and more want to join the theater workshop.

What is my life like? Well, it just goes along. One day after another. Money troubles are irritating.

Postcard to Tut

Magdeburg
June 24, 1927

Tomorrow my talk, with photographs. The Dance Congress: Laban is a good man (the only one of the committee besides me to come). Still, this committee will remain in existence for future undertakings, congresses and such. Too bad we could not perform anything; there was a dance competition, and we would have done very well. I am staying until Sunday morning; Saturday thirty Bauhaus people are coming, and I am to head the delegation.

To Tut

Dessau
July 2, 1927

I am strongly tempted to stay here for two weeks and do some painting, once the vacation begins and Meyer and Gunda are away and absolute peace returns. I would enjoy my vacation much more that way than if I left without having worked. When will I get another chance? What do you think?

Yesterday the Schepers gave a farewell party in honor of Muche. Speeches. Presentation of a portfolio of contributions by the masters. At the beginning a sort of funeral. Later dancing. And finally general high spirits, once the stiffness-experts had left. Meyer flung himself down on the floor, ripped off his jacket, and shouted joyfully that now one could be human!

To Tut

Dessau
July 5, 1927

It is midnight and I have just come home from a rehearsal. The performance will be very funny. Many people are participating in the "Figural Cabinet." Holding the company together takes some doing. I had to break off work on the "play" because we would have needed until autumn. But the experiment we started on was very valuable, and others realize that it makes better sense to use what we already have than to keep experimenting. Now we are concentrating on dance, pantomine, and things that are easily transportable, and that is all to the good. The "play" had a gigantic apparatus, making it almost impossible to perform anywhere else. And would have cost a great deal of money for equipment, leaving aside the fact that most of our people cannot speak lines. A tremendous amount of work, which has a slightly paralyzing effect in the long run. No, in spite of everything, prospects do not look too bad for the Theater. Several people from the beginners' course also want to join the company. Still, I shall adopt a different policy next semester. Maybe. More courses in the form of lectures; dance, not much workshop. And leave myself time for painting.

To Tut

Dessau
July 10, 1927

July 9th we had a great time! A brilliant performance. Which was reflected in the dance that followed in the cafeteria, marked by unusual high spirits and exuberance. The Theater has gained great prestige. And psychologically it provided an excellent conclusion before the vacation. The Mayor and his wife were also there. The box office receipts will come close to 200 marks, which I plan to distribute among the cast. The whole thing caught on like wildfire! A repeat performance! The "grotesque," the diver was also good. I rehabilitated and legitimized myself as a dancer. The "Figural Cabinet" without the cabinet, just twelve figures, went off beautifully. Too bad you were not there to bathe yourself in the glory and be able to regain a little belief in me! For the final effect was really good: to get that off the ground, to begin at eight sharp and finish at ten sharp, with twelve numbers, meanwhile keeping all the little elves backstage in line. All they said was that it was clear, and drastically so, that only I could dance my roles. Even a dubious Gropius cannot deny that.

The party in the cafeteria lasted until three, then a group set out for the Meyer-Schlemmer house, and there it went on until five. Frau Feininger stuck it out to the very end; she was wildly enthusiastic.

To Otto Meyer

Ascona

August 18, 1927

The incoming tide brought my arrival and various new experiences. Then came the flood of people come to see my wife. Four-headed relatives. A tumultuous young musician has just left; the tide is going out. But the children and the still considerable number of strangers provide more than enough distraction; still: "Keep smiling!" said the bird to the worm and gobbled him up.

So, staying, stranded, or just here in Ascona, are (among others): Dr. Giedion, Moholy and his wife, Marcel Breuer-Bauhaus and his wife. Another Bauhaus member and his girl-friend, Emil Ludwig, Hausenstein, who has just written five hundred pages on Rembrandt, the Cromelinck family, drama-tists, modern, formerly of Paris-Brussels. The poet Nebel of the "Sturm," various singers, barons, counts, dancers, dancing countesses, painters male and female, native Asconians and Ticinese, fishers and boatsmen, chauffeurs (do you get the picture?). Further the conductor Hermann Scherchen and his wife, the actress Gerda Müller. I know both of them. Every day I spend some time working with him on a theory of music-dance-numerology; he conceived the project, and it is stimu-lating. For both of us, I think.

The trip went well. Tut and the children are tanned and obviously thriving. The freedom and mobility one has in Ascona are unique for this area; the Asconians are used to everything, thanks to the eccentrics, saints, nature worshippers, and painters, so that nothing and no one causes so much as a raised eyebrow. In addition there is a collector here, a Baron von der Heydt, who owns the Monte Verità; and nearby Locarno is the local metropolis.

So I am involved in discussions with the abovementioned conductor, and they are to bear fruits. It began with my asking him to write music for the ballet. But he is not composing now, or only a little. He wishes I would try something new and not cling to the "Triadic"; that is easier said than done. While searching for material, an object, a motif, he came up one day with Beethoven's "Great Fugue," the whole of which he hummed for me (not played; and in general, I never hear music from him in any other form!). He has an extraordinarily high opinion of this late work of Beethoven's, and I must say that the development and variations on the theme, not to forget the dramatization, strike me as glorious. I was tempted by the idea of doing a graphic rendering of the musical notation, and he did such an interesting drawing along these lines that I instinctively asked why scores were not written this way. Harder to read, he replied. Then he suggested that this fugue be danced, without music; the dancers would follow the music in their heads, which would produce an extraordinary effect. I wondered whether music, which was after all intended to be heard, could and should be used as the inaudible basis for purely optical impressions and movements. He then continued that the whole thing should be done not with human dancers, but with mechanical shapes, and this forms the heart of most of our discussions. More important than the forms themselves is their color; he conceives of a construct of form and color in space, mechanically propelled, which would act out the fugue. He would like to make a model, but I have no tools or materials here, and besides I know only too well what a good, accurately functioning apparatus costs. It would have to be fairly large; Beethoven's size at least, I should say. Today we shall see what we can do with four colored pencils—red, blue, yellow, green—and a piece of graph paper.

Of course I also brought in Handel—he admitted that in spite of Handel's relativity in a temporal sense, music is moving in that direction. Beethoven, he thinks, was simply the more modern man; I imagine he means the more tragic one; I, on the contrary, specifically prize the untragic nature of Handel, which in him became high style.

To Otto Meyer
Ascona
End of August 1927

Today is the third beautiful, cloudless day, and one reads with surprise of torrential rains in South Germany, flooding in Berlin, etc. I am sitting on the sand at the beach, the family taking a nap in the nearby grass. It is noon and "brooding time," so to speak; brooding time for the eggs of thought, too, which I have serious doubts of laying here, since I feel rather benumbed. It is not exactly laziness; it is the back-and-forth with the family, the children often quite out of hand, and then the constant new arrivals, for now Baumeister and his wife are also here (in Locarno), as well as a Dutch architect belonging to the Stijl-Kreis (van Esteren), the Emperor's second son, Prince Friedrich, and so on. The Bauhaus, one may say, has departed. The Dutch architect, who teaches three days a month at the school that followed the Bauhaus in Weimar, is just here for a rest. The Prince is very sociable, plays with our children; rather un-Greek in stature. I met Baron von der Heydt, who owns mountains of money and land; the Hohenzollerns' banker, who owns a very handsome collection of sculpture: African masks, Buddhist art from Bali, Greek Archaic things, China, Japan. Also a Munch, an early Gauguin, and a very early van Gogh—an almost academic still life with a little pitcher and apples. And in his bedroom he has nine drawings by Seurat, some of them very beautiful, especially one, a sort of preliminary study to *Chahut*.

I have never felt much desire to do frescos. I do feel the urge to be a plastic artist. The Maggia Valley is a fantastic statuary collection, with blocks of marble lying all around; for a while I played with the idea of retiring into the farthest reaches of the valley, finding one of the many seemingly abandoned peasant houses and staying there, carving stones in a solitude that would even surpass that of Amden.

210

But such thoughts remain mere thoughts, for already I can hear theatrical and city matters calling; in October I am supposed to design the production of a modern opera at the Dresden State Opera. I shall also hear from the Frankfurt theater whether anything is being considered, and if so, what.

Here I live animalistically, unintellectually, "naturalistically." Except for expeditions with Tut, with and preferably without the children, the days are spent on the Lido, on the Lago, sleeping, eating, drinking. My colors, brushes, and paper remain untouched. Conversations with others skim along the surface. Deeper ones might be possible, but I do not seek them out.

To Otto Meyer

Ascona

September 3, 1927

Fresco: one starts thinking unmodern thoughts here—they are simply in the air. What is this, now? Atavism? Relapse? Anti-Bauhaus? I would have found it extremely gratifying to paint large figures on large surfaces, taking themes similar to those of my pictures, but lavishing particular study and experimentation on the surface quality, on the conditions set by the fresco form (the natural scale of tones that would result), the gradations of space, the statuesque quality of the figures. Themes: the horizontal, the vertical, the diagonal; standing, lying, sitting; posture, gesture, movement; the type.

To Otto Meyer

Ascona

September 15, 1927

Let me first of all explain why I am still here: the work I am doing with the conductor has advanced to the point that we are adapting a piece by Igor Stravinsky, *Les Noces,* with the idea of illustrating what happens in music by means of continuous color projections; we hope this will produce a more intense effect and avoid the complications of pantomine performed by human actors. This "adaptation" is as fascinating as it is difficult, for although the technical question is settled (the picture projections), I still have to approximate a Russian style, not my usual sort of thing. Still and all, I find the task stimulating. How can I do justice to the Russian style without losing my own in the process? Should one reject such a job? In the interest of guarding one's own preoccupations, of furthering and purifying one's own work? The question is only how I can bring the two together, this new task and my own.

I have never been as passionately eager to paint as now. Praise, purchases by museums are of course encouraging, but at the moment my mission lies clearly before me. I sense that following through on my theatrical concepts will require a temperament very different from that of the "unheroic" painter. And trying to do both things at once would produce constant inner conflict. Good intentions of organizing one's time, of being industrious, help pave the proverbial way to hell—but go ahead and make them anyway. If the idea were actually driving me and I could simply give it its head, I would be insane to relinquish such a position.

It is growing quieter in Ascona, also cooler. It seems probable that Tut will rent a little house for the winter, where she will be sheltered in truly ideal fashion.

To Tut

Dessau

Beginning of October 1927

Well, the house is freezing cold; Frau Meyer goes around in her fur coat, and even so her nose is blue.

The cafeteria is not paying its way, because the students cannot or will not buy meal tickets two weeks in advance. They prefer to go into town to eat; so it may be closed down. I am eating at the "Swiss House" again. It is so pleasant to sit at a table with a white tablecloth, having one's food brought to one, read the newspaper, and not see any Bauhaus people for a while. I have the feeling I was not made for the South. I did not feel as comfortable in Ascona as one is supposed to feel; it was time to leave. If I had stayed longer, something would have snapped. It may well be that in this harsher, fresher, more northerly clime I shall feel more myself. I am curious; let's wait and see. I still need some time to become acclimatized and find my old groove.

To Tut

Dessau
October 6, 1927

Gropius is ill. Last faculty meeting without him. Course offerings. We have no continuation course for the advanced fourth-semester students. I suggested "figural drawing," which was well received and adopted at once. So I will now probably have to give that once a week. I hope to work up this subject, which I like so much and the students greet eagerly, with the idea of formulating a "Compendium of the Figural."

To Tut

Dessau
October 17, 1927

I have just returned from my first class in figural drawing, which went very well. I am doing it quite informally, and there is plenty of material—anatomy and so on. Tomorrow the theater rehearsals begin again, every evening from nine o'clock on. I really have no idea when I shall find time for my own work.

Another person has joined the theater group, so we are now five or six. And a good spirit prevails. We are tidying up the workshop and preparing a program: a light piece, a sound piece, a salon play, something comical, something classical, something political, theater of horror, all to be done in the form of selections; the range of possible selections, so to speak, short and pithy, with the goal of a performance for the Bauhaus and friends, perhaps later on for others, to bring in some money. When funds are distributed to the workshops, the metal-working shop will get a thousand marks, for instance, the Theater twenty-five(!), likewise the sculpture workshop; we are protesting.

To Otto Meyer

Dessau

October 20, 1927

Elections are coming up here in Dessau; there will be a bitter struggle, the city government will go rightist, and when cuts come, which seems unavoidable, unnecessary items like the Theater will be the first to go. Theater, alias Schlemmer, who may be a German but counts for nothing in the Fatherland. Besides, Gropius does not exactly warm to my work. But the students are once more sounding a warning and plan to go over the whole operation with a fine-toothed comb and, we hope, with élan, borrowed at the moment from Russia, which one of them has visited, to inform himself of events there. That in itself would make quite a story.

Diary

October 1927

The mathematician lives on roots and has an easy time of it. The astronomer has a somewhat harder time; he lives on stardust and ore-bits. The sailor has his problems with naughty lusts. The chemist has it best of all; he spends his time with Anna Lissus.

To Ernst Gosebruch,
Director, Folkwang Museum, Essen

Dessau

October 13, 1927

Herr Scheper has just conveyed your regards and the gratifying news that you have decided on the picture *Römisches* ["Roman Theme"]. If you really plan to buy it, I am as grateful to you as I am pleased that you have chosen this picture. You seem to have acquired the privilege of being my "savior in time of trouble," thanks to your welcome help in days of war!

The economic depression has never been as crushing as now. But now I shall be able to work undisturbed: I have all kinds of new things I want to paint.

To Tut

Dessau

October 28, 1927

The happy event is that Essen has bought the *Römisches* for 1500 marks. That is 500 more than the asking price. The biggest sum I have ever been paid for a picture!

We are rehearsing every evening again.

To Tut

Dessau

October 31, 1927

I get sudden cravings, yes, that can happen, and there have been bad days when I couldn't see my way clear of the debts, which simply refuse to disappear; something new always comes up; even Bollmann sent a bill for the goose we had in December 1926(!). I do not know what I would have done if Gosebruch hadn't bought the picture. Now I have a breathing space, and outside it is very lovely, one day like the next.

I am so glad that you are looking forward to coming home—are you really and honestly? In that case I am looking forward, too. You know, it is not very cosy sometimes. When I see the Meyers using our coffee warmer and think involuntarily: we have one like that, too! That is just how it is.

I am buying myself a peg frame and canvas, and Scheper will prepare it for me. I have a longing to do some oil painting, am even stimulated by the motifs of the Stravinsky piece. The hair fantasies especially—they will turn out beautifully. Hair does play an important role with me, although, or perhaps because, I have none of my own.

To Frau Ida Bienert

Dessau

November 2, 1927

I was delighted to hear that you have decided to buy my *Tischgesellschaft* ["Dinner Guests"]. Experts consider this picture the best among my recent work, and it means a great deal to my highly critical friend, Otto Meyer-Amden, whom I should very much like to recommend to you. He felt the picture achieved almost effortlessly something he had long been striving for.

To Tut

Dessau

November 10, 1927

The Bauhaus is humming. Article in the newspaper. Elections for the Gemeinderat [City Council], attacks, a statistical run-down showing that too much has been spent, etc. The Mayor will have to choose sides; things are going to be hot for him; he foresees a swing to the right and bad times for the Bauhaus.

The figural drawing is going well. Excellent training in clarity and self-awareness. I am doing this for myself, after all.

To Tut

Dessau

December 1, 1927

Preparations for Saturday, December 4 (first anniversary of the Bauhaus building, and Kandinsky's birthday). "Fête of Slogans" is the title I chose for the evening, and it looks as if I have hit on something; everyone is bustling around making preparations. The introductory course students are making gigantic posters for the cafeteria, and we are rehearsing a bittersweet play, *The Weimar Affair,* with a "climax," "conflict," etc., except that everything relates to a slogan. For instance, the director *(Leiter)* becomes the ladder of feelings (*Gefühlsleiter*—Moholy), each step being a material—sausage, wire, broom, wool. Moholy uses such "ladders of feeling" in the introductory course: different materials are attached to a piece of wood, over which one runs one's fingers, eyes closed, and "feels." And of course the word cooperative, Meyer's favorite, will come in for a good laugh. The entire architecture department, in fact!

It has the potential to be great fun. All sorts of current things will be satirized. However: this morning I saw Gropius, who is in a sour mood. The elections were bad, he said, because

216

our party, the democratic one, lost half of their seats; cuts; things can't go on this way; he would like to throw the whole thing up, and so on.

To Tut

Dessau
December 5, 1927

Well, yesterday was the "Fête of Slogans," and it was really pretty good. The "play" went smoothly and pleased the audience. Unfortunately someone had forgotten to invite the masters in time; it was not done until that very afternoon. As a result, Moholy and I were the only "old ones" there. Breuer was an admiral again, Herbert Bayer a Hiasl, Bavarian; there were all sorts of good tidbits, little relevance to the announced theme, which was expressed only in gigantic written placards (made by the basic course). I was in tails, a red paper collar with white cravat which read, "the tie that binds us." On my shirtfront was a red cardboard dot which read, "the dark, sore, cardinal point." On my shoes red pieces of cloth labelled, "the loose tongue."

On the stage Schawinsky and I played the two gentlemen. Biedermeier trousers, Lohengrin armor, gray top hats with bouquets; Lux and Röseler the two servants in livery; a girl, prettier than she was talented, in crinolines.

Gunda played a servant in a white apron, on which was written, "the social question." On her back she had "social security," and "liberty, equality, fratellinité" (the Fratellini clowns are in Berlin at the moment). Kat Both came as "Naked Truth." It ended at three o'clock. Today a walk down to the Elbe, where I had not been in a long time, beautiful, cold, many field mice. Then to Kandinsky to wish him happy birthday.

To Otto Meyer

Dessau
December 6, 1927

It is too bad that you did not have a longer, more intensive discussion with Kandinsky. It would certainly have been valuable. His teaching here often arouses dissent, due to the aesthetic he tries to impose, due to his dogmatic approach: the circle is blue—and other things (but that can be blamed on the generally contentious atmosphere around here). He is our great lawyer and diplomat in dealings with the prominent citizens of the city, with whom hardly anyone else has any contact.

Unfortunately the Scherchen project has ground to a halt; I had to go to Leipzig, where he was giving a concert on his way back from Budapest; that was my only chance to see him. He liked what I had brought along, and his wife liked it even more, but he felt the tenor was too serious; there should be something to make people laugh. Ha! This project showed me more clearly than ever before where my talents lie, because it called for such versatility; and the serious, fully thought-out scenes were precisely the ones I felt were important, and they have to have a serious effect. When it is a question of making people laugh, I freeze up. The job provided a number of fine ideas for pictures, and these I should like to salvage. I am quietly adding this opus to my chain of ill-fated attempts, of which I have a nice collection.

To Tut

Dessau
December 8, 1927

Shall speak with Piscator. Schawinsky, Lux Feininger, and the secretary are going along; they plan to buy a saxophone. Gropius just told me he has been arguing matters of principle with Piscator "until it comes out of his ears," discussing me as well. He said Piscator had been on the point of dismissing his stage designer, Traugott Müller, and appointing me. But for the moment we must wait and see. I have the impression that the theater will not get built. A slight tiff with Gropius because Piscator published the project without his permission.

On December 17 the Bauhaus celebrates its Christmas. "Silent Night"—no one is allowed to speak a word. But flash cards will be available, for one word (one pfennig), ten words, one hundred words. Communication only by gesture, enforced by the Wopo (Word Police). Too bad you can't be here!

To Tut

Dessau

January 6, 1928

No one knows a thing about the projected party, thank God; I hope it will be cancelled. The Mayor replied negatively. I am partly laughing up my sleeve, partly cursing. In the meantime the Mayor is allowing himself all kinds of liberties, has closed down the cafeteria, forbids us to stay around after five o'clock—until ten according to another version—and that includes the Theater and the stage! Gropius has already protested. When the Mayor had a notice to this effect posted in the cafeteria, the students ripped it off the bulletin board.

To Tut

Dessau

January 14, 1928

Yesterday we had the first meeting, and from Monday on we shall have one daily, starting at four o'clock. Sallies by the students, the Hannes Meyer program, a call for everyone to lay his cards on the table, so to speak, and thus pave the way for a new beginning. Some declare their readiness to do so at once, others first want to know what the name of the game is. Others: Kandinsky, Klee. This is meant for you in strictest confidence: Breuer and Bayer have formally resigned. I very nearly did likewise, but caution and patience prevailed. I simply reckoned up what the Theater had actually accomplished, and the results were not encouraging; there is no hope unless things change drastically. I intend to make that perfectly clear.

Now plans are to be laid for the new building, just as though nothing had happened, utopian plans, but formulated in such a way that they could be carried out within the existing budget. Hannes Meyer has his program ready in his pocket. He would tell me only that he set aside plenty of room for the Theater. My negative analysis of the situation still stands, however; the theater workshop carries no weight at all. I have to hear what Meyer et al have in mind. The human, spiritual element is supposed to be placed in the foreground once more; in fact it was almost comical to see how everyone insisted on these things, probably out of the realization that we could not continue much longer on our present course.

All Gropius said, summarizing the results of the first discussion, was that we had to set up an architecture department with a budget and some flair to it and appoint Hannes Meyer.

The emphasis on spiritual values and related matters of course plays right into the hands of the theater group, giving it great relevance. I shall listen to all the debate and then say my piece. Explain what I had hoped to accomplish and why it has turned out to be impossible.

Tomorrow the two student representatives are coming to talk things over with me. There does seem to be a general conviction that the Theater is necessary.

To Tut

Dessau

January 15, 1928

"All praise and honor to painting!" Today was a veritable celebration; at heart I really am a painter—enjoying the happiness of harmony, contentment, being at peace with the infinite. Here I am in my element; it is the thing I value most (next to you!), this is my kingdom. If I could really work undisturbed and concentratedly, something valuable and important would result, of that I am convinced. The picture literally flowed from my brush, and it came out right (I think) and will have an impact (I hope).

To Otto Meyer

Dessau

January 23, 1928

I am trying to note down a painter's thought processes. I realize once again how important it is not to get out of practice. For when I resume work after an interruption, a certain number of attempts always misfire. And after my various side-excursions and wrong turnings (Scherchen, theater, Bauhaus), it is difficult for me to find myself and my true interests again. It looks as though there will be changes at the Bauhaus. There have been changes in the City Council, which is less favorably inclined toward us since the elections. The budget is not sufficient, simply too small.

Hannes Meyer will fill his post well; he is staying, of course, even though he acts coy about it. The Mayor wishes him well, more so than he does Gropius (to the point of overrating him). The Bauhaus will reorient itself in the direction of architecture, industrial production, and the intellectual aspect of technology. The painters are merely tolerated as a necessary evil now.

You know how ambivalent I am about this whole affair. Especially here in Dessau, where circumstances have conspired to stifle my free development. I have now pronounced the death sentence for theater at the Bauhaus. And in fact the City Council has issued a publicly read decree forbidding parties at the Bauhaus; including, for good measure, our next party, which would have been a lovely one.

Perhaps, if I were plunged into the middle and given the prerequisites, my desire to paint might come back stronger than ever.

Diary

January 24, 1928

What can I do? Try to reaffirm my own values, the things I and I alone can do. In the absence of a religious framework restrict myself to the simplest, to that which lies close at hand. That means: the human figure standing, sitting, lying, walking. A theme capable of unlimited variations. I should hold myself to a simple range of tones. Transitions of these into dark and light, more or less color; blue determines the reds and browns, the lighting . . . .

Objective in new pictures: ever purer, more primary color.

In general: simplicity. (It says nothing yet everything.)

To Tut

Dessau

January 27, 1928

Meetings at the Bauhaus for the zillionth time—the students call it the six-day race, but there have already been more than six! And still nothing definite has emerged! Constant back-and-forth. The resignation of Bayer, Breuer, and Moholy is not sufficient. Not until the new curriculum is set up will we see how many teachers are needed. Albers may take over the cabinet-making shop in addition to his other duties; the print-shop in its present form will cease to exist. The question remains whether we can get by with teachers only for the basic courses. Theater: I myself proclaimed its death sentence. But what will happen? What am I to teach? Some mention was made of mural work. But that is by no means the last word. Gropius merely said that he wanted to keep me; I wish I were not staying.

The student representatives keep raising the subject of communism. Reduction of the teaching staff to a bare minimum, renunciation of outside sources of income: everything for the Bauhaus! That demand has naturally encountered stiff resistance. Agitated debates. Volger: the students in a desperate situation. So and so many are leaving unless their demand is met. Volger claims to speak for the student body, but I believe he actually speaks only for a few individuals. Hannes Meyer is very successful in his dealings with the Mayor. People are already saying that he has done more for the Bauhaus than anyone else. One cannot exclude the possibility that Hannes Meyer will someday stab Gropius in the back. Or perhaps he will go himself. No new meeting until Monday or Tuesday.

Moholy will not be staying. The clash with Hannes Meyer created too much bitterness. The two can no longer stand being under the same roof.

But the main thing: I am painting and becoming a good person once more. Molzahn was right when he remarked mournfully that we used to be better people (he meant earlier, when we were still painters). I am making progress, toward something new, but it will take work. I already have many drawings and watercolors finished.

Went through my watercolors, coming to the following conclusions: the most recent ones are off the track; too much indulgence in impressions; careless form. The ponderous, gloomy-colored ones revealed their strength in structure and wholeness; this is "high style" and must be hung on to. Struc-

222

ture, composition, irrational treatment of space, irrational treatment of the human figure, not with exaggerated plasticity, and also not with actual lighting—that leads to impressionistic effects. Pursue the grand line, the Handel model.

Diary

January 28, 1928

It has become clear that the watercolor, when pushed to extremes, impinges on the realm of the oil painting, appearing heavy and thick when by nature it should stick to light, bright, transparent tones. Glaze!

The goal which still remains hidden from me.

Diary

January 29, 1928

Baumeister: just ornamental neo-Baroque after all. Especially the non-objective paintings. That is a new form of commercial art. Ornament, asymmetrical.

By contrast I am more spiritual, more intellectual. The *Tischgesellschaft,* which has found a good home with Frau Bienert in Dresden, is typical. It is also the picture that Bauhaus people like. In others, like the *Frauentreppe,* a tendency toward the baroque. One of the risks when one produces in quantity.

I belong more to the line of Caspar David Friedrich, Genelli, Füssli, Munch. The picture *Homo* is also typical. At the time, a sense of a resonance deep within me. Likewise *Bild K.* By contrast, my more recent ones are often decorative. Still: they make up for it by their great sonorousness. The former have the monotony of Chinese song.

For a "posthumous exhibition" I would insist on: the *Homo,* the *Tischgesellschaft, Der Sinnende.* Also the *Mythische Figur.*

To Tut

Dessau
February 4, 1928

The latest, most important news, which will appear in Monday's papers: Gropius is leaving! You are surprised? Yesterday he told me, then announced it to everybody at a hastily called meeting, in the following terms: he is resigning in recognition of the fact that many issues have crystallized around him to the detriment of the institute, and that the constant skirmishes keep him from his own work, and that he hopes to promote the interests of the Bauhaus better from a position on the outside. Well, you will see the full text. He of course names Hannes Meyer his successor. He, Gropius, can think of no one better suited; he has considered all the possibilities, and both within the Bauhaus and among independent architects no one else seemed right. So it will become a reality, as of April 1.

Diary

February 4, 1928

Ideas for pictures are finally flowing, even entering my dreams, so that pictures come to me between waking and sleeping. I can do full justice to only one pursuit at a time. Either painting or the theater. I have now resolved not to lose the thread of painting, and to consider all else secondary.

It is essential to work hard and make use of every minute. That is the secret. But without frenzy.

My kind of painting requires Olympian serenity and calm, a peaceful, well-tempered mind. So if I wanted to be a real painter, and it would probably be worthwhile, a position at an art academy would be the ideal solution for me. That as the basis, and then theater work, dramatic projects, dance, and so on; this would be an excellent arrangement.

I want a topic that suits my predilections and would permit of improvement ad infinitum. The sitting, standing, walking, lying which I chose as my topic is almost too broad. Although it could yield a great deal if treated with "concentration" in mind.

To Tut

Yesterday Giedion was here and gave a lecture with photographs. Afterwards there was to be a dance in the cafeteria. But around town and among the students the news had got out (prematurely) that Gropius was leaving. People were completely taken aback, and the band refused to play, for reasons of tact. But then Gropius spoke to the students in the cafeteria and persuaded them that this was just the moment when they *should* dance. After that the evening turned out very jolly, although there was considerable tension in the air. Gropius was most cheerful. Towards three o'clock Andi sat down at the piano and sang his old Hungarian songs, and a melancholy mood set in. Then Kuhr addressed the company. To Gropius: "You have no right to leave us! We have starved in the name of our cause here and shall, if need be, continue to starve; the Bauhaus is not a knicknack that can be dropped and picked up by someone else; the Masters' Council is reactionary, all the students stand behind you; we have a mission to fulfill, the mission set forth in Schlemmer's manifesto for the Bauhaus Exhibition of 1923. That is our program, the program of the Bauhaus, yours and ours. Hannes Meyer as director of the Bauhaus will be a catastrophe! That is our downfall!" Gropius replied that although *"in vino veritas,"* Kuhr was wrong. Nowadays nothing stood or fell by one person any more; one should take a positive, not a negative attitude; the students should show what they could make of the Bauhaus, and so on. Kuhr replied. Then came a long speech by Gropius on pedagogy, on the sense of community, at its best when it consisted of tacit agreement, not grandiose pronouncements. By then it was five o'clock, and people were tired. But it was indubitably a remarkable confrontation, and everybody went home still perturbed by the unreconciled conflicts that had emerged.

This affair is certainly causing tremendous turmoil among the students. When the publicity campaign is unleashed tomorrow—the opposition has apparently put up posters—things will start rolling. Everyone seems to think that the old Bauhaus has breathed its last.

The next, most immediate task facing the Theater is to prepare a big farewell production for the end of March, and I think this is the time to put on the chronicle, *Nine Years of Gropius.* The oldsters are all participating. So Bosk must put his mind to it!

To Tut

Dessau
February 13, 1928

Saturday morning in Berlin: first the Léger exhibition at the Flechtheim Gallery, then a Manet exhibit, two totally different worlds! In the evening Piscator's *Schweyk.* Pallenberg is in charge of the whole thing, genre comedy, very effective. But the best part of the book does not come across—the things one reads between the lines, the intimate details. In the play one finds clever snatches of barracks style; some of the scenic effects are simply bad, actually a comedown from the first play (the Toller). Sunday morning the *vernissage* at Itten's: Otto Meyer. Unfortunately not everything, and no "paintings," but some pretty little studies. I knew them all, and they seemed if possible even more delicate than in Amden. Actually Meyer's work does not have an "effect" in the conventional sense. One Léger can overwhelm an entire exhibit of Meyer's—but that is not the point! Then on to Chaplin's "Circus," which is magnificient. Unbelievable things he does, tragi-comic.

To Willi Baumeister

Dessau
February 15, 1928

Gropius is stepping out into a broader public, going to Berlin on his own. Hannes proposed as his successor. The case is still pending, i.e. awaiting approval by the City Council and the Board of Trustees. I am dangling by a thread, but I *am* dangling, which means I am in a safe position, even if theater work should become impossible, due to the shortage of funds that will result from the planned expansion of the architecture department. My duties are to include publishing, public relations, and unfortunately also pedagogy-demagogy. With "great trepidation," for that is not my sort of thing. I don't like playing the schoolmaster. But it is my only hope just now. I am often simply worn out from all the goings-on here, and if I want time for my own work I have to steal it. I have begun painting again and pray I can keep it up.

Even Hannes Meyer is pretty much frazzled by the recurrent crises and his own duties; the first part of his stay here was the part I enjoyed most. If he takes on this running battle, it will be no laughing matter, for things can get pretty rough.

To Tut

Dessau
Ash Wednesday
February 22, 1928

Well, *Fasching* has come and gone, and it was good, with many fine masks; the theme was "Beards and Noses." Even Kandinsky had a Sudermann-style beard; Klee had muttonchops; Hannes Meyer a big nose. We had set up a barbershop, where Clabi went to work dressing hair and perfuming. On the stage: first a serious dance by the Kreibig girl, white-stockinged feet, rose-colored hand holding a silver head (and black head cap so that her face disappeared completely). Then movements using these three things, illusionistic, against a black backdrop. It was excellent, and we plan to take up this vein right away. She is very hard-working and feels her way quickly into a role, also adding a great deal herself. All this by way of preparation for the "Triadic." Then the "Wing Play," which I conceived and Schawinsky designed and painted. First setting up the wings (this time to phonograph music), then Schawinsky as a sort of Adam, in a white leotard with a figleaf; he disappears into the wings (painted with articles of men's clothing) and comes out fully dressed. Then a waltz with the Kreibig in toe slippers and two men (Röseler and me), then the Kreibig in a wooden mask made by Lux (Chinoiserie), Lou with a big child's head, I in a white wooden mask by Lux, then a dance by the whole ensemble: Charleston. Everyone liked it and said that it was the best thing we had done and most successfully staged. The problem

227

will be to get rid of dilettantism in our theater, have the technical instruction take place in a workshop, and receive 1000 marks per annum for acquiring and installing the necessary equipment.

Today the studio is clean, the cleaning woman having given it a good going-over. It had reached the point of being squalid, and for the first time I really felt how totally I had been abandoned by my little elf! Come back!

To Otto Meyer
Dessau
February 27, 1928

Because your paintings are showing in Berlin at the same time as Léger's, they are often compared. He is a decorative barbarian, certainly, a master of poster art, the bull to your china shop, one might say. Crude technique, strong, blatant effects, handsome colors.

To take up your points in order: the Bauhaus, briefly. Hannes Meyer the new director, clearly an important turning point in the stormy history of the Bauhaus, which I now have the privilege of portraying dramatically, in a play, *Nine Years of the Bauhaus.* Moholy is also leaving, Gropius' faithful drummer boy and teeth-chatterer; likewise, less directly in connection with Gropius' departure, Breuer. Gropius, celebrated and mourned, cursed and hated, will first go to Berlin, then perhaps later to America on a lecture tour. Hannes Meyer, himself no uncontroversial figure, will keep things going in his realistic, calm, sensible way. When Gropius leaves, there will be a mite less aristocratic atmosphere, a mite less élan.

I am staying for the time being; Hannes Meyer nobly took my part, and I am slated for a full-time appointment, the same as Klee's and Kandinsky's, although that of course means more duties. My subject will be a lofty one: man and everything connected with him: the nude, figural drawing, art history, hygiene, etc.

The Theater! Still the subject of much argument and on the verge of being closed down—something I myself want. But it will continue in its present form as an extracurricular activity.

228

However: Frankfurt is still playing, Dresden as well, where in April I am supposed to do the sets for Verdi's *Macbeth*.

To Willi Baumeister

Dessau
March 1, 1928

'Scuse me for not writing 'til today. But I was waiting for a letter which, according to Gosebruch, was supposed to be on its way from Professor Sauerlandt; you and I are invited to enter a competition for a ceiling painting in Essen. A change of course is gradually making itself felt here; certain things will be very different, but I don't yet know in what way. People think Gropius' departure will improve the general situation.

To Tut

Dessau
March 1, 1928

As far as one can tell, things have settled down. Provided the budget goes through, but it will. True, I have a teaching load—quite a bit more than before, but so do the others! The debts considerably reduced. It gives me satisfaction to stamp "paid" on them; soon everything that comes in will be there to spend. I cannot even imagine such a blessed state any more!

How does this strike you: my future subject of instruction will be "Man." I must lay in all kinds of books on the topic. It is an enormous area, and I shall have to make it worthwhile for me, treating everything from the point of view of what I find interesting. I shall also have to keep the third-semester students excited and busy: Kandinsky has the first semester, Klee the second, I the third. Heredity, racial theory, reproductive biology, ethics, and so on; at least that is how I picture it. That will form a nice totality; supplemented by nude and figural drawing and anthropology. And theater! And painting! oh, oh. And publishing! no!!

To Tut

Dessau
March 13, 1928

Well, Karin has been accepted at the school!

The Kandinsky evening was very jolly. Breuer, Scheper, Wittwer, and I appeared as Schillian officers, Moholy as an old Dessauer, Bayer as an Austrian officer, Andi as a Jesuit priest, Ludwig Grote as a member of the City Council, Hannes Meyer as a people's representative, Klee as a Turk, Kandinsky as a half-breed, comical. The women were mixed. The basic idea: the Kandinskys have become real Anhalt natives, Germans. Humorous toasts to this effect.

To Tut

Dessau
March 26, 1928

So the farewell party for Gropius is over. The picture part was bungled completely. Nonetheless the play went over well, a huge job with many humorous details, occasioning much laughter, and people pitied me, the chronicler in academic robe and white wig, for the idiotic mistakes by the technical crew. So be it! That is the last time I am going to try to do anything with the whole Bauhaus. In the future just the Theater, with a small ensemble.

But from now on I am going to have a great, great deal of work. Teaching and the Theater will keep me more than busy.

After the performance there was a dance, wild shouting. Gropius was dragged and carried around more than he could stand. Everyone was screaming and yelling. I was on edge and exhausted and went home alone at four-thirty. It continued until morning, and many did not get to bed at all. This morning Gropius and Pia left.

The Chronicle will be printed, because many people wanted a copy. Kandinsky had high praise for the performance. Even so. On Sunday the Gropiuses visited and thanked me for all my efforts. Hannes Meyer laughed the loudest of all.

Now I have had a chance to relax and am feeling more myself. I am taking a breather, even though there is no end of new work to be done. Articles, letters, the sketches for Essen, preparation for my courses.

Diary

March 26, 1928

Manet-metaphor: oyster, asparagus, peach. Léger-metaphor: clamp.

One cannot ask the former to be the latter, and vice versa. But one can say that although the oyster, the asparagus, and the peach may not be "more beautiful," they are eternal. The clamp, though made of iron, will "pass," made obsolete by a newer invention, but the peach will remain, demonstrating each year anew the law of organic growth.

To Otto Meyer

Dessau
April 13, 1928

Please forgive my delay in answering, but the family came home, Easter was just around the corner, then over Easter Hannes Meyer gave the house back, to be swept out and reclaimed. In addition I used the vacation period for painting, taking pleasure in being a poor correspondent, something I might indulge myself in completely if I were able to be a pure artist, which is to say an eccentric. What a prospect!

The Hannes Meyer Era has now begun. It will be a while before we see whether the change brings about a relaxation of tensions between us and the city administration and a certain part of the citizenry. Meyer is moving slowly and cautiously; a valuable innovation is the new curriculum; instead of the previous hodgepodge of subjects, we now have two days devoted exclusively to art and theory (Monday and Friday), and then three workshop days with classes right through the afternoon. This was not the case formerly, and we now have Saturday completely free for sports, excursions, and the like. My teaching is concentrated on Thursday and Friday, so that I have the rest of the week pretty much to myself.

The "Nine Year" chronicle raised a lot of good laughs, but

there were many irritations. The actors and the lighting people have seldom failed so miserably. To top it off, everyone laughed uproariously at the sight of the Bauhaus standing on its head in the slide projection! For me, the era of "parties" at the Bauhaus is pretty well over. I shall put aside my clown's garb and turn to serious matters. The Theater can devote itself to precise, earnest work, which need not for that reason be any less valuable. On the contrary, I hope to have more influence on the outside world than we have had with our private, one-shot festivities which cannot mean anything to outsiders.

I am doing some painting. It is curious to see how dependent I am on space, setting, and general mood. I now know that the studio in Weimar was in large part responsible, in the good sense, for the form my pictures took at the time. Here things are more cramped, there are many interruptions, and I find it difficult to recover the mood I had then.

Diary

April 16, 1928

Last night a visionary dream: large (architectonic) surfaces (black-and-white lacquer) with little, finely molded figures of great delicacy. Dangers: the "holy," angelic, Richard-Wagner-like! William Blake (somewhat).

My mystical tendencies should actually place me somewhere near Chirico, Carrà, and related Belgians (but in German terms).

It requires absolute clarity of purpose to fight one's way through to the typical.

The new picture, *Begegnung* ["Meeting"], has ready appeal. Why? In contrast to the serene, perhaps too serene, interiors, it is explosive, eruptive; mighty contrasts of types and chiaroscuro (not felt to be bathetic, as I had feared).

Perhaps it does show something characteristic of me, peculiar to me: the tension, the loaded quality, the affect. And then a new element: the strong mass of white taking shape against a dark, imaginary space.

I must figure this out and discover where the crucial elements lie.

232

Diary

End of May 1928

My teaching gives me both joy and sorrow. This latter because the students react so little to things that really should interest them, partly out of incompetence, partly out of the laziness for which this place is notorious. Joy, because I am dealing with areas which may not be absolutely essential but which fascinate me: internal anatomy, physiology, and especially psychology, not to forget philosophy in general. I have to dig all this out for myself; some of it is hard to get at, due to the complexity of the various branches. I am curious to see where it leads, what picture of the world will emerge by the end of the semester, and whether anything both personal and universal can be extracted from the contradictory opinions of the scientists and philosophers. It will not be love's labor lost, I think, and will represent a certain addition to my general personal scope. The nude drawing also gives me pleasure, and the students likewise. They themselves model, on my suggestion.

To Willi Baumeister

Dessau

June 29, 1928

The Dance Congress in Essen is over: we performed four numbers which were well received by those whose opinions count and also by the general public. Applause, especially for the "Dance of Staffs." On the way down I contracted a super-cold, which then developed into a general catarrh, making it uncertain whether I would be able to appear "in person," but I managed, except that today I am feeling the after-effects and am moping around all numb and vague.

Diary

June 1928

Art is dead and done for; that is what they are shouting from the flat rooftops of modern architecture.

New Objectivity: the "most difficult" art achieves the greatest precision. Abstraction: dissolved into the Nirvana of architecture. And for that reason "understood" by architects. The spirit you can grasp.* Common causes meet on commonplaces.

Diary

July 21, 1928

Have taken up oils again, a picture with figures in reddish-brown. Arrangement always my forte: heads and hands, lightly modulated in tone, on a white surface. Then come the essential follow-up tones. Up to the clothing everything is all right. But sometimes the interior undoes all the fine effects that have been achieved. Then it becomes necessary to pull everything together, to neutralize, in order to get back to the initial state of affairs.

The color range is worth mentioning: pink faces, dark-brown to black hair with burnt siena as an added shade, then white or cream. Efforts to execute an entire picture in one basic color range—red, brown, black, white, yellow, etc.—thus doing without the (cheap) contrasts of cold and warm, red and blue, etc. Or if these are used, then in very pure form. No English red with ultramarine. Result: the picture *Gegeneinander* ["Oppositions"].

To Otto Meyer

Dessau
September 11, 1928

I face the future with tranquillity, so to speak. Something will turn up, somewhere, sometime, and the way I want it. My desires incline toward as much freedom as possible (in art and in time) and more toward painting than toward the theater. This particular orientation may be the result of recent events: a few sales, which are being used to pay off debts (contracted in the course of theatrical work), a Gold Medal in Düsseldorf, accompanied by a money prize, and last but not least the likelihood of a commission in Essen on the Ruhr: doing paintings for a hall in the Folkwang Museum.

---

*An allusion to Faust's conversation with the Earth Spirit. — Translator

Heckel, Baumeister, and I were invited to compete. Heckel was soon eliminated, having apparently dashed off a few pointless sketches. Baumeister seemed to be in the lead, since certain discrepancies between the building and the assignment made me unable to come up with any serious suggestions. In the meantime the character of the assignment was changed drastically; there was still time and I heard that they really wanted me to win. I offered a new proposal and at the moment the situation looks more than favorable for me.

It is a little circular hall with a rotunda; the center is occupied by a fountain by the Belgian sculptor George Minne (whom I have long known and been fond of). The theme: "the adolescent spirit of the age" (formulated thus by the director of the gallery). There are nine large panels (about eight feet by six and one half feet), of which five are to be treated importantly, the other four as subsidiary. I would like to insist that the painting be done as a fresco right on the wall (the medium attracts me), and conception and technique will have to be kept simple, likewise the amount of painted surface, so as not to overload the room. The result will be simple groupings of figures in the style of my recent works, one of which, *Römisches,* the Museum owns; the director has displayed it repeatedly in the rotunda and never tires of telling me how effective it is. Nevertheless I am somewhat nervous in the face of such a major assignment. I wish I had time, time, time to do something relatively good (the entries are to be opened at the end of January).

Apropos of theater and things human: at our last performance here I played a musical clown (against my will and only because no one else would have done it right); the total effect (charming) was achieved through simple humanity, i.e. on-the-spot improvisation. You are absolutely right: most people are familiar only with the mechanical, and our times like things that can be grasped instantly.

To Otto Meyer

Dessau

November 11, 1928

A brief run-down:

A ballet at the State Opera in Dresden, music by Tschai-
kovsky, the title of the revised production being *Spielzeug*
["Toys"], (but they were toys for somewhat older children);
painful and irritating days there, quarrels with each of the
technical experts. This now belongs to the past, that is to say,
the ballet will "run" through Christmastime. The next project
will be a ballet in Hagen in Westphalia: *Vogelscheuchen*
["Scarecrows"], short, original, much more so than the Dresden ballet, since the music was written especially for it, as was
the text (there are spoken parts). This will involve days of
gruelling work. Virtue is its own reward—the monetary reward
will be a pittance, the moral one by compensation substantial.

In the meantime there was an exhibit at Nierendorf's in
Berlin.

Dresden wants to try something different and more demanding; altogether, Dresden is a city to keep an eye on. Like
those two other former royal seats and cultural cities, Munich
and Berlin, Dresden has lost some of its glory; in place of royal
patronage it now has a ruling bureaucracy. But its size and its
past give it a certain something which Dessau lacks entirely. I
realize that most of my dearest friends are in Dresden. And
here? More than enough work and claims upon my time, and
the atmosphere always touchy. Perpetual crises, often covered
over, often out in the open. I am sick of "it." Perhaps no one
should serve longer than the biblical seven years. Hannes Meyer
well disposed and helpful, but also demanding. "A doer." Certainly exceptionally hard-working, energetic, organizing, providing, a real man of the people, and thus sometimes more peasant
than nobleman, if I may characterize him in such a flood of
epithets. But he will succeed, and since Gropius' departure the
situation seems much improved.

To Otto Meyer
Dessau
Beginning of December 1928

Today I must be very brief, because my head is literally spinning. Aside from temporary ache, it is filled with a thousand urgent tasks; the matinee of the Bauhaus Theater at the Berlin Volksbühne, scheduled for March 3, 1929, calls for all sorts of rehearsals, workshop, organization, but also music, some of which I must do myself, and so on.

Painting has been pushed far to the back of my mind, after being well in the foreground for a time. The fresco sketches! Due to a cold wave, painting in Essen is out of the question. Postponed until warmer weather, almost summerlike weather, which is fine with me—it gives me time.

The theatrical work in which I am totally involved at the moment prevents me from getting to anything else. One idea leads to the next, as always happens when I do something with enjoyment, exclusively, and with complete dedication; I am confused again, no longer sure which is my true calling— painting or the theater; I always succumb to the theater's wealth of figures and the fascination of dance, music, color, personality. Also the stretch for a climax, performance with its joys and sorrows. Joys and sorrows, and that in the company of others, upon whose ability, enjoyment, love, loyalty, etc. success depends.

In March and April I shall still be in the clutches of theater. Prague, Dresden, Frankfurt, Stuttgart, Basel, Zurich, Breslau are all cities being considered for guest performances.

Then a break and, I hope, complete dedication to painting.

To Gunda Stölzl
Dessau
January 1, 1929

New Year's Eve was very nice. At first we were home alone. At midnight the Schepers invited us over for champagne, Italian salad, and meat pasties; then at one to the Kandinskys', where we found a few Bauhaus people. We danced until three.

Diary

February 1929

At long last another party at this troubled Bauhaus, and it was undeniably unique. The airy rooms of this building, festive in themselves—in fact almost too festive for everyday purposes—impose a certain style which always prevails no matter what theme is chosen. Not a "Bauhaus style," as the unavoidable cliché would have it, and which our imitators always so gloriously fail to achieve. The Bauhaus style which sneaked its way into the design of women's underwear; the Bauhaus style as "modern décor," as rejection of yesterday's styles, as determination to be "up-to-the-minute" at all costs this style can be found everywhere but at the Bauhaus. Here the evolution is, and must be, so far ahead that those following in our wake are caught napping. Naturally!

The early parties in Weimar, at which Expressionism produced its wildest, most fantastic effects, marked the happy, festive stations along the otherwise thorny path of this institution—I am also thinking of the "White Festival" in Dessau (before the new building), at which white dominated and the only other colors allowed were red, blue, and yellow, and these only "striped, dappled, and splotched"; and now there is the "Metallic." Tell me how you party, and I will tell you who you are; or: every generation, every social stratum gets the parties it deserves. When young people throw a party, one can certainly draw conclusions about their character, and the Bauhaus represents a group who, it is to be hoped, will one day play a leading role. One can note with satisfaction that the Bauhaus people set to work with self-sacrificing enthusiasm to "pull something off," and it certainly succeeded!

The original idea: a festival of "bells, of all sizes and functions," but the very thought or cacophony made it impossible to hear one's own thoughts: the thought of cowbells, and bell towers, musical bells, collection boxes, booming, ringing, rattling. To ward off the danger of too much noise, too much clanging, we decided to adopt the theme of the metallic in general, and that proved the right decision. The unfettered imagination now wrought miracles. A children's slide covered in white sheet metal led one past innumerable gleaming silver balls, lined up and sparkling under spotlights, right into the heart of the party, but first one had to pass a tinsmith's shop. Here the need for every sort of metal could be filled; there were wrenches, tincutters, can openers! A stairway, of which every step gave out a different tone, a true "backstairs joke," (in the course of the evening there emerged virtuosos of stair-climbing) led to the lottery; here one could not, to be sure, win folding metal houses and "Livingmachines," but things almost as good: steel chairs, nickel bowls, aluminum lamps, lovely cakes with a bit of glitter, and natural and unnatural art. But then on to the realms of true metallic pleasure. Bent sheets of foil glittered and reflected the dancers in distortion, walls of silvered masks and their grotesque shadows, ceilings studded with gleaming brass fruit bowls, everywhere colored metallic paper and the ever-beautiful Christmas-tree balls, some of enormous size.

The Bauhaus band had dressed festively in coquettish silver top hats, and it launched into the music with great élan, rhythm, and verve. On the stage, bolts of foolishness dropped from leaden tongues; there was an amusing "ladies' dance" performed by men, and a sketch in which, to be sure, metal was represented only by the spike of a helmet; these two numbers satisfied everyone's desire to laugh and look. I should also mention the best costumes at the party: a death's-head Hussar in black, with an aluminum pot and scoop as a helmet, his breast garnished with two crossed tin spoons; a woman in flat metal disks who coquettishly wore a screwdriver on a bracelet and asked each new escort to tighten her loose screws; a pair of brothers wearing beards and hair made out of bronzed wood shavings and metal funnels on their heads, in the point of which each had a cigar which he puffed on through a metal hose leading to his mouth! On the stroke of midnight the "Bauhaus's Iron Ration" marched in, twelve knights in shining armor, etc., clanging and stomping.

The Bauhaus looked lovely from the outside, radiating into the winter night. The windows were pasted on the inside with metallic paper; the white and colored light bulbs were concentrated according to room. The great block of glass permitted long vistas; and thus for one night this house of work was transformed into the "high academy for creative form."

The next morning there were frozen ears; the escorts with ladies oriented toward the west had their left ears frozen, while those with ladies oriented toward the east had their right ears frozen.

But everyone agreed with Paul Scheerbart when he said, "Where would we *all* be without met*all*?"

To Willi Baumeister

Dessau
March 6, 1929

We returned from Berlin moderately covered with glory; you might say it was a success. The theater sold out; the audience enthusiastic; the press, too, for the most part. That helps reconcile me to this nerve-wracking undertaking. A guest performance at the Schauspielhaus [Theater] in Frankfurt as good as assured for sometime in April.

Then to Breslau on March 24 for a lecture. This in confidence: they are interested in me there.

All in all, it looks as though my days at the Bauhaus are numbered! I am ready to leave. People—the students and I, too—are dissatisfied with Hannes because of his boorish behavior and tactlessness. The atmosphere in the house is not good. Add to that the fact that the whole Bauhaus question will soon come up before the Landtag. But don't breathe a word of this to anyone!

Flechtheim wants to do an exhibition of my work. Asks when I want it, in the fall or next spring. An excellent pretext for painting; here I am simply going to the dogs, because I cannot tear myself loose from the Theater. Unless I escape now, it will only get worse. I think I shall be able to treat my theatrical concerns more casually in a new setting; I cannot give them up entirely—I have too deep a sense of commitment.

Diary

April 1929

If the signs do not deceive, a renaissance is underway in the portrayal of man in art. First the Futurists' manifestos swore

death to moonshine and death to the naked human figure—
"painting nudes will be banned for ten years!"; then Expressionism and abstract art swore death to the object and to any reference to nature; when the human figure nevertheless ventured a reappearance, it was deformed to a greater or lesser degree, in the good as well as the bad sense. Then *Verismo* and the New Objectivity movement portrayed man, but in a sort of Biedermeier style or in extreme naturalism; after such an evolutionary process it seems only natural that we should witness the return of the ideal to which Hans von Marees devoted his whole life, the ideal of high style in art. Its most noble subject will always be man, man as a beautiful art object. There will always be examples of what Goethe equated with Classical Antiquity: creations which spring from the combination and perfect balance of abstraction, proportion, law on the one hand, and nature, emotion, idea, on the other.

To Willi Baumeister

Dessau
April 8, 1929

Forgive the long silence! Bres—I shall use this code, for I am superstitious in this matter and dare not speak of it out loud—is shaping up. The city proved a pleasant surprise. Handsome streets, broad squares, a citadel of Catholicism, something I had not realized, with its own cardinal. The either-Oder, the Century Hall, etc. So I enjoy working this vein. Am more fed up with this place than ever. Hannes a disappointment. Not only to me. Gropius was a man of the world, after all, capable of the grand gesture, of taking risks when it seemed worthwhile. The other fellow is petty-minded, a boor—and, most important, not up to the job. Toward the Theater, my special area, he is "personally" negative; he wants a social and political slant, which rubs me the wrong way. And besides, I have received such unanimous praise for what I have done thus far that I see no reason to change my course, What I say is: just let him try to get Klee to be a George Grosz!

On May 4 the opening of the competition entries in Essen,

but my entry consists only of sketches, which are being mounted. I will have to paint the panels on plywood when I have some time this summer. The frame not yet settled on. Unfortunately have to make all kinds of concessions to the Minne fountain, which Gosebruch could not see his way clear to removing. As a result I must hold myself in check. Restrained effects, shades of gray. This project has given me many new ideas, and some of the by-products have turned out even better, because they are free of restraints.

Postcard to Otto Meyer

Stuttgart
April 24, 1929

It has just been settled that a matinee by the Bauhaus Theater will take place on Sunday, the 28th at 11:30 A.M. in the Basel Stadttheater. Zurich did not work out because the expenses involved would have been too great. Can you, will you, would you like to come? I would be so glad if you did! It looks as though I shall be in Basel from Friday on, but unfortunately I have to be in Essen on May 1. So no possibility of coming to Zurich. We have already performed in Frankfurt, and tomorrow we will be at the Landestheater here.

Diary

May 1929

Notes on the Bauhaus Theater's new dances:

"Why is the audience so enthusiastic? Out of primitiveness, out of a spirit of opposition, out of a sense for contemporary culture? Or due to a misunderstanding of the comic aspects, a love for *variété*?" thus asks the noted ballet expert, Professor Oskar Bie, and Dr. Artur Michel, likewise an expert in the field, adds even more question marks: "What is this?" Mechanistic cabaret, metaphysical eccentricity, spiritual tightrope walking, ironic *variété*? Is it perhaps all of these together, sometimes more of one, sometimes more of the other? The debut of the Bauhaus Theater in Berlin was a surprising success, surprising not the least for the director and participants, because all of them had been gripped by the traditional stage fright and were only saved from it by the applause that greeted their appearance. This surprising success set up a pleasant situation: the theoretical defenses and considerations were justified in practice and made unnecessary. Or: the theory passed into the hands of the critics, and the performers ("doers") can now sit back and watch the critics quarrel. For Oscar Wilde is right when he says that when the critics squabble the artist can be at peace with himself.

The recipe the Bauhaus Theater follows is very simple: one should be as free of preconceptions as possible; one should act as if the world had just been created; one should not analyze a thing to death, but rather let it unfold gradually and without interference. One should be simple, but not puritanical. ("Simplicity is a noble concept!") One should rather be primitive than over-elaborate or pompous; one should not be sentimental; one should be sensitive and intelligent. That says everything—and nothing!

Furthermore: one should start with the fundamentals. Well, what does that mean? One should start with a dot, a line, a bare surface: the body. One should start with the simple, existing colors: red, blue, yellow, black, white, gray. One should start with the materials, learn to feel the differences in texture among such materials as glass, metal, wood, and so on, and one should let these perceptions sink in until they are part of one. One should start with space, its laws and its mysteries, and let oneself be "captivated" by it. This again says a great deal—or it says nothing, if these words and concepts are not felt and made reality.

One should start with one's physical state, with the fact of one's own life, with standing and walking, leaving leaping and dancing for much later. For taking a step is a grave event, and no less so raising a hand, moving a finger. One should have deep respect and deference for any action performed by the human body, especially on the stage, that special realm of life and illusion, that second reality in which everything is surrounded with the nimbus of magic . . . .

All these are the precepts one should follow! They will

lead, if not to the key, at least to the keyhole to the riddle which the Bauhaus Theater seemingly poses.

To Otto Meyer

Dessau
June 9, 1929

I hope you arrived back safely in Zurich. The evening in Basel was well worthwhile, although I would have done better to come after ten o'clock. For the star, Josephine Baker, only arrived at the end and was very beautiful, an experience. I even had a part in it: she flirted with the audience; apparently likes bald heads, for she adorned mine with one of her pearls, which I have kept as a talisman, and with petals from her costume; another head, this one with hair, she combed and coiffed, using the contents of a little pot of coffee as brilliantine. But her singing and dancing were most impressive.

In Essen, at the opening of the Folkwang Museum, I met Dr. Wartmann of the Zurich Kunsthaus [Art Museum]. He seemed to be much taken with my designs for the frescoes, and would like to mount a special exhibition of wall paintings. I accepted somewhat hesitantly for the spring. We had quite a long talk.

Breslau seems to be going from lukewarm to hot. There is now just one more hurdle to pass (the Prussian Ministry of Culture). Given the mood here, I can only say thank God. I have never felt more alienated from the Bauhaus than now, thanks to Meyer's total failure as a director. A pity we did not discuss him properly. The "executor of the estate," as he calls himself, will prove its executioner yet.

At the moment I have it easy at the Bauhaus, furloughed from theater work because the "youngsters" are doing a play of their own, a Bauhaus revue intended to express the revolutionary program of the new Bauhaus. Something like this: a soviet republic of the Bauhaus, the "masters" being capitalistic kings who must be deposed and stripped of their privileges ("I'm on my way out!"). So my enthusiasm for painting is very high. I have some new ideas, and it is not easy keeping myself on a tight rein.

To Otto Meyer

Groß-Dirschkeim

July 17, 1929

Have you already set off on your travels? Like us! Or rather, we have already reached our destination, and not a bad one: Groß-Dirschkeim, mailing address Groß-Kuhren, Samland, East Prussia.

There are six of us and one dog. Me, Frau Tut, Fräulein Marie Schlemmer (the daughter of my brother in Stuttgart), Karin, Jai, Tilman, and, as I said, the dog Buck. The first few days were full of discoveries and surprises. The ocean, which glistens far out into the distance, the pounding surf, its rhythm, the secret of which we have not yet plumbed, swimming in it, the things it washes up on the beach, the most remarkable of which is the amber; the landscape pleasantly hilly, unfamiliar vegetation, and almost overly rich color in the flowers, like Amden. Altogether, many echoes of Amden and parallels, not least of all in the general attitude toward life, the types of food, the rhythm of the day, with its long, productive lulls. A pleasant change from Ascona, the Allgäu region, and Lake Constance, and not exactly detrimental to our general well-being: fresh, salty air (and fish—very cheap and fascinating to watch being caught). We plan to stay at least until the 10th of August.

Basel must have its "Odeon discussions," too. They had them in Stuttgart, very fine ones, but now they no longer take place, or only very seldom. And in Amden of course they go on all the time! Dr. Georg Schmidt was part of the lively group in Basel, and the time was probably too short for me to perceive the differences very accurately. I was surprised that he understood our theatrical attempts so well, judged them calmly and sensibly, appreciated the formal aspects, which actually are the key to the whole thing. For my dear Bauhaus colleagues, including Hannes Meyer, do not grasp this truth; they keep urging "relevance," historical, political—contemporary in any case. The rump Bauhaus Theater will now be free to follow this course; I shall pick up our previous projects en bloc and take them to Breslau. (The Bauhaus people seem glad to give them to me, i.e. to get rid of them).

France: you know that the Germans are well looked upon

in Paris at the moment. In fact, they almost seem to be setting the tone; this is said to be the case with Klee and Max Ernst. Picasso's strange new creations are often ascribed to their influence. Klee has apparently had tremendous sales there—what explains this? Have the French tired of classicism; do they feel they have exhausted their resources—how else could one account for the incredible fact that they are embracing something German? Only these two artists, to be sure. They close their minds to anything else German, just as they always have. The very German quality which the French reject strikes me as being central to the work of those more or less descended from Kirchner.

Kandinsky—form with color! My guess is that the whole issue arose out of the problems which van Doesburg made acute. For it dates from this period, as does Kandinsky's specialization in the primary colors of red, blue, and yellow. Mondrian (and van Doesburg) had urged that these colors be used exclusively for right-angled planes, and Kandinsky "corrected" them in accordance with his notion of the form that properly corresponds to each color. I see a connection between all that and the unmistakable influences and changes in point of view one can trace in his pictures.

Yesterday we took a lovely excursion to the Kurische Nehrung. A long stretch of dunes, East Prussian Africa. But this excursion was so expensive that other things (Finland) are out of the question, including Hamburg. That is a shame—I have such a yearning to see Hamburg, Lübeck, and Bremen, which I do not know at all. Especially since I will probably not be likely to come north from Breslau (where I now have an appointment at the Academy), for that region holds the lure of the Riesengebirge and the High Tatra.

To Alfred and Trudl Arndt

Groß-Dirschkeim
August 12, 1929

To kill two birds with one letter, since we keep having to go down to the seashore and look for amber. We also have to go to Danzig, a venerable old city, with non-contemporary architecture. And then we keep venturing into the devil's casino in Zopot, where one can gamble one's last two gulden and watch them go like hotcakes! But the memory lingers on!

Time is passing, and so are we. On September 1 the last Groß-Dirschkeim hour will have struck. Then with knapsack and dogpack off to Nimmersath in the Riesengebirge, which we chose for its name,* since it will be the bridgehead to Breslau. Once the battle has been won there (the apartment), the rear guard will be brought up cautiously. In September we shall be packing in Dessau, where we hope to find the last remains of the glorious army. How is your little Napoleon's Royal Majesty?

To Otto Meyer

Groß-Dirschkeim
September 8, 1929

I am lying in the beautiful but impractical position described by Oscar Wilde, on the sand of the Baltic coast, tortured by flies, shone on by the sun, repeatedly challenged by the dog Buck to throw his stick for retrieving. In the distance the cries of the children, in permanent ecstasy over the sand and the beach and its excavatory possibilities, in which I have occasionally shared. Altogether, I have extinguished myself here as a mind, a person, a painter, and a theater man, going back to a state which much resembles a recapitulation of childhood. It began with the wonderful wind, which suggested simple parachutes of tissue paper; these soon led to a kite. For days the kite kept plunging head-over-heels to the ground, until finally adjustments on the tail, weights, and a first-class wind bore it astonishingly high. This kite, three-quarters the height of a man, had to be replaced by a smaller one for the children, made of gold paper. This one flew and never crashed. I remembered the curious Japanese box kites, of which I had never made one myself. We put one together, and this one too soared, remarkable in its lack of a tail and its still way of hanging in the air, even without wind. But where are you without wind? We had a tissue-paper balloon, hexagonal and colorful, lovely to look at,

---

*"Never full." — Translator

but it tried twice without success to climb. It had to be heated inside with alcohol and filled with gas. It still refused to climb. This setback, and the fact that we only have a few days before we leave, induced me to lay aside the game.

It was lovely here. The coast, unique in its way, forms a right angle here, peace on two fronts, so to speak.

I told you that Hannes Meyer and a group of students reject the Bauhaus Theater productions as irrelevant, formalistic, too personal. And that this was one reason for my being glad to leave. Kandinsky supported and defended me, as did Klee—and both said: the people at the Bauhaus will only later realize what they have lost. Kandinsky openly shows his sorrow at the end of the Theater in its present form. I asked him if he wasn't tempted. He shook his head in resignation. Obviously he is frightened off by all the work, which is by no means inconsiderable, perhaps also by the controversial position this particular activity occupies at the Bauhaus. Kandinsky certainly saw many of his own ideas realized on my stage; after performances he would let me know through his wife how close I was to his conceptions.

On the other hand, I created the "Triadic Ballet" before I came to the Bauhaus (thank God!), and that contained much of the basic material and the stylistic simplicity which I later was able to build on. The trias = triad (of the colors—red—blue—yellow, of form, and many other things) dates far back; it later became common property at the Bauhaus through Mondrian (I can see that tracing this kind of history is very difficult!).

The painters at the Bauhaus are not waging open battle against the opposition, which consists of architecture, advertising, "relevant" pedagogy. Meyer's dernier cri: "sociology!" The students are supposed to do something on their own, fulfill a commission "with the maximum feasible minimum of direction"; even if the results are unsatisfactory, the sociological factor is considered an asset, something *new*. (I always think involuntarily of the joke: "Master, the trousers are finished, should I mend them now?") The goal of these attempts: a (master-less) Republic of Students. ("With the salary of one master I can give happiness to X number of students!"—Hannes Meyer.) This and everything related was, and still is, the subject

248

of long debates. I do not yet know whether I shall escape such problems entirely in Breslau, or whether they exist in a different form, or whether the light touch of the director and the general laisser-faire attitude make for a sort of unpretentious atmosphere of academic freedom. I shall have more than enough work to do.

I shall be able to paint, and if I am out of range of the Bauhausian racket for a while, I shall not miss it. The question remains whether our hectic times actually call for uninterrupted commotion, so that solitude and silence are as good as death, and anyone who seeks them out should be dismissed as out of the running. Nonetheless: I shall certainly be more than enough in demand, especially for theatrical projects (with the students, which will keep me in a constant state of alert). And perhaps also for social doings, which are quite lively in Breslau. Right now I cannot make any predictions, but everything is in my hands, and I can arrange things to suit myself.

BRESLAU AND BERLIN
(Autumn 1929 to Autumn 1933)

1929: On October 1 the Bauhaus gives a farewell party for Oskar and Tut Schlemmer. In the middle of the month Schlemmer begins teaching at the Academy in Breslau, his topic "Man and Space." A studio theater is planned. At the Academy he comes to know the fellow painters Oskar Moll (the director), Alexander Kanoldt, Carlo Mense, Johannes Molzahn, and Otto Müller—one of the leading members of the "Brücke." Schlemmer lives alone in Breslau until an apartment has been found. He works concentratedly on the wall paintings for the Folkwang Museum and prepares the production of an opera and ballet by Stravinsky, which are performed at the Breslau Stadttheater [City Opera] in December.

1930: The first months of this year are devoted entirely to painting. Continued work on the wall panels; large compositions completed. In April the family is reunited in Breslau. Gropius, who is directing the exhibition of the German Werkbund in Paris, puts three figurines from the "Triadic Ballet" on display. Schlemmer goes to Paris in May for their installation and then on to Berlin, where he designs the production of Schönberg's *Glückliche Hand* ["Lucky Hand"] at the Kroll Opera.

Friends in Dessau report on the changes at the Bauhaus: Klee is leaving for the Academy in Düsseldorf, Hannes Meyer has been summarily fired and is on his way to Russia with a group of students. Mies van der Rohe becomes director of the Bauhaus. In September Otto Müller dies. At the Breslau Academy the first effects of the world-wide depression begin to make themselves felt: academic chairs that become vacant are not to be filled, the studio theater is not approved, salary cuts are in the offing. Schlemmer concentrates on his painting. In October the alarming news arrives from Weimar that the paintings and reliefs he had done in the workshop building for the Bauhaus Exhibition of 1923 have been destroyed, the first foreshadowing of the wholesale destruction of art works by the up-and-coming Nazi Party. At almost the same time Schlemmer exhibits his finished panels for the Folkwang Museum in Breslau's Silesian Museum.

Major pictures of this period: *Eingang zum Stadion* ["Entrance to the Stadium"], *Figuren im Interieur* ["Figures in an Interior"],

251

Frauenschule ["School of Women"], *Duo, Vierzehnergruppe in imaginärer Architecktur* ["Group of Fourteen in an Imaginary Architecture"], *Festliche Zwölf* ["Festive Twelve"]. Exhibitions: Breslau, Stuttgart, Berlin.

1931: The general political and economic situation is confused and puzzling. Nevertheless Moll manages to bring Muche to Breslau. In March the Academy throws a happy, lighthearted party, with Schlemmer contributing decisively to its success. In March a reduction in income forces the Schlemmers to give up their large and expensive apartment and exchange it for a little row house in the Werkbund colony. At the April International Theater Exhibition in Zurich Schlemmer exhibits his theatrical works—the ballet and the Bauhaus Theater; the exhibition at the Kunstgewerbemuseum [Museum of Arts and Crafts] opens with a lecture by Schlemmer. At the same time the Zurich Kunsthaus offers a representative show of his paintings. Meeting and conversations with Otto Meyer-Amden. In May Schlemmer displays examples of paintings and reliefs intended for wall decoration at the Berlin Architecture Show. Through the architect Adolf Rading, he is commissioned to decorate the house of Rading's client, Dr. Raabe, in Zwenkau. He decides on compositions in wire which attach to the wall, the first time he has used such a technique for wall decoration.

This productive year yields the paintings *Gruppe am Geländer* ["Group at a Railing"], *Junge in Blau-Weiß* ["Youth in Blue-White"], *Gruppe mit blauem Ekstatiker* ["Group with a Blue Ecstatic"], and a series of large watercolors.

The political horizon becomes increasingly clouded, and toward the end of the year all hopes of fruitful work in Breslau are smashed by an emergency order that the Academy be closed by April 1, 1932.

1932: Filled with sorrow, and not only for his own fate, Schlemmer opens in January the exhibition of the Silesian Künstlerbund [Artists' Guild], of which he is chairman: he stresses that a period of artistic hardship lies around the corner. At the Berlin Art Library he achieves great success with his lecture on the elements of theater. At the end of March, after the closing of the Breslau Academy, the Schlemmers have to give up the little house they had come to love. In June comes an appointment to the Vereinigte Staatsschulen für Kunst in Berlin.

On July 4 the "Triadic Ballet" has its debut in Paris at the International Dance Congress, and it receives a prize. Fernand Léger has high praise for the ballet. Schlemmer takes leave of his friends in Breslau with an atelier party. During the last period in Breslau he paints the major works *Treppenszene* ["Staircase Scene"], *Rote Mitte* ["Red Middle"], *Szene am Geländer* ["Scene at the Railing"], and the large picture *Bauhaustreppe* ["Bauhaus Stairway"] (now at the Museum of Modern Art in New York).

In the autumn the reunited family moves into an apartment in the Siemensstadt district of Berlin.

252

Schlemmer presents his inaugural lecture in the main lecture hall of the Vereinigte Staatsschulen, on the topic "Perspectives." His pleasure in the new opportunities open to him is dimmed by signs of the approaching political cataclysm. His works are displayed at the Frankfurt Kunstverein [Art Guild], along with works by Willi Baumeister and Otto Meyer-Amden. Other exhibitions: at the Hanover Kestner Society along with works by Picasso, and at the Flechtheim and Cassier Galleries in Berlin under the title "Living German Art." But these are among the last attempts to exhibit modern art pubicly.

1933: On January 15 Otto Meyer dies. With him Schlemmer loses his best friend and an intellectual partner whom it is impossible to replace.

Under the pressure of political developments, changes begin to take place at the Berlin Art Schools. Schlemmer expects to be dismissed. At the beginning of March he does, however, recieve invitations to Wiesbaden and Saarbrücken to lecture on the elements of theater. On this occasion he visits Baumeister in Frankfurt.

An exhibition scheduled to open on March 14 in the Stuttgart Art Guild is banned by the SA and remains closed.

On April 30 Schlemmer is provisionally dismissed from the Consolidated Art Schools. In June he manages to take part in an exhibition of the Berlin Secession. In August he is fired summarily from his teaching post. In November the apartment in Berlin is given up, the family once more separated, and Schlemmer leaves Berlin.

To Gunda Stölzl

Breslau
October 20, 1929

The going-away party was nice, jolly, exuberant, but, but. Too bad you were not there. It was a gas! Everyone was very kind to us. The requisite speech was bursting with high points. Then on Saturday evening a humorous toast by Hänschen, the usual portfolio, a piece of weaving turned out by the weaving shop and presented by the mourning widow Otti, accompanied by a kiss from blackened lips. Ha, flowers for Tut, black balloons from the "colleagues." A play—for internal consumption, not funny to non-Bauhaus people. Well, it will lay the ground for real deeds. All in all, it was nice, and we might almost have been moved—except that in spirit we already feel that this is now "home."

Here, too, much work and confusion, due to the transition. In my "Art of the Theater" class there are seven men and two girls, and they are frightfully busy painting and making things. They seem to like their new broom and its sweep.

I have quite a bit to do for the theater; two Stravinsky pieces which are supposed to be put on in two weeks.

To Otto Meyer

Breslau
December 22, 1929

Do not think my silence is symptomatic of Breslau—it is not. It is simply that there has been much hustle and bustle with the local theater, where I just had my first—and successful—opportunity to stage something; now the tide is slowly ebbing, and I am coming to my senses again; but this letter today will have to be brief. I do not want "Christmas to pass without my having written you," really I don't.

The beginning here looks auspicious. I am alone in Breslau, while my wife and children stay in the Riesengebirge until an apartment has been found, but they are enjoying the wait, 27,000 feet high, with snow and skiing. We plan to spend Christmas there. I have a fine studio here, larger than the one in

Dessau, and conditions look favorable for working, the painting part of which I shall resume after the holidays.

To Otto Meyer

Brückenberg

January 31, 1930

Two pieces by Stravinsky at the Stadttheater here, stimulating, interesting; like everything in the official theater it required certain compromises which were not necessary at the Bauhaus Theater; it proved a success for me, especially the second piece, ballet-style, for which I was co-director—one could feel the difference between that and the first play, which the manager of the theater himself directed. These theatrical activities took up a good deal of time at the beginning. Plus general confusion as a result of the move, setting up the studio, new people. Now that is behind me. Christmas vacation with the family in the mountains, tomorrow being the last day. After that I am hoping to settle down in Breslau and devote myself to painting, a necessity, since the Folkwang Museum project is pressing; preliminary and follow-up sketches must still be completed. I am free to put theatrical matters aside for a time, and I shall do precisely that. The moment has come for painting, although certain circles still expect great things of me in the way of theater and are offering me all kinds of assistance. No matter! That field is really not very rewarding—the mime functions within such narrow limits: a brief moment of magic at considerable cost in terms of time and nervous energy, and all for something fleeting, linked to and dependent on other human beings!

I hear that in Dessau they are already bemoaning the theatrical productions that ceased with my departure; the new, political brand seems doomed to failure, and rightly so, I feel.

For my part, I take a certain satisfaction in having made the Bauhaus Theater good enough to tour several cities. This mission has been fulfilled. Some say I am now committed to continue what I started. Unfortunately I have another love, painting, and I cannot do both things at once if I hope to produce anything powerful and consistent. But for the immediate future and until further notice: painting, and theater only en passant.

In the spring the exhibition of the German Artists' Guild will take place in Stuttgart—in June I shall probably be in Munich staging a little dance performance for the Dance Congress.

I was surprised to learn that in Switzerland you are also experiencing political interference with art and the schools. The big advantage here is that the Academy comes under the jurisdiction of the national government in Berlin rather than that of the city government. The city takes umbrage but can do nothing. I, too, am concerned about the students here, although in a much pleasanter way than in Dessau. Here they are almost servile by comparison with the impudent Bauhaus students; one finds real interest and a strong desire to learn, quite unlike the arrogant and argumentative spirit at the Bauhaus. I find that what I have to offer is so new and unfamiliar that all the students are eager to take my courses. This fact gives my teaching a boost, and I am getting invaluable practice in presentation and precise expression. At the same time I can expand and deepen studies I could only touch on in Dessau.

"Space and Man" is the general topic, broad enough to put the fear of God in one.

Recently Theodor Däubler gave a lecture; he is a hymnic, oratorical poet with the physique of a Jupiter or an apostle; he spoke beautifully about Greece, one of his points being that the Greek example is periodically revived—he mentioned Hans von Marées—and me. On the strength of this talk we decided to plan on a trip to Greece with Däubler as our guide. Maybe next spring. Would you like to come along?

I have started to work. Peace has been restored—I am curious to see how my paintings will be affected by the new surroundings in terms of city, people, studio, setting.

Diary

February 12, 1930

The first paintings in Breslau.

My very first combined all the faults that I must try to

256

overcome. Excessive crowdedness, undisciplined, exaggerated forms. And: a poorly prepared canvas! Just give me the ideal preparation—or ideal for me—and all will be well! Now I have to do it myself. The canvas itself is excellent. The second series should be better (?). At first: vacillating between extremes, fear of copying myself, irritation at others' opinions. The greatest pitfall. The conception must always be fresh, reflecting the present moment, the milieu, the prevailing mood. Following an emotion-laden picture, something stark and simple, like the *Tischgesellschaft*. Everything emerges in the course of the actual work process. So now, thanks to the good canvas, I shall probably achieve the bright, light pictures for which I have been aiming so long, the delicate glaze effects. I am eager to see how they turn out.

Oh, this heady sensation of working! How wonderful it is to have to tear oneself away in the evening (as used to be the case), to be surprised anew each morning. The first glimpse of the picture! Priceless elation. This alone would be reward enough for the painter. And if his work then reaches out, makes others happy, does honor to its maker, he is but a few steps away from perfect happiness on earth.

Diary

February 21, 1930

Essen, Folkwang: the result of the new version: asymmetry as a deliberate principle to offset the symmetry of the architecture. A dynamic element. The central picture likewise asymmetrical. Furthermore, emphasis of the horizontals and verticals: not in vacillating groups of figures, but as an architectonic framework, into which the few figures are fitted, with which they are coordinated.

Effect: these few essential structures "hold down" the surfaces, extending to the outer reaches (in contrast to the earlier design, in which everything was floating!) and thus create tension over the surface. Thus the figures are also held taut, transfixed against the surface.

Postcard to Tut

Paris

May 14, 1930

I am sitting *seulement* on the Place de l'Opéra, letting Paris stream past me. Stores close at 7 P.M. A fantastic city. I look at the women and *je cherche toi, Tutine.* Apropos, Valesca Gert is also here. She will dance tomorrow. I have fled the exhibition because it made me angry.

The German section of the Werkbund exhibition is the only one that is finished! Very striking.

Postcard to Tut

Berlin

June 5, 1930

Oh, painting! How much more comfortable, more total, more responsible an activity it is than work in the theater, which is a mad helter-skelter. Schönberg in a milder mood today, many technical details still unsolved—a good learning experience for me. Am not perfectly satisfied. Still alarming uncertainties—threats of postponement, cancellation, etc. But by dint of night rehearsals from midnight to four we shall manage. I would have handled the directing better. Never got a chance.

Diary

June 11, 1930

Gropius and the Bauhaus took the decisive step of linking the question of modern art to the reality of handicraft, thus showing eager young artists that there are other possibilities for artistic expression besides painting. This valuable perception has caught on, and some wise instinct led certain art academies to institute workshops as well; for the academy, a holdover from the days of royal patronage, was in danger of creating an artistic proletariat, something it could ill afford in an age of intense economic hardship. When the young artist has a chance to paint walls and to become acquainted with the different materials (wood, textiles, etc.), he begins to perceive the limitations of his standard tools (color, brush, canvas). He learns to think in terms of materials, and sometimes he realizes that a craft suits his inclinations and abilities better.

To Freiherr von Schenk,
Nassau Art Guild, Wiesbaden

Breslau
June 19, 1930

Yes, let nothing be said against Stuttgart! A native city one can really treasure, and hold in reserve for one's declining years. But the younger years must unfortunately be spent in foreign parts. Breslau is not bad, thanks to the extraordinary patience and perceptivity of the director, thanks also to the unprecedented almost five months of vacation! And since Moll insists on filling every vacancy with a modern artist (as long as the supply lasts), prospects look most encouraging.

Gosebruch! He acts as though my slowness were annoying him, but whenever I want to really get started, which happens often enough, *he* applies the brakes. Now he has suddenly decided that either the pictures or the fountain have to go. But the latter is impossible, he says, because the hall was built around it and the fountain has become the emblem of the East Wing. But he has known that for a long time. Wouldn't mosaics or hangings be more suitable? Painting is certainly the cheapest solution, capable of anything, even to the point of being totally inconspicuous! Well, this summer I shall paint the panels and send them to Essen as a fait accompli, the only way to put a stop to Gosebruch's vacillation. When the museum directors meet in September, they will find the deed just about done.

To Gunda Stölzl

Breslau
June 20, 1930

Yes, I was in Berlin several times, for a production which went relatively well and to discuss various other projects that still await completion; some wall paintings, nothing pressing. I saw Carla, Clemens, the Siedhoffs, and Andi briefly from a distance, since I had to lunch with the celebrities, Schönberg, Klemperer, et al. I know we have many things to say and sigh over together, but why rub salt in old wounds when there are new ones; or rather, we have almost none, or only when we want to have them, which we do not. Breslau is mild, hot at the moment, but only in the air. I am doing some theater work, some theory, some man, some wall painting; I lecture on it about once a week but often don't bother.

How are things with the Schepers? Will they be coming back? My regards to Arndt and Albers—how about Hannes Meyer; he seems strangely quiet. Hadn't he planned to demonstrate against the Werkbund Exhibition in Paris? Will he carry through on that? Will the Bauhaus? The exhibition of work by Gropius and the others is really good! Almost unbeatable. Although I was annoyed at Gropius and at Moholy, who is more arrogant than ever, I still enjoyed the five days in Paris. The excellent catalog by Herbert Bayer must be making the rounds of the Bauhaus, right? So the Loew girl, Winter, and Ehrlich have also left? Forming an "YZ Group" in Berlin? Who is left? Anyone new? Anyone good? Collectivists, socialists, or what sort of -ists?

What if the Kandinskys are granted a leave? I have to check up occasionally and make sure things are all right—or all left. Schmidtchen? Nonne? How are they doing, how do they feel about the Bauhaus? Eh? Albers, when he writes, does not sound happy either. What is the problem? How about the Bourgeois Admiral—what is he doodling these days?

To Otto Meyer

Breslau
June 29, 1930

So: I had to turn down the Dance Congress in Munich because an important theatrical project in Berlin came up, as well as an exhibition here at the Academy; and things became simply too hectic when my plans for Munich were thrown off by the woman dancer's injuring her knee. Too bad; the basic conception was good, well worth pursuing, but it would take time. No one here has sufficient training yet.

260

Paris was improvised; I, too, was taken by surprise. Three of my ballet figurines are on display there, and I was asked to supervise the installation. Gropius and Moholy had been put in charge of the Werkbund Exhibition at the Grand Palais, and had invited me to participate. Probably they just wanted to get whatever would make the greatest impression. It is remarkable to see what Gropius always manages to produce, a good example being this exhibition in Paris, the first since the war, which was, all in all, pretty impressive. There were a few rather unfortunate personality conflicts, especially in connection with Moholy. Still, it was my first visit to Paris in sixteen years, and I saw Pellegrini for what must also have been the first time in sixteen years!

Noteworthy new acquaintances were Mondrian, whom I unfortunately saw only briefly, because my French is too weak, and Arp, whom I liked very much. Then the art dealers and the works they have on display. I saw a good exhibition of Picasso, Braque, Léger, and Marie Laurencin.

Picasso: he seems experimental to the point of madness when one compares him with Braque, who is settled, "beautiful" (in his large, well-constructed pictures which gush out in deep, rich harmony and display beautiful technique). My feelings were very ambivalent, except in the case of one picture done in big forms and colors, showing painted sculpture.

I know Léger quite well; Moll in Breslau has a good collection of him, including three large new pictures. What I saw of his in Paris was more decorative than ever. The other new things I saw were not especially striking. A very interesting Delacroix exhibit, revealing what was new about him at the time and then blossomed in the works of others. Also saw new and interesting work by Chirico, some of it very baroque, Roman, historical. I was reminded of a thought I often have in connection with Baumeister: how strict one is, how difficult one makes it for oneself, how little one lets oneself go (for "one" read "I"!). Also: many of our early Stuttgartian abstract tendencies are turning up among the modern French, making these early abstractions seem modern again. So Paris was certainly stimulating, perhaps giving me a push in a new direction—as yet undisclosed.

Moll, the director of the Academy here, rules quietly and wisely. Things are much calmer than at the Bauhaus, although there are pros and cons. Friends who remain in Dessau have remarked several times that we should be grateful to be gone. The communism (of the students) seems impossible to extirpate, despite the numerous victims, i.e. expulsions or voluntary withdrawals.

To Ludwig Grote,
Director of the Dessau Museum

Breslau
July 7, 1930

You will also have learned that despite the new army directive to the effect that no one may leave the Bauhaus with impunity, Paul Klee is going to Düsseldorf! Well, well, well! "Who will teach my sons to cast the spear and honor the gods when I am gone . . . ." Klee's son, Felix the Cat, just celebrated his debut as a director here. Things are going well with me at this Academy. Wonderful relaxation after the boiling cauldron in Dessau. No student revolts, no all-night meetings, no discussions that go around and around in circles. When one has one's own problems, one has one's hands full.

To Tut

Breslau
July 7, 1930

Well, *Grande Sensation:* Paul Klee is leaving on April 1, 1931, for Düsseldorf! Just imagine! The silent one. And: we have been proved right!

We also stopped in Salzbrunn, which has the biggest warm springs in Silesia. Large parks, promenades, everything bustling. Otto Müller came down from his room but went no farther; had to sit down, totally exhausted. He looks very bad, pitiable; I could hardly bear to look. At night he has to sleep sitting up, and then only three or four hours.

To Tut

Breslau

July 9, 1930

I am beginning to paint, little studies. The canvases will be ready tomorrow.

I feel as lonely as a widower. It is unbelievably empty and silent in the house, where in contrast to Dessau I miss having life around me. It really is nice to come home and find a change of scene, life. I am recovering from the stresses and strains of the past few weeks and preparing for the next Saison .... I miss my vis-à-vis morning, noon, and night; am reading Flake's *Marquis de Sade.*

At the moment I feel at peace with the world, a condition ascribable merely to our financial state. We cannot complain, but an example like Kanoldt proves one should never sit back and rest on one's laurels; each day brings new trials. But just now I do yet not feel like my own executor, but rather in the very midst of it all, as far as paintings are concerned. I have a preliminary sketch yet to do. I am keeping records and feel relatively happy.

Adieu, my sweet turtle dove, my little ring-tailed swallow! Take good care of yourself and the children.

To Wilhelm Schlemmer

Breslau

July 18, 1930

We have discovered a real marvel: not far from here, near Bunzlau (famous for its pots) is a place with the name of Schlemmer! What d'ye say to that? True, it turned out to have neither a railroad station nor a post office, but it does have a *Kraftpostation* [bus station]. So you see: the grandparental name lives on! for their name was "Kraft," a much handsomer, prouder name than the ominous Schlemmer. Actually we wanted to surprise you with a postcard or a photo of the Schlemmer station, but it is easier to get to Wölfelsgrund than to Schlemmer. We also wondered if we should move there; the address would be so simple: "2 x Schlemmer."

263

Since the beginning of the vacation the family have been in "Wölfelsgrund, County Glatz, Alixishof, am Urnitzberg, care of Frau Loparta," and they will stay there for the whole vacation. I give you the address in all its glory on purpose, for it conveys an approximate idea of this truly lovely stretch of landscape, which is not in the Riesengebirge but in the Glatzer Bergland, more idyllic, softer, more South German, than the Riesengebirge. They are staying in a magnificent big farmhouse, wooden Swiss-style construction, with balconies running all around it; it lies in an open meadow but is surrounded by woods, a quarter of an hour from the village. I hope to go there some time this week and make sure all is well.

In the family's absence the house is being put in shape. Furniture also has to be made, not to mention other things we still lack, for we are secretly preparing ourselves to celebrate enduring ten years of a relatively happy marriage which in Tut's opinion has not really been long in duration.

To Konrad K. Düssel

Breslau
July 20, 1930

Your unstinting praise means all the more to me because I know you judge things on their own merits, in the positive sense. Given the present chaos in the art world, selection naturally becomes all-important if any standards are to be established and personality appreciated, personality in art, I mean, and whatever points to that noble goal known as style.

You have probably heard that I have also had a picture at the National Gallery in Berlin since this spring, an earlier work from 1924 called *Konzentrische Gruppe*.

Although we are on vacation, I am staying in Breslau for a while to finish the wall pictures for Essen at long last. But I plan to come to Stuttgart in the fall, in early September.

Diary

August 13, 1930

How dependent I am on my materials. The different forms of canvas preparation lead to totally different results. The very smooth ones lead to almost excessively flowing painting, a pitfall for me. Delacroix says one's material should be as unyielding as marble, so one can conquer it with patience. This dictum means as much to me now as it ever did.

I incline more in the direction of a Chirico or a Carrà and their Belgian successors than in the direction of a Léger. At the moment I am very far from plastic abstractions, and I believe my early abstract pictures point that way.

Restlessness is preventing me from meditating. Once again something has come to a conclusion, and something new seems to be in the making. A state I often experience, a sign of regeneration.

Diary

August 23, 1930

The artistic waters have become fairly tranquil, stirred and muddied only in one place—could there be a more perfect example of stagnation? Only one issue can still raise the critics' hackles: the issue of style. The tide of Expressionism has long since run out, only abstraction still has little waves licking around it: an evening of rare beauty! Paul Klee, yesterday still a little shrimp, is today already considered an "island." Kandinsky, once one of the wildest, impossible to classify, has entered the ranks of the classics, clear and unruffled as a mirror. Only in one place? Why? Because here the issue of the figural crops up, the problem of style, which is actually the issue central to the art of all ages; yet precisely that is taboo. "Wooden dolls!" "Doll painting!" The slogan, once formulated, "makes the rounds." But no one ever passes the word that wherever such problems have arisen, during all periods of grand figural style, one can easily detect the proximity to a doll-like conception of the human figure. Aren't Indian, Egyptian, Archaic Greek statuary and painting perilously close to this image of man, which, because it is art, not nature, and because it is produced by artistic means, necessarily entails abstraction: the doll, the reflection, the symbol. (The sculptor Marcks always speaks of his "dolls," and by no means ironically). Aren't the figures of Seurat, that great anti-Impressionist master of composition, suspiciously close to the doll-like; and do they not owe their greatness to this very form, which was purified in the crucible of abstraction? And is it surprising that the same symptoms appear today, wherever we find the struggle to master grand artistic form, subject matter, concept, style—a struggle unfortunately waged in all too few places. When painters finally stop imitating, i.e. painting from a model, when they learn to work and compose freely, drawing on their knowledge of nature and the human figure, a sacrifice will be necessary; naturalistic truth will have to go, but only to make way for something better: artistic truth.

Must one state these simple things nowadays? It would seem so. Then why are the critics so reluctant? What are they afraid of? The field of art is in beautiful order, thanks to its stagnation, and one risks one's neck if one attempts to upset the prevailing status quo. Nonetheless: "Everything is in flux . . . ," and for all their lamentations, our dear contemporaries will not be spared this last bitter cup: the way to style leads via the doll!

To Otto Meyer

Breslau

September 2, 1930

Unfortunately I shall not have time before the 14th to go to Stuttgart. I must finish up some of the panels for Essen, and if possible also get to the ones I have not yet started, unless I decide to wait and see what impact the finished ones have in Essen. Perhaps I shall receive orders to halt immediately! The hitch to these panels is, as I mentioned previously, that the center of the room contains a fountain (by George Minne), with figures of boys kneeling on its rim, white marble. The paintings must appear discreetly muted, almost as if they were not there at all. The best I can do is to dip these fresh, sometimes really good-looking paintings in gray, covering them with veil after veil until the desired effect seems achieved.

Baumeister seems dissatisfied with my present anti-abstracts. Last time he had already begun to ask sotto voce: how long will you keep this up? I imagine I shall eventually reach a new form of abstraction via the specifications of the architects, which involve not painting as such but compositions in material, adapted to the given architectural situation. The clear distinction between "painting" and "composition in material" suits me very well. I am certainly far from any sort of abstract painting in Baumeister's sense, at least for awhile.

And politics! What do you think of the confused state of affairs in Germany? When will the new Stresemann appear? Do you still take an interest in these things as you used to?

To Gunda Stölzl

Breslau

September 2, 1930

The children are enjoying life, going to school and learning, or not, as the case may be: Karin avidly, Jai wouldn't dream of it, their little brother in kindergarten. They are also taking music lessons from a lady. We have an angora cat and two toads, but we are releasing them for reasons of feeding. Tut will be going back to Wölfelsgrund with the children for the "potato harvest" vacation, while I still hope to do the Stuttgart-Munich-Zurich route.

I am working my head off on those everlasting Folkwang panels, which are finally getting finished—all good things come to an end. But so much work, and so much up-and-down on the ladder, because the panels are so large. I get plenty of exercise. Sometimes I dash over to Berlin, where there are architects who seem interested in Schlemmerisms. If Dessau were only located on the Oder, one could perhaps sail by, but it is too far out of my way.

Good heavens, what reorganizations you will all have to put up with under a new director (I assume you have returned) —adjustments, as they say, discussions of where things stand, will stand, and should stand. I abstain, as I did at the recent elections, from giving my opinion.

Gropius irked me, Hannes irked me, and I am good friends with both, the party of the middle. I should like to see the middle strengthened! Well, you know how it is. We have only rumors as to what happened and what is happening now. There was something in the papers about a mediation board, but we never found out what was decided. Baumeister will be appointed, to "support" Kandinsky, who now stands alone; peace and quiet will reign, for this was the idea behind summoning Mies van der Rohe to Dessau.

You will all be bedded in roses, there will be no more deadlines, not a political creature will be stirring, even to leave the sinking ship. That is about the way I picture such a change of régime, first left, now right. Are you launching any protest? One hears that the entire student body stands firm behind Hannes—is that true? How does Mies handle such a front? Is Fräulein Reich already there? (Thy Reich come!) Naturally we are all ears when it comes to any news of you all and Dessalia.

By the way, Hannes' swan song in the *Tagebuch* was very good. Who could help laughing? The wolf has finally slipped out of his sheepskin, and one may well ask why he waited this long. And why has he waited until now to kick "Uncle Kandinsky" into the Adriatic? What does Nina say to that?

This has to stop. You should have a newsletter printed up. What has happened to our lines of communication?

To Willi Baumeister

Breslau
September 30, 1930

Otto Müller is dead; he had been very sick. The lungs. He was shrinking before our very eyes, although he himself ascribed no importance to his condition, or did not choose to. He was a good man and an original, probably the best of the Brücke painters, along with Kirchner; he had been at the Academy eleven years. We have laid him out in his studio and draped it with the black Triadic curtains.

Moll is in Berlin until the middle of next week, trying to find out from the authorities what happens next, for unpleasant rumors are making the rounds to the effect that vacated positions are not to be filled and that no one is to be promoted. But this would be catastrophic for the Academy, since Müller is dead and Kanoldt is leaving; we will thus have two positions vacant. If the rumor turns out to be true, it will mean a considerable blow for Molzahn and me, since the salary is simply not adequate, and will be even less so if there are cuts and other sacrifices.

Moll's last words about you were that he dare not tempt you to leave a better position and come here, especially since financially Breslau can hardly promise anything. Once it could, but now there is nothing at all. I already feel myself a victim of the situation, since the promises made me when I came have not been kept. The Breslau Theater fulfilled its commitment for only a year, and that after a struggle. The intended studio theater at the Academy was not approved by the Ministry. So I gave it up, and not even with such deep regret; now I am concentrating on painting, especially wall painting.

To Paul Westheim

Breslau

October 8, 1930

You might be interested to know that last week my wall paintings and reliefs in Weimar, for which you were once such a powerful advocate, have been either removed or painted over. I received this information from the building superintendent, who managed to carry some of the lighter pieces of sculpture to safety and writes in his letter, "Everything has been painted over in white, which I and many others deeply regret. But who can block the march of history?" I have not been able to discover who initiated this particular march, whether it was Director Schultze, born Naumburg, or freaky Frick of the Ministry of Culture. In any case, these products of mine had withstood the storms and the march of history for five years.

But let us not despair, for "new life blossoms among the ruins." I recently finished the nine wall paintings for the Folkwang Museum in Essen; they will be shown here in the Silesian Museum for a short while before being shipped off to Essen.

I suspect they represent something of real significance.

To Otto Meyer

Breslau

October 9, 1930

You have probably realized that your doubts were, alas, alas, justified; I shall not be able to get away. Even a very reduced program of just a few days in the Riesengebirge before the 15th will probably not work out. I would be finished, but then I shall have to stay here to help carry the heavy panels back and forth, touch up details, and so on. So I have to forego the pleasure of seeing you; I have been trying to accustom myself to this idea for three days, as the situation became apparent. The time would simply have been too short. I would have needed at least a week in Stuttgart, I would have wanted to see Munich again, and that would have left too brief a time with you. So we shall have to postpone it to next Christmas.

I wish you could see the finished pictures for Essen! My colleagues at the Academy and my friends in the art world express great admiration. They are extremely reserved in the use of color, for that was how it had to be. Four of them were sprayed with a spray gun, and I would have particularly liked you to see the effect. They seem almost unreal, "hand" painting reduced to a minimum; by contrast, but not a great contrast, the other five are brighter. I am very curious to learn what impact they have in Essen. Also what impact they have on the future of wall painting, a genre to which they represent a considerable contribution. Strange coincidence: at almost the same time as I finished them, my wall paintings and sculptures done in Weimar were destroyed, painted over by the Nazi Kultusbewahrungsanstalt [Institute for the Preservation of Culture].

Another reason for my not coming, although an indirect one: the financial straits in which we unfortunately continue to find ourselves, despite various strokes of relative good luck; for these hardly change the picture at all, so rapidly does any apparent gain melt away.

In the meantime the rightists have won in Germany. I hope this does not mean a turn for the worse!

To Willi Baumeister
Breslau
October 21, 1930
We are still fooling around with the frescos. But starting Sunday everything will be on display at the museum for two weeks. Then off to Essen. Ha!

In the meantime a lot of water has gone under the Academy bridge. Moll was in Berlin reconnoitering, met Muche and seems to have taken a liking to him. Others, among them Scharoun in Berlin, helped matters along, and since Muche agreed to the salary offered, he emerged as the leading candidate from a unanimous meeting of the Academy. And that decision will probably stand. Nota bene, he was our choice; the appointment still has to be approved. What tipped the balance as far as Moll was concerned was the need for a candidate with strong pedagogic credentials, and those Muche had, having worked for Itten and the Bauhaus. The second candidate, to replace the departing Kanoldt, has not been chosen. The (confidential) list of possibilities runs as follows: George Grosz, Heckel, Huber, Schmidt-Rottluff, Masereel, and of course you. Kirchner, too. The suggestion has been made that someone should be appointed from the Brücke, in memory of Otto Müller. Moll is partly open to such suggestions, partly closed; sometimes he lets one in on what is going on, sometimes he acts behind closed doors and surprises everyone.

Diary
October 1930
Proportion and the basic laws: experience has taught me that proportion and the basic laws signify something very noble in art, but also something very dangerous. It is utterly fatal to treat them as a convenient recipe or dogma, to invoke them before the picture itself has been visualized; instead of "freedom under law" one ends up with inspiration in handcuffs. No! The initial impulse should be emotion, the stream of the unconscious, free, unfettered creation. The more latitude feeling receives, the more readily it will gravitate toward precision, compressing the picture into final form without help from the laws

of proportion or measurements. If mathematical proportions and measurements *are* called in, they should function as a regulative, first simply to confirm what instinct has created and then, proceeding from this confirmation, to establish new rules (which combine feeling and objective principles).

The scientific bent in modern art should not be considered a product of our allegedly intellectual and rationalistic age; this becomes clear when one examines similar attempts made in earlier eras: the Egyptians and early Greeks with their measurements; Leonardo; Dürer, who measured with passion and real German thoroughness; and also Philipp Otto Runge, who tried to trap his romantic visions with the help of "strict regularity."

In our own times, most of the Bauhaus masters, each more or less on his own, studied the fundamental laws of order in art, partly out of the necessity for basic principles that could be taught, partly because ever since Goethe, painters have longed to discover the equivalent of musical harmony and counterpoint and to achieve a precision of form similar to that in music. But lovely dreams of this sort always remain unfulfilled. To this day, a common denominator has not been found for the innumerable, highly individual, and constantly shifting forms of the plastic arts.

We moderns lack the great symbols and beliefs of the old masters because we live in a period of decay, shifting values and, it is to be hoped, of renewal; what else can we do but remain simple and straightforward in our manner of portrayal, open to all the conscious and unconscious impulses that take shape within us, so that gradually they can forge an appropriate form?

Diary

Mid-November 1930

State of affairs in Weimar, 1923:

For the first major Bauhaus Exhibition in Weimar I decided that the workshop building designed by van de Velde, with its walls, niches, stairways, and hallways, offered the most promising setting for a unified and unifying complex of wall paintings and reliefs. At the time, the Thuringian Volksbildungs-ministerium [Ministry for Popular Education] stipulated that the walls be returned "to their original state," but this stipulation applied only to the main building, which in fact was restored to its original state as soon as the exhibition was over. Among the many innovations which the Bauhaus displayed at the time, my work on the interiors and the "Triadic Ballet," performed in conjunction with the Exhibition, received great recognition and were acknowledged to be among the few important modern attempts to revive the long-lost bond between architecture, painting, and sculpture.

In the entrance hall, a pentagonal space, two forty-eight-foot-high relief figures were applied in mortar directly to the wall. A similar but flatter relief was mounted on the ceiling. The adjoining corridor was done in flat painting. One central figure on the short wall of the corridor in white, black, and various bronzes; on the two side walls several large linear figures, upright and recumbent.

The first stairway from the entry hall led past niches to the left and right which contained small metallic figures (metallically treated reliefs) against a dark background. A corridor facing this stairway was adorned with a figure on the ceiling and linear compositions on the side walls.

A broad winding staircase with a skylight led to the upper floor. The curving wall of this stairway was given over to a frieze of figures, full of movement but delicate; viewed from the dark hallways of the upper floor, this frieze was especially striking. The coloring adhered mainly to earth tones, a range which seemed natural for wall paintings on a large scale. And then the metallic surfaces and reliefs.

Well-known critics praised my contribution as the only positive feature of the entire Exhibition. It bore not the slightest resemblance to expressionistic excesses. In fact, the radical young Bauhaus members reproached me for my "classical" bent, my ethical approach, "the knights and heroes I had painted on the walls"!

State of affairs, Weimar, 1930:

During the seven years of their existence, the paintings and reliefs went untouched, except for a small portion removed in connection with some new building done under Professor Bartning, the successor to Gropius. Then Professor Schultze-

Naumburg and his colleagues caused them to be totally destroyed. Even if Professor Schultze-Naumburg asserts that my works were totally alien to his tastes, that he considered them "exercises devoid of artistic value," and that "their present condition justified their removal," I still feel it was culturally barbarous to have them destroyed without informing their creator. Now elsewhere in Weimar, in the museum, the removal of the entire modern collection has been ordered, so it is becoming apparent that there is a method to the madness.

Diary

November 27, 1930

The horrible thing about this cultural backlash is that it is not directed against works of a political nature, but against purely artistic, aesthetic works, identified with "Bolshevism" merely because they are new, unusual, different, original. In fact, the purge of the Weimar Museum has affected artists whose profoundly German mentality and loyalties no one in his right mind would question.

If this movement should spread, the great danger is that spontaneous artistic creation, the old tradition of artistic freedom, will be destroyed and the artists robbed of their naïveté of thought and expression. One cannot replace the work of today's artists by masterpieces of the previous century, for Caspar David Friedrich, say, or Schinkel, were misunderstood in their own times, when they were innovators and the heralds of the future.

To Otto Meyer

Breslau

December 1, 1930

Only the first six of the nine panels have arrived in Essen, and the director writes that they are so wonderfully beautiful, especially in terms of technique, that they should be guarded with one's life. That sounds promising, but I also detect a note of concern: how are they going to protect these pictures, which people will be tempted to touch? Yes, how? Well, they have

274

been paraffined, which will guard them against grasping hands, and in general pictures in museums hang in the open without being "grasped." The other three panels are still here, but they will be sent off this week. When everything is installed I should like to go and see, but only if the Museum invites me.

I do not know whether you in Switzerland can picture what is going on in Germany these days: whatever it may be, it is far from gratifying; on the contrary, very murky and possibly threatening. The mood abroad in the land resembles the one during the inflation. Perhaps intensified here in Breslau by the political clashes. Skirmishes, police alerts are the order of the day (disorder of the day).

In Weimar—perhaps you have read about it—there is an art scandal raging because Frick, the National Socialist, has ordered the removal or storage of all the modern art, and Schultze-Naumburg, Bartning's successor, has had the paintings and reliefs I did in 1923 painted over.

Will one have to retire to the Bohemian Forest when the Nazis take over, or will we proceed *directement* into the next war?

To Gunda Stölzl

Breslau

February 28, 1931

Thank you for your letter and the balm to my spirits, your assurance that I am a welcome guest, one of the tribe of the Bauhaus-people, who do not die when they depart. That I am only seemingly happy, that you are only seemingly unhappy, because one always thinks things are better elsewhere. Be comforted! Here, too, not everything that glints in the sun is rotten; here, too, one can bemoan human failings, the general atmosphere, money problems. Yes, I, we, are interested in everything connected with the Haus, to the bitter end. Also the Bauhaus newspaper, now alas so shrivelled, when it was supposed to expand, thanks to American funding, no? Who will be the first to join the American branch?

The party at the Academy was also nice. Tut and I went as Moors, accompanied by Otto as Queen of the Night and Day in

275

a smashing costume made of curtains; in the absence of other good costumes, we were the hit of the party and much enjoyed ourselves. At 5 A.M. we visited our friend and benefactor: hot sausages, coffee, and other delights. Was your Bauhaus party closed to the public? There was no report of it in the paper.

For lack of lack I have not been back to Berlin. Only indirect sales. The triumph a purely moral one, more, it would seem, than Kandinsky's, who has been given a pretty hard time, I gather. Coming up an exhibition in Krefeld, after that one in Zurich, where I shall go at the end of April for a lecture, "Elements of the Theater." They are also having a theater exhibition there. We want to move, because this place is too expensive. We would like to build but cannot, for lack of money. Are alternately happy and unhappy. What will this Easter bring?

To Willi Baumeister

Breslau
March 6, 1931

We had an Academy party here, in which I participated. Then I wrote something on Otto Meyer, the essay evolving into a lecture which I presented here last Tuesday, with ten photos which when enlarged proved extraordinarily effective. Simultaneously there was an exhibition of Otto Meyer's works in the corridors of the Academy, the contents of a portfolio he had sent me.

Lecture: on April 25 I shall deliver my "Elements of the Theater" in Zurich, for the opening of the theater exhibition there; I was invited by Altherr. I am pleased to be able to go to Zurich, for this way I shall also visit Otto Meyer. There was also an exhibition at Flechtheim's; now there is one in Krefeld, and there will be one at the Kunsthaus in Zurich. Success? Only a moral one, thanks to Glaser, Osborn.

This creative lull, resulting from a combination of circumstances, should give me the impetus for new work. The exhibitions have an encouraging effect. And my temperament urges me to work and demonstrate my worth. You know how it is.

The only abstraction recently was a wire figure, which may appear sometime, when everything else is finished, that is. My paintings tending toward even more relaxed, representational stuff. Everything is in flux. I shall probably not return to pictorial abstraction at all. But in solid materials I will.

The money situation is unbelievable at the moment. We shall probably give up this place and exchange five rooms for three; there is a possibility of our getting something in the Werkbund colony more like what we had in Dessau than our present lordly marble staircase. True, we will only be able to manage by applying American space-saving methods: folding beds or bunks, etc. After all: we need a thousand and are getting five hundred!

Today we have visitors from the Ministry in Berlin; grand inspection for the Academy. Moll will describe his sorrows, to the effect that since the loss of Otto Müller's class everyone else has been bearing a heavier load. What we really need is a sensible curriculum, which we plan to put together shortly. Oh, yes, I not only am a member of the steering committee of the Silesian Artists' Guild; I have been made its chairman. Silesia for the Stuttgartians, I say! Ha, ha, ha!

I am somewhat at odds with the kind of self-indulgence I find in the *Cahiers d'Art* ["Art Notebooks"] —Picasso—it is getting on my nerves. Masson likewise highly suspect. The fact is: I am moving away from anything fantastical, abstract, uncontrollable, and am trying to master natural shape governed by formal necessity.

Diary

March 18, 1931

A baroque period!? Not without risks, desertion of strictness, of static-constructivist structure, in favor of dynamism, intense feeling, resulting perhaps in romantic ecstasy.

This is not (only) an answer to the critics—who always reproach me for the stereotype quality, the doll-like, decorative traits—it reflects my own impulses. Perhaps pre-spring impulses to break out of the old shell and rigidity and flow outwards.

277

Diary

Doctrine: what suits me is the richly flowing, sonorous, pastoral "organ sound." A pitfall: the expressive; theatrical posturing. And now, with my new pictures, the danger of falling into mannerism. How does Schinkel put it? "One is really original only when one is searching."

To Willi Baumeister

May 29, 1931

So you have already been in Berlin, where I must go on Friday to see where I stand, since it seems impossible to get sufficient information on my walls for the Bauhaus Exhibition. Twenty-four feet long, twelve feet high! Have you ever been confronted with such proportions?

In Zurich and Switzerland I had a lovely time.

Otto Meyer in his venerable beauty, citizen of a city, teacher at a school—a completely new way of life, partly enjoying it, partly suffering, struggling, resigned. To each of these participles one could add a long sentence: it seems to me he is happy with his life, fairly comfortable in terms of security; he suffers from things in general, and more specifically from his health, which did not strike me as very sound: difficulty breathing, a sense of physical and mental oppression; but he ignores it whenever possible, fights for his cause, the cause of art itself, defying his enemies, resigning only at the point at which we, too, resign, when the last drop has been drained.

Altherr, the director of the Kunstgewerbemuseum, a very decent, obliging man; and in fact everyone connected with the School and with the Museum, where the theatrical exhibition took place, was very nice to me.

I am continuing this letter in Berlin, where I shall be from morn to midnight to find out about the Bauhaus Exhibition. The art part is being handled stingily. Hofer will do, but most of the other paintings are lousy. The "connection" with architecture has not exactly been established; the paintings should have been placed in real rooms, painted for them. As it is, one sees all too clearly that the architects don't give a damn about painting.

Handsome rooms by Marcel Breuer, some rather interesting advertising material by Moholy. I made the rounds only once and intend to return. Over Whitsuntide I shall do some painting on panels in Breslau and mount these.

This evening *Tales of Hoffmann* and from there to the railroad station; I shall get into Breslau at seven tomorrow morning.

To Willi Baumeister

Breslau
Ascension Day
June 4, 1931

I am thinking of travelling via Frankfurt, but no, it will not be possible before the holidays. A pity that we will not see each other. Tut may pass through Stuttgart in July on her way back from the south, where she is being allowed to take a brief vacation for a change.

Have you heard how the Russians are building cities! Here we had *Stahlhelm* demonstrations, assassination, unrest. What is going on, anyway? Tut is making an inspection tour to find an island where we can be out of harm's way when the great convulsion comes. What wicked fairy placed these gifts in our cradle?

Diary

June 22, 1931

After "completions" of all different sorts (finishing the three wall projects: Folkwang, Zwenkau, Berlin Bauhaus Exhibition), after the Flechtheim and Zurich exhibits, after the last "baroque" envoys to the Exhibition of the German Artists' Guild—now that vacation has arrived, something new must be undertaken.

New things and old. Old in the sense that "back to the simple forms, to the elements" remains the eternal old = new requirement. I must become simple again. For in my recent work I abandoned simple pictorial elements in favor of natural elements, figural motifs, which were never nature enough to satisfy as such.

My good pictures could be reduced to a few simple forms, to one good, full chord. One needs so little in the way of good composition to make a picture! Otto Meyer often chooses the elementary geometrical forms as the basis of a picture. This must be the foundation of my further work. For it implies a return to integrating the abstract with the elementary, simple pictorial forms; it banishes the naturalistic plague, which had begun to spread unchecked in the later pictures. With this hope for success I enter the summer holidays of 1931.

To Otto Meyer

Breslau
July 2, 1931

Perhaps I have just discovered this core in myself; the opposite of really original creation often seems to involve beginning with an original thought, only to go astray later on; others, maybe I among them, begin confused and stabilize later on. I know of several examples. One hopes to "stabilize" in the good sense of the word. It is up to fate and one's own strength, always subject to doubt and latent insecurity. In these past few months I have completed so many projects, now things are settling down; I, too, am settling down, waiting, relaxed at last, for something new to develop.

The gist of the critical digest: the (art) world has taken note of me. The "beautiful" works I did in 1924. I have, or seem to have, created a type, most authentic where "my movements resemble my pictures." Can one return to a state which was good once, or must one move forward into uncharted territory? We shall see.

The "wire picture" displayed in fragmentary form in Berlin interested the architects there very much. It is now installed in three parts.

To Willi Baumeister

I stayed home—in the new house, which is as good as a vacation trip. Tut, on the other hand, was in Dalmatia, whence she returned very cheerful and buoyed up. It was her reward for bearing ten years of marriage with so much pluck. I have finally sent off the essay on Otto Meyer to *Kunst und Künstler* ["Art and Artists"], where it should be appearing soon. When I saw Otto Meyer last, his health not good at all; probably he will decide to undergo an operation, which represents a big decision for him; let us hope all goes well. It is no simple affair.

Essen, wall paintings. I really ought to see how they look in their present state. It is possible that the transition from the figures to the right angles is insufficiently motivated. I sense that now myself. True, my intention was to avoid architectural-perspective-painting. Is the tone of the pictures too cool? To offset the warm color of the columns somewhat this cold gray seemed called for. Didn't you notice the difference between the cold gray tablets and the reddish ones (five gray to four reddish). Gosebruch criticized the dissimilarity, and is even thinking of having all nine reddish with single figures or all nine gray, with several figures. I feel that some syncopation, some interruption is essential. I had this five-four contrast in all my sketches. Gosebruch has not yet said anything about making the pictures "warmer," although he has commented plenty on everything else. He seems almost obsessed with the subject. He comes up with the strangest ideas, such as hanging tapestries by Kirchner over them "for ceremonial occasions," since the panels are very delicate (they are washable!). In actuality he wants to compensate for the fact that Kirchner was originally supposed to paint the adjacent great hall; a special fund was set up for Kirchner for the purpose, but now the room is to remain unpainted. Kirchner apparently reacted violently to this idea, criticized him sharply for the way the architect had ruined the hall with the fountain, but defended my work as the only way to save this mistake of a hall.

Essen, Artists' Guild. Yesterday I read the report; the final outcome: no sales. Not a single picture, not a single piece of sculpture. Sign of the times: things are going from bad to worse. One wonders why one continues exhibiting, why one even goes on producing. Oh, what at idiotic age we live in!! I, too, have had no sales for a long time. And no prospects, since the museums are in their last gasp. Another salary cut, so things look grimmer than ever. (Gave up on the theater long ago.) What can one do, where can one go? Moll is trying to work some improvements. Success highly unlikely.

The project for the figures in metal really looks fantastic. Photographs do not do them justice. Unfortunately rather far from civilization in Zwenkau, a village near Leipzig, the house of a medical doctor, built by Rading. That's the sort of commission we should be getting! And probably would be getting en masse if—we had won the war! Yes, that may be the crucial point, for who knows what Germany would have looked like then.

The wire sculpture, or better, "Composition in Metal," a figural composition made of different kinds of metal wire, consists of three figures: the large figure carries a smaller one in its hand; to the right of the wall in relation to the first figure is the metal profile of a face, over fifteen feet high. The figures stand out three inches from the wall, and the changing light creates interesting shifting shadows (on the sundial principle).

Diary

September 7, 1931

At the Bauhaus Theater we used to have something we called spatial dance, a series of movements which traced geometrical figures painted on the ground (square, diagonal, circle), this geometry being rendered by three dancers in differing tempos and steps. This dance expressed the space with an astonishing intensity, merely through the differently timed movements of the dancers and through the kinetic aspect of the progression. There were no "static tableaux," except at the end, which was reached when the three arrived simultaneously at the center. Much of what we did was surprising (to us as well). For instance, we determined the center of the space by stretching ropes, and the "tensions" radiating out from them resulted in entirely new configurations of space and movement. Another surprising effect resulted from something as simple and obvious, but unusual, as attaching poles to the body joints, "elongations of the instruments of movement," the biggest surprise of all being the movements executed with them. For static postures, "living tableaux," meant nothing here. "Let him who has eyes to see, see," for it is useless to try to understand this sort of thing in intellectual terms.

The concepts "mechanical" and "mechanistic" created the greatest misunderstandings. The world of forms I employed in the "Triadic Ballet" rested partly on the fundamental theories of geometry and stereometry, transposed into new, intriguing materials, appropriate to our times; and partly on the basic laws of the human body, which, as I constantly reiterate, is both a being of flesh and blood, mind and emotion, and a remarkably well-functioning apparatus of joints. When I took this particular aspect of the human body as the basis for certain unusual displays, without, however, maliciously disregarding the synthesis of both qualities. that was only my attempt at redressing the balance in favor of what is usually neglected in what we normally know as the dance.

I never created a "mechanical ballet," intriguing though it might be to construct figurines and sets directed by an automatic mechanism. The relatively slight gain in types of possible spatial movement would not justify the high cost of the apparatus. Even the mechanical qualities of the puppet are only relative, since it is not an automaton like E.T.A. Hoffmann's Olympia; the movement is produced by the articulation of the human hand. The disk figures in my "Figural Cabinet" are carried and manipulated by disguised dancers: thus the fluid human element always forms part of the game.

I readily concede that I came to the dance from painting and sculpture; I appreciated its essential element, movement, all the more because the expressive range of the former two arts is restricted to the static, the rigid, to "movement captured in a fixed moment." I have no need to prove that the plastic artist's world of forms and emotions can perfectly well be combined with that of the dancer, and in fact such marriages of one specialty with another usually prove very fertile. To be sure, the artist must have a lively sense of the body, which only awaits an opportunity to express itself directly.

The concept "abstract" also led to misunderstandings. For me, abstract simply means style, and style, as we know, means polished form, the greatest possible degree of perfection. Attaining it necessitates overcoming naturalism, rejecting all unnecessary flourishes, moving toward greater and greater conceptual precision. The paths differ according to the point of departure. If I start with the body, and gradually develop the dance form out of it, my path will differ from what it would be if I started with form, with a formative concept, and then attempted to realize these by using the body. Beyond a doubt, the present mood is hostile toward experimentation of any kind. Nevertheless, misunderstandings should not be allowed to arise. For what does this experimentation represent but the next step into the future?

To Otto Meyer

Breslau
September 8, 1931

How are you? Have you decided to undergo the operation? Could it already have taken place? Where was it, where will it be performed? You have all my best wishes.

Your praise for the wire construct made me very happy. The discordant elements in the architectural painting will be removed. The architect realizes that the two things do not mix. While doing the wire sculpture I became deeply involved; this form would be the medium for abstraction: materials. That helps keep the two realms separate: I can be a painter when I paint, but a calculating constructivist when I do that kind of work.

In the meantime all sorts of things have happened in and to Germany. Self-help, economy measures, special emergency legislation are the daily fare in the newspapers. We at the Academy are also aware that something is in the offing. Prussia will probably have to sacrifice one or two of its five academies. Jobs are threatened, uncertainties on all sides. Money worries add to the many other worries. A bitter winter is predicted, or rather, it is assured. Paintings are not being bought.

To Otto Meyer

Breslau

November 17, 1931

I was very glad to hear that you have been working well. More nature; nature in general, or landscape-oriented? It sorrows me when you say you would come if you could, because it is not to be and probably will be impossible for a long time, for it looks, doesn't it, as if the boundaries will be closed, with God knows what still to come. And this spring was so sunny and unclouded! Now I shall be unable to visit you until far, far in the future. The country is in a political fever: "something has to give"; these world events are certainly interesting. If a catastrophe may be so designated! "National communism"—why not find such a level on which to resolve the differences? I, who admire many things about Russia, do not like to see maxims that are valid for Russia applied uncritically to Germany; and as to "national," well, I can identify only too clearly with the good, typical German things which they want brought out even in art. A long story, and one which in all likelihood will unfortunately be written only too soon. How do these German, and, more especially, these international happenings affect you?

To Willi Baumeister

Breslau

December 1, 1931

The Academy here remains in the throes of uncertainty. We are weighing every eventuality and looking for a place to build a refuge or move into one already built. And are considering Lake Constance! Will you two come along? And where should we go? Überlingen? And what will we live on? Sauerkraut with or without meat? Or a South Sea island? Or Spain? Or . . . . For certain pre-war emotions come back to me: something has got to be, should be, will be done! Or do you have different premonitions, more pleasant, optimistic, gloomy, or fatalistic?

We are arming for the march of the academies on Berlin, to take place January 15; the five Prussian academies will try to demonstrate what they can and will accomplish if allowed to remain in existence. A pity, though, that the five must go together to avoid competition; it might be quite a challenge to present our case in all its uniqueness. I shall probably be going to Berlin some time soon; have not been there for ages.

To Willi Baumeister

Breslau

December 23, 1931

The closing of the Breslau Academy is one characteristic omen of this year's Christmas. Sorrowful times! We can learn only that the closing was ordered under emergency legislation. We are still waiting for details as to the actual procedure, maintenance of contracts, whether individuals will be sent somewhere else. Nothing specific yet.

One gets the impression that all this by no means marks the end; there will be more decrees—have to be; and in these times even contracts that seemed safe can be threatened. However: the Kunstgewerbe- und Handwerkerschule [Commercial Art and Handicrafts School] here is safe (for how long?), since it comes under the Ministry of Trade, which could not reach an agreement with the Ministry of Culture. That is what they call jurisdictional conflict!

How are things with you in Frankfurt? From Essen one hears that Buchartz has been fired and the Folkwang Schools are to be closed. Moll hinted something to me about my being transferred to Berlin, thinks in fact he can promise it with certainty; I would not mind that in the slightest, although at the moment I find it impossible to believe. For a great many valid contracts are still in effect, and I would think they would have to receive first consideration. Let us wait and see. By New Year's I should know more than I do now.

Dresden: Frau Bienert took something, far beneath the asking price. I had to accept because of her genuine love for and interest in the picture. I am still bickering with the Patronats-verein [Patronage Guild]. For what may be my best picture, *Vorübergehender*, they want to offer me 750 marks (!); I am protesting on my own behalf and suggesting they should take a smaller picture at the same price. But now even the price seems shrouded with uncertainty. What has happened to standards, to human decency?

How did your little affair come out? Grohmann wrote that he was staunchly taking your part and was surprised to see how controversial you remain.

Lake Constance etc. has been put aside for the moment by Tut, the canny housewife, on the grounds that nowadays one can live and lodge more cheaply in town. The latter I would question, the former probably not. We shall have to tighten our belts and move into a small apartment, which will be painful, since the present house suits us so well. Fleeing the country, fleeing to the country depend entirely on what develops. Yes, when no choice remains. One does not plant one's own cabbages lightly.

To Gunda Stölzl

Breslau

December 23, 1931

We are being closed, the beautiful Academy will exist no more, likewise Cassel and Königsberg. Only Berlin and Düsseldorf will be permitted to live on. My contract is of course the first to expire! In October I shall join the ranks of the unemployed! Unless others join in February and March. Such questions await the decision of grim fate. On December 29 comes the meeting in Berlin which will settle the lot of the individual faculty members, mine included. Then I shall know more definitely where the shoe will pinch.

To Gunda Stölzl

Breslau

February 8, 1932

So you want to hear how we are? Yes, the Academy will be closed down to all intents and purposes on April 1. We have still heard nothing any more specific. Apparently the people in Berlin have not, either. Now I gather that there is a considerable movement underway in Berlin to fetch me to the Academy there. Bruno Paul there has apparently had an eye on me for quite some time. And I always did want to go there. This is how we see it: no matter which way things go, we shall give up our sweet little three-room house on April 1. The children will be put in a boarding school in Warmbrunn bei Hirschberg—good and fairly cheap. Tut will travel hither and thither, perhaps to Dalmatia where the wife of a teacher at the Waldorf School is moving shortly. I shall live in my studio for the time being. Until October, unless I have to go to Berlin before then. Only once everything is settled will we rent an apartment, somewhere near Zehlendorf. The reason being that nowadays one can still live better and more inexpensively in a big city than far away from everything in the country. That is our thinking at present, because the children need a good education. But where, and how will we pay for it? One needs some money no matter where one is.

But who knows what political developments the spring will bring. Will the Nazis come to power? In that case it will be all up with "Eastern-Bolshevistic-Judaic-Marxist art" . . . . The Bauhaus seems perpetually endangered. The Nazis even want to "tear it down"! I am surprised that the Schepers haven't uttered a peep. According to a final issue of the Bauhaus newspaper, Klee would seem to have left for good. Right?

So in April or October the Breslau period will draw to an end. How many more? We are gradually becoming expert at moving and getting used to new surroundings. It would be nice to settle down someday. Once Berlin has been conquered, that phase should last a while. Or perhaps not?

To Otto Meyer

Breslau
March 4, 1932

Theater lecture in Berlin on March 7, and in connection with it an exhibition. Shall be gone a week, shall make discreet inquiries, to the extent one can interfere with the secret workings of government agencies; and along with this, museums, exhibitions, friends. Also a brief visit to Dessau. Which is electing a president Sunday. The Nazis in Anhalt not only want to dissolve the Bauhaus—they want to tear it down. And this when the Bauhaus has been becoming tamer and tamer, hardly even recognizable, according to eyewitnesses. A historical misunderstanding: the sins of exuberant youth (Weimar) are visited upon innocent old age (Dessau as it is now).

I think I can foresee that I shall plunge myself anew into theatrical work, for the theater city promises a powerful incentive. The—creative(?)—interlude of Breslau will have to prove its worth. I now feel I can plunge in without drowning, that producing one good theatrical piece a year will be enough to keep me in practice. That should be ideally suited to Berlin, which is so critical and demanding. But all this still belongs to the future. Best wait and see.

I must bear in mind that the *Vorübergehender* ["Passerby"] has in the meantime passed on to the State Gallery in Dresden, the *Sitzende in Weiß* (if you recall) going to the city of Breslau, but at prices which you can derive only approximately from the level of our unemployment statistics, using key figures or a numerical key which will fit the spring of last year or the beginning of this year! Enough said.

Postcard to Tut

Berlin
March 15, 1932

My lecture was delivered: a great deal of applause, an ovation, in fact! Apparently unusual here. Berlin is gradually fading away; tired of theater, tired of people. Everyone saying that Oskar Schlemmer will be coming to Berlin!

To Otto Meyer

Breslau

March 21, 1932

I was away, theater lecture in Berlin, which, revised and improved, was an unexpected success—I was afraid of the opposite, knowing how theater-conscious Berlin is and how critical toward anything experimental; then in Dessau. Dessau: to my surprise still, or once more, violently politicized, the Communist clique terrorizes the otherwise indifferent student body, and is backed by the Party, which in Anhalt can apparently tip the balance and will decide the death or life of the Bauhaus.

To Tut

Breslau

April 5, 1932

Yes, that is how it is. Here I sit in the empty house, walk on tiptoe at night, and only then notice that the children are gone! The house looks spic-and-span, like the quarters of a childless bachelor. How are the children? How are they adjusting to Warmbrunn? No tragedy, I hope? Are they already thinking back to the past, or only forward to the future? Adieu!

To Otto Meyer

Breslau

May 7, 1932

Please forgive my silence: moving out of the house, a rush job for a Berlin weekend exhibition (was turning out paintings on the assembly line) did not give me time to catch my breath, and now that the last yard has been painted I must steel myself for going to Berlin to help mount the exhibition and open it.

I find political wrangling upsetting to an unusual degree; one simply has to put one's feelings on ice. Which is not to say that said feelings are not defended warmly, even with passion. Why must the Germans make such a to-do over their nationality; it results in a kind of distortion where other nations (England, Switzerland, America) take such matters for granted. It would be so nice to be able to say: nationality is nothing to get excited over; one has it, or should have it, as a matter of course, since one is a German and was born one. And if one lives in one's native country, is surrounded by fellow countrymen, necessarily thinks and feels as they do and cannot help sharing their ideals since it is in one's blood—then why should one lay such stress on something so natural, especially since history has taught us more than enough about what happens when nationalism gets out of hand? For as much evil has been done in its name as good. But the nationalistic tide seems to be sweeping over the world; neighbors are reinforcing their fences instead of pursuing the beautiful goal of breaking down barriers; this attitude promotes the creation of conditions in which "even the most devout cannot live in peace."

At the moment people of good will and good faith here are turning away from National Socialism, which holds a terrible threat for our cultural life. One can perhaps take comfort in the hope that Hitler may not be the final representative of German thought, and that people cannot look only backward in art and culture. If they turn their spotlight on Frederick the Great, they will inevitably come upon Voltaire, Watteau, and others like them, too.

The burning question of the moment is: will the Nazis join the government or not? If they do, it will be because they have to (because of the innumerable people waiting for government positions who refuse to wait any longer), and then the Center will hold them back, "rein them in," whereupon a schism will develop. If they do not, the possibility will remain of their someday winning an absolute majority, which will result in something which actually corresponds better to the thrust of this movement: a dictatorial seizure of power and, as with Russian Communism, a clean sweep before the final push. At the moment the cards are still being shuffled.

Postcard to Tut

Berlin
May 13, 1932
Tomorrow is Saturday already, the opening of my exhibition at Flechtheim's, and I have not yet finished everything.

291

Met Gerhard Marcks; also Hindemith in the subway last night; he was very happy that things are turning out well for me here. This morning with Sorensen (Academy), discussion of the contract: mine is apparently the first to incorporate the new guidelines which have been in the works for three years; the Ministry will have to be consulted, but that is supposed to involve no risk, since the "transfer" has been "acted upon." Contract thus to be more favorable. This evening a concert at the Singakademie [Academy of Music], modern music.

The national line-up for the Dance Congress in Paris: four Germans, only two French, then Poland, Switzerland, Czechoslovakia, America, Russia, and so on.

To Gunda Stölzl

Breslau

June 2, 1932

Tomorrow I must be off to Berlin. Yes, the moment has come. To Bruno Paul's School of the Arts on Hardenbergstraße, not Liebermann's. It is an extraordinary stroke of luck, which I hope will not be undone by the Nazis. Schultze-Naumburg will be the big man from now on—the one who had me painted over! Do you in your fortunate Switzerland feel any reverberations from events in Germany? Something or other is going on—one does not know what. But it is going on!

Well, since April the children have been in Warmbrunn, situated in the foothills of the Riesengebirge, in a good, inexpensive boarding school, where they are enjoying themselves. We gave up our house in mid-May. Tut is living with friends, I in the studio. The battle is still raging to save a remnant of the Breslau Academy.

I must go to Berlin to fetch my contract, and also to rehearse the "Triadic Ballet" with a ballet troupe there; it is to be presented for a modern ballet competition in Paris, July 2-4. We are working busily on the costumes. Tut sews and plays Girl Friday. Just like old times. The studio milieu also contributes to the sense of "like old times."

Depending on how Paris turns out—whether well or badly—I should like to get rid of the ballet at last and get on to

292

something new—sell it if possible!—so depending on Paris it will be either back to the sticks or off via Arles—Aix—Avignon! And that will determine whether I spend the summer in Breslau in the studio.

Then Berlin! Rent or build? Depends on Paris. Build if possible. The children are already drawing floor plans. That is our tune for the future, something everyone needs, after all.

Felix Klee has gotten married! A singer at the Breslau Theater. Mama Klee is overjoyed. Came over while I was in Dessau for a party at the Schepers' (oh, memory!); she was suffused with the happiness of a mother-in-law. Paul Klee happened to be in Düsseldorf. Saw Albers only briefly. Met Mies van der Rohe at the Schepers'. He was there because of the "mess" in Dessau: the Communist cell is still giving him trouble. How things stand there now? A Nazi government. Saw Otti Berger only briefly. Is still there. Did not see Peterhans. Was fetched at the railway station and conducted to the cafeteria with flags a-flying, so to speak. Still: the old spirit is gone, only the memory remains.

For the Berlin summer show I was asked to do some large backdrops, working with students. The remuneration is now going on the ballet. Tut scolds and lets me go ahead. I say: "my last folly." I am pinning everything on this card. A jury on which René Clair and Léger sit must be good. A plan exists to film the ballet. And then Paris, after all. If it fails, I shall close up shop and swear eternal remorse—until the next time around. By then I shall be in Berlin, which besides the Academy has the Musikhochschule [Music School], with Hindemith, a handsome stage and theater! It would be a crime to let that go unused! If the times were not so wretched, one could do all sorts of things. But maybe even so.

To Otto Meyer

Breslau
June 2, 1932

In Breslau for only two short days, the rest of the time in Berlin, less involved with the future school than with a new performance of the "Triadic Ballet," being prepared for an international competition of modern ballets in the Theatre des Champs-Elysées. It is a last attempt, in what may be the eleventh hour, to set this creation, which deserved a better fate, on its feet, abroad, I hope. If it fails, I shall gain wisdom, lose a hope, learn from a folly. But if it succeeds, everything will be the other way around (can one be made foolish by a learning experience?).

What happens after Paris depends entirely on what happens in Paris.

What do you think of our reactionary sweep? It is slowly creeping up on the cultural area. My escape to Berlin came in the nick of time. When the parting of the ways comes (and it looks as if it will) . . . .

To Tut

Berlin

June 7, 1932

Yesterday we reviewed the troops. The two female leads have been found. "Spiral" is rehearsing today; she is not yet definitely hired, so careful with the measurements. "Wire" and the "White Lady" we are sure of. Almost certain are two gentlemen for "Disk," "Diver," and "Goldspheres." There is still controversy over Wagner, who can and wants to dance the "Hampelmann" and would be simply great. The "Abstract" is still missing; if no one else can be found, I shall take on the role myself. Upon popular demand. Ballet shoes can be had only at Zuberle's in Stuttgart. Yesterday I performed the whole ballet for everyone, to general amazement and hilarity; I was in excellent form, and it is fortunate I can demonstrate how everything should be done, which, as Wagner says, is the simplest, surest, and quickest method.

Bruno Paul wants me to pick what appeals to me, design my own course; it may provide a springboard to all sorts of things. He wants me to draw up an outline. I promised to work on that over the summer; I might, for instance, present my findings in an inaugural lecture on "Perspectives"; Bruno Paul reacted very positively to the idea.

Yesterday: I am flawlessly dressed in black, and then, oh

misery! I discover that I have no black shoes! What to do? I went to the opera in my black house slippers and light-colored spats. The Schlees laughed themselves sick when I told them the truth. Just imagine: I was making the rounds of the foyer with Fräulein Trümpy and various other ladies! Would anyone find me out? Self-consciousness aside, the lack of heels made for a peculiar sensation. I was happy to reach home without mishap (they might have slipped off!). But since Berlin is becoming increasingly relaxed, and a premiere is simply theater, one is not obliged to meet any standards—at front row center sits a gentleman in tails and next to him (I kid you not) a man in a baggy pullover.

To Tut

Berlin
June 9, 1932

Yesterday no breakfast, or at least not until one o'clock, due to rushing around, headache, general confusion. Today back on a sensible schedule. Took the first room I found. Gloomy weather, which always affects my mood. Yours, too, I fear. Don't let it get you down! Leg up, Tutsch!

Saw Wagner-Regeny yesterday; he is very busy with a Neher opera and could only offer me something he already has on hand, certainly at least as suitable, as well as new and unusual, like Pachernegg. It would probably be impossible to compose something ideal from scratch, no matter who tried! Today we shall continue playing things through on the piano. What he offered me would fit the Paris Orchestra as far as the instrumentation goes.

The rehearsals are progressing well. The people catch on quickly.

Postcard to Tut

Berlin
July 23, 1932

Returned to the scene of the crime. In Essen I met Gosebruch and several others. My wall paintings looked splendid to me. We had lunch in the Gruga, later I saw my *Festliche Zwölf* at the Henke Villa, hanging in the handsome addition designed by Mies van der Rohe. Then by car to the station and now here.

Berlin is a fine place, too; it stimulates me.

To Willi Baumeister

Breslau
July 27, 1932

Léger was charming at lunch. Only three pictures in his studio, nothing new. Ozenfant seems to be restricting himself entirely to pedagogical matters. Otherwise I did not see anybody. And why should I have? Picasso, the Kreuger of painting (!), not a bad bon mot. Terribly impressive. A huge mass of painting, skillfully mounted by him (Ozenfant, his rival, claims that Picasso quickly dashed off the lacking pictures), but, as Tut rightly remarked, he offers a cross section of the entire evolution of art rather than a unified presentation of his own development. His work represents polemical confrontations with other artists and artistic trends. But always amazing. Marvelous coloration. Best displayed, I feel, in a series of excellent still lifes. Braque and Picasso. Strange parellels cropping up between these two again. A riddle! But: we shall not be able to see any of this in Germany from now on; the whole trend will be proscribed here, at the very least. Horrible to contemplate!

Chartres: there everything the modern French are doing is anticipated. What beautiful unity of style even in the posters in the Métro, in the smallest things, in natural harmony with French painting (in contrast to the Berlin Underground). The city stays marvelous, especially in the evening with spotlights illuminating the buildings. Manet exhibit also very good. And all such things well frequented by the public.

To Christof Hertel

Breslau
July 28, 1932

Paris was unfortunately a fiasco. Bronze medal, to be sure, and sixth place (among twenty international troupes), but disorganization and plain bad luck prevented us from placing higher which, according to the jury, we might well have done. Well, when I am settled in Berlin, I shall arrange the ballet for the *variété* and then let it die. I am longing to do something new for a change!

Tell me, how does it stand with the Bauhaus, what is in the cards? It looks inevitable that it will be closed down. In spite of Mies van der Rohe's attempts at depoliticization, the toll will have to be paid for past sins. And yet: can't the closure be revoked? A disgrace! And a disgrace, too, that the entire cultured world does not rise up and firmly say no. But apparently we are all so worn down and resigned that we have no power to stop anything.

To Tut

Breslau

August 7, 1932

The Breslau sky hangs as heavy as lead—and the rain keeps coming down. That makes leaving less painful. What is your weather like? The talk I am working on should turn out very well, I think. It will give me an opportunity to formulate quite a number of general principles. Perhaps I shall arrange to give a lecture every month, about an hour, with slides. Then, too, I once more feel the urge to paint, and I plan to do precisely that, because I need some new pictures for this fall. Exhibition with the Secession and at Flechtheim's. So you see! If the autumn is unusually beautiful and I finish up in time, a quick trip to the Baltic. *Avec vous?* or *seulement? Comme vous voulez.*

This is how I spend my time: "Perspectives" and the lecture in the morning, painting in the afternoons. I still have a full month's grace. Baumeister wrote that Otto Meyer's condition is alarming. He is under medical observation but acts as though nothing were wrong. Takes unkindly to suggestions. Is keeping himself on a starvation diet, has become very thin.

To Otto Meyer

August 26, 1932

First to less immediate matters: the ballet. We had bad luck in Paris, as a palmist had predicted: "Undertake nothing on July 4." The day of the performance could not be changed. The orchestral scores were not yet ready when we left, so we had them sent airmail, and they were lying around the customs office at the Gare du Nord from July 1 on—but not a soul could find them. They were finally unearthed the day after the performance by the courier from the German Embassy. That was misfortune number one. Then we needed a black dance carpet. Practically an impossibility in Paris. Until finally money and good French secured us one, which we finished painting right before the performance; except that it was so slippery that the dancers were in constant danger of slipping and falling. The nervous tension generated by this streak of bad luck communicated itself to the lighting, which failed, since the lighting supervisor had to be at the piano. And we were all so tense that it must be counted a miracle that we won a bronze medal and sixth place among twenty-two competing nations and troupes.

The first prize was well deserved. It went to the Folkwang Dance School troupe from Essen; I was surprised and mystified to see what a good, strong production they had put together. (It was not I who suggested that without the visit of our Bauhaus troupe in Essen this would have been unthinkable.) Gradually reconstructing it for myself, I now perceive that their *Grüner Tisch* ["Green Table"] has certain elements in common with our "gesture dance," and that the basic steps by the dancers (warriors) might be identified with our "spatial dance"— especially since nothing of this sort had ever been done by the school previously. But: what we used to celebrate *in abstracto* they presented in concrete form.

As to the "Triadic Ballet," Léger expressed the opinion that he as a painter had found it the most appealing presentation of all, since it was a "ballet," whereas the first prize had been *"un spectacle"*—he felt that all the optical resources should be used much more fully—lighting, projection, transparencies—to concentrate one's attention on the optical marvels rather than on the quality of the dancing. True, but neither in

Berlin nor in Paris did I have the opportunity to do much with lighting; that would almost have resulted in a second ballet—a ballet of light! In Paris we had only half an hour's worth of lighting rehearsal! In Berlin I had no theater where I could rehearse and try out such things.

A fundamental discovery prevents me from returning to my former method of abstraction: the potential the canvas surface offers for achieving spatial depth and a great range of color—a potential which is either sacrificed or insufficiently explored in abstract painting. I can no longer bring myself to take a canvas with a good pebbled surface and draw the black contour of a figure on it—and nothing else. That sort of thing I prefer to execute in "materials," as I did with the wire composition. There abstraction really seems called for, and one finds wonderful possibilities for employing abstract, streamlined form. Even Arp has the right idea when he dips string in glue and pastes it onto the canvas or attaches pieces of wood to achieve contour. I am concerned with what one legitimately can and should do with a canvas.

In my own work I am groping in confusion. I would like to start again from scratch, or at least to renounce the liberties I have allowed myself of late, which have gone to my head. Perhaps I should draw the curtain again and retreat into dimness. For some of the things I tried may have been too much too soon. But then again, the present political events may account for my inner uncertainty.

So at the moment I am pausing to take stock, in the hope that a resurgence of strength will follow.

Arp seems to be winning considerable recognition. In Paris and also in Switzerland. I believe Klee also recommended him as his successor at the Bauhaus, something which by then was already out of the question. And now the Bauhaus's fate has been sealed by the Nazis' majority in the elections. It is supposed to be "absorbed" by Leipzig or Berlin. The only question is: what is left to "absorb"? Hasn't it already shrivelled into a miserable little heap?

Arp: his simplicity the diametrical opposite of Mondrian's. Doesn't it seem poetic justice that after spending so many years in obscurity he should now emerge victorious with his simplifications? I met him two years ago in Paris, but only briefly; he spoke appreciatively of my theatrical photographs.

Lessing and the German character. But wouldn't you agree that Lessing was dealing with a world structured very differently from our present politically hectic one? I have heard the hateful song* of the political loudmouths, but hardly a peep out of the ethically and artistically minded circles. I am sure that the flood of print now inundating Germany must contain something on this subject, but I have not yet come upon any formulation of a national program for the arts. After all, a revival of the classics in music, writing, and painting is nothing new—they always provided an alternative to modernism. It almost looks as though modernism will now be considered unpatriotic. We shall see. The Bauhaus will lead off. I also believe, however, that the nationalists' unadulterated conservatism will almost have to generate some form of revolutionary modernism, either within the Nazi camp or in an opposing camp; for Hitler's fourteen million followers cannot possibly all be poured from the same mold. I was amazed to learn of the numbers and different types of youth groups that exist, largely representing various minorities, the nuances of which extend all the way to communism.

Since the individual cannot change the course of destiny, he must think of his own fate. Perhaps mine will catch up with me soon, who knows. For the number of Nazi governments in Germany is on the increase, and they will show which way the wind is blowing. By their fruits we shall know them. The next few days will show whether Papen can hold his own. The people indubitably want a strong man and the kind of decisive action which led them to vote for Hitler: "Things have gotta change!"

I am curious to see how I shall be received in Berlin, at the school. The semester begins around October 15. I shall make my debut with a lecture on "Perspectives," being careful not to make too many pejorative comments about perspective. I hope I soon have a chance to apply all this to real theater, as the

*An allusion to a line in Goethe's *Faust: "Ein politisch Lied, ein garstig Lied . . . ."*—Translator

director planned—provided the neighbors hold their peace. I mean the eunuchs in the school itself, not next door, where the actual stage is, in the Music School.

Diary

August 1932

My painting: either finished or on the verge of something new. Conflict: should I continue in the "baroque" vein, which suits my tastes and comes easy—or go back to the simplicity of abstraction. Or at least: to simple clarity (which tends to take on metaphysical implications). A sense that I cannot go on this way, that a rebirth is just around the corner, although I cannot yet tell what form it will take.

Diary

August 26, 1932

Well—after much fruitless back and forth, after thinking I was in a hopeless rut, after losing confidence in my ability to plunge in at any moment regardless of my mood and circumstances—after days of emptiness and aridity, an attempt finally succeeded, when I least expected it, the gift of some unknown benefactor (probably an outgrowth of this very depression). This painting captures impulses I had feared would simply be dissipated; it definitely reflects my very own style, and therefore embodies something absolutely straightforward and pure. Are these "strokes," these moments of grace and luck, becoming rarer and rarer? Or is the explanation that the spiritual and manual motor must constantly be broken in anew until I have it running smoothly? Might my bad habit of forgetting everything, of always ignoring what I learned from earlier attempts actually be an asset; maybe this naïveté, this freedom from preconceptions is essential, to prevent paralysis from setting in?

Diary

September 4, 1932

Crisis: either I draw the curtain once again and plunge myself into total darkness (for purposes of meditation), or I

commit myself to all-out use of color, not for decorative purposes but as an essential element of the painting. But to reach
this point I shall have to work like a fiend, trying experiments
which would perhaps benefit more from being done "in the
dark."

To Freiherr von Schenk

Berlin

October 20, 1932

We have been established for quite some time now in the
Siemensstadt housing development, which we find very pleasant. On Saturday I shall move into my studio on Hardenbergstraße. We are gradually becoming acclimatized. Breslau lies far
behind us, off somewhere in the East. Muche and Molzahn are
still there, sitting out their contracts. The building will be taken
over by the Kunstgewerbe- und Handwerkerschule. And the
Berlin Bauhaus! I have not yet seen it or any of the members.
One more gesture toward centralizing everything in this capital
capital!

To Willi Baumeister

Berlin

November 17, 1932

Just a few words to bring you up to date on events here. I
delivered an inaugural lecture, on "Perspectives," partly because
I was asked, partly because I felt the urge to introduce myself
and explain "the heart within my breast." And now I am
preparing my courses. Perspective, which I am trying to approach from a new angle, mainly from the point of view of
color, an approach which seems promising. I have the backing
of Bruno Paul, who introduced me in most flattering terms; to
be sure, he has his enemies, especially in the "free" depart-
ments, to which I, on the other hand, belong (architecture
consists of both a free department and an applied department).
The school has a very complicated structure, which it will take
me a good while to analyze. But once one is here, no one seems
to pay much attention. Bruno Paul makes himself scarce; often

one has no idea whether he is still in Berlin or off somewhere in India. The (likable) student body received me with high hopes. More than sixty have signed up for my course; such a heavy enrollment presents more than a simple problem of space! I hope I can concentrate my teaching into one hour's lecture per week plus studio sessions.

My studio is smaller than the one in Breslau and the others I have had in recent years. Still, I hope to arrange it pleasantly. An idiotic building, all stairs, windows, and corridors—with no rooms, or only those held by the long-lived, honorary occupants of the masters' studios set aside for the Akademie der Künste [Academy of the Arts].

We have a nice place in the Siemensstadt development, where Scharoun and Rading also live, near the Jungfernheide Park and the woods, not far from Lake Tegel, which awakens dreams of a motorboat in Tut. I can reach my studio in eighteen minutes by streetcar.

To Otto Meyer
Berlin
December 14, 1932

This is the first day I have had a chance to catch my breath, the last day of classes after a strenuous semester of teaching.

I had considerable difficulty finding my bearings in the field of perspective, and shall continue to have difficulty. But the subject interests me, and I get real pleasure from searching through the old theoretical texts, illustrated with copper engravings and dating back to 1700, of which the school library has a fine collection. I have been working up colored studies in perspectives, to demonstrate how it is done, and the more I do, the more eager I become for more. I am almost grateful to have such a neutral subject; I can remain aloof from all the factions and their different directions, although "direction" also enters into perspective. Once one has one's curriculum set up (which I have), one need hardly fear interference. It makes the director happy to see things getting done at all and the machine running smoothly. The Palazzo is larger than anything in my previous experience and has so many students that one can never get to know them all; under such circumstances one's individual life takes on a certain gratifying anonymity.

At present I am completely out of touch with the theater, but I hope to establish some connections soon, although not all at once. Yet people seem more interested in my painting these days, and my head is filled with things I should like to accomplish in this area; thus the old push-me-pull-you effect is once more preventing me from going back to the theater while distracting me from painting. So the theater remains very much up in the air. I have the feeling that I would go right back to the theater if I no longer had the security of my "job" at the school and had to face the music—or the footlights. So I am holding it *in petto* as a sort of insurance against more turbulent days.

I sense distinctly, more so than in Breslau, that the students have a program of their own. To an extent this manifests itself in their political hostility toward teachers gone bourgeois and the society in which they will be obliged to live. The students need, or rather demand, something to live for, something which will make their upbringing and their training meaningful. The stirrings among the students reflect a phenomenon which can be seen throughout the country in all sorts of forms and variations: unpolitical revolutionaries, neither Nazi nor Communist by inclination, are nevertheless involved in those two movements; they form secret societies which are struggling in desperate earnest to control the future course of events.

In Breslau, as the departure and the loss of my beloved studio drew nearer and nearer, I did some work which I consider quite good. It is on display at an excellent gallery here in Berlin and has been praised, more or less as an island of calm amidst the general artistic whirlpool. Klee, Kandinsky, Kirchner (with a strong Picasso influence), Baumeister, Dix, and others. Klee: more caught up in abstruse games than ever; Kandinsky: so close to Klee now that at first I thought Kandinsky was missing and only later realized that I had taken his paintings for Klee's; Kirchner: bold, strong, poster effects, lacking the fine touch of Picasso even at his boldest: highly controversial.

The Picasso exhibition in Zurich must be breaking all the records, even if one looks only at the number of visitors. Does it form a unified whole, with shape and direction, or does it offer a cross section of modern art, as Tut puts it, something this artistic Napoleon is ideally equipped to provide?

Yesterday my first party at the school (our Christmas celebration). The serious part was followed by a relaxed one, with jazz, dancing, and wine. But: almost all of the teachers were absent. The mentality of an arts and crafts school. No comparison with the Bauhaus parties, already of blesséd memory, or even with the parties in Breslau. The prevailing tone and manner were such that Tut's reaction was, "Come, let's quit!" What can one do: isolate oneself, limit one's contacts to the family and a few friends?

Politics: so many bridges already crossed, and look where we are headed! Our government crisis—Germany's claim to full sovereignty—France's refusal to pay. These are major events, history-making events!

Diary

End of 1932

Il professore: I profess!

I believe:

That:

anything one of us writes in his own defense merely gives his enemies a rope by which to hang him; i.e. an excuse to judge him by his words and not by his work. Nevertheless I write.

That:

in this frantic, anti-artistic age it is sheer folly to keep increasing the supply of painted canvases ad infinitum, and that the order of the day calls for performing more urgent tasks. Nevertheless I paint.

That:

the permanent crisis of standards in art has been exacerbated during the present nationalistic frenzy to the point that now anything different, individual, or new is considered un-German, "Eastern," politically suspect. There are fields of art in which politics has lost all meaning.

That:

one must struggle unremittingly to untangle the confusion

that prevails in artistic concepts, not dogmatically, but quite simply by the example of one's own work, by firm commitment to irreproachable methods and clarity of conception.

That:

the old Goethean distinctions between imitation of nature, manner, and style are as valid as ever, except that today the first two are fairly well understood, while hardly anyone sees the concept of style as a challenge, as an objective, or as a phenomenon; instead, people apply the standards of the first two to style. Result: misunderstanding to the point of malice—disastrous chaos of all artistic concepts.

That:

painting still offers tasks for which it is worthwhile to live and strive.

To Lily Hildebrandt

Berlin

January 26, 1933

Otto Meyer is dead! The thought makes the mind go blank. A tragic life!

The children had diphtheria but seem to be making a good recovery.

Poelzig has now replaced Paul as director of the Academy, but they are out to get him, too. Gruesome times.

My course on "Perspectives" keeps me pleasantly occupied. We do not yet know Poelzig's plans for the school, whether he will take measures or let things remain as they are.

We are not taking many excursions. That always happens when one comes to live in Berlin. No theater. My own decision! No time for painting just now, but the enthusiasm is there if I ever find a free hour.

To Willi Baumeister

Berlin

Beginning of February 1933

Up to now Nazi policy has not affected the Academy. But now it is being felt at the Akademie der Künste, where the

Marxists are being forced to leave. Poelzig will probably be labelled a Communist, too. When things get critical I may find that "perspective" is my salvation! It is non-political! The political climate in Southern Germany is gratifying. One wishes one could be there instead. Good old South German democracy has come through, and I imagine they will defend it to the death against the Prussians.

To Julius Baum,
Director of the Museum
of the City of Ulm

Berlin
March 1, 1933

Someone sent me a newspaper clipping. I am constantly surprised that people perceive so little "nature" in my pictures, when I consider them to be full of it, and that they hardly acknowledge my application or use of the basic principles of art. All I can say, like Luther, is: "I cannot help myself," and hope that what now seems puzzling will little by little come to be taken for granted.

To F. C. Valentien

Berlin
March 18, 1933

I called up Curt Valentin at Flechtheim's, and he informed me there had already been incidents in Düsseldorf; his advice was not to try an exhibition there. I share his opinion and shall write Düsseldorf off. I wanted to close up shop entirely and have no more exhibitions for the present, my feeling being that one should ride out this storm and keep calm. What weapon does one have against passions?

On the other hand, I cannot ignore your suggestion that this business should be blown up into a "case" while there is still time, i.e. immediately; we should enter the lists and fight the good fight. For the worst has not yet come! It would be terrible if yesterday's paper were right in asserting that Party Member Hinkel will be put in charge of the Art Division of the

Ministry of Culture. I recently heard him speak next door in the Music School, and all I can say is: it was dreadful! A sergeant addressing his men.

I have written to the Art Guild that I would like them to keep the interned exhibition under their wing a while longer and to display it until I have determined whether Düsseldorf is still in the running, so some friends of mine have a chance to see it. The big question remains whether one should react to the Nazi provocations or hold one's peace.

If a "case" is made, I would like to see it done in my native Stuttgart, the city in which I completed my studies and which I still love, in spite of everything. I am also convinced that my case involves major principles.

To Willi Baumeister

Berlin
March 22, 1933

How are things down your way? Events are coming so thick and fast. Who has taken over the government in your city, and what is he like? That will probably determine whether you hang or go free.

Speaking of hanging: I did; and was taken down. In the Stuttgart Art Guild. Then mounted in two back rooms, accessible only to insiders of unquestionable character. Count Baudissin, a longtime devoted National Socialist, apparently wrote to Hitler immediately, but couching his letter in terms of principles instead of exposing himself on my behalf. Valentien in Stuttgart had wanted to show my paintings at his gallery even before they went to the Art Guild. Still wants them. I am wavering between "closed until future notice" (there were threats in Düsseldorf, too, and my exhibition, which was supposed to go there from Stuttgart, had to be cancelled) and standing to fight; at the moment, so much tension is in the air that the latter course seems very risky, although it would certainly force a decision on principles and future policies. Hofer tells me that there are apparently some decent people among the Nazis, but the ruling clique consists of petty-minded characters who know no tolerance. Nothing has happened here yet. Just rumors. The decision could be dragged out for quite a while. Bad times are coming. What course should one take? Cultivate art only within one's four walls, on Sundays? Find some practical second profession? But what?

The excursion to the Rhine and the Main was lovely and sorely needed. One should do such things more often, and be able to. But it will soon be almost out of the question. And it was good to see each other again and talk. The intensity of your work seems to gain from the extremely difficult circumstances with which you have to contend.

To Willi Baumeister

Berlin

April 2, 1933

It is absolutely crazy! We heard about Wichert, and Swarzenski, and worried about you. What now? Where to?

Yesterday a large poster appeared here in the Academy, describing Hofer, E. R. Weiss, C. Klein, Gies, Reger, Wolfsheld, and Schlemmer as "destructive Marxist-Judaic elements." "Boycott these teachers!" I complained to the local Gruppenleiter of the Nazi Party, and he made a note of my protest. Poelzig lodged a protest with the Reichskommissar.

That is all for now. In the end we shall probably be fired. I just wonder what form it will take. Everything will depend on that. Where to? What then?

Flechtheim has taken down all my pictures. They are stacked against a wall, shown only to people he knows he can trust, and only after they have inscribed their names in a guestbook.

To Willi Baumeister

Berlin

April 25, 1933

Today the newspaper report corroborated what I already knew: here Hofer and Scharff have been dismissed, in Düsseldorf Klee (!) and Moll (no reasons given). "Further dismissals are expected." I shall bear that in mind.

309

The iconoclastic frenzy seems to be spreading. Dessau, Mannheim, and now Dresden. "Chambers of artistic horrors" are being set up in the museums. No one has seen fit to protest.

What will you do with your cow?

Letter of Protest to Minister Goebbels

Berlin

April 25, 1933

Deeply shaken by what I hear from numerous cities in the Reich, including Dessau, Mannheim, and Dresden, where the museums' collections of modern art are to be placed in "chambers of artistic horrors," each picture labelled with the sum paid for it, exposed to the mockery and indignation of the public, I take the liberty of appealing to you with an urgent plea that you call a halt to these measures.

Please allow me to direct your attention to the period before the war, to the years between 1910 and 1914, when simultaneously all the artistically vital countries, like Germany, Russia, and France, experienced a spontaneous revolution of consciousness in the arts; the works which grew out of this revolution could not possibly have anything to do with Russian Communism or with Marxism, because these concepts did not yet exist!

It was a period in which the windows of the musty chambers of art were opened wide, when the doors suddenly stood ajar, and the artists were caught up in a delirium of enthusiasm for the new spirit they sensed being born.

It was in this enraptured mood that we young academy students were surprised by the war. We marched off to battle filled with genuine enthusiasm for a noble cause, for the ideals of art! In the name of my fallen comrades I protest against the defamation of their goals and their works, for those which found their way into museums are today being desecrated.

That was not what they died for! After the war, the survivors, now in their forties, continued their interrupted work in the pre-war spirit, largely oblivious to and uninterested in the political occurrences around them.

These days pictures by both living and deceased modern painters are being systematically defamed! They have been branded alien, un-German, unworthy, and unnatural. The political motives ascribed to them are in most cases totally inappropriate. Artists are fundamentally unpolitical and must be so, for their kingdom is not of this world. It is always humanity with which they are concerned, always the totality of human existence to which they must pay allegiance.

To Willi Baumeister

Berlin
June 12, 1933

Write and tell me how things stand with you, with all of you. My pictures are on display at the Secession along with Klee, Feininger, Kirchner, etc.—causing violent controversy; one still cannot tell who will emerge on top, the Kampfbund [German Fighting Union] or the good side. The latter remains within the realm of possibility here; for instance the Palace of the Crown Prince has not been tampered with.

I still have my studio and it looks as if I shall be able to keep it for a while. My course on "Perspectives" (!) is cancelled for this semester. I am not painting—am good for nothing these days. By the way: my taste in style inclines to extravagant abstraction, rather than to making concessions.

To Gunda Stölzl

Berlin
June 16, 1933

Yes, Halle, too, has bit the dust. They all sent me a card, the Marckses, the Friedländers, the Ottes, and so on. Marcks is "leaving Halle in a week, never to return." It is all up! The Berlin Bauhaus has been deflated in another way. They are no longer receiving salaries from Dessau, and they must return their borrowed furniture by July 1. And the whole thing allegedly stems from a "misunderstanding," which, however, took so long to clear up that the students have left almost to a man. We have just seen Wassily Kandinsky. He has been less directly affected than most; he still cannot believe it has happened—but I have just heard that the Bauhaus will remain closed for good. All up!

I have been "temporarily severed" and shall go on receiving my salary until the fall. Time in which to think things over. At the moment my connections are still under investigation: ancestors, party, Jew, Marx, Bauhaus . . . .

Stuttgart—no, at least not for the time being. Berlin, where we happen to be, and settled for good, is still more lively and presents more possibilities. Stuttgart, Swabia; fine for retiring to some day. But first some real work has to be done, since one never receives something for nothing in this world except in the lottery, and there one has no right to get one's hopes up!

Despite our cheerfulness our situation is rather grim—we often lack the most immediate necessities, and wishes and dreams go unfulfilled. We have a nice apartment in the settlement built by Scharoun, near the lovely Jungfernheide Park and swimming pool, vis-à-vis the school where the two youngest go; Karin goes to school by streetcar. Nearby we have Lake Tegel; we spent Whitsun on one of its islands, the Schaffenberg. Berlin is so beautiful . . . . The "so" refers to the natural surroundings, the lakes, the forests, the variations in the character of the different parts of the city. Otherwise: an ominous silence has fallen over art and cultural circles. But then, of course, it is summer. Not until winter shall we see what the "purged" brand of theater, film, and so on looks like.

The Klees finally left Dessau on April 1. The Feiningers are in Deep. Their furniture was left in storage, I gather. The only ones remaining in Dessau: the Schepers. Felix Klee married, working as a trainee at the Düsseldorf Opera. Yes, one wonders what the army of fired teachers will do? There are hardly any signs of concerted action. Each person is searching for a hole to crawl into, a spot all to himself. For a while there was talk of a new Bauhaus to be established in Nice by Mendelsohn. But now not a word. It is a great pity to have everyone scattered to the winds. With this thought in mind we decided at Andi's last night to set up a chain letter system to link our dispersed friends and colleagues, a sort of Bauhaus newsletter.

To Ernst Gosebruch,
Director of the Folkwang Museum in Essen

Berlin
June 19, 1933

Your suggestion that my murals be sold strikes me as absurd. I could never consent of my own free will, and I would have thought the same would apply to you. It is something else again if you are being compelled to remove or to sell the murals. I feel that one can justifiably give in to this cultural barbarity only under pressure, never voluntarily.

Diary

End of June 1933

I have been a practicing painter for twenty years. When one pursues an activity for this long a time, it becomes part of one's flesh and blood. I live through my painting. Often filled with despair, just as often with joy. Like Gauguin and Delacroix I say: "Painting is the most beautiful of the arts." But the skepticism characteristic of modern man often tarnishes our pleasure. Painting is experiencing the crisis of our times. Occasionally I lose faith in it, precisely in view of the times in which we live. To whom does painting address itself? The ranks of the happy few have been alarmingly thinned. The great bond with the people which formerly existed no longer does.

And yet I love painting. It still contains elements which can be found nowhere else. After the recent flood of "isms" it might seem as if painting were finished. But I believe painting is merely making a fresh start, having temporarily lost its bearings as a result of hovering between heaven and earth in the realm of abstraction.

Diary

July 11, 1933

Art and nature—the problem will never be laid to rest as long as art exists. These are the two poles to which the various styles gravitate; any given style receives its character from the preponderance of either the natural or the abstract element.

313

Someone who sheds considerable light on this dispute is Goethe, for although the infallability of his ideas about art can be questioned, he formulates a few concepts which really help clarify the issue. They are worth recalling if we hope to give naturalism, manner, and, most important, style, their due.

The fascination with abstraction displayed by artists from artistically alive countries signifies a desperate attempt to escape from the dead end into which naturalism had led them. One method they chose was to seek out the roots of all art; another was to fall back on the fundamental principles of art; these attempts were carried out gradually by different groups, all at odds with each other. Thus arose the concepts of impression and expression, of impressionistic and expressionistic art, and in connection with the latter, theoreticians decided that all great art was expressionist.

Returning to the roots, one of the escapes from over-extended naturalism, meant conjuring up the elemental in nature, in feeling, and emotion, as well as in artistic method. The result was expressive art when it came to portraying basic emotions; it was constructive art when the emphasis lay on the basic and universal quality of the artistic method and techniques. What decided the artistic value of a work was always the intensity with which and out of which it was created.

Mannerism crops up in every age and clime, as much in naturalism as in any other sort of art. Therefore it seems inappropriate to designate the attempts at abstraction found in modern art as mannerism. There is a form of abstraction which goes beyond the merely negative and seeks to preserve the supreme values by purging all impurities, abolishing all inessential flourishes, and revealing the essence of a thing in as pure a form as possible.

To Willi Baumeister

Berlin
July 17, 1933

Although we come up with new plans every day and every week, we keep reverting to the same resigned question: what does man live by?

Schmitthenner's transfer to Berlin must have had an equivalent impact in Stuttgart. The whole affair is certainly significant. His lecture expressed great hostility toward modern styles of building, of which he displayed the most unflattering photographs imaginable; his gabled roofs, on the other hand, were shown dripping with lovely flowers, etc. Well, he is the new and coming man, so we can see the direction that will be taken: cult of the Biedermeier, or, in other words, reactionary taste. But that is precisely contrary to the desires of the Nazi students, who recently staged a very lively rally at the university. They took a unanimous stand against Biedermeier and reactionary taste. Dr. Schardt, the provisional director of the National Gallery (for how long? at the moment he is refurbishing the Crown Prince's Palace) spoke in the same tenor. True, he fairly one-sidedly assigned a predominant role to northern, Germanic art, seeing a direct line between the earliest North German ornaments and modern forms of ornament. He was also one-sided in his extravagant praise for the ecstatic, Faustian vein, which he described as genuinely German and *völkisch*, by way of contrast with the Roman, classical style, which he designated as "subverted by foreign influence." Nolde, Barlach, Marc, and Feininger are his men. Is it really a question of going back to the Expressionist style? Things did not stop there—others came afterwards, we included! But Schardt states calmly that postwar art has nothing much to show for itself (!)—so he contradicts himself, but is still better than the other alternative (Schmitthenner). Both the Nazi rally and the Schardt lecture were heavily attended and much applauded. An exhibition staged at Möller's by Nazi students was not allowed to open until today. The students also wanted to put on an exhibition of kitsch and then one which would provide an outlet for the malcontents, the "Rauschebärte" and "Kulturbund members." All of this will probably not take place. The decision reportedly corresponds to the wishes of Schultze-Naumburg-Schmitthenner.

I still have my studio, probably until October at the latest. I cannot work and am not trying to, at least for the time being. Everything has become rather meaningless. Yet one will hew to one's line and "now of all times" defend what one feels to be essential.

To Gunda Stölzl

Berlin
September 1, 1933

Hovering in the back- or foreground there is always the question: what does man live by, and how about the four dependents? We also have a plan for parcelling out the children. Karin with her Göpp aunt to America, her brother in a boarding school; we are so buzzing with plans that I myself am curious to see what we come up with in the end.

The Bauhaus has been dissolved for good.

To Willi Baumeister

Berlin
October 9, 1933

They say that on October 18, in connection with the planned program at the Deutsches Haus in Munich, certain very important matters will be clarified. For the Nazi policy on art remains undefined. The Crown Prince's Palace has been closed down. Schardt is backing us, but now he must stick to the Nordic—Expressionist line, to remain consistent with his recent speech. Klee, we hear, will not be eligible for a pension, and is thus fired, as is Grohmann, whom we have seen again in the meantime. Kandinsky, who has been forbidden to teach, writes from Paris that the art crowd are bewailing the lack of sales and interest, the chauvinism! He will be returning soon, with Berlin the first stop. Molzahn, also dismissed, is trying to earn his living here doing graphics.

As to me: "reapplying" apparently out of the question.

To Gottfried Benn

Berlin
October 22, 1933

Although I am aware that you are probably besieged with letters, I feel I must write to you and plead the case of the fine arts against some of what you say in your book, *Der neue Staat und die Intellektuellen [The New State and the Intellectuals]*.

316

You address yourself as a writer to the literary emigrés and devote particular attention to the situation of the intellectual. This aspect of cultural life seems to have been dealt with very promptly: the Akademie der Dichtkunst [Academy of Literature] was the first to be reorganized. The blacklist was drawn up with relative unanimity, the climax being the official book burnings.

There has been no clarification of the policy toward music, although the Minister of Culture has repeatedly declared that an announcement is forthcoming. The policy toward the more famous musical figures is clear, but not that toward the representatives of new and progressive tendencies in music. And especially unclear is the attitude toward the plastic arts. What could account for this?

I do not wish to point out the alarming discrepancies in the Nazi attitude toward art that can be gleaned from Adolf Hitler's speech in Nuremberg, from the proclamations by the National Socialist students, and from the speech by Dr. Schardt. In point of fact, two sides are at present confronting each other in an undecided battle over the plastic arts: a youth which commits itself unreservedly to anything modern, innovative, bold, revolutionary—and then your sixty-year-olds, who, you write (on page 20 of your book), no longer understand this youth! Ah, if only what you say about today's revolutionary youth were true! But in our field, the plastic arts, the situation is dreadfully complicated.

For now the sixty-year-olds have the last word. They, who were in the field in 1870 but not in 1914, are celebrating another victory; they celebrated one before the war, during the war, and now again! But those who barely had time to grow up before the war, to find their identity, who are carrying the torch for the new art of the future, these men are being persecuted; they offered their lives during the war, and after the war they found themselves thrust into a world for which they are today made totally responsible! What did we do but carry on the heritage of our fallen comrades, more in spirit than in form; for their hectic Expressionist style, a premonition of the coming war, now had to be replaced by a new premonition, by an artistic style oriented toward order, strictness, and fundamental principles. Could this generation help it that they came of age during the post-war period? Concepts like Marxism, liberalism, destructivism, in fact anything connected with politics and political jargon, were completely foreign to them. But I dare you to name one National Socialist artist of any recognized worth! All about me I see blind persecution, crazed destruction of paintings, chambers of horrors, but to this day nothing which could take their place, not even the barest rudiments of any such thing. Well, perhaps we must wait and be patient.

But the conditions which have been created do not look promising. Noted artists with significant achievements to their names, as well as young artists about to acquire recognition, are being laid off and removed from all government positions. They are not being replaced by courageous revolutionaries; on the contrary, tried and true purveyors of kitsch are being resurrected—like old Vollbehr, who reportedly plans to immortalize the Nuremberg gathering in travelogue style, so that the National Museums of the future may be filled with such stuff! When the education of our youth is at stake, the nod goes to the proponents of Biedermeier-like New Objectivity who, with their wooden academicism or their highly diluted imitations of Casper David Friedrich, claim to speak for the new epoch! At the moment we are being treated to the spectacle of banal naturalism triumphant (naturalism *can* achieve greatness at times); and one sees no idealistic élan, conquering audacity, or true romanticism in the field of the plastic arts, which, after all, is an extraordinarily important one. Important because it is precisely art which is called upon to express the irrational, unconscious intuition, the metaphysical dimension of life; in this area intellectualism and literariness represent a real danger, yet they are about to invade it flags a-flying. For "art as propaganda" endangers the cause and the purity of true art, and Germans, who in any case are prone to over-profundity, should make a special effort to appreciate and to cultivate a visual perception and understanding of the world. In our field the great fundamental questions as to the meaning and value of art are once more being broached. But the only response I detect is regression, fossilization, obscurantism.

Revered Herr Doktor, these frank opinions may help you comprehend why so many artists and connoisseurs of the arts are gravely concerned for the future of art in this country. The artists' idealistic hopes are clouded by sobering doubts, and more and more men despairingly see the ideals in which they believed and for which they fought frustrated on all sides; they are seriously considering whether they should likewise escape to the "bathing resorts" where the intellectual emigrants are now enjoying the climate of a warmer, a less anti-artistic land. Must we really suffer a return of the old Wilhelmine curse—the phenomenon that the art which represents the nation in museums and academies must hide its face in shame before history, and that the true representatives of the nation lead a miserable existence in garrets and hermits' cells, recapitulating the fate of their fellow artists of earlier epochs? Or is this just an inevitable adjustment of the relationship between the artist and the state, and does this sort of ostracism earn honor and glory for the artist before a higher court of appeals?

To Tut

Berlin

November 6, 1933

Kandinsky just telephoned. I am supposed to go and see them again. But there won't be time. He will also be in Bern and Zurich in mid-December and hopes to meet me then. He says there are interesting new developments to discuss. Yesterday Muche was visiting them, is back here today. He and the others apparently have no prospect of having their dismissals revoked.

First comment at the Unemployment Office: "Well, you only worked eighteen hours a week when employed." At that rate I would not be entitled to unemployment compensation in any case. I replied that it was brain work, and none of the teachers were required to work more hours. Hm, well, they would have to check into that . . . . At any rate: I shall have to get onto the rolls if I want to receive anything. Otherwise the family will go hungry.

EICHBERG — SEHRINGEN — STUTTGART — WUPPERTAL
(Autumn 1933 to April 1943)

1933-1934: In November Oskar Schlemmer accepts an invitation from a brother of Otto Meyer's to come to Laupen, near Bern, in order to go through the estate of his friend and put it in order. On December 22 the memorial exhibition prepared by Schlemmer opens at the Zurich Kunsthaus, later to be shown in Basel and Bern. Schlemmer delivers the memorial lectures. A monograph, "Otto Meyer-Amden—Aus Leben, Werk und Briefen" ["Otto Meyer-Amden—a Chapter from his Life, Works, and Letters"] is published in 1934 by the Verlag der Johannispresse [St. John's Press], in Zurich; in it Schlemmer sums up his thoughts and previous written notes on his revered friend.

In March Schlemmer is the guest of Ernst Ludwig Kirchner in Davos. He manages to find a little house to rent in Eichberg bei Dettighofen (South Baden). In April the family is finally reunited there.

For months mental stress and strain, coupled with the necessity of performing country chores, prevent Schlemmer from doing any artistic work.

1935-1937: Not until 1935 and 1936 does Schlemmer produce any new paintings: oil paintings on oiled paper, a "new, blooming painting embodying many new possibilities," in which Schlemmer seeks to strike a balance between nature and abstraction. On the side he designs ballets, preparing colored drawings of each stage of the dance, for there appears to be an opening for some theatrical activity in Zurich. Madame de Mandrot, a patron of the arts who each summer plays host to artists from around the world, invites Schlemmer in the summers of 1936 and 1937 to her castle, La Sarraz, near Lausanne.

In January 1937 the Ferdinand Möller Gallery in Berlin risks exhibiting his new works, and that same year a gallery in London mounts a retrospective exhibition. In addition, the garden architect Hermann Mattern commissions Schlemmer to do a mural for his house in Bornim.

Encouraged by these events Schlemmer is seized with a burning desire for a suitable place to work, and thus he decides to build a frame house with studio in Sehringen bei Badenweiler. Badenweiler—an international bathing resort, where René Schickele and Anette Kolb also live—the proximity to Switzerland, and a projected artists' and writers' colony strike him as a favorable constellation. The house, built at great sacrifice, is ready for occupancy in the autumn. But about the time of the move there arrives the catastrophic news of an exhibition of "Entartete Kunst" ["Degenerate Art"] in Munich, which includes paintings by Schlemmer.

The hopes which Schlemmer had pinned on the house are destroyed at one blow, and it becomes evident that his fate as an artist and the fate of modern painting in Germany are sealed. The dream of having his own studio comes to an abrupt end, and there is hardly any possibility of selling pictures. He is unable to make up his mind to emigrate to England or the United States, where there might be possibilities for earning a living. Now he must face up to the necessity of finding a source of income.

1938 1940: In 1938 and the subsequent years Schlemmer earns his bread by working for a painting concern in Stuttgart, for which he does mainly decorative jobs and, after the outbreak of the war, camouflage markings for buildings. This involves exhausting physical work, some of it on scaffoldings and out-of-doors.

In the winter he paints pictures behind glass for his employer, sometimes following religious motifs, sometimes inventing his own themes.

His artistic production comes almost to a dead halt. In his native country he becomes the object of defamation and humiliation, while outside the country he receives considerable attention. At the great Bauhaus exhibition at the Museum of Modern Art in New York and the "German Art" exhibition in London, the significance of his work is duly noted.

1940–1943: Around the middle of 1940, Kurt Herberts offers Schlemmer and Baumeister positions at his paint factory in Wuppertal, where he provides persecuted artists with a refuge and an opportunity to experiment on their own. Among Schlemmer's fellow workers in the paint laboratory are the architect Heinz Rasch, the art historian Hans Hildebrandt, and the artists Gerhard Marcks, Edwin Scharff, and Georg Muche. In September Schlemmer begins his job, which consists of testing new paints. In Wuppertal and nearby Krefeld he finds many of his old friends and acquaintances. At first he feels comfortable in his new surroundings and his morale is high. But soon this feeling begins to evaporate, and the available opportunities cannot offset his increasing unhappiness with this setting and his duties. He feels inwardly isolated.

In the spring of 1942 he paints the so-called *Fensterbilder* ["Window Pictures"], small in format, "marvels of the visual" which offer new possibilities and thus strike him as a hopeful omen.

But he is torn between his duties in Wuppertal and jobs he must still carry out in Stuttgart, often wishing he could break these ties and live as a freelance painter in his studio in Sehringen; thus he exhausts his vital forces. He falls ill, and hospital treatment in Stuttgart, Freiburg, Bühlerhöhe, and Baden-Baden can no longer save him.

Oskar Schlemmer dies in Baden-Baden on April 13, 1943.

To Tut

Laupen bei Bern
November 15, 1933

Here I find myself completely under the spell of Otto Meyer. There are many works here I had never seen. His brother has done a good deal of work and sorting already. But it is very important to make sure that the major works, which are often small in size, are presented more forcefully than many of the sketches which are larger in format.

What are your thoughts on a future location? How does Berlin look to you? The Siemensstadt district was lovely, of course. I still think that time ripens and clarifies things. For the moment I am taken care of. When I am through in Switzerland, there is always Stuttgart. That I find very tempting, perhaps better than with relatives.

To Tut

Laupen bei Bern
December 26, 1933

I had a lovely and exciting stay in Zurich. The last evening there was especially fine. Otto Meyer's doctor was there, then the Kündigs and the Paul Meyers. The doctor often drives to Germany, to Dettighofen; it takes him forty minutes. That is the German customs-free enclave. The beauty of the area was much praised, and it was generally decided that that should be my future place of abode! And of course my own feelings naturally lean toward such a plan. The only question remains: where will our daily bread come from? Otherwise I am completely in favor of living in the country and painting.

When I have mastered my last cause for worry, the lecture, I shall be completely free in spirit and in deed. I am burning with eagerness to write about Otto Meyer. I now feel very much at home with his life and work and will certainly be able to say something worthwhile. People seem very glad that I am going to speak, since otherwise there is no one else, or no one willing to do it.

What lies ahead? I keep wondering what will happen to me

after January 15. What do you think about this, and about things in general?

To Tut

Laupen bei Bern
December 29, 1933

Of course I cannot leave unanswered the courageous sally in favor of painting you sent as a Christmas and New Year's greeting. I find answering easy, since my preoccupation with Otto Meyer has plunged me right into the midst of the subject and has also made me perceive my own special mission more clearly than ever before. A large portion of my leaning toward the theater can be ascribed to the fact that I feel obligated to provide for the family, no matter how uncertain the theater is these days. But since nothing appears to be available in this area, whereas there suddenly seems to be a chance for selling some paintings, the issue looks to be settled. *Man tau!*—I am taking the leap, and that should give you a plain answer if you wish.

To Tut

Sihlbrugg
February 12, 1934

Today the blue wonder is finally due to occur: Dettighofen. I arrived in Zurich and am now waiting to be fetched by car. Glorious weather.

Dettighofen. Or rather, Eichberg. Surprisingly lovely landscape with a view of the Alps. The cottage a *bijou*. It is situated not in the village but three kilometers above it; near the farm, however, is the village of Eichberg, consisting of several farmhouses. Unfurnished. Electricity, running water; a bathtub.

There is a lot to fix up in and around the house. For instance, some of the farmers make their entire living by growing strawberries, which flourish in the area. Many fruit trees. There is also land along with, which one could lease to farmers, thus cutting the rent by about half.

To Tut

Zurich

March 16, 1934

Not until today, early Friday, did I get back from Davos—because it was so lovely there! Wednesday, just when I was ready to leave, proved the most beautiful day yet. Sun for the first time. So up we went with the Parsenn railway to the Weißfluhjoch, the starting point of the ski trails, I with Frau Kirchner, who had not been up there since they came to Davos seventeen years ago. Kirchner has never been! Then, the next day and again today, snow, lots of snow, still going on when I left. The Kirchners' house, 40 francs' rent per month, very peasantlike but roomy, primitive but beautiful. His wife an exiled Berliner; that is, she dreams of comfort and big city life, has had a very difficult time of it with Kirchner, who has been seriously ill. He a "Viking," as Pinder described this sort of artist in his lecture. He has retired altogether, but is certainly the most important member of the Brücke.

To Willi Baumeister

Zurich

March 17, 1934

The die has now more or less been cast: we are moving to Eichberg, mailing address Bühl, Post Office Waldshut/Baden, until April 15. Addition: c/o Schaub.

At the beginning of next week I shall move in temporarily, which means I shall take a room in the village of Eichberg and do various things around the house: paint the rooms, get it cleaned up, and so on.

I spent six days in Davos visiting Kirchner. He is feeling better now, has done colossal amounts of work, a dash of Davos plus Picasso, but he also has some paintings very much his own. Lives in relative isolation, on bad terms with everyone. Finds himself suspended between two worlds, Switzerland and Germany (he is still a member of the Prussian Academy).

But now my Swiss period is over. Off to prepare the house to receive my wife and Jaina, and then the furniture and then the deer, foxes, rabbits, wild boars. When can we expect you two???

326

To Tut

Dettighofen
March 23, 1934

"Don't curse, that makes it worse," is the house's motto!

Think of others' fate these days! Ours is far from the worst, But you aren't that depressed, are you?

So: the decision to leap into certain uncertainty has fallen. And now bad weather, too. Cold and rainy. All I can say is: the place has great potential (if it ever gets warmer!). Perhaps that is the source of my "cooling off."

To Tut

Eichberg
April 17, 1934

Dear Tutsch, so you're amazed, are you? Eh? Yes, yes.— The move has been effected! About three in the afternoon the four loads arrived, two at a time, that is, and by half-past eight this evening the moving men left, I at nine by moonlight. Just this note in haste, for it is half-past nine and the Löwens are tired—the best time for the three of you to come would be Saturday!

The painter left me in the lurch and I still have some chores to get done. Must clean up. When you come, you should at least find a somewhat bearable atmosphere. That is what I have in mind.

*To the Administration of the Folkwang Museum
in Essen, in care of Count Baudissin*

Eichberg
April 19, 1934

I recently learned that you have announced a competition for designs intended to replace the wall decorations I did for you some years ago. If this is true, I assume that I must count on the definitive removal of my pictures, in which case I should be interested to know how you plan to dispose of the panels. At the moment I am not sure of my legal rights in the case, but if it were a question of destroying or painting over the plywood panels, I would take the appropriate steps to prevent such an action.

To Count Baudissin

Eichberg

May 22, 1934

Thank you for sending me the conditions of the competition, which made it clear that I am already too old to qualify. But I am grateful for the assurance that nothing will happen to the panels as long as you remain in office.

You might receive the impression that I was embittered. That is not the case. I am looking forward with great composure to seeing the present confusion over art resolved, and I have considerable faith in the indestructible German qualities which will certainly survive. Probably I shall one day thank Fate for transplanting me from the hustle and bustle of the city to the peaceful countryside. For the freedom from petty irritations in which I hope to live and to think here should make it easier for me to draw on the insights obtained through my previous work. My composure is disturbed only when I see myself the victim of patent injustice.

For I often have the feeling that the pre-war and post-war artists are treated like shoddy goods from a discount store: they are weighed and usually found to be too light, and there can be no doubt that grave mistakes are being made of late. Who can legitimately claim to be an infallible judge?

To Count Baudissin

Eichberg

June 17, 1934

I asked you once before to describe the type of painter which National Socialists would consider exemplary. I have asked others this same question and have been referred to Kanoldt, Schrimpf, and Lenk. My conception of German style and stylistic greatness happens to differ from what these three artists have to offer. Why, then, have I no right to state that the Messiah of new German art is still awaited, since at the moment he cannot be found and thus still represents only a hope; and when he appears, he will have to suffer the fate of the Messiah: he will go unrecognized, be mocked, nailed to the Cross, and finally venerated. If "the mission of a great artist is a gift of grace," you yourself testify to the messianic character of the artist. Why, then, your remark that my words amount to "a mockery of Germany's desperation"? That I do not understand. Why shouldn't the Messiah be born of Germany's desperation? It *will* come about that way, without a doubt, and you share this belief, for you place all your hopes on the young people and on the future. I am also convinced that he will not descend from the heavens but will live an earthly life, full of pain and toil. But all the talk nowadays about artistic craftsmanship, solidity, and training in materials strikes me as dangerous. Of course those things are necessary, should be taken for granted, but by themselves they nowhere approach real art. Well, let us wait and see what the younger generation can do, and whether the new incentives, the lockstep, belief in Germany, can surpass what has been done up to now.

"Art serves!"—Yes, in an ultimate, lofty sense. Not literally; otherwise art enters bonded servitude. If you deprive art of its freedom, it dies. If you deprive it of the joys of play, of spinning tales, of freely inventing and shaping, then it will vegetate, not live.

May I take this occasion to inquire whether you have also had my picture *Römisches* put in storage and if so, whether it was for those reasons of principle you mentioned in your first letter? I do not know the situation at the Folkwang Museum these days and whether justice is being done to the intentions of Osthaus, the founder, that is, to his choice of pictures, his German idealism, and his fervent belief in art, to his courage and audacity?

To Willi Baumeister

Eichberg

December 3, 1934

Things are about the same here—how are they with you? We hope for the best. The major issue of the day is nothing more nor less than a ram. Since Tut's birthday we have been the proud possessors of a milch sheep, which grazes and eats and gives milk—every two or three days a liter of good milk with plenty of butterfat—this until the end of the month; then she will be "dried off," since she will be "lambing" in March. But then, when the two or three lambs have suckled, she will place her two daily milkings entirely at our disposal, and we shall enter the ranks of the self-sufficients, autarkists, state sheep-holders.

Now we have been offered a ram for 35 marks. But since at the moment we have to watch our spending closely and winter makes heavy demands on one's resources, we have arranged to proceed as follows: 15 marks down payment now and 3 marks to cover the feeding until the end of the year.

In short: if I could ask you to send a check for 18 marks immediately, to the below address, half the ram would be yours. In case we slaughtered you would receive half the ram, either salted or canned; his name might be WIL-OS, to express your share in him, as would a ring in oil paint the length of or around the ram.

I hope and trust that this is agreeable to you. Apropos, you would also receive a share of his fruits: lambs! How many, if ever?

I have done some painting and hope to continue when the most urgent gardening chores are out of the way: digging, the deeper the better; manuring! Thinning trees, hoeing, liming, fertilizing!

But it is as lovely as before, even when we have frost. The peace of winter is gradually settling in. Winter and the stoves make their daily demands.

To Albrecht Kämmerer

Eichberg

January 1, 1935

I am placing my hopes on the summer. With me it always takes a long time before something has taken hold and my mind is filled to the point that I can go to work.

Right now we are going through an uncomfortable period, probably the hardest of the year, but here in the country even this holds no horrors. The damp, cold, misty weather must be uncomfortable elsewhere, too. We are waiting for snow! In the meantime my wife's donkey has arrived, in the form of an East

Frisian milch sheep, which grazes in the meadows in all kinds of weather. Some day soon a ram will be arriving, likewise East Frisian, but coming from the Black Forest; we wanted to save him from the butcher. So the national slogan "Keep sheep!" has not gone unheard in these parts! The farmers of Eichberg are already watching closely to see whether they should not do the same.

Diary

January 15, 1935

Impressions in the Munich Pinakothek:

Caspar David Friedrich and Hans von Marées: the earnest profundity (dark tones, almost black in C.D.F.'s paintings). Is it the melancholy of these two masters? Why are masterworks often characterized by such noble mournfulness?

Titian's "Mocking": full of gloom, mighty, formless by comparison with El Greco, who seems so form-conscious. When the degree of emotional intensity is so great that one forgets to think about form, then one has a masterpiece. To be sure: C. D. Friedrich struck his contemporaries as artificial, constructed. So the unfettered child of nature Courbet should be considered the stronger of the two?

In the Glyptothek the archaic Greeks, the Apollos. One wonderful one, patched together, said to have been chopped in three pieces by the man who found it so that he could transport it unrecognized. One can see where it was glued.

The breath of fresh air one gets from these early works, then a predominance (numerically) of the middle and (naturalistic) declining periods of Greek art.

Marées: the great new example of grand style, the parading of which puts his contemporaries in their place (to each his own!). Feuerbach an academic painter, Leibl a miniaturist (of high quality) and portraitist, Thoma a folk painter (native of the Black Forest), Böcklin a fantast, Lenbach—well, now!

Diary

January 18, 1935

In the end a painter's life boils down to something which one designates as "characteristic" of him. Or: in the last analysis the individual's particular features center around one element; the personal factor can be reduced to a common denominator. Or: what the individual attempts to add to the existing body of art is a trifle, a tiny particle. The question: is it winnowed chaff or dormant seed; is it an end or the beginning of something new? Or: when one filters and distills a painter's life work, one is left with what is unique to him, his essence. How does it appear when viewed from the highest vantage point? profound? new? (merely new?) comprehensive? narrow? simple and clear? or unfathomable?

Diary

January 22, 1935

Outside there is snow, white snow, clear blue sky, bright blue shadows from the pale orange sunspots on the snow. The dark green fir trees—the well-known beauties of nature. Who can resist the sight?

Indoors my palette with its nature-given colors, ranging from black to white, from brown via red to yellow. How lovely is the terra di siena, how glowing the Prussian blue, then the umbers and ochre, the English = Venetian red. It is the other world, the other range of tones. It would be criminal to portray one's experience of nature with them, for it does not correspond to the essence and the nature of the palette. Why did the Old Masters paint nature in brown? Out of love for the artistic media: and they linked their love of nature to that. The (bad) Impressionists did violence to their palettes without ever achieving the verisimilitude and the so-called truth for which they strove. But aren't these old truths which have become commonplaces?

Diary

Another project: to paint Eichberg and everything connected with it, all the familiar, beloved things, in such a way that everything becomes anti-natural, all the things one clings to in human and artistic terms.

Doesn't old experience suggest that such projects are doomed to failure from the outset, precisely because the actual painterly elements do not receive their due? Or is it only a question of mastery, of finding the appropriate form, of transposing reality into the fitting media?

The fascinating quality of chance splotches of color on the palette or other accidental phenomena such as the oil spots left when one wipes a brush off on paper.

Is it the stimulus these chance occurrences give the imagination or—taking the spots on the palette—isn't this "pure painting" as it should be, that is, a combination of colors juxtaposed in a way more pleasing to the eye than anything created on purpose?

I know of no painting as attractive, as distinctively *peinture pure,* as these spots on the palette. Of course one would have to add a meaning, something relatively concrete; then one would have performed the great feat of turning a piece of art into a work of art.

When I think over the best, most beautiful paintings I know, I can come up with nothing that could equal the splendor of these chance effects. Or: I know of no painting both meaningful and good, i.e. representing some object, which reveals such beauty of material.

Is that not a goal devoutly to be wished? As far as I am concerned, the question of pigment is solved (coloring tones on the palette, pastose). Pursuit of this goal would take one away from the graphic outline filled in with color, for it would be full-blooded pure color.

I shall attempt it!

Diary

February 7, 1935

Little things can prove decisive. Once Otto Meyer hung my little Landenberger nude in his attic room and remarked that it struck him as more modern than the cubistic experiments I was involved with at the time. For him this nude doubtless afforded a decisive revelation: for him, who was bound to the graphic approach, it opened up vistas of the painterly, visual approach, and its modern possibilities; and in fact I see one of Otto Meyer's merits, though not his chief one, in his unique combination of painterly *peinture pure* and an unusual element of intellectual content.

Diary

February 23, 1935

My "studio" is too cramped. I painfully miss the space I had in my previous rooms. So I must escape to the great outdoors!

Coming from Corot and Courbet—my initial successes in Stuttgart based on a cultivated palette and a natural proclivity to simple media—I at first found acquaintanceship with the "Sturm" modernists in Berlin confusing. However, it was Derain to whom I always returned. Here I felt the strongest affinity, and probably a genuine one, since Derain remains within tradition and reflects, if you will, Corot, Courbet, Cézanne. And his world offers soothing nobility. At the time I feared falling into premature narrowness and fled to abstraction. I also tried to escape the French influence, sensing the existence of a (rigorous) German mode of expression and searching for it, (subconsciously at the time).

Am I today, after, oh, so many detours, once more approaching the French model? The pigments and the attempts to achieve depth are leading me ineluctably in that direction: that explains the sudden appearance of romantic elements.

Diary

Was Corot completely at ease with himself?

There can be no doubt: the dynamic, ecstatic mode does not come easily to me, whereas the calm, self-sufficient, composed mode does. Is that a law of art or a matter of personal inclination and talent?

I sense that the calm, static aspect of painting calls for similar subject matter more than for movement and kinetic impressions. Nowadays we have another art form to portray the lapse of time.

The Futurists did attempt this—but to my mind without success.

Pictures are piling up, sketches for ideas for pictures; the log is rolling, I must act—the best method for sorting out thoughts.

To Karl Nierendorf

Eichberg
March 13, 1935

Have no fear: I do not plan to attempt an exhibition! I am sunning myself in my defamation, which with me seems to have taken a particularly virulent form. Why is that? Can you explain it to me? Perhaps you can make me see what people have against me, why I am not included in the Berlin Secession; but I see that your Fuhr, and even Nolde, are not included. Now I see in *Kunst der Nation* ["National Art News"] that you, too, have "stricken me from the list" (this was the title of a picture by Klee, whom I visited in Bern). Why? Feel free to tell me.

No, for the present I do not want my work exhibited. Perhaps in a year's time. Perhaps, if I hold out that long, not until my fiftieth birthday (1938). But I shall work and am working like a demon, with, to be sure, the famous classical bias with which I was apparently born. What was it one used to hear: I was considered predestined to evolve the style of our times. All I can do is continue cultivating my natural abilities and, as a child of the times, give them free rein. I hope to draw strength from my pariah status, for strength is usually the gift of grace bestowed on those who are wronged.

I face the future with composure. Something would be amiss if the peacefulness and isolation of country life did not have a beneficial effect on the painter and his work. I still refuse to kowtow to the sort of naturalism which assures an artist of success in the Germany of today. As in the past I shall continue to dedicate myself to large-scale composition and its principles, and to believe in the magnificence of a type of painting which I now envision more vividly than ever.

Diary

March 15, 1935

Depression, psychic and physical. Am I on the right track, am I on any track at all? The crampedness of the studio is reflected in the form the pictures take. My earlier pictures were in no small part a product of the setting in which they were created. At best the new pictures will turn out more concentrated. I don't want them to be "narrower."

Keep having premonitions of new kinds of beautiful painting. A good sign, actually.

Diary

March 18, 1935

And once more: Seurat! How often his ghost has hovered over my studio! The clear, simple, plane-bound quality of his painting has repeatedly drawn me under its spell.

To Willi Baumeister

March 31, 1935

The art world, the German one, that is, is in tumult. Hither and yon, and I paint on! You will have discovered by now that your country has pretty much turned its back on you. Foreign countries beckon to you. But where do I fit in?

In Berlin: Marcks, the constructor, a great success, so he has nothing to worry about. Barlach less so. Dix, under the patronage of Lenk, is reported to be painting slick, bourgeois landscapes of Hegau (near Singen), and has sold one to a collector from the Rhineland. Feininger has sold watercolors, several. Muche is also content.

Diary

April 9, 1935

After a long interruption, an attempt to start afresh. After such interludes the first efforts usually succeed, as if something really had been stored up, or at least a freshness of emotion achieved which tends to wane if one works constantly. In the works I consider good and important I achieved a sense of tranquillity, and therein probably lies my hope for the future. The field I have to work with is narrow. That I know. Still, I should be able to achieve greatness and perfection within its confines (and perhaps precisely thanks to them). It will not be a cornucopia as it is with Klee, who is so fertile.

There will be a secret element of melancholy and a trace of terrestrial "eternal hunting grounds," to which I am returning after extensive wanderings.

And Seurat's monumentality will be my guiding star, never the bombast of a Thorak, so favored these days in Germany! Brightnesses born of the depths, breaking into the depths (of figures).

To Jules Bissier

Eichberg

May 9, 1935

We are completely under the sway of the milk of human kindness provided by Minka. It flows as in the Promised Land; up to five liters and more per day! To be sure, Frau Blessing has to come and milk her three times a day, since Frau Mam has not quite mastered the art yet. Also one has to cajole her to let down her milk, since we have separated her from the four lambs, to which she responded with long-drawn-out baa-ing. But that is already over, and everything points toward a peaceable solution of this existential question. A further step in this direction was taken when we decided to lease out part of the land and only keep what we could conveniently work ourselves. Otherwise we would simply be unable to manage, and it would not make economic sense. Potatoes aren't worth what you put into them, the most intelligent of our farmer neighbors says, and the same goes for other crops. In short: we are making things easier for ourselves, because art is difficult enough.

We are girding ourselves to receive the three ice saints along with cold Sophie and send greetings from amidst snowy carpets of blossoms and May dew!

Diary

June 3, 1935

Landscape exercises. Impressions. Impressions of how I plan to work from nature from now on. Shorthand notations of impressions, optic and geometric, extracts of the essential (essential to me), lest I succumb to the multiplicity of the vegetative; in order to achieve a stable posture.

The sketches have the added attractions of freedom, which will perhaps be hard to maintain when I am working directly from nature. Still, I plan to "study" from now on, and perhaps such studies and fragments will gradually lead me to the form of landscape I envisage. Perhaps I shall eventually achieve the freedom in landscape painting which I had achieved in the portrayal of figures, and then I might successfully bring the two together.

Diary

June 9, 1935

Artistic truth—natural truth! Yes, yes, faithfulness to nature is not enough. One form of faithfulness to nature necessarily ("naturally") results in pictorial abstraction, for it consists of extracting, attempting to render one's real impression, the one received by the inner eye. Here the ways part, and the results are, of course, "directions."

Diary

June 17, 1935

The fascinating thing about Henri Rousseau is probably that he achieved perfection, the ability to finish a picture, in short: painting a beautiful picture without, it would seem, having to agonize over it. By contrast, all modern art remains a fragment, if not a wreck, something which breaks off and seems to shun completion.

To Julius Schottländer

Eichberg
July 6, 1935

Farming can take up a great deal of one's energy; actually one should devote oneself to it full time. As it is, I hurtle from one extreme to the other, for that is what art and nature are: extremes. To achieve balance and harmony would indeed be "a consummation devoutly to be wished." For instance, I am still unable to do what my friend Kirchner in Davos advises: base my work on my present surroundings. I cannot paint sheep instead of human beings, or my family. I have a precise concept of figural painting which I still subscribe to; it was the objective of all my painting up to now. Nor have I yet found a suitable artistic form for farming, one that would conform to my figural ideal. A cheap way of going about it would be simply to sit down facing the landscape and copy it; but I am looking for a more sophisticated approach, and have not yet found it. Besides, I'm not even fifty yet!

Diary

July 6, 1935

Cherish the ideal! The vision I often have these days of new, beautiful painting. It is a rich, deep-toned, blooming painting, full of an inner glow, although not modern on the surface.

Pursue this lovely vision. It should provide the basis for something uniquely mine and for a truly fine modern art.

A "problem" arises when the artist strives for something which does not match his inclinations but which he finds stimulating in its newness or originality.

Picasso thrives exclusively on problems, on inventing ever new ways of posing the basic questions, constantly doubting anew, perhaps even despairing of ever achieving a definitive formulation.

339

Others calmly proceed from step to step, registering what means most to them personally—Corot, Vermeer, presumably. So the question arises: were these old masters free of inner torment? But who can answer that question for me?

July 15, 1935

For I come from the brightness, the all too bright, and am headed into the darkness—for natural, I might almost say political, reasons. Natural because the extremes are always linked, and an excess of light must be followed by deep shadow. Political? Yes, in order to enter the darkness intentionally, to reserve my strength, which I think will be possible if I allow just a little brightness to glow against a near-black background.

The ordinary person will turn away from the blackness without taking the trouble to look for something in it. The man with genuine interest will be able to find meaning in it and will put together what he wants to see.

August 31, 1935

Over and over again I have visions of a non-expressive form of painting, full of import and intent, which really points the way to a kind of perfection. How lovely, splendid, the tranquil Chinese scrolls are. How lovely their simplicity of portrayal (nature pictures, mood pictures), how invisible the technique.

It is basically "decency" (an ugly word for a well-meant thing) which prevents me from allowing myself liberties and audacities like those of the Expressionists, say, or Kirchner or Baumeister. I understand all their audacities without being able to indulge in them myself. Not out of decency but out of a sense of obligation to an ideal, which was present in C. D. Friedrich and mighty in Otto Meyer; out of a passion for strict discipline.

Diary

September 19, 1935

Just read Nolde's *Jahre der Kämpfe [Years of Struggles]*. The battle for his cause and the passion with which he waged it are extraordinary; he certainly has won the right to regard everything egocentrically, from his and only his point of view, and to pass judgment on other artists. He had an ideal, or one took shape in him, and he rendered and evaluated everything in relation to it, as in fact should, or must, be the case. Seen in this light *he* is *the* German artist whom the National Socialists would make their standard bearer, if they knew what they were doing.

I never really liked Nolde, with the exception of his water-colors, which were often very rich and lovely; in his oil paintings he tends to be coarse and brutal. He describes a dream in which he is in a studio and sees pictures by an unknown painter stacked against the walls, incredibly beautiful, inconceivable and totally unfamiliar; as I read the passage, I thought to myself that this must be the very kind of great painting I envision in my inspired moments. But mine is constructivist, i.e. with horizontals and verticals. Cultic, and simultaneously glowingly colorful. Nolde can bloom only in the absence of strictures, which he sees in negative terms, even in Cézanne; he shuns system, and that is why his book contains not a single word on the laws of painting. Strange. My feeling would be that one cannot have a perfect picture without them. Either he wants to let chaos prevail—or else his concept of law differs completely from mine; for one cannot create a single picture, a single artistic statement without constructive relationships within the picture, a point of view, a fixed pole.

Diary

October 22, 1935

The National Socialists are instinctively attracted to the New Objectivity school of painting. This puritan style, which copies nature and abjures any attempt at capturing significant form, will prove unsatisfactory in the long run. Force and aggressivity are not enough. So where will ground be broken?

If only one could create something new without smashing the old forms, as the majority of modern painters do, thereby giving their art its distinctive character?

Diary

October 23, 1935

The constructive rigidity of my earlier works (some of my best): Chirico's constructivism relaxed progressively into an ever more flowing, baroque line; similarly Kokoschka's original graphic precision yielded to a baroque pointillism and sometimes even to the intoxication of a landscape. My tendency toward more relaxed forms probably stems from the same pattern of evolution.

To Julius Schottländer

Eichberg

November 3, 1935

The new paintings I have done here I would rather not part with until I have tried to get them displayed in Berlin at Nierendorf's or Bucholz's. One keeps imagining, or begins to imagine again, that one has something to say after all and that it would be heard amidst the hullabaloo of opinions.

You cannot imagine how wary I am of the landscape! It is lovely here, glorious in fact, but I have such inhibitions about plopping myself down in front of it with an easel and painting in green, a color which I banished from my palette years ago. Kirchner in Davos gives me advice on how to go about it—for instance: to get rid of the inhibitions, I should paint pictures only in green! Even so! Perhaps some day; and yet the fall coloration is especially lovely right now and would match my predilection for earthy tones.

I was in Zurich recently to discuss the planned matinee of the "Triadic Ballet." They treat me with great consideration there, and they expect my ballet to create the next theatrical sensation, once the success achieved by Stravinsky's *Histoire du soldat* has worn off. However, it will not be exactly easy to launch a new production with dancers whom I do not yet know, who, in fact, must yet be found.

Diary

November 4, 1935

If I had my old, bright workroom back in these changed times, would I produce anything different?

It is criminal to stifle the artist's joy in creation and his artistic freedom!

To Julius Schottländer

Eichberg

November 15, 1935

The artistic trends of the day are catastrophic, and thus cannot provide any sort of standard or guide. Let me refrain from getting worked up. I always believed that within the evolution of modern art (which de facto no longer exists in Germany, or only under the name of "Bolshevism") I represented the genre which concentrates on the question of composition, ultimately the source of all style, a goal some of the best minds happen to consider worth striving for. Frankly, I still consider it that, despite the present mood, and my faith in composition gives me ample reason for not sitting back and twiddling my thumbs. I also keep hoping to find a satisfying solution—even in the absence of resonance or encouragement, sheer *l'art pour l'art*. Because men like us (I am definitely not the only one) have literally no other possibility but to keep doing what an unknown God or daimon commands.

No, this belief has not yet been extinguished, and persecution will make it grow and strengthen, not perish. Painting still offers the extraordinary possibility to make visible things of which the mass of humanity has not the faintest conception. Goods for the masses are available in huge supply and have been for a long time; they are turned out on the assembly line, so no struggle goes into their production. But we must go around with a lantern searching for anything rare, fine, out of the ordinary.

Eichberg
November 13, 1935

First I must make one thing clear: my painting is not in such bad shape that you can dismiss it entirely. After all, I have been able to earn my living by it until recently. I wish I could soon inform you that we can manage on our own. Do stop by the art dealer Tannenbaum's some time. He actually managed to sell something for me, and there are other people who also want to help; help in this case means acknowledging my special brand of art as an essential component in the development of modern art, supporting it, and, if possible, buying it. There are other artists like me (thank God, is all I can say!) who are playing a similar pioneering role, most of them under the most difficult circumstances imaginable and at the sacrifice of such comforts of life as food and clothing. These few, I would contend, are the ones who count! If they keep on working determinedly and their best work turns out to be new, unique, progressive, then in all probability Germany will some day be proud to call them its own. So you see, we few moderns have a mission to fulfill. Here, too, one can be a deserter; but I want none of it.

One reason for my being persecuted today is that in the past I aroused too much controversy and had become established as an important figure. My less distinguished colleagues have all kept their snug little jobs! Sometimes I wonder what they are really thinking, whether they don't suffer pangs of conscience; for they are well aware who I am and what I stand for. And everyone sees that those who in the past, justly or unjustly, lacked success, are now enjoying prominence. Unfortunately this group includes those whose lack of success was entirely deserved—they were nonentities from way back!

Diary

November 16, 1935

Werner Gilles; he sits up there so devout and pure in his solitude, giving shape to his vision, seeking the form = formula for the hieroglyphs with which he tries to make the inexpressible visible. But not even the elect understand him, let alone the people. Yes, probably his landlord and landlady there understand him, for they watch this man at work and can see his work growing, share his emotions; and by following the curve of his character they can come to grasp what he is doing.

It is a delicate lyricism, like that of Georg Trakl, for instance, with perhaps a dash of Hölderlin; in any case, something spiritual, non-intellectual, naïve, and unspeculatively pure. And thus also purer, more German than Kirchner, who has now so clearly been drawn into Picasso's orbit. And further along than Nolde, too, since he eschews Nolde's often clashing colorfulness and wildly distorted figures. But somewhat on the same track, and in that sense anti-classical, not "over-run by foreign influences." The classical and classicistic are my domain, come naturally to me in the course of my search for order and clarity.

But that, too, is cultural Bolshevism! Where will this lead? In architecture we already know what to expect. What style of painting would correspond to this kind of architecture? Perhaps artistic development will be throttled, resulting in an eclectic building style and painting which merely repeats, rather than, as Schinkel puts it, seeking, i.e. *consciously* seeking the new. Perhaps this suppression of healthy development will one day produce a vehement and categorical demand for the new, the futuristic, the mysterious, and then it will be good to have something like that around. Perhaps a natural hunger for it will develop, since it is unnatural to deny for any length of time the latent powers of creativity, which even the people possess.

Diary

November 24, 1935

Once and for all: I cannot and must not work "impetuously," with murky ideas, with unfamiliar tools, but rather with a clear notion of what I want to achieve and the appropriate tools. In short, I must proceed cautiously, carefully, slowly. I am no Dionysian—I find my ecstasy elsewhere. Where, then? In the holy "shudder" that comes when I succeed, when I perceive the glorious confluence of will and vision.

Diary

November 29, 1935

Talent keeps to a pre-established path, although it often displays great skill. Genius overleaps the boundaries of convention, finding even the greatest skill insignificant in comparison with the ideal.

Diary

December 8, 1935

I envisage clearly (or is it only approximately?) glorious pictures that should be painted or would be rewarding to paint. They resolve the conflicting elements of modern art within a "beautiful" style of painting, one without the type of problematic features that impose themselves on one's awareness and call attention only to themselves; not Expressionism, for this contains assimilated fragments and gestures, and not New Objectivity, with its leanings toward the Biedermeier. This new painting has a rich inner resonance; it contains as many new elements as old, and should convey as much harmony as the works of Mozart and Raphael. Who will create this art? Is my lovely vision of it sufficient? If so, one's only worry would be how to make it a reality.

To Hugo Borst

Eichberg

December 11, 1935

Your travel report on the politics of art is both interesting and gratifying. I heard something similar recently from Dr. Kaesbach, whom we saw in Schaffhausen; his opinion, however, was somewhat more negative; he felt, for instance, that Hanfstaengl was in danger and that modern art would continue to be taboo in official art circles. So how do you explain this hunger for the forbidden artists? If a hunger has really developed already, that would be a good sign. Does it constitute a protest against the suppression of living forces, or, as someone has asserted, a search for objects of value? That need not concern us artists; our task is to work, true to the motto of William of

Orange, which Sauerlandt quotes in his book: "One must begin one's task without hope of success, and keep to it even if recognition fails to come."

About a year ago I became involved in a rather long correspondence with Count Baudissin; it began when my wall panels in Essen were taken down and put in storage, but I broke it off eventually because misunderstandings kept piling up.

Yesterday, when your letter arrived, I had just struggled through to the decision to take up at the very point where I stopped in Breslau in 1932 (ever since then I have not managed to do a single large picture). For all the detours and devious approaches which became necessary when my naïveté and spontaneity were impaired proved fruitless; what is required is naïve and spontaneous devotion to the one, exclusive, and essential thing.

We shall not be able to spend much time in this congenial place, for the owner plans to move here himself eventually. So we must look for another place to live, although that has not become pressing yet. But my wife wants to make this zillionth move our last if possible. Where should we go? We enjoy country life so much that we would like to continue this way. An "appointment" hardly seems to be in the cards any more, and so far we have felt no longing for the city.

Diary

January 12, 1936

The most impressive experience of this past Christmas was the dress rehearsal in the old Catholic church in Dettighofen: the singing of the peasant boys, their partly rehearsed, partly improvised performance of several songs I had never heard ("What then doth that signify?" and "Ye shepherds, ye men and women").

Christmas Eve in the "Lion": the great experience was hearing "Silent Night, Holy Night" spoken, to a soft piano accompaniment. I would not have thought such intensity possible. The old song acquired a lovely, very piercing significance.

Diary

January 15, 1936

Anniversary of Otto Meyer's death.

I no longer have anyone who provides such a welcome sounding board for my nature, mind, turns of phrase, my puns, my humor, as Otto Meyer did.

I no longer have anyone with whom I can discuss the deepest artistic and human mysteries, with the certainty of being understood correctly and answered.

He was the one responsible for creating and preserving the right atmosphere—which I now lack, despite friendships—and thus I now suffer from its absence. Now I have only my diary! So in the future I shall have to use the diary for working out my ideas.

Among my friends, Kirchner seems the one most ready and willing to help me think through certain problems, although his massive subjectivity would prove an obstacle. The main thing is to aim for something clearly defined.

Diary

January 18, 1936

When besieged with doubts I must try to recall what I really want, what I prize in my previous work and what seems appropriate in light of the current situation of art in Germany.

In answer to the subservient role assigned to art one should insist on total autonomy for art. Topical but mostly inferior pictures of soldiers and athletes are being produced en masse; one should reply with works that achieve their effects solely through artistic means and have a purely optical impact. The elements of composition, so clearly perceptible in the great masters, and, in fact, the ideal and goal for which they fought long and hard, should be defended firmly and energetically. Marées—Seurat—Cézanne, cannot be allowed to have lived and struggled in vain.

And then the painter's media should be treated as integral parts of his work; color must come into its own as a form of expression. In pure form (the glowing earth tones!) and, when mixed, mixed transparently, i.e. in superimposed layers. The prerequisite for this would be extremely precise planning, an orderly system, which, however, should not appear "too transparently" on the surface, should instead remain somewhat mysterious.

The next step is to find the subject matter appropriate to these prerequisites and requirements, a deliberately chosen content. Straightforward composition and color call for directness of content: the simple mode of being of a given figure, its basic emotions, its still pulsations in space. New material grows out of the new tonality which is being aimed for (tonality of living shadows, light distribution).

But I must make sure I remain on my own path.

And then I must try to determine in what ways I am original, so I can pursue that which is unique in my work.

Are such reflections the "extra-optical element" which the painter must have if he wishes to exchange his juggler's balls for new ones?

Diary

January 19, 1936

I cannot do a thing, i.e. paint. It is as if I were right back at the beginning. My recent work seems a cul-de-sac, in which I end up going around and around in circles.

This feeling is intensified by the freshly prepared canvases, which now confront me in their blinding whiteness. "An empty canvas." They deserve only the best—and that does not mean covering them with color, but, on the contrary, preserving their whiteness and purity.

It is the "Felicitas" mood of Flaubert; the mood produced by white plastered Catholic churches setting off the black of the pews, the gold of the holy vessels, the red of the banners and the decorations. Also the aura of certain old, tinted window shades, of old illustrations of perspective, of old engravings. It conjures up touchingly primitive archaic objects which practically drip with antiquity; it is the mood of clever compositions done in hair by artistic hairdressers, it is their (old-fashioned) mannequins. It is the mood of the *Homo* and other early works, things sensed intuitively at the time and later translated into formality and abstraction.

Ah, if only I could manage once and for all to see my goal and my course clearly and then concentrate all my energies on them.

But can one use one concept as a starting point and expect to be nourished by it all the way to the goal? And what then?

Diary

March 1, 1936

The concept of progress in art does not provide a wholly adequate explanation. The familiar formula: Courbet-Corot contained the seeds of Cézanne, he the seeds of the Cubists, after which came a dead-end, a witches' cauldron; now all that is left is abstraction, exemplified in its purest form by Mondrian. But what comes after Mondrian? Can one go further, or are we faced with the alternatives of endless variation or an end to art?

The extremists of this persuasion (Giedion, Moholy) swear by the Surrealists, the abstractionists, and await the consequences. Some artists are taking the logical next step by switching to architecture or advertising. But the "painters"? Why shouldn't a genius appear like a bolt out of the blue someday and take everyone by surprise, demonstrating a form of painting so miraculously rich that the painters and extremists will stand transfixed with amazement?

Diary

March 8, 1936

"Memorial celebration for fallen heroes"—and on the previous evening the first "Village Community Evening."

What a discrepancy between what I do at home and the community's celebrations! The connections do not lie out in the open; rather, they are undercurrents, hard to recognize, which merge somewhere out of sight. On the surface they appear as a contradiction, the same contradiction, I would guess, as existed between the ideas and ideals of my fallen comrades—Ott, Stenner, Wirth, Widmann, Stemmeler—and the way they met their deaths, not necessarily heroically, certainly

not consciously so or intentionally, some of them very courageous in their individual actions when the circumstances favored
such things, some of them simply victims, struck down while
asleep, or shot. Heroic in bearing the sufferings of war, often
unnamable, indescribable; this heroism was indubitably an attribute of all who were at the front.

If they had returned from the war they would have picked
up where they had left off and would probably have found
themselves facing the same artistic problems as I, and the others
would most likely have sensed the discrepancy, as I sense it,
between the cult of hero worship today and the absence of
respect for the intellectual and spiritual values they represent,
the values which made their lives worthwhile.

The artist and the state. It is hard to be a yea-sayer in a
state which deprives the artist of his artistic freedom, hard to
have to watch how the growing power of the state increases the
state's boldness in prescribing what the artist must do. This
contradicts the iron laws of art—or it would require a titan to
weld together the ideals of art and those of the nation.

Where do we find anything approaching that? De Chirico in
Italy? Hodler in Switzerland? Monumentalists who constantly
run the risk of producing heroic drivel, because their epoch, far
from containing the heroism of old, is but contradiction, disso-
nance, and calamity.

Diary

March 12, 1936

Classicism, that much is clear, falls like a ripe fruit from the
tree of the Baroque and the Gothic: it feels like the quiet
breathing and calm rest that follow the crisis of an illness.

If classical calm were my only objective, I would have a
narrow field of endeavor, for perfect products are rare. The
field broadens when the gates are opened to admit the metaphysical and exploration in uncharted territory.

Diary

April 2, 1936

The motif? The psychology of the present. Can one escape it? And of what does it consist? War or peace. You or me. For or against.

Can the sensitive artist bury his head in the sand and stumble through a calamity-ridden present like a virtuous fool?

At the very least the tense atmosphere will be reflected in his pictures.

Diary

May 13, 1936

I suddenly realized what I want to do: link the (German) artistic tradition with the new abstract mode. It must be possible! It must be possible to unfold color in all its power and glory (broad-surfaced, full-toned) and to derive form from that. Yet I know that form remains the primary element for the time being; graphic form is still decisive, not the mass of color, the fluid medium of painting.

Diary

May 18, 1936

Nowadays Hans von Marées is praised and held up as a model by the young. But in his day the notables were the Lenbachs, Böcklins, and Makarts.

Now many such will step forward and be notables, and the new Hans von Marées will languish in the dark, only to be resurrected again when the time comes.

I want an exuberant style of painting, born of color, of light and shadow, of structures and laws, both overt and clandestine ones, i.e. conscious and unconscious ones, but especially of the unconscious ones that contain the secret. That is what I as a "pure painter" want.

But at the same time I should like to unleash a furor which would unmask baseness and force perfidy to its knees. I believe in a justice which will one day put to shame—at the very least—those who today claim victory.

This desire should not let me rest until I have achieved some of what I set myself as a goal.

Diary

Whitsun
May 31, 1936

Finished the *Symboliken* ["Symbolics"] ; having done the preliminary sketches, I painted one Saturday, the other three Sunday. What does this series signify? An act of liberation, or just an excursion into abstraction? A Whitsun miracle?

I am amazed by the power of simple form. It contains forces which the materialist and many of his ilk would never suspect. This much is certain: these are no mere aesthetic products; they are the external expression of the very inner compulsion which Wassily Kandinsky, the inventor of the concept, himself so often belied later on. When the concept was formulated he must have believed in it.

They are compositions so simple that one could draw them in the sand, as Hans von Marées said. They have, I feel, the strength of Mondrian without, however, being formalistic. They are ornamental, but again not "merely," for their chief function is to help portray something unconscious, and *that* molds their character and their characteristics, rather than considerations of external beauty.

Diary

June 13, 1936

I am wondering whether my abstract symmetries correspond to the chorale in music. Or what does one call it in Bach's "Passions" when the finely branching arias are followed by the massive towers of the chorales, and then, too: what would be the equivalent of the recitatives?

Diary

June 17, 1936

Everything is opening up again, as at the time of the early abstractions in 1916.

The possibilities of portrayal achieved by these so-called abstract, i.e. unnaturalistic, means to be sure have nothing in common with traditional painting along the lines of Cézanne (and his predecessors), since they draw on all the available methods and employ each where it fits best.

Thus one can have a group of figures in which one figure appears in silhouette, another for psychic reasons as pure line, a third "painted," that is, rendered in the form that corresponds to the inner necessity and function of the figure.

Abstraction is as much a break with traditional painting as van Gogh, and it opens up new perspectives; such prospects persuaded me in 1916 to reject the (supposed) temptation and ultimate dead-end of painting à la Derain and to throw myself into the arms of abstraction. The situation today is similar. I seem to be experiencing a new breakthrough, a bursting of the bonds and the confinement which result from exclusive dedication to one genre of painting.

If it proved possible for both kinds or several different approaches to exist side by side, that would probably provide the best solution to my inner conflicts.

Postcard to Tut

La Sarraz

August 5, 1936

Mes chers—I have been here since Tuesday evening. Castle has a glorious location, weather has been fine since yesterday, very lovely today. Later a drive with Madame de Mandrot. I share a bedroom with Max Ernst, but he is sick, has a cold, and shuts the windows so tight that I almost suffocate. Now we are reshuffling the sleeping arrangements; I shall sleep elsewhere, but again sharing a room. Thus far there are seven of us, with two or three more expected. Xanti also wanted to come for a short stay. Madame says I should undertake something with Prampolini in Milan. *Je ne sais rien.*

I am or seem to be the youngest here. A few graybeards, Max Ernst very gray and much aged. He strikes me as larger and especially older that I had remembered. He looks handsome, distinguished, like an old *Abbé*. There is a great deal of discussion, but because of the French I have difficulty following it. Still, I am learning.

To Tut

La Sarraz
August 12, 1936

Last night was very jolly. I was dressed in an old coat of armor, and all the spaces inside were stuffed with such items as graters, toilet paper, flowers, etc. Max Ernst, Flouquet, and Bognier played comical doctors, and subjected me, coming as a *blessé* from a tournament, to a gruesome treatment involving water, flour, tongs, and so on. When finally cured I executed a little dance of joy! Number two: they painted me up horribly à la Grock, I played on the completely rusted-out old square piano (still very lovely on the outside), while two others sang a grotesque accompaniment. Finally six of us went down into the village and had a drink.

The social atmosphere is warming up; thanks to the arrival of new elements—an English surrealist writer from London, who knows Gropius and the others there (also Slutzky), and a young interior decorator from Paris—new relationships keep forming. The young Parisian, very distinguished and reserved, brought his three-year-old little daughter along, since he has recently been divorced. The man who understands me best is Monsieur Kühlmann of Colmar. I sense that he has great sympathy for me, as do most of the others, and even Max Ernst seems to join in, although under different circumstances he would probably have a very different attitude toward me. My work on Otto Meyer had a considerable impact here, by the way. The Belgians have already invited me to come to Brussels. But how will that be possible?

And how are you getting along, all alone? This never happened before, that you were left alone with sheep and rabbits!

La Sarraz
August 23, 1936

Xanti has received a telegram and must return to London at once. He earned a lot of money in Milan and apparently has a good contract in America. He thinks we should follow him there! Albers has reportedly already turned down two teaching offers at American universities, despite the better pay, because he is in the midst of building up Black Mountain and very much enjoys being there. Xanti asked me if I might want to come. He feels France has nothing to offer. Italy much better; he says there is a mood of nation-building there, much élan, and there is a demand for the latest and newest.

Seen from here, things look pretty grim in Germany, and not very hopeful, if even Hamburg is now being closed off. That naturally makes some impact on my "clear-thinking." It is very difficult to remain consistently optimistic. And yet I want to try.

Diary

September 23, 1936

Have reached the stage of having Hans Fischli submit his building plans for approval! Looking forward to the new house and the accompanying (and necessary) garden. But also financial anxiety, in addition to the mortgage problems.

Therefore: desire for theater work, hopes. Realistic thinking, leading to the goal of earning enough to fix up the inside of the house and keep alive. The theater represents something I can fall back on, as commercial graphics and advertising do for others.

I let my mind rove, and it finds no shortage of ideas. For instance: a comic ballet, or that of the clown. Not one Grock, but ten! Why are such things never performed? Has this kind of imagination died out?

But what a different world compared to my dark-hued painting, and then a different world in turn: the new house, the "garden as magic key"! One has to live in all these worlds, create order, organize, find and invent, bring things to a successful conclusion.

Diary

Transformation! *Variété* through and through. One person enters a monastery—these days—while another joins the *variété*.

"Blooming folly!" It cannot be denied that I am in my element. Inventing comic types: these are the same feelings I had in Stuttgart as a little boy when I visited the Eden Theater, whereupon I put together a little Eden Theater at home, feverishly excited.

Some of this must run in the blood! Where does it come from? From the pastry bakers, goldsmiths, and preceptors, or is it my father's passion for the theater? My father and old Knie in Stuttgart! What an experience!

All this is very peculiar.

To Hugo Borst

Eichberg

November 27, 1936

I don't know if I wrote you that we have now purchased a good-sized building site and that the plans for the house are at present being checked over by the building authorities. The new blueprint corrects everything objected to in the first plan we submitted, which was rejected. Unfortunately winter has come in the meantime, so that we cannot possibly get all the structural work done this year, as we had planned. Nevertheless, we hope to have a roof over our heads by spring. I am looking forward tremendously to the studio, which should do great things for my work; for I see more and more clearly how much my painting has suffered from my working space's being far too small. True, the phenomenon of the dedicated painter is becoming a rarer and rarer commodity, but once my existence has been placed on a fairly firm footing, nothing will prevent me from obeying the voice of inner necessity. And how much I still have to accomplish!

Since earning a living is becoming problematical, given the situation in the art field in Germany, I am at present considering various theatrical ventures, which, however, would necessitate my working abroad; Zurich would provide a starting point, and the resources I need. The theater, even *variété*, would be the most suitable second profession for me. I must do something, and this winter I shall probably try out this possibility.

Diary

December 27, 1936

Muche agrees about the "richness" of the ten recent pictures exhibited at Möller's in Berlin. So pictures born of a long and painful struggle *do* have this quality; they of necessity appear richer than "improvised" pictures; and in fact I am convinced that solitude, absorption, slower, more painstaking work manifest themselves in the picture.

Maxim for these days: try to create difficult, delectable painting, "fruit-laden," hard to match by anyone not working on similar or even more demanding premises.

So let this be my task for this period; to summon up my utmost and render it as rich, ripe fruits.

Diary

Beginning of January 1937

"Let man bestir himself, while it is yet day. The night is coming when none shall make his mark." (Goethe)

Diary

January 20, 1937

I must say: after the quiet patter of the past days and weeks, events of both positive and negative nature are suddenly heaping up.

Connected with the stars?

To Hermann Müller

Eichberg

February 5, 1937

At the moment I have pictures on exhibit in Berlin, and some of my friends and acquaintances have reacted with great enthusiasm. Paint, paint, continue at all costs, that is what is most important now: this is what I abstract from their letters. Well, a first step has been taken, and others may follow. Once I have a decent place to work again, things will look up. I am quite firmly convinced of that.

To Fritz Nemitz

Eichberg
February 17, 1937

Since you reviewed my exhibition under the significant title of "The Question of the Mural" and raised a number of fundamental issues, I feel compelled to reply.

First of all, I was amazed that you took these pictures for studies for murals, when in fact these pictures—the products of cramped conditions—were never conceived of in connection with mural work; this should have been clear in purely external terms from my use of thick, textured oil color, which I would never use for fresco style. In wall painting I also strive for a different sense of pictorial space from the one I attempted to achieve in some of the pictures on exhibit, and I would never mount a wall painting in a frame, or would definitely keep the frame to a minimum. But if these pictures nevertheless contain some mural character, as "panel paintings," which they are intended to be, this must be due to their constructivistic inner order, which I cannot regard as a drawback.

And I am always amazed to be reproached with "calculation, constructivism." Does that reproach come from the stereotype of the Hoelzel School with which I am often associated, a stereotype based on the fact that Hoelzel was a passionate theoretician and constructivist? Or need one merely observe certain elementary rules of form, the decisive function of the horizontal and the vertical for instance; need one merely preserve certain basic color combinations to fall under the suspicion of employing construction and intellectual calculation? Or are the present standards of art in Germany so opposed to any sort of discipline and order that feeling for nature, expression of emotion, and spiritual experience are esteemed far above the only approach that can really regulate these factors and make them effective, an approach which was so highly developed during the greatest epochs of art that everyone took it for granted? And if this is the case, why shouldn't there be a few individuals who have been given an assignment by Fate, and for this reason, not for base motives, devote themselves to finding the tools without which we shall never have the mural which is supposed to embody the spirit of the times?

Construction! I confess that I almost never work from preconceived principles and calculated formulas, but rather "out of the riches" of an inner conception, "a premonition of and for something beautiful," the origins of which remain a mystery to me.

There are genuine constructors in the field of painting, the "constructivists," who display what one might call the naked facts, pure, unconcealed measurement; but I am worlds apart from them, and by contrast I would seem a romantic, if romanticism can be interpreted as free creation out of the imagination, as making ideas visible through applying the media of form and color to the human figure.

The conclusion and crux of your discussion consists of your appeal, addressed not only to me, for a "revision of attitudes which have long since lost the social and intellectual ground under their feet." This does indeed touch on the substance.

Without income after the loss of my teaching position, with three young children to support, I was faced with the necessity of reducing my needs to a minimum. So I retired to the country. I also gradually returned to painting and proceeded to review what I had hitherto accomplished and to plot a course for the future. During three years of outward passivity, I could find no task and problem more important than what I had already formulated in the past. Since I belong to the generation which experienced its storm and stress and also its first successes during the "system period," I had a handicap from the very outset. The untrammelled freedom which permitted anything and left no stone unturned in the search for new avenues of art (and often merely for the sake of innovation) was misused by many, that I know, but the freedom also guided responsible artists to laws, to measure, to order. Why, then, should these virtues in art be so despised now?

I am interested in creating human types, not portraits (although I occasionally practice this art, too), and I am interested in the nature of space, not in "interiors." By no means do I declare myself "independent of the object because I cannot do it justice"; rather, a higher obligation restrains me from paying more attention to the object than the form and the intent of the picture allow. My themes—the human figure in space, its moving and stationary functions, sitting, lying, walking, standing—are as simple as they are universally valid. Besides, they are inexhaustible. My propensity for grouping human beings in the picture, showing their relationships, their contrasts, their gradations, likewise struck me as timely and appropriate, as do certain classicistic tendencies; I must thus ask: what in the world should I set about revising?

Nor do I believe that I am such an eccentric or so unintelligent that I am guilty of mistaking the tenor of the times. In this respect the artist is the seismograph, even against his will. Besides, the artist will always be more or less intensely interested in the art of other epochs and will feel attracted to those which accord best with his own nature and intentions. And in this connection I really cannot prize the copying technique of Naturalism as highly as I prize the examples of high style, which are necessarily anti-naturalistic. When I say this, I am well aware of the formula (my formula?): abstraction—synthesis—naturalism, just as in practice I maintain a balance and attempt to bring all three "possibilities" into harmony. Here I model myself on Otto Meyer-Amden, who succeeded admirably at achieving such equilibrium. I agree with him that the Archaic Greeks were far better than the Greeks in their period of decline. I admire the severity and greatness of the ancient Egyptians, the medieval church statues (the most glorious example being the apostle figures blended into the columns on the cathedral of Chartres). I know that we moderns are not and cannot be Greeks or Egyptians or devout artists of the Middle Ages, "because the social and spiritual foundations have long since vanished." But the body of inherited tradition, the richness of life in all its aspects. the subconscious included, and then the range of the imagination, the new, lovely, and daring possibilities: are these not content enough? We need only find the form which, in the artistic sense, can express all of this.

And why, I must also ask, do you not turn your very negative discussion into a positive one by setting forth what you mean by a revision of obsolete views, since your demand applies to others besides me? Given the present confusion of artistic standards, such an explanation could have proved most useful.

I do not believe that you are simply advocating tendentious art. Some painters lend themselves readily to such things; I am not one of them. There remains the issue of popular [*Volk*] art. For this, too, some people have a natural gift. I am not one of those so blessed, and I am skeptical toward a game so transparent that from the moment a new work appears its rules are understood immediately by the people in the broadest sense. The star witnesses of history speak against such phenomena, and I still believe in the "terrestrial pilgrimage of the artist."

That was what I wanted to write you—and myself, the latter in order to remind myself of where I stand and what I want.

To Hugo Borst

Eichberg
March 18, 1937

I am once again left high and dry, so much so that I am seriously debating what will happen if this continues much longer. True, I received a down payment for a sale at Möller's, but that was the proverbial drop in the bucket.

So what should one do? Teach drawing among the Botocudian Indians? Who would arrange that sort of thing? The German or the Botocudian consulate? Something must be done! I recently applied to the Eduard Arnhold Fund for Artists in Berlin, which a friend mentioned to me two years ago and from which I once received eighty marks. The answer I got this time was that my application could unfortunately not be considered. Nothing more in the way of an explanation. I shall register with the "Philanthropy for German Art," apparently the catch-basin for all the dilettantes and unknowns. Perhaps I will be admitted. I have tried doing short stories and caricatures and find that I am totally unsuited for that sort of thing.

And in the meantime I am burning with eagerness to paint the pictures that only I can paint. "German fate!"

Diary

March 31, 1937

Just finished Jean Giono's *The Song of the World.* In the line of Joseph Conrad, only more nature-bound, more colorfully plastic, more trenchant. How is that possible? It seems as if the true masters in unspoken agreement pass the basic creative elements from hand to hand, trusting that the next man will add his bit and whatever else is generally necessary along the path to fulfillment and perfection.

Who grasped Cézanne in all his complexity and continued in his path with the full significance, preserving all his greatness? It was certainly not Derain. Picasso, Braque—don't they turn somersaults instead of standing up straight and walking?

Where can one find the heavy richness, the powerful sweetness, the blooming unfolding, the sated profusion of a grandiose, inclusive, beautiful style of painting?

To Julius Schottländer

Eichberg

April 30, 1937

The construction of our house has finally begun, after much back and forth (rejection of the plans, new plan, changes, final version); nothing fancy, but it will still be August before we can move in. We want to stay here for the harvest, especially the fruit. Our sheep-raising is flourishing: through their combined efforts the three ewes have produced eight lambs! A happy time for little ones, now that the weather has finally taken a turn for the better. I am not pushing ahead with the dance projects. In Zurich I could not get anything off the ground. In the end there is never enough money to stage a production on any scale; so the question of America has been animatedly discussed: should I go there and see what I can accomplish in person? Two Bauhaus people (one a student of mine) have jobs at American colleges. Gropius has received an appointment at Harvard University. There is a college in Santa Barbara where Feininger and Mary Wigman spent six months. I am trying to see if something of the sort pans out for me.

To Willi Baumeister

Sehringen
August 3, 1937

I imagine both of you are back home by now. In the meantime a few more details have emerged on the destruction of pictures and "degenerate" art. Willi's name did not appear in the reports I read; could he be less well-known than I, who am mentioned in every newspaper? One expects to be expelled from the *Reichskulturkammer* [National Chamber of Culture] any day now, but nothing so far.

"Neverthespite" we are building our house. We were extremely lucky to get the pipes for the steam heating; according to the Four Year Plan they are officially unavailable in July. I am spending most of my time here, where I can do all sorts of things in and around the house.

Aside from this, there remains the question of a new profession, now that the "trained" painter has had the rug pulled out from under him. I have pretty much decided to lay this profession aside until further notice and look around for some more lucrative field of endeavor, if possible one that will leave my personal freedom relatively unimpaired. But Tut already pictures me working in an office or a factory (also forms of security!). I am still thinking in other directions, but I realize that experiments are now out of the question. I must earn money, no two ways about it.

To Ida Bienert

Sehringen
October 25, 1937

At last I shall try to give you the full report I promised. Please forgive me for taking so long. But the move and all the confusion prevented me from catching my breath, and I am still painting furniture and pushing it back and forth, aside from the equally necessary outdoor jobs such as digging and earthmoving. Today, for instance, we are building the sheep shed, which will also house the rabbits and, in the spring, the hens. The children are terribly pleased with the new house, with their little rooms, with the changes, for here things are naturally different from our previous cottage. If it were not for the unexpected blow in Munich, our happiness at owning our own house would be almost perfect. But this affair troubles me.

My wife's mother would like, as she so nicely puts it, to see her children happy and all under one roof during her own lifetime. So we started the search, and after visiting Badenweiler one day I made it my choice. My wife also looked the area over and came home with a building site! We told ourselves that proximity to a city of some size was certainly desirable. The resort life and the tourists in Badenweiler, from which we are twenty-five minutes on foot, prevent one from feeling as lonely as in other spots farther from civilization, and here we can continue our country life, partly out of necessity and partly because we have come to enjoy it greatly.

The sales of pictures have of course been reduced to an absolute minimum, and in the future I shall probably be unable to count on Germany at all. I had an exhibition in London. The majority of the pictures are still there. Some of them went on to New York and will be displayed there in November, along with a collection of theater photographs and stage designs. The question of theater seems to be taking on new immediacy for me. In March the Museum of Modern Art will put on an exhibit of "Industrial Art" (in reality: "The Bauhaus and its Development"), and my "Triadic Ballet" is slated for performance at the opening. Remarkable how this thing goes on and on! How often performances have been planned recently, and each time it came to naught, partly due to financial problems, partly because of the dancers. But I shall leap at the possibility of doing it in New York. Thanks to Gropius and Moholy the whole Bauhaus business has taken on new immediacy, and the prospects for finally getting to the United States now look good.

I shall also report briefly to you on the family. My wife is fine in the sense that she does not let the circumstances get her down, even when they are difficult or practically hopeless. She now refuses to be parted from her sheep! We have three, two ewes which give milk and a half-year-old lamb. In the spring there will be new lambs. This spring we got eight lambs from three sheep, most of which we sold, one of which we ate. Wool is a very desirable item these days, and the milk has a very high butterfat content, without the slightest unpleasant taste. Right now our wool is being woven into blankets. At the moment all three children are home. Karin, the eldest, has been living with relatives in Stuttgart, where she wanted to study dancing at the Theater Ballet. But the ballet school there is not of the best, and we do not know if we should let her continue. Then comes Jaina, one year younger, who is still attending public school here. What comes next we do not know. Perhaps her passion for animals will lead to some profession in that area; the angora rabbits are entirely under her care. Twelve-year-old Til has a talent for handicrafts; when he finishes school he will probably be apprenticed to a cabinet-maker or electrician—something practical. He plays the trumpet, Jai plays the violin, and Karin the piano; unfortunately they have never had time to work on their music much—that should be easier to manage here.

Post scriptum

November 2, 1937

My letter has not yet been mailed, one of the reasons being that my wife objected to my portraying our situation to you in too rosy a light, when she sees it as very dark indeed. So instead of rewriting the letter, I shall add to my original remarks.

Herbert Bayer, who recently returned from New York, wrote me that the ballet performance was just an idea, nothing definite. But he gathered the impression that conditions were very favorable and that such a venture stood far greater chances of success over there than in Germany. And I know from experience that it takes a long time before anything is settled. Well, I shall do what I can to follow the recommendation I have heard from its very inception: take it to the U.S.A.!

I see almost no way we can stay here, lovely and also necessary though it would be, for the house and the farm need taking care of. People advise me to do picture books and cartoons. For the former I would need a publisher; as to the latter, I have already tried something in that line which is supposed to appear serially. So this vein may be exhausted, too. Advertising, but for that one would have to live in the city.

Diary

November 27, 1937

What a summer! A house-building! Munich and "Degenerate Art." A big, beautiful studio—useless and pointless.

Diary

December 1, 1937

A time for small landscapes. The important thing is the microcosmic and shorthand element; otherwise banality cannot be avoided.

A glance out the window must be sufficient for capturing a small, intense totality, without the hunt for motifs.

To Heinz Braune,
Director of the Württemberg State Gallery in Stuttgart

Sehringen

December 7, 1937

Please permit me to write you a few words on my present situation.

To begin with, it was not clear to me why I was grouped in Munich among the degenerate, destructive, fundamentally and intentionally malicious painters. But there one appeared in a body and could take comfort in the company of a man as respectable as Christian Rohlfs. But now I hear from Berlin that I have also been selected for the major anti-Bolshevik exhibition "Bolshevism without a Mask," where my picture is one of ten on display. It is one of my best pictures from the year 1924, *Vorübergehender,* which I stand by to this day, and the choice of which for this exhibition I simply do not grasp. This time the danger lies in the fact that the exhibition bears the brand of Bolshevism.

As I say, I see the situation as dangerous, although I am unable to picture precisely what might happen. If I were alone, I would not consider this such a tragedy; but I have a family. And now a little house as well.

Does this mean one will be forced to emigrate?

Diary

January 1, 1938

Utter confusion. Should we stay here, which would be in the interest of the house and the farm—or go somewhere where I could earn a living? A question that is never answered to my satisfaction. It should be possible to stay in this house and in this area, to do good, creative work in the studio, thus taking advantage of the space and justifying my being here. But then there are the "options." Primary at the moment is the United States. My ballet and theatrical matters in general. Dare I place all my hopes on that? More projects like the "Comic Ballet"? Today—the beginning of the new year—I see these as the only course open to me.

Where will I be a year from now, and in what circumstances?

To Heinrich Lauterbach

Sehringen
January 17, 1938

To keep the thread of friendship from breaking off, we want to bring you up to date again, and then perhaps we shall hear something from you two. Well, we are established in our own house, wooden, warm, with central heating, and we are relatively happy in it; in fact, our happiness could almost be called complete, if it were not for our worries about simple survival. Worries about our daily black (and white) bread; art takes second place, for it has now become a highly dubious proposition; all the more painful since in the spring, when we were building, the wind seemed to be blowing in a very different direction from the one which manifested itself during the summer in Munich. Now I am mulling over whether I can somehow earn a living without leaving my happily acquired house and studio, without being forced to go far afield, which in this case could probably only mean crossing the great blue sea to seek refuge in the arms of the Statue of Liberty. The latter would be feasible if I were assured of work in the theater. The "Triadic Ballet" costumes are rolling, or rather swimming across the ocean, sent out as messengers to query the future as to what it has to offer.

In my other avocation, painting, I would at the very least have to convert to landscape, which can certainly be done with dignity and decency and should perhaps be welcomed as an intermezzo, a return to the bosom of nature, a comfortable resting place. And then copies, free ones, of good old Dutch masterpieces, a sort of artistic cottage industry.

At present the family is reunited. Tut, the mother, feels alternately happy and unhappy, thinks we should have stayed in the city after all, because of the children's education and also because of my obligations as a provider. But who can tell?

How do things look in Breslau these days? At the Academy? The Artists' Guild? We would be so glad to hear something from you. And how are the buildings? Shortage of materials? We just barely managed to get the heating for our house. By the way, some time ago the museum sent the *Tänzerin* ["Female Dancer"], rolled up in a narrow crate, and now it is on its way unopened to New York. In March the Bauhaus exhibition will take place there. Let's see what this new year brings us. A belated toast to it!

Diary

February 24, 1938

The usual conversation at breakfast, which always ends with my determining to look around at once for a source of income, no matter what, and to leave this house and the dreams it engenders. I gaze out into the landscape, slowly taking shape under the morning sun: the pale violet-brown strips of forest, the blue-white snow, the black tracery of the bare trees. This landscape is lovely, even when seen in conventional terms, with memories of landscapes painted by some of the Naturalists.

But a slight adjustment of vision, simply blinking, suffices to bring out other, no less beautiful elements of form and color. These are the ones apparent probably only to me or to the schooled eye of the painter. This is no longer the landscape as people usually see it, boring because it is so familiar; suddenly one has the imaginative interplay of secret geometries, of linear forms which merge to form colorful surfaces, a "feast for the eyes," an ornament full of the rarest, most marvelous relationships.

This form of vision should be cherished, cultivated, and developed to where it acquires universal validity and comprehensibility.

To Tut

Stuttgart
March 18, 1938

Now a piece of news for you, and please do not get too upset. On the way back from Wertheim I squashed my right ring finger, which is now bandaged up and unfortunately prevents me from working. Still I shall try to do some of the work waiting for me at Kämmerer's, although I am not especially optimistic. Perhaps I would think differently if my hand were all right. There seems to be a steady supply of work here, but I am not sure whether I can adjust to what they want of me.

Can you believe my actually being in Kämmerer's painting business, having "a job," with you four out there in Sehringen? The question remains whether I can handle it.

Diary

April 21, 1938

Vacillating. Am I ever wholly dedicated to anything, "heart and soul"? To my painting, yes. And of course to the free play of the imagination, to visualizing paintings and working them out in my own inimitable fashion. This I still have, and this type of creativity affords the artist and the connoisseur the purest form of pleasure. It gives one an opportunity to cultivate the values which ultimately are all that matter, which matter more

Backstairs Joke, production at the Bauhaus Theater, 1928; Oskar Schlemmer is the figure with the globe. *Courtesy of Tut Schlemmer.*

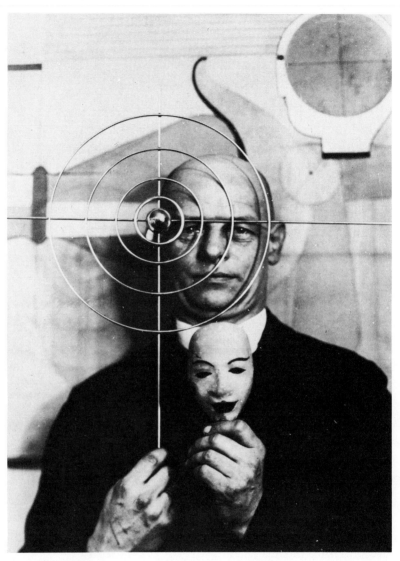

Oskar Schlemmer, ca. 1930. *Courtesy of Oskar Schlemmer Archiv, Staats-galerie Stuttgart.*

the more they are endangered, the more dubious their survival seems. And here, too, all the maxims that deal with the mission of art are valid, both the old ones and the new ones. Everything else seems cockeyed by contrast.

To Tut

Stuttgart
May 24, 1938

Monday evening I got back from Wuppertal. A pleasant trip along the Rhine. The people in that industrial pocket are very nice. I have with me the plans for two murals Herberts wants painted in the new laboratory being built onto his paint factory in Wuppertal. The building should be ready in August, so there will be time to work out the designs, which I shall do quickly here, at least in rough outlines. The factory is very spacious, modern, built by Rasch, whom I know from Stuttgart. Everything very restrained. I have the impression that this can lead to other things. Baumeister has done a sgraffito job, a wall-scratching, i.e.: drawing.

To Tut

Vaihingen bei Stuttgart
July 19, 1938

This week I am not going into Stuttgart every day; instead I am picked up at 7 A.M.. by Kämmerer and taken to the railroad station in Vaihingen, whence I take the train to Böblingen, where I am painting the tricky wooden ceiling of the air terminal with many little figures and perspectives. In the evening I drive back to Vaihingen either with Kämmerer or with the architect in charge, my neck so stiff I can hardly move it. Every evening I am dead tired. I hope to finish by Thursday. Then back to the pictures in the big hall of a brewery, figures, an Orpheus and a dragon killer, lifesize. And then? The job will continue about the same. In addition I have the little armoire for Elberfeld, and then Frau Borst wants the doors to her dining room painted, but I just don't know when I shall get to that! I wish you some of my optimism! Without that I could not survive here.

371

To Tut

End of July 1938

It is glorious weather—and I have to work! Mars hangs red and threatening in the sky; he "rules the hour." No one can make out the political constellation. Some claim there are powerful counterforces in Moscow. The reason for the failure to reach an accord, who knows?

Postcard to Tut

Stuttgart
October 2, 1938

Here, too, tension of course ran high. Men being called up, and then the miracle came to pass. Amazing! In spite of it all, work continued here in the great hall, where a figure gets done every day—but we shall need at least a week more, if not ten days. Sundays I work on the little armoire in Elberfeld. Karin wrote me a nice letter. I intend to launch a correspondence with this daughter of mine. As to the other: I thought school began on October 1. When I finish up here I plan to take a few days' break, at home.

To Tut

Stuttgart
October 29, 1938

I shall be home the 12th. If the jobs in Würzburg and Elberfeld pan out, that should carry us through Christmas.

At the memorial for Barlach in his studio in Mecklenburg Gerhard Marcks spoke in the name of the sculptors.

To Tut

Stuttgart
November 10, 1938

You were born into tumultuous times; all sorts of things are going on, and have been going on these past few days. Not the least on November 9: last night they set fire to the synagogue here, as well as to the one in Cannstatt, and they smashed

372

the windows of all the Jewish-owned shops. This morning it looked pretty desolate, and the Hospitalstraße took a beating. Kämmerer's shop faces the synagogue and the Jewish school, out of which they took all the documents, to be carted off in trucks. Also the Jews, during the day. It has stopped being funny! And this from a people that considers itself cultured!

To Heinz Rasch

Sehringen
January 3, 1939

Anonymity is of course essential. We can pretend we are following the example of the cathedral builders . . . .

Only in this light can I understand your optimistic interpretation of the situation for Willi Baumeister and me. We can continue working only if we do so anonymously. I, for instance, must now explain to the Reichskunstkammer [National Arts Chamber] why I took part in the exhibition in London. Or: Gropius writes that a Bauhaus exhibition has just opened in New York to tremendous crowds; my ballet figurines were pictured in the *Times*, and altogether my work played quite a dominant role. That might conceivably make things even more difficult for me here. But let us wait and see.

Postcard to Tut

Stuttgart
April 21, 1939

The work at Kämmerer's keeps breathing down my neck. The Munich job really should be started on next week, since the scaffolding is up and costs us extra every day.

To Tut

Stuttgart
May 2, 1939

What is going to happen with Poland? A risky business!
The weather is so terrible that one cannot do outdoor work

anyway. I should keep my mind completely on the task at hand, but I keep thinking about the garden. So many things left to be attended to! Are the peonies growing? Is the lilac making headway? I really should have transplanted the tulips and hyacinths, since one is supposed to cut them when they blossom. Otherwise it hurts the plant. That's why they are called cutting flowers! Are the rambler roses opening?

I get dizzy at the thought of all one should and could do. Kitchen herbs! The whole vegetable garden! Well, at Whitsun I shall be able to pick up a hoe again.

To Tut

Munich
May 11, 1939

To judge from the job up to now, which is pleasant and goes easily, I shall not be finished until Whitsun, and then only if I keep very busy, which I plan to do, for Whitsun means a break when I can go home and then start on a new project. Here in Munich there are sixty-seven Schlemmers, thirteen of whom have a telephone, among them the Siamese consul!

To Tut

Munich
June 9, 1939

Back here again. I came via Lindau. The Lindau-Bregenz area is certainly the loveliest on the lake. The mountains! But Lindau is full of military personnel, SA and "Strength through Joy" units. Very different from bygone days! Of course the lake is very beautiful. Still, the Badenweiler Lake does not suffer from the comparison. Bissier was happy to see and smell the woods again. The "Landi" in Zurich very lovely. Amazing what this little country has managed to produce.

To Tut

Stuttgart

June 30, 1939

War rumors: people are muttering that July 23 will be the day. But that is just muttering. And one hears again and again that we are doing something with Russia. Hard to believe.

To Tut

Stuttgart

Beginning of July 1939

The London exhibition ("German Art") has apparently opened, to judge by the Führer's speech and the general agitation.

To Tut

Stuttgart

July 9, 1939

After working until nine-thirty Friday evening to finish up the job at Benger's, I slacked off for the first time on Saturday and did nothing. The work itself turned out well; the response was enthusiastic. But I finally decided not to go to the dedication celebration because I do not care to have people discussing me. In any case, word has it that the storm over me will burst soon—because I am still active.

So Saturday morning I went to the pool in Feuerbach Hollow, located in a quiet, pretty spot on the edge of the forest, and there I lay in the sun. In the afternoon the crowds started coming, so I went home.

Draft of a letter to
an unknown recipient

July 23, 1939

I cannot overcome my doubts and worries, although I know it is not healthy to be agonized and at odds with oneself. If I were an emigrant and living abroad, and if I had to undergo what M. underwent, all the doubts would probably vanish and I would think just as he does. But under the circumstances, being here, compromising daily, voluntarily or involuntarily, with the state of affairs, I cannot help feeling ambivalent, not to say torn, and I am concerned about the long-range psychic effects of such anquish. At the moment I cannot pursue my artistic vocation, but I shall have an opportunity to measure these psychic effects if and when I am able to return to my individual pursuits. Sometimes I think that my personal vision will assert itself all the more directly and ruthlessly now that it is suppressed and proscribed; I need no longer take the preferences of the public into account, and can retreat entirely into the realm of the imagination.

In my work I am presently experiencing a degree of self-alienation I would not have considered possible, and I am curious, in an impersonal way, to see whether this state of mind in the long run yields a stronger sense of self. This condition might prove symptomatic for the mind and spirit of the age where culture is concerned.

Diary

September 3, 1939

Since September 1, 1939, war with Poland.

What will the Western powers do?

Will there be a world war, more terrible, more murderous than the last one?

War!!!

To Tut

Stuttgart

October 22, 1939

Well, the train was very full, many soldiers, on leave for the Sunday. The blacked-out city looks uncanny. At first I hardly dared poke my nose out of doors, but one gets accustomed to it. I now think I shall be coming home first, to attend to the autumn chores and if possible to paint a few pictures behind glass, and only after that back to Stuttgart for a while.

I hope to scrape together enough money so I can hold out in Sehringen another three or four weeks.

Rumor here has it that we have troops in Italy and Spain lined up to march against France, and that Italian troops are deployed in the Black Forest. Sounds highly unlikely. People see a major offensive against France in the offing, to isolate England. Keep it to yourself. What does the radio say?

Ida Kerkovius is here. Her family had to leave Riga, too. Conditions there are said to be terrible.

To Tut

Stuttgart
November 9, 1939

Now your birthday is upon us, and I stand here empty-handed. You will say: as usual; you are used to it.

My only present will be as follows: this morning there was a conference to discuss my designs for decorating a hospital, which were well received. The contract I have requested will be drawn up, and then I shall go to work. That is, of course, something for which to be grateful. The job will take about a month and will bring in ten times as much as my work for Kämmerer. An example of the advantages of freelancing. If only nothing goes wrong. One never knows when trouble will erupt and what form it will take.

To Tut

Stuttgart
November 17, 1939

Well, tomorrow morning at seven I'll be off for Giebelstadt with a truck and two soldiers. Once there I shall have to experiment with camouflage on a grand scale. I feel that this empirical method is the only useful one.

By Christmas I hope to have everything done, then return home and stay there for the immediate future. If the situation permits: let's hope so!

Giebelstadt
November 21, 1939

Spent an hour today way up in the air. It was very lovely. Glorious but cold weather. Giebelstadt is located on a sweeping high plateau, and a fresh breeze prevails.

The job itself is very interesting. But there are many difficulties: the frost is a great nuisance; one cannot paint before ten in the morning, and then only until three, otherwise the color peels off; an insufficient amount of scaffolding, with the result that the work progresses slowly, given the vast area we have to cover (two hundred seventy feet wide, fifty feet high, seventy-five feet deep), and there are seven barracks that size, not counting the many outbuildings, all of which have to be camouflaged, and as quickly as possible. I shall see if I can make little models in Stuttgart which the painters could follow, so that I would only need to come now and then. The camouflage itself is turning out well. Gigantic paintings.

The icy cold air takes one's breath away but feels very healthy. Everyone has rosy cheeks. The last few days we worked straight through because of the threat of a freeze.

Today, Saturday, there is snow, which changes the situation, although it is already blowing away. Right now I am sitting in the station restaurant in Würzburg and shall be on my way to Stuttgart Sunday.

To Tut

Stuttgart
December 2, 1939

After a night in a hotel I looked around for a room today and have rented one for 30 marks, third floor, 65 Eberhardstraße, c/o Bäuerle. After all, I need a place to leave my stuff, and it would be too expensive in a hotel.

I may keep the room just for the month of December. It happens to be part of my parents' old apartment. What memories! Forty years!

To Tut

I am simply furious, because I had scrounged together everything necessary for making breakfast, and now I am left high and dry. Not even on Sunday morning do I get breakfast: the old lady has to go to church. I had eggs and wanted to make a fire, but no wood. Yet it would not make sense to give up the room, because then I would have to store my things somewhere and go hunting for a room again when I come back in mid-January. So I must simply grin and bear it. I sleep well, and that is the important thing, after all.

To Dieter Keller

Sehringen

January 17, 1940

Whenever I had the chance to paint murals as I wished, without making compromises, I decided in favor of abstraction, and that is what one should do, especially in an age which forbids one to. The result is a form of symbolism which cannot be explained logically and yet must grow out of some secret inner necessity which causes one to paint one way and not another. One becomes the tool of the subconscious, not, it is to be hoped, of "the degenerate," for there are no standards by which to make certain. So we are groping in the dark, and it is certainly valuable to know one is not alone.

I shall always aspire to and defend a form of abstraction which, far from being a composite of undefined forms and colors, strives to create symbolic elements, thus necessarily surpassing the merely formal or formulaic. My belief is that the ultimate, supreme matters can be portrayed only by purely abstract means.

But at the same time I believe in the necessity of (or the necessary connection with) the human figure, seen as the measure of all things, as the link which makes understanding possible. Pure, non-representational form means ornament to me. It gives pleasure to the eyes, and is intended solely for the beholder. Might one say that abstract music is by nature a feast for the ear? Music works upon us by its regularity; we perceive the banality and the nobility; by analogy, abstract, non-representational painting should awaken this range of feelings and convey a sense of nobility when it refers to something noble. Is there such a thing as noble ornamentation? Noble decoration? I doubt whether such phenomena could match the force that can be transmitted through the medium of the human figure.

Diary

April 7, 1940

Germans are not visual in the artistic, contemplative sense. During the period from 1919 to 1933 an attempt was at least made to educate them in that direction. Nowadays nothing at all is being done. Naked, brutal reality, crass materialism rule supreme. With phoney concreteness people acknowledge only what they can touch, what the technical and perhaps the practical realm have to offer—this attitude means a stab in the back for anything artistic.

Let it at last be said: cultural philistinism is and will remain the Achilles' heel, if not more, of this regime. I shall see it as an incredible tragedy if young talent or genius can no longer unfold in freedom, but instead is hemmed in on all sides by political considerations so narrow that they can never aspire to the name of "ideological schooling."

To Tut

Stuttgart
April 25, 1940

Your call for money coincided with a visit to the doctor, who established that I had a temperature of 102.1° and inflammation of the kidneys and sent me straight to bed. I hope to be up and about again in three or four days and to get the detail drawing for the fourth mural done before Whitsun.

To Tut

Stuttgart

June 15, 1940

So this week I shall paint two legends of St. Anthony of Padua for the choir loft of the little church in Hohenheim.

People are saying that preparations must be made as quickly as possible for the peace conference in Berlin, or perhaps for a dictation of terms! People are likewise saying that a "Temple of Peace" is to be built in Berchtesgaden and must be finished by July.

To Tut

Stuttgart

June 22, 1940

Three restful and stimulating days in Wuppertal. In the evening a party at which Frau Rohlfs showed us some large, beautiful watercolors by her deceased Christian.

The second day a visit to the future "paint museum," now being remodelled, and in the afternoon a Japanese film on lacquer painting was screened in Herberts' factory. Then Baumeister tacked his sketches on the wall (I am not absolutely satisfied with them).

Rasch proposed that I go there for three months and devote myself entirely to lacquer painting, paint as much as I wanted with complete freedom. He invited me for September and October. It would certainly be a peaceful task. Rasch believes that lacquer keeps for thousands of years!

Diary

June 23, 1940

In the days to come I shall devote myself to the cult of the surface and the delicate nuances of color, catching up on something I have neglected far too long, trying to recall what I once knew. Technically it requires a smooth, glazable preparation which, once achieved, naturally compels one to treat the surface cautiously and refinedly (as in the *Frauenschule* and the *Geländerszene*).

July 6, 1940

A week of illness, for the second time this summer. What is causing it? The stars. Fever visions, fantastic, close-ups of South-Sea Gothic, colorful carvings; then too, racing by, stone sculptures as tall as a building, blackish-gray, Assyrian-looking. And then of course the angels, the Anthony of the Church in Hohenheim. Also the number 56. What does that signify?

Today the news that Paul Klee is dead! Only a year after he turned sixty. Too early, and yet it seemed to me that, judging by the catalogue of the last exhibition, something in him was finished. A loss of strength or a natural process? What a visual and spiritual contribution he made to the world of the artist. And what wisdom! Will his death mean the end of an era? Where will abstraction find a refuge when Paris falls? In the U.S.? In little Switzerland?

Diary

August 20, 1940

I perceive how I could decorate the walls in Offenburg with fragments of landscape, amorphous bits of various landscape moods. Advantages: the necessity of painting out-of-doors, taking walks to find motifs. In a larger context: I once upon a time wanted to translate my figural oil paintings, for instance the *Figuren-Katarakt* ["Cataract of Figures"] into landscape, or alternately, to transpose the elements of the figural picture into landscape. Furthermore: nowadays artistic neutrality, camouflaging one's real intentions, is necessary or appropriate; one should convey one's message through the universally comprehensible medium of landscape.

So this day may acquire a deeper import.

To Tut

Offenburg
October 23, 1940

Arrived safely of course; it was pitch dark. This morning I began by bumping my head against the scaffolding, sat still for ten minutes, and then started work fresh and cheerful. The wall is now impeccable. If everything goes according to plan and I paint a landscape every two days, I shall be finished in ten days. Prepare to come and fetch me, "with or without dress."

I hated leaving, of course, but I do adjust easily and have already gotten over it; I plan to spend the 12th in Sehringen, but on the 15th I must go to Wuppertal at long last, for in six weeks it will be Christmas, when I want to be back home.

To Tut

Offenburg
October 29, 1940

Well, today all the remaining Jews were deported. Within two hours, with one hundred marks each and twenty pounds of luggage, they were shuttled off to the border of the unoccupied territory. The "sun" is horrified; they are making no attempt to conceal it, announce that it was tried only in Baden, as an experiment. Dreadful!

To Tut

Wuppertal
November 25, 1940

Here I am sitting at my diplomat's desk, with stone writing utensils, stifling steam heat, a box sofa with built-in shelves overhead, a bed, somewhat hard but with a lilac quilt, a large armoire, running water—but 43 marks, with only coffee included; anything else costs extra. It was the only acceptable room of the fifteen offered. I got in a generous survey of repulsive streets and ditto landladies. I hope that when my studio is fixed up things will improve; perhaps I shall be able to live there. My work, as I said, takes a pleasant form, in a friendly atmosphere. There are tantalizing possibilities if I accomplish anything, which I believe I shall, since I intend to study lacquer very thoroughly and will certainly come up with new ideas: I am even secretly thinking of a lacquer ballet!

To Tut

Wuppertal

December 4, 1940

Money! Here I need more than in Stuttgart. There the weeks go by, one earns a little, and it is never enough. I know that you, too, have to live and that your welfare is most important. And what does Your Grace desire? A winter coat; of course, but I am powerless without a clothing coupon, and even then. Patience!—but that you have had for twenty years. I tremble before you, Christ Child. Well, just organize whatever you can.

To Tut

Wuppertal

December 8, 1940

Muche sent a telegram that they were expecting me in Krefeld. He has aged. After the meal we went to the school, an old brick building. Way up under the roof Muche has his rooms, which are not connected with the rest of the building. His own budget from industry. He showed me fabrics being made under his direction, some of them quite beautiful, of a sort one sees seldom or not at all. Certainly an inspiration for the textile industry, which buys them up and mass-produces them. He also showed me his own work, paintings, mostly still lifes. At least the atmosphere is good. We also stopped by the museum, where an exhibition of arts and crafts is in progress: Wagenfeld (glass), Lindig (very lovely vases), wall hangings by Benita Otte and Frau Mögelin, Tümpel, too. Kadow, who directs one of the classes at the school, is likewise a Bauhaus product, as is his wife, who teaches silk embroidery. Some of these people came for coffee at Muche's afterwards, and in addition Volger, the town architect of Krefeld, the husband of Lisbeth Beyer. That was really a surprise! Of course they wanted to hear all about me. Isn't that amusing, so much Bauhaus all in one spot, and all of them productive people? Time sped by; I had to leave at six in order to reach Wuppertal before night.

December 8, 1940

When I was young and in my prime, I thought that if my intensity of inner vision and of creative energy ever failed, I would call it quits. I have indeed fallen low. I would have an arduous climb to reach my former state. Here in Wuppertal I have everything necessary for a regeneration, for finding my way back to myself. For here I am not being asked to deny my nature, but rather to do what I find most congenial! The best possible conditions. Now comes the test. Will my creative energy fail altogether? Am I already too old? Unlikely, since I do not feel old; on the contrary, I still see everything spread out before me; my imagination remains active. To have visions, inner images—that is the decisive thing, after all. Afterthought: to be able to give them form: that is no less important.

Diary

December 15, 1940

My depression persists, unabated. This "applied" work I am doing haunts me day and night. Now I know what an inferiority complex is. I once read *Die Prinzessin [The Princess]* by Bruno Frank. In it, a man who has undergone all sorts of adventures in the course of a stormy life one day turns his back on everything and retires to the Zoological Station in Naples, where he tends the fish and lives in modest solitude. This image keeps coming back to me. If anything, I should have disappeared in 1933, gone somewhere abroad where no one knows me, instead of going through the undignified performance of selling my soul before the throne of artistic conscience for a few pieces of silver.

Will I ever overcome this gnawing feeling? Ever prove I can act responsibly?

Diary

December 31, 1940

Paintings are relevations of the divine through the medium of the man known as the "artist," who employs a language of form and color mystic in origin, which kindles the "revelation" in others and permits them to share in it indirectly.

To Tut

Wuppertal
January 22, 1941

Today is Baumeister's birthday, and we must celebrate with him. Besides, Grohmann just arrived; he has to be in Düsseldorf for three weeks on business; somewhat aged. We shall see each other once more while he is in the area. He always has many interesting things to talk about.

People are saying that the invasion will be launched in the spring. Greatly intensified air war. We should probably prepare for a devastating war; peace seems very far off. Everywhere shelters are being built near the railroad stations, Düsseldorf included. In Krefeld heavy attacks, huge fires, vast quantities of synthetic fabric said to have been lost.

To Tut

Wuppertal
February 5, 1941

I have shifted my bed around for the third time and am now sleeping facing east; strangely enough I find I am finally sleeping well. In the evening I usually eat at home, and actually feel quite comfortable in my second apartment. The apartment and the external circumstances often remind me of the Bauhaus days—and I am really trying to rebuild, not just the lacquer, but also my own concerns (here I manage to fit in my painting with no trouble, even with the house still in mad confusion). Once things settle down, peace will return, and I have high hopes, for I must build up a backlog of work for the days to come.

Someone met Dr. Grote of Dessau in Munich, where he is having an exhibition at the Lenbach Gallery; he reported that the remaining "degenerate" pictures belonging to the Dessau Museum had all been burned. If that is true, it is enough to send one into a state of shock. Do they really have nothing more important to do, now that there is war, than to burn pictures? Incredible.

Diary

March 19, 1941

Finished Lawrence's *Seven Pillars of Wisdom*. Started Leopold Ziegler's *Apollons letzte Epiphanie [Apollo's Last Epiphany]*.

Discussion with Rasch about the morbid element in today's art. The sculptors do torsos because Greek statuary is dug up with parts missing. The painters create an artificial patina. This passion for antiqueing is not the mark of a vigorous, youthful art; even when the works in question are of high quality, it is a sign of decay, a perversion in the worst sense.

Diary

April 25, 1941

I could now become a painter of the German forest *(Freischütz)*, German insofar as I would paint the forest I see all around me. I would seek out the heart of the woods, the depths, where the richest resonances were to be found. I would trace the mystical forms of the tree roots, reproduce the rich browns and greens and grays and blacks. I would paint little fragments, which would convey my intentions with utmost purity, and perhaps only gradually would I combine these into a total picture. This woodsy darkness (tones of green, brown, black), combined with my red-brown-black figures would yield the clear chord of red—green, in a minor key, to be sure, dipped in melancholy, rendering the inner and outer mood of contemporary man, certainly not exclusively that of O.S.

I would, if I were free of the necessity of earning money. But as it is, I am tied to duties which never concern me deeply, which I manage to perform, but without any final commitment, without my heart's being in them. How much longer?

Postcard to Tut

Stuttgart
May 12, 1941

What grows and blossoms in my garden?
Shall continue my journey Thursday morning. How well

one can still eat here and in Munich, and how dreary the food is in Wuppertal.

A new wave against degenerate art is sweeping across the land. I myself read Ziegler's directives. Cheers! And then alongside it one finds hymns for Schmückle, who holds the exact opposite position. Hess has flown off to Scotland. Terrific!

To Tut

Wuppertal
May 23, 1941

Yesterday Muche and Watenphul were here. On Sunday or Monday Marcks is coming. So there is good company, and it is amusing to see how this company attracts others. In that sense the atmosphere is much improved. I am supposed to participate in the summer exhibition here and do various other things as well. Günther Francke in Munich did, however, urge me very strongly to keep out of the spotlight; I should consider myself fortunate to have such a job. Basically I don't want to attract any attention.

Yesterday Willi Baumeister left to take charge of the printing in Stuttgart. The important thing to Dr. Herberts is that one do something original. That explains my success with the new techniques which I now also plan to try out for wall processes (lacquers on plaster).

Diary

May 26, 1941

Close similarity between handwriting and painting style (Hildebrandt thinks this especially noticeable in my case). East Asians!—Perfect identity is something I should struggle even harder to attain; and my unique hand should embody the essential features of my painting.

Diary

June 14, 1941

How much the French have taught us with their many varieties of style (since Cézanne and van Gogh): Rouault—a demonic type with his deep black-blue-red-brown-white combinations, and what themes! Bonnard—the painter most sensitive to optics and optical impressions. Seurat—archaic discipline, applied to highly unusual themes! Each one of these painters complete in his own way. Each one the representative of a distinct genre; all these genres together run the gamut of artistic—and human—multiplicity. In light of such possibilities can one ever say: this is it? This is *the* painter? This is the purest, this is the greatest? But that is a matter for the art critics and the grand juries of the Creation. My task is to be an artist and produce.

Diary

June 22, 1941

War with Russia!

A day spent in total apathy.

We artists are simply incapable of grasping the contradiction between the organizational "miracles" performed by the government and its persecution of painters and their works. The war against Russia will revive the old formula which equated political with artistic Bolshevism—but what misunderstandings this equation harbors! Nevertheless, it will remain incontrovertible as long as "the rats in the valley mingle for a long time to come" (Otto Meyer).

Then I think of my avenues of retreat: of the forest interiors, of "Les Mystères du Forêt-Noir," also of certain portraits, painted in "masterly" fashion, which could, if need be, absorb all sorts of secret aspirations, portraits conceived in such a way as to calm my present irritation and unrest by recourse to nature, where I might reorient myself.

Diary

July 8, 1941

Splotchography! Inspired by what appear to be microscopic photographs of natural objects such as sponges, bark, etc., but are actually splotchographies, blotting paper style. I have run experiments in this technique with oil on paper. Once again I have hit upon a unique creation "from somewhere," it sits there, not painted; one sees no trace of the wretched paint brush; it appears to be a piece of nature, perceived and formed by a phenomenon. A strange by-product of what we call "nature"! I wish I could paint as if it came "from somewhere" and not from the human hand.

Diary

July 9, 1941

Remain true to my theme of "figure in space" by humanizing, spotlighting, drenching with color, intensifying the imaginative element.

Humanizing = releasing from abstract, geometric rigidity. Spotlighting = bringing out of the darkness, and also rendering the miracle of optics (Seurat's drawings). Drenching in color = instead of hectic "tone," consistent color. Intensifying the imaginative element = never again sinking into banalities; instead, consistently striving to capture the inner image, the visions.

Diary

August 5, 1941

I must regain my balance, find my center of gravity, before everything can be set "right" again.

To Tut

Stuttgart
August 31, 1941

Am eager to hear your reports on Eichberg and Strassburg. Unfortunately I shall now have to spend my birthday here; there is no help for it. And on the Blues? And the trip to Lake Constance? And . . . and . . . .

Here we have frequent air raids. We are entering the third year of war, and one becomes accustomed to dismal forebodings. At the moment a pessimistic mood prevails, and we hear a foreign radio broadcast cutting in on the German station.

To Tut

Stuttgart
September 4, 1941

The birthday is in full swing. Your special delivery package was brought to my room early this morning—many thanks for the contents. What lovely letters!

My work here is gradually drawing to a close. Of course they expect me in Wuppertal.

In general I am feeling better, especially today—no wonder. Last night I saw the Hagenbeck Circus: the animals were wonderful. Charming ponies! They really are your animals, or perhaps in an earlier life you *were* a pony. With that in mind I fed them pieces of carrot during the intermission.

Today I am fairly happy, and I wish I were a dancer. Too bad this cannot last.

Diary

September 30, 1941

What is characteristic of Marées, of Rouault? The compositional, figural element clothed in pure, fluid, painter's style. What produces pure painting? The painter must succeed in mobilizing on his canvas all the elements which bring out the substance of the color (color in the fullest sense of the word), and with its help create space, volume, and solidity.

And the figural element? This always furnishes the framework, even when barely recognizable, or raised to the level of the legendary, far from everyday naturalistic happenings. Myth, legend, mystery—those are the categories within which greatness occurs.

To Tut

Wuppertal
November 4, 1941

I have let myself in for an adventure. I could not resist. The opportunity was too tempting. For the anniversary celebration on December 6 I am doing a lacquer ballet. I mentioned this once some time ago, and now I am being taken at my word. Actually I am by no means reluctant. One can work up something very interesting with the simplest of resources. Just colorfully lacquered cardboard plaques, little balls, staffs, and so on. The Barmen Theater will be rented; first we shall hold our private party there, with the local chorus, a chronicle, and a speech, preceded by this little ballet. We still do not know whether we shall be able to get the eight girls from the theater's corps de ballet. But in any case it will be less a matter of fancy dancing than of measured pacing and showing the costumes.

And be forewarned: you are invited. Do you have a gown? Might Karin's perhaps fit you? This is the latest news. I shall have a few upsetting weeks, but in any case I hope the ballet proves effective; that would be something. Just the thought of it made me go all warm inside. This seems to be a germ in me that refuses to be killed off. So don't scold!

To Tut

December 9, 1941

The party has come and gone.

The little "Round Dance in Lacquer" lasted a bit over three minutes, was danced to a Handel sarabande, slow and stately. Six ladies, each in a different costume made of glass balls, cardboard coasters, cardboard shapes, etc. They did the best they could. More one could not ask. Dr. Herberts liked the round dance very much; he wanted the costumes kept so that they might be displayed some day. It was also mentioned in the newspaper account as having "unique charm." The educated people were much taken with it, the simple people asked: "What is that supposed to mean?" But that is the usual fate of such things.

Diary

December 15, 1941

The Gebhardt Collection in Wuppertal (with Baumeister, Rasch, and Krause). Handsome things—and I am seized with the desire to do something similar. When will I overcome this lethargy and—will I overcome it? When achieve full composure? This nervousness is killing me—what causes it?

To Gunda Stölzl

Sehringen

December 28, 1941

Yes, all of us were together for Christmas: Karin, who has reached the first stage as a solo dancer in Strassburg, and Jai, who is studying theatrical costuming at the Kunstgewerbe-schule. Til is at the trades school in Freiburg, but plans to go into farming, something he always wanted. Tut already pictures living on an estate and having her donkeys at last! Now she often has to spend long stretches completely alone here, which does not suit her temperament in the least. For I, too, am away most of the year, at the moment in Wuppertal, where I am involved in artistic work with lacquers, with an enviable amount of freedom and the best working conditions; if only the city were not so ugly! It is up to me to make this job something of longer duration. Muche, as you probably know, has settled in Krefeld, not far away, as has Watenphul, and they seem to be having considerable success in industry. I have seen Marcks once.

It is of course a shame that I cannot be in Sehringen, for this way it hardly makes sense to have the house. We were not counting on the family's being so dispersed. But with the war going on one cannot contemplate any changes. In the summer I was on Lake Constance, as lovely as ever, and seeing Konstanz on the Swiss side lit up was quite an experience.

Diary

January 1, 1942

New Year's!

Politically: a bad mood throughout the country. In the East, violent attacks instead of the expected winter lull, not to mention the fact that the campaign was supposed to be over by winter.

393

In North Africa vicious battles, and Bengasi (or even more) reconquered. Delayed wool collection, church bells, fuel shortage, tin. Will we be able to recoup all these losses in the spring?

Artistically: I can capture the essential only by taking circuitous paths, by employing several different processes. I must find my way back to immediacy. How? Through concentration, inner tranquillity? I must do much more free experimentation.

In general: one must seize hold of the positive, hang onto it, intensify it, and one must steel oneself, shake off the weakness that besets one, and summon up all one's vital forces. Also put aside sentimentality. The Old Masters were devout and unsentimental (the delightful freshness of old peasant art, for example).

An interesting time chart: born 1888 + 7 = 1895, + 7 = 1902, + 7 = 1909 (around this time the first independent nature studies, Corot, Courbet, etc.), 1909 + 7 = 1916 (the abstract series during the war!), + 7 = 1923 (in 1924 the new series of *Galeriebilder, Vorübergehender,* and all the others, perhaps the best I ever did), 1923 + 7 = 1930 (the Breslau period, *Bauhaustreppe* and others), 1930 + 7 = 1937 (the oil papers, also building the house in Sehringen). And now 1944 would be the next promising year!

Diary

January 18, 1942

Nota bene:

From now on order-pictures, constructed in such a way that they convey the essential as a symbol, even as an emblem. And then: order, order-pictures on the one hand, in which symbolic forms, perhaps private ones at first, are arranged by virtue of the artist's faculty for envisaging and rendering. Unambivalent-ambivalent, displaying precise variations of form and color!

And by contrast: pictures for the eye: meant to be looked at, drawn from nature, perhaps even nature pictures, also phantasmagoria. I must perceive these possibilities clearly, register them, know where they must fit in if they are intended to exist side by side (I always envisage a plan in which various areas are blocked in, parts of a greater whole as seen by a temperament that loves order).

Stuttgart
February 4, 1942

I need my surroundings, the room, a few pictures, the warmth of my nest. And now I have become a nomad, the opposite of my true nature. This much I know, the milieu here is more stimulating. Here I have good ideas and become productive. Such things should be decisive. But I also wonder: have I no choice but to enter into servitude? God, if only I were a free agent! I could simply paint, which is what will count when I am gone, not the work I forced myself to do, against my will, in the wrong place, and with the wrong means! Between now and Easter I shall keep a very sharp eye on Wuppertal so as to finally clarify the situation for myself. Everything will become clear eventually, for some day the lid is bound to blow. For the moment I am indulging in deliberations, and not fruitless ones, either.

Diary

February 14, 1942

Addition to the seven-year pattern (of January 1, 1942): the sevens do represent unmistakable, evident stages in the course of my evolution, without, however, my being clear on which stage represents the values that will stand up before God and man. Today I asked Baumeister if he had anything similar. He was not aware of any such rhythm in his own life.

Postcard to Tut

Stuttgart
February 25, 1942

Here in Stuttgart I am once more experiencing visions, "the premonition of something beautiful," or rather, such a state of mind is just around the corner, on its way.

Diary

March 8, 1942

I keep wondering what would happen if I had to appear before the throne of God, and everything that did not belong to me dropped away, leaving the true form, which here on earth is veiled, buried, hidden, cramped, twisted, and which can express itself on the one hand through the unconscious (subconscious), in actions free of such inhibitions, in gestures, in expressive forms (the dance!) and on the other hand through art. For in art man tries to give vent to his soul as purely as possible, to project the uniqueness of his soul through the medium of forms and signs. But the soul would have to stand before God's throne in all its clarity and glory, stripped of all doubts.

Salvation, then? Beatification?

Some achieve this even here on earth: the blessed (in art), while others struggle their whole life through and never rid themselves of their earthly shackles.

Incident: we are leafing through the *Minotaure,* and Baumeister spots a Klee, which he sees as conforming absolutely to his own principles. I cannot support him in this. Or: I have a sense of responsibility which sets limits for me. If these boundaries may be crossed, anything goes. The question will be whether art remains within its limits or goes beyond them. For my part I am trying to find a path within the world of the visible. Like Cézanne, Bonnard, Rouault, Otto Meyer, whom one could never accuse of being materialists, in contrast to the abstract, non-representational painters in signs.

I feel like a pregnant woman, "expecting" to bear a new child, watching it take shape. I hope it will be neither a premature birth nor a miscarriage—and not a hysterical pregnancy! An immaculate conception?

Diary

March, 18, 1942

Was there ever a painter who managed to create a Work, *the* picture, or at least aspired to seminal work to which all later paintings would refer, directly or indirectly. Cézanne tried desperately (his bathing women); Seurat: yes! Marées: yes! Otto

Meyer: yes! Matisse: no! Klee: no! Baumeister: no! They make many pictures, but no Picture. O.S. wants to try his hand.

> *To Dr. Posse,*
> *Director of the State Gallery in Dresden*
>> Sehringen
>> March 19, 1942

For some time now I have wanted to inquire whether you can give me any information as to the whereabouts of my picture *Vorübergehender,* which was once given to the museum by the Patronage Guild and which you had displayed very handsomely in a modern room on the Brühl Terrace. I later heard that it had been shown at the Reichstag in an exhibition entitled "Bolshevism Unmasked."

It is one of the most important pictures I produced in 1924, and I have repeatedly determined to track it down.

My pictures from the Folkwang Museum and from the Museum in Mannheim have reportedly found their way to the Kunstmuseum [Museum of Art] in Basel.

> *Diary*
>> March 22, 1942

Piero della Francesca is said to have perceived delightful forms and colors on a wall spat upon by patients in a hospital (as Leonardo is said to have done on a wall splattered with mortar). My *Bild K* had similar strange origins.

This strengthens me in my concept of "from somewhere." Everything not made by human hand, or made indirectly, unconsciously, is thus "nature" (photography included), can contain mysteries of form and color which enrapture anyone able to perceive them. Other examples: the merging colors of a used palette; smears made on paper while painting, and the like. Look for more such phenomena!

April 6, 1942

Easter Monday.

My essence consists in the pared-down classicism which emerges more and more unambiguously as time goes by.

Alongside this "classical" Golden Mean, I have also done baroque-romantic and psychological or sentimental works! Also some which are merely banal and representational.

It is the same effect as when one leafs through the *Minotaure* and suddenly finds, among the Surrealists and other monstrosities, a Seurat. This reveals at one blow that the world of the visible and the perceivable, that portrayal based on visual impressions is far from exhausted; it remains eternally capable of renewal, like nature. The painting seems a victory of the *"monde visible."* This is my domain, and I should be loyal to it and never swerve from the true path.

This Golden Mean does require inner calm and a state of grace. The other form more or less flourishes on agitated nerves. The romantic-baroque style derives largely from a psychological or literary conception, an intention, whereas the Mean sings with Goethe* "and nought to seek, that was my plan." I am anti-surreal, pro-Seurat and those like him. I seek the legendary, the Pan-like European elements, yes, the German. And I perceive these things more and more clearly as a basic distinction.

To Jules Bissier

Wuppertal
May 11, 1942

Since we are on the subject of children and parents: Til is in Friedingen, near Singen am Hohentwiel; from his room he looks out over the lake, with occasionally the Alps in the distance; every morning he carts the milk with the horse, which he sometimes also harnesses. It is not quite clear from his letters how he is managing and whether he is physically equal to the work. One thing seems certain: he is well fed. He also has charge of the pigs. Tut is in Strassburg at the moment, summoned by

---

*In the poem "Gefunden."—Translator

our daughters, who are both in bed with sore throats. By the way, Tut had to register for the Landhilfe [Agricultural Auxiliary Corps], which I would probably be unable to avoid, too, if I were home for any length of time. Probably.

I think I have somewhat overcome my state of depression. Only now do I realize how severe it was, and that it was inner necessity which made me turn to my friend for advice. An astrologer (unknown and unasked) did tell me that I would remain in this state until September 1942 and should not be spoken to before then; that an upturn would not come until 1943 (I would even say 1944, remembering the seven-year pattern!). Well, even so I am cheerfully letting new emotions and sensations flow over me. I am a painter, after all, and have recently completed a series of pictures, inspired by what I see right around me: views from my window into the neighboring window, done in the evening between nine and half-past nine, shortly before the blackout. When night is falling and clashes with the scraps of interior beige-orange-brown-white-black, it produces amazing optical effects.

I am experiencing with unfamiliar intensity the mystic force that resides in the optical effects of nature, and I observe that with the passing years one keeps learning to see in new and different ways. In the style, say, of Otto Meyer-Amden, who strikes me more and more as a phenomenon. I often recall how around 1910 I painted a little nude on unlimed paper in Landenberger's painting class; I did it quite unsuspectingly, but to Meyer-Amden it proved a revelation. He asked to have the sketch, and for years it hung in his attic room. At the time he said that this little picture contained more modern elements (to his way of thinking) than the rather inflated so-called modern art which was then coming into fashion; and today I think I am not mistaken if I see a connection between this little sketch and many of Meyer-Amden's important later works. Nowadays, when I no longer believe in the infallibility of Picasso-style abstraction and also cannot find the courage to applaud the moderns of those days, I find the world of the visible opening up to me in a remarkable fashion, in all its density and surrealistic mystique. Furthermore: the insight that we cannot match the intensity of what nature constantly produces. In addition I am doing little plaster statues, modelled in plasticine, in the negative, and then cast straight off in plaster, which is then painted.

May 12, 1942

Constant flow of new ideas. In the future I shall do more and write less.

The window paintings: the miracle of the visible, the mystique of the optical. At least in its un-inventability, i.e. one cannot invent that sort of thing. Source of inspiration for free composition.

Concerning the window paintings: I feel like a hunter who goes stalking every evening between nine and ten o'clock. And then: here I can be sure that I am only painting what I see, but the important question is *how* I see it and especially how I paint it, and that brings up the old question: "what is truth?" Truth in art—truth in nature . . . .

May 23, 1942

When the creative spirit comes over one, and it comes on like an attack, it obsesses one with ideas which cry out to be put into practice; one becomes nothing but a medium, a tool; one feels beside oneself, a transitional agent.

When the destruction of pictures and the overthrow of all previously accepted values set in, I wished for a bible to which the persecuted painters could turn. For religious disputes there is the Bible; for artistic disputes one must fall back on that which has gone before, the Old and the earliest Masters, their works, and also their words and their spirit. For instance, when Leonardo advises his students to look at a mortared wall and to discover the figures swarming there, that is a daring piece of advice, since these figures are extremely strange and unusual, and indeed visible only to one predestined to see them. He, too, sees figures "from somewhere," of unknown origin, not made by the hand of man or inventable by calculating reason. In today's jargon they would be "Bolshevistic" and "nihilistic" figurizations, well worth further examination.

To Tut

Wuppertal
July 2, 1942

The food situation here is becoming catastrophic. I cannot stand going without food. That would soon do me in. If I am hungry, I simply cannot accomplish anything. And right now the work and cooperation could be getting along very nicely.

Diary

July 11, 1942

My smallest sketch ever started out as a test of the effects of oiled paper: a few spots took on the shape of an imaginary interior. It is the purest portrayal of myself, in the sense that I cannot outdo this tiny piece of paper, no bigger than a child's hand! It has élan, life, reality, without being those things exactly; it has richness, yes, even greatness—and yet its dimensions are so small. So the sum of a life's work can be demonstrated within such a tiny space . . . .

My own tested recipe: after the unchosen task, in this case a bureaucratic one, of classifying the different wallpaints, my new-found freedom affects me much more intensely. Praise of change? A painting done in the aftermath (the Saturday afternoon of my liberation) was very rigorous, very much a free painting. Or might I also be influenced by reading Ernst Jünger's war diary, in which he often alludes to the "terrible majesty" of the world's destiny and evokes various mystic heights and depths? Jünger is also a German type; he betrays himself to a large extent, as so often happens in personal revelations. Where would one find something equivalent in today's painting? Dix? As types he and Jünger have external resemblances. They share the trait of cool objectivity coupled with romantic yearnings.

Of course it is unhealthy to try to force into one Sunday afternoon work which should take a week, if not more. It remains in the form of improvisation, of nervous groping, un-concentrated. And what contrasts! The strict window paintings and the turbulent figural fantasies! Can no connection or recon-ciliation be found for these stark tensions?

What would the Hölderlin of painting be like?

Diary

August 6, 1942

In the cellar of the "Post" (air raid). Depression, complexes of the worst kind, which I only bear so easily because of my "general physical weakness." So this is August's blow! And September? To which doctor of the soul should I entrust myself?

Diary

September 3, 1942

Is my present restlessness a condition that should be con-sidered psychically dangerous, or is it the restlessness Otto Meyer used to praise? Be that as it may: I have the impression that I have found the themes for my future pictures and that I must now do everything I can to put them down on canvas. Am I wrong in thinking this? Have my most recent attempts not shown that the true values transcend all ideas and elements imposed on the picture from without (extra-optical elements!). To assent to this means confining myself to a small but certain sphere; the former possibility opens up avenues to something unknown, to a symbolic world on a grand scale such as we lack today and yet so desperately need. And is this longing a matter of destiny, and if the will and the drive were strong enough, would it not have to reach its goal?

Diary

September 15, 1942

Leibl—Marées:

Leibl loved detail, used it as his point of departure, and failed to capture a whole.

402

Oskar Schlemmer, 1937. *Courtesy of Tut Schlemmer.*

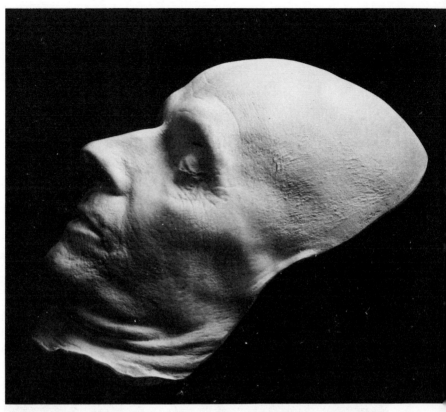

Oskar Schlemmer's death mask, 1943. Eta Lazi Farbfoto. *Courtesy of Oskar Schlemmer Archiv, Staatsgalerie Stuttgart.*

Marées loved the totality and failed (more or less) when it came to detail.

Both painted portraits. Leibl with Holbein-like precision, exactitude, lifelikeness; Marées in the spirit of titanic Titian, plunging into the midst, slowly "taking hold of" the phenomenon.

Can one aspire to a middle course? Does one exist? How about Cézanne? He, too, painted portraits and large compositions. Does he stand in the middle between the other two?

To Gunda Stölzl

Stuttgart-Untertürkheim
September 16, 1942

One night recently we were looking out from Bürgeln castle—we live between two castles—and saw the lights of Basel glowing like a happy island in the surrounding night. We used to see the lights of Zurich, but at that time we ourselves were still lit up. When will we be lit up again? Tut is alternately cheerful and wretched, the latter because she is alone so much of the time, although she escapes this condition by shutting up the house for the winter and going to look after her daughters in Strassburg. And then she is unhappy that I have to be away from home most of the time, something about which I am far from happy myself. Just now I am looking for some solution which would guarantee me more freedom. But that is not so easy in time of war, and my present work is "important for the war effort."
New friends—ah, they are few and far between, and you are very right that one gets the greatest pleasure from seeing the old ones, who have already become part of history. I saw Felix Klee this summer in Würzburg, unfortunately only at the railroad station; he urged me to come along to the premiere he was going to.

Postcard to Tut

Stuttgart
October 7, 1942

Last night intestinal colic, this morning fever. The doctor says it is the intestinal flu which is making the rounds here. Have to stay in bed, follow a diet; must count on several days of this. Don't know if I shall be able to leave for Wuppertal Monday. Now I have time to think.

To Jules Bissier

Stuttgart
October 21, 1942

I am allowed to get up, take walks, go home soon, and even smoke, which was forbidden for over two weeks! My guess is that the whole thing was a shock brought on by some complications with the food I was eating; it did cost me the three weeks which were needed to clear up all the side effects and imbalances, among which I count sugar and bile. They were three almost precious weeks of involuntary rest and contemplation, replete with fever fantasies and a certain courting of madness. I draw strength from madness, from the madness of the mystical, the legendary, also the madness of grand style, and I cherish visions of things which I think should be done in this direction. I feel we have the duty = obligation to deal in essentials, or at least to render our conception of the essential as well as we are able. This implies ethical standards rather than aesthetic ones—and yet we cannot escape the aesthetic, any more than we can escape impressionism, considering that we derive our best stimuli from sense impressions, especially those received by enchanted eyes. I experience this time and again (not only with my "windows," but also here in the hospital: nighttime impressions during an air raid, the nurses swarming like bees to move the severely ill patients to safety, and such things).

At the end of this week I hope to return to Sehringen for a week or two.

Diary

November 9, 1942

Almost like a solution to all my inner and outward anguish: illness!

To Jules Bissier

Sehringen

November 13, 1942

The issues do change with the years, almost explosively! and if my old friend O.M. were to return today (and not just in a dream, as he did recently), there would be endless discussion—or else he would utter just two words and put everything in proper perspective. Be true to yourself! Remember who you are! And be yourself!

That is so easy to say and so difficult to do. But why hesitate? We have so little time, and we must make the best of the gifts we have, given the four posts to which, as becomes clearer and clearer, we have been hitched. Does that mean we may no longer reach for the stars, yearn for the impossible, and "honor the gods"?

In Wuppertal I painted a little thing, no larger than a child's hand, a few spots of color, a memory of a window interior—everyone who sees it is captivated, and I myself must say: within this tiny space I have offered my utmost. Is this the wisdom of age, to elevate such restraint to a principle? It almost seems as if one came full circle: such a painting reminds me of similar ones done in my early youth; they did indeed contain everything that was unique and characteristic at the time and subsequently remained so. In the intervening period a great flapping of wings, reaching for the stars, daring and boldness, which, despite all the drums and trumpets, could not match the simple little song. All this still strikes me as a form of shrinkage; I cannot yet accept the idea of quiet withdrawal—I do not want to resign myself! That's it! But for the future I should probably aspire to just such a condition of self-restraint, chosen in freedom and without resignation.

I did the "window pictures" in a state of real enthusiasm, and it is curious that my feelings apparently have a direct impact on the beholder, always the best touchstone for the value of a work of art. Perhaps the window pictures helped me find the long-sought key, which I had either mislaid or lost and must now quickly put on a key ring, a ring of similar paintings, for safekeeping.

One more thing, the window pictures were drawn from reality; they offer impressions of the external world, seen, to be sure, through a "loving temperament."

How can I produce so much bile, I who am the very image of composure? I cannot get over it. By the way, I am getting progressively better. Soon they will run another test for sugar, which I hope was merely a side effect, since a diabetic's diet is difficult to maintain these days. I have a vigorous appetite. Apparently we, too, go through a sort of menopause. For the first time I feel I have grown older, become more deliberate and cautious. But I am resisting the sensation and do not want to admit to any changes.

Diary

November 24, 1942

Today I once more envisage a sort of painting with the "Breadth of Greatness" I mentioned earlier, large and sweeping, symbolic and yet glowing so beautifully in its material that no one bothers about interpretation. The most recent French paintings have something of this quality, but only hinted at, for they have it at their fingertips but lack spiritual profundity at present. I was reminded of this by the sight of the rusted kettle against the winter landscape. I immediately recognized its "from somewhere" quality, the East Asian element. Compared to this mode of art I envisage, many past and present paintings would look like the products of a petty mind . . . .

To Tut

Wuppertal

November 29, 1942

It is not nearly as cold here as it was in Sehringen. The trip was pleasant; it is interesting to travel second class, for the people have different and better minds from those who travel third. Generals and general managers. Soft upholstery. Arrival on schedule.

Here I shall first have to become acclimatized again.

To Jules Bissier

Freiburg im Breisgau

University Clinic

January 17, 1943

In the meantime I barely "skirted the abyss," as the doctor in attendance expressed it. I was brought here on the 4th. Immediate insulin treatment probably saved my life. This will have to continue about three months (home treatment program). I shall be released in a week, at the earliest.

This affair will bring about a decisive change in my life. Sehringen will be my future domicile = center of activity (something Tut has been demanding for a long time). I shall come to Stuttgart and Wuppertal only as a visitor; my contracts are still in effect. This somewhat unusual path seems to be finally leading me back to myself and my painting—and I am trying to imagine it and this whole way of life. How shall I exist? By trial and error. One has friends, after all. *Vita nuova.*

To Jules Bissier

Bühlerhöhe bei Baden-Baden

February 6, 1943

Read and stand amazed at where fate has landed me, or: where Tut's elemental energy (in such cases) has brought me in spite of all obstacles. No bed was to be available until the end of

March, but mentioning the name of a friend from Badenweiler, who had been here recently, proved effective, and thus I have been here since February 1. It is naturally a "costly" business to be here, but in such situations Tut knows no false shame; money is of no account when it is a question of my health.

As to that, I am still a convalescent, due to the strange phenomenon that when I stand up I get cold legs (not only feet), which makes me shaky and easily tired. For this reason I wish to state that I shall not leave this place until I can walk out. All the measures they applied in the clinic proved to no avail. When I am lying horizontally in bed, however, my legs feel warm.

The other guests (members of the upper class—where do *we* belong in social terms?) range from reserved to stiff, partly because of their illnesses, partly because of their sense of social rank. That might change, although I feel no need to start conversations or become involved in any way. On the contrary: this is a welcome opportunity to chip away at some of my ossified forms of thinking, to dissolve them, and if possible rearrange my thoughts; also, to plan for the new life ahead, down to the details of vegetable garden and kitchen. It is a challenge to manage with the permitted and the forbidden items, two hundred grams of graham bread and two hundred grams of potatoes per day, almost a Bircher-Benner regime.

I naturally tend to assume that Wuppertal played a part in bringing this on; I even fancy that one particular thing was responsible for hastening the progress of the disease. It is very possible that the disease was latent for quite some time. But it would take a psychiatrist to unravel all these connections and interrelationships. I also feel that this is the price I have to pay for ten years of irritations, mistakes, rootlessness, alienation from my true concerns. I wonder if the life left to me will suffice for putting everything back in order, for summing up my intentions? Actually I should not have to decide to use my last strength for this task. I must build up my world around me again, my visionary world and also my existential world, which

I always had around me until 1933, which I reconstructed once more in Eichberg, only to lose more finally than ever. It remains to be seen whether the Sehringen experiment succeeds. Tut plans to guard my privacy like a Cerberus!

The children: Til is in Breisach in the Arbeitsdienst [Public Works Corps] and is being driven very hard. Jai is doing quite well in school, gets small commissions through her teacher, has prospects for a scholarship. Karin went to Stuttgart to launch her trial balloon in the the theater, but will apparently be returning to Strassburg.

Tut accompanied me here and stayed a few days, but today she returns to Strassburg and will stay there with the girls as long as I have to stay here. Then, depending on how things go, we shall return home together.

In Freiburg I once again delighted in the beauty of the cathedral.

Diary

February 7, 1943

I had a sudden vision of my future style of painting: deep-toned earth shades, block-like forms out of which a head emerged.

Diary

February 9, 1943

To perceive and to further:
Purest feeling
Purest emotion
Purest thought
The purest heart
and likewise: what is uniquely one's own . . . .

Diary

February 20, 1943

If I think of the various "available" gods I could adopt in order to reach the tranquillity I now find desirable, I keep coming back to the Buddha, plump and composed, at ease with himself.

It is the mouth! Anything but a distorted Gothic one or a theatricalized Baroque one. And the large size of the Buddha statues strikes me as significant in terms of style; the Buddha is frequently larger than life, an extraordinary figure stretched across the landscape, gigantic in its dimensions (the sole of his foot larger than a man). Does any other art offer anything similar?

To Tut

Bühlerhöhe

February 22, 1943

I hope my project for this summer is not frustrated by the civil defense alarms which make such a racket that anyone still running around loose or even taking a walk has to feel guilty. For I cannot tell every child and Kreisleiter that I am sick. There should be a sign as there is for the Jews: s = sick!

Free of sugar! Carbohydrates are being increased some more and the insulin dosage reduced accordingly. Very gratifying! Now you can draw up a plan for the trip. We shall meet in Appenweier, right?

To Tut

Freiburg

March 21, 1943

I am in bed with a slight fever, probably the result of too much gymnastics. So I doubt I shall be released next week. I would prefer to eat only the apples; don't feel like eating anything else. Don't get worked up; it is just one of these setbacks, although not especially pleasant.

Diary

March 28, 1943

In the meantime the coma at the beginning of January, then four weeks in the Freiburg clinic; after that four weeks at Bühlerhöhe; scarcely was I home before the flu set in, so back to the clinic in Freiburg. Now home again, cleaning up, organizing, preparing things.

Postcard to Jules Bissier

Sehringen
March 31, 1943

I am trying to create some atmosphere in the studio. Set-ups . . . setbacks. But this restlessness is probably a necessary prelude to the true and longed-for tranquility. But I am still literally too weak for real work. That is no way to be and must stop. Next week I am supposed to go to Dr. Malten in Baden-Baden for a cure. I am trying to keep up my spirits and am counting on him, my fifth station on my road to Calvary.

Last entry in the diary

April 1, 1943

". . . to consider art not a piece plucked out of the world, but the complete and utter transformation of the world into pure glory . . . ." (Rilke).

INDEX OF NAMES

413

416

419

424